William Desmond's Philosophy between Metaphysics, Religion, Ethics, and Aesthetics

Dennis Vanden Auweele
Editor

William Desmond's Philosophy between Metaphysics, Religion, Ethics, and Aesthetics

Thinking Metaxologically

palgrave
macmillan

Editor
Dennis Vanden Auweele
KU Leuven (University of Leuven)
Leuven, Belgium

ISBN 978-3-319-98991-4   ISBN 978-3-319-98992-1 (eBook)
https://doi.org/10.1007/978-3-319-98992-1

Library of Congress Control Number: 2018958416

© The Editor(s) (if applicable) and The Author(s), under exclusive licence to Springer International Publishing AG, part of Springer Nature 2018
This work is subject to copyright. All rights are solely and exclusively licensed by the Publisher, whether the whole or part of the material is concerned, specifically the rights of translation, reprinting, reuse of illustrations, recitation, broadcasting, reproduction on microfilms or in any other physical way, and transmission or information storage and retrieval, electronic adaptation, computer software, or by similar or dissimilar methodology now known or hereafter developed.
The use of general descriptive names, registered names, trademarks, service marks, etc. in this publication does not imply, even in the absence of a specific statement, that such names are exempt from the relevant protective laws and regulations and therefore free for general use.
The publisher, the authors and the editors are safe to assume that the advice and information in this book are believed to be true and accurate at the date of publication. Neither the publisher nor the authors or the editors give a warranty, express or implied, with respect to the material contained herein or for any errors or omissions that may have been made. The publisher remains neutral with regard to jurisdictional claims in published maps and institutional affiliations.

Cover design by Ran Shauli

This Palgrave Macmillan imprint is published by the registered company Springer Nature Switzerland AG
The registered company address is: Gewerbestrasse 11, 6330 Cham, Switzerland

There is simple gratitude for the sweetness of being that no one merits and that no act of thanks can ever repay.
William Desmond

To William
Teacher, friend and inspiration

Preface

William Desmond held an appointment at the Institute of Philosophy at KU Leuven (University of Leuven) from December 1994 until his retirement in 2016. In the spring of 2017 (April 19–20), an international conference was organized in honor and recognition of his philosophical achievement. The turnout was—both for speakers and for attendees—far beyond expectation, and the subsequent quality of keynote and split sessions presentations was impressive. After the conference ended on a high with a round table including John Milbank, Cyril O'Regan, Sander Griffioen and William himself, the organizer—yours truly—thought it more than appropriate to collect some of these excellent contributions, adding some essays commissioned especially for this volume, in order to give life to the present volume.

Why such an undertaking is of philosophical importance, now more than ever, will be discussed in the introduction and the chapters to come. There are, however, also reasons of a more personal nature why I think that this book, both critical and honorific, had to appear. When I had become a master's student at KU Leuven, I had my fill of German idealism and hoped to work on Nietzsche. Only two courses in the curriculum promised discussion of Nietzsche, both of which were by William Desmond, but to my regret they also promised ample discussion of Kant and Hegel. Grudgingly I decided to weather those discussions of 'transcendental critique' and 'absolute spirit' once again in the hopes of hearing the sweet rhetoric of Nietzsche. To my surprise, I was taken in by a new way of thinking about German idealism, one not merely expository and reconstructive, but critical and engaging, serious and playful. I was excited about this class many weeks before Nietzsche was even mentioned. This explains the image on the cover of this book: the serious playfulness of a child, on the beach, running after birds.

I mention this anecdote because it might give readers a first impression into what makes Desmond's philosophy unique: it allows new discussion, new thoughts, and new engagements, with topics and authors that are, by some, assigned to the dustbin of philosophical history. Many colleagues have told me that they similarly felt revitalized by the metaxological approach to philosophy. While I had no plans to continue philosophy after my master's, I was to finish my studies in law, William's classes inspired me onward, toward a research master and even a doctorate. To this day, I am still engrossed in philosophy, which would not have been the case without William—whether this is for better or for worse, I have no clue. Throughout these years, he was my gentle doctoral supervisor (as they say in German: *Doktorvater*) and we slowly became friends. Much like William's teaching, our conversations mix the high and the low, the critical and the appreciative, the metaphysical and the profane. Years later, I learned that William adapted his style to the needs of his students. One colleague of mine once described William as a gardener, tending to the garden with insight and finesse. Some of us needed confidence, others needed constraint; some needed a firm hand, others needed to be let free. Most appreciated William's style, which is evident from the good number of former students who flocked from all over the world to William's retirement conference.

I hope that this volume would get his gentle approval. Ironic. When I write, there is always music playing on my computer. The songs 'shuffle' randomly, which sometimes works well, sometimes not. When I came to this paragraph and was looking for a way to close this preface, the song 'Life Is Good' by the Irish-American folk-punk band Flogging Molly started playing, and that seems appropriate. The song is itself expressive of a desire for someone who would bring peace, but the search for that someone tends to be a gamble. The chorus repeats 'life is good', even though the advances toward the other are not always successful and life will come to an end someday. The song is bittersweet, but it truthfully expresses intimacy and displacement, love and estrangement—similar sensations emerge when reading through metaxology. Flogging Molly comes to the bridge now, and the chorus will soon repeat: "But I could walk across the ocean / Find ourselves a little peace / Where all our troubles are forgotten / And wars will someday cease / Life is good, life is good / Life is fine, life is fine / Life is everything we loathe and so unkind / They say death is cruel, / But death unwinds / It comes naturally to all us here alive".[1]

I feel confident to say that this volume is good as well, which is to some extent the case because it came to be under fortunate circumstances: many had written excellent papers on the topics of metaxology. There was an abundance of good work to select from, and I express my heartfelt gratitude for the commitment and diligence of all contributors to this volume. Although some negotiations with regard to deadlines were in order at times, the process ran fairly smoothly. When I contacted the editorial staff of Palgrave Macmillan, I was happy to find that Amy Invernizzi was enthusiastic about the project. The book proposal passed a favorable review, and I am very grateful to the anonymous reviewer for his or her comments and suggestions, most of which I have incorporated in this volume. The editorial staff at Palgrave Macmillan works very efficiently, and I do want to voice gratitude toward all of them.

Leuven, Belgium   Dennis Vanden Auweele

---

[1] Flogging Molly, 'Life Is Good'. From the album *Life Is Good* (2017), released by Vanguard, Spinefarm.

Contents

1 Introduction 1
   Dennis Vanden Auweele

Part I Being, Knowing and Intimacy 13

2 Number and the Between 15
   John Milbank

3 True Being and Being True: Metaxology and the Retrieval
   of Metaphysics 45
   D. C. Schindler

4 Hermeneutical Selving as Metaxological Selving: Bridging
   the Perceived Gap Between Theological Hermeneutics
   and Metaphysics 59
   Daniel Minch

5 Metaxology and New Realist Philosophy 77
   Sandra Lehmann

Part II Absolute Being and Talking God   93

6 The Metaxology of the Divine Names   95
Brendan Thomas Sammon

7 Metaxologizing Our God-Talk: Desmond, Kearney, and the Divine Between   113
Mark F. Novak

8 Espousing Intimacies: Mystics and the Metaxological   129
Patrick Ryan Cooper

Part III Autonomy, Porosity, and Goodness   149

9 Evil: From Phenomenology to Thought   151
Cyril O'Regan

10 Retrieving the Primal Ethos of Life: (Bio)Ethics in the Love of Being   177
Roberto Dell'Oro

11 Silence, Excess, and Autonomy   195
Dennis Vanden Auweele

12 Reactivating Christian Metaphysical Glory in the Wake of Its Eclipse: William Desmond Contra Giorgio Agamben   209
Philip John Paul Gonzales

Part IV On Wholeness, Hegel and Pan(en)theism   227

13 The Real and the Glitter: Apropos William Desmond's *Hegel's God*   229
Sander Griffioen

14 Transcendence in Metaxology and Sophiology   243
    Josephien van Kessel

15 Panentheism and Hegelian Controversies   257
    Philip A. Gottschalk

Part V Creation, Embodied Being and Beauty   269

16 The Gift of Creation   271
    Richard Kearney

17 On Speaking the Amen: Augustinian Soliloquy
    in Shakespeare's *Metaxu*   285
    Renée Köhler-Ryan

18 Metaxology and Environmental Ethics: On the Ethical
    Response to the Aesthetics of Nature as Other in the
    Between   303
    Alexandra Romanyshyn

19 Responding Metaxologically   317
    William Desmond

Index   337

List of Contributors

Patrick Ryan Cooper Saint Meinrad Seminary, Rockport, IN, USA

Roberto Dell'Oro Loyola Marymount University, Los Angeles, CA, USA

William Desmond KU Leuven, Leuven, Belgium; Villanova University, Villanova, PA, USA; and Maynooth University, Maynooth, Ireland

Philip John Paul Gonzales University of Dallas, Irving, TX, USA

Philip A. Gottschalk Tyndale Theological Seminary, Badhoevedorp, Netherlands

Sander Griffioen VU Amsterdam, Amsterdam, Netherlands

Richard Kearney Philosophy Department, Boston College, Chestnut Hill, MA, USA

Renée Köhler-Ryan The University of Notre Dame Australia, Sydney, NSW, Australia

Sandra Lehmann University of Vienna, Vienna, Austria

John Milbank University of Nottingham, Nottingham, UK

Daniel Minch KU Leuven, Leuven, Belgium

Mark F. Novak McMaster University, Hamilton, ON, Canada

Cyril O'Regan University of Notre Dame, Notre Dame, IN, USA

Alexandra Romanyshyn Saint Louis University, St. Louis, MO, USA

Brendan Thomas Sammon Saint Joseph's University, Philadelphia, PA, USA

D. C. Schindler The John Paul II Institute, The Catholic University of America, Washington, DC, USA

Josephien van Kessel Radboud University Nijmegen, Nijmegen, Netherlands

Dennis Vanden Auweele KU Leuven (University of Leuven), Leuven, Belgium

Abbreviations

AA	*Art and the Absolute: A Study in Hegel's Aesthetics* (Albany: SUNY Press, 1986)
AOO	*Art, Origins, Otherness* (Albany: SUNY Pres, 2003)
BB	*Being and the Between* (Albany: SUNY Press, 1995)
BHD	*Beyond Hegel and Dialectic* (Albany: SUNY Press, 1992)
DDO	*Desire, Dialectic and Otherness* (New Haven, CT: Yale University Press, 1987)
EB	*Ethics and the Between* (Albany: SUNY Press, 2001)
GB	*God and the Between* (Oxford: Blackwell, 2008)
HG	*Hegel's God: A Counterfeit Double?* (Aldershot: Ashgate, 2003)
ISB	*The Intimate Strangeness of Being: Metaphysics after Dialectic* (Washington, DC: The Catholic University of America Press, 2012)
IST	*Is There a Sabbath for Thought? Between Religion and Philosophy* (New York: Fordham University Press, 2005)
IU	*The Intimate Universal: The Hidden Porosity among Religion, Art, Philosophy, and Politics* (New York: Columbia University Press, 2016)
PO	*Philosophy and Its Others* (Albany: SUNY Press, 1990)
PU	*Perplexity and Ultimacy* (Albany: SUNY Press, 1995)

CHAPTER 1

Introduction

Dennis Vanden Auweele

Of late, philosophy appears to have become a business of trends, including trend watchers who make us aware of what counts for these days—hot and what not. There are trends that promised to be the next big thing but now seem passé such as deconstruction (which seems to have passed its sell-by date), but also trends that grow from older fads such as neo-Thomism. Nostalgia can be a trend too: endlessly and voraciously scavenging in texts of yore, looking to apply old insights in new contexts. Philosophical trends make philosophy not only a business but also an epochal practice: there is a time for this, and then there is a time for that. What would it mean to stand outside of all of this? How is one ever not in the business of doing philosophy, not in the business of following the latest trends and not in the business of reducing philosophy to its merely epochal concerns? In such a case, one would be an *outsider* who transcends the business of the day whilst donning a mischievous grin. Culture is replete with images of outsiders, and many believe themselves to be one of these. Perhaps the literary most pronounced outsider is Dostoyevsky's anonymous protagonist in *Notes from the Underground*. In raising the middle finger to polite society, he puts himself on the fringes, shamelessly abusing all others. Not coincidentally,

---

D. Vanden Auweele (✉)
KU Leuven (University of Leuven), Leuven, Belgium
e-mail: Dennis.Vandenauweele@kuleuven.be

© The Author(s) 2018
D. Vanden Auweele (ed.), *William Desmond's Philosophy between Metaphysics, Religion, Ethics, and Aesthetics*,
https://doi.org/10.1007/978-3-319-98992-1_1

Nietzsche felt immediate kinship to Dostoevsky's most misanthropic character. Both of them were in recognition of the overwhelming strength and authority of the business of the day, but refused to blend smoothly within it: "Of course I cannot break through the wall by battering my head against it if I really have not the strength to knock it down, but I am not going to be reconciled to it simply because it is a stone wall and I have not the strength" (1918, p. 59). I have come to believe that such outsiders are parasitic upon the *insider*, desperately seeking recognition through their dissidence. Ultimately, these blend into epochs of their own; they will have their day like Schopenhauer who in his old age finally received the recognition he believed to deserve. Nietzsche said of God that He is *not now our taste*. Are the outsiders Nietzsche, Dostoyevsky or Schopenhauer now our taste? Or have we, as Nietzsche suggests at times, forsaken all discerning taste and have now become voracious gluttons incapable of saving ourselves for the finer things?

For sure, William Desmond is an outsider in the business of philosophy, but not in the same way as the agonal rebellion of a Nietzsche or the nihilism of Dostoevsky's man of the underground. Desmond's thought is not parasitic upon existing ways of doing philosophy and not in any trend or business, though he does clearly enjoy kinship with phenomenology and its theological turnings, dialectical philosophy and neo-Thomism. He is this, and more. In a word, William Desmond's philosophy is metaxology, and metaxology is metaphysics. Metaphysics is not only not now to our taste, but it is not a matter of tastes of trends. Metaphysics is of all times and of none; there is always a time for metaphysics, but no specific time from which to do metaphysics. Perhaps this is the cause of why Desmond has been slow to receive mainstream attention, simply because of standing outside and above such mainstream? Metaphysics is attentive to its own history, but it is not exhausted by its history. This is so because metaphysics must always start again from wonder, which Plato told us is the true beginning of all philosophy. But if wonder is the beginning of philosophy, is there a way for thought to move beyond wonder determinatively? Can we just take wonder as a brief moment of perplexity that can be determinatively overcome by scientific or dialectical thought? Is there a return to wonder after wonder? And is our philosophical attempt at determinacy then not chastised by its inability to cut the cord with wonder?

These are some of the issues that are at the fore of metaxological philosophy: a metaphysical and therefore timeless returning of philosophy to wonder, again and again refreshing thought beyond its self-complacent systematics. These brief introductory pages hope to serve as an initial guide through the maze of metaxological philosophy. Even Dante did not stop short at one guide and neither should the student of metaxology. After our initial descent with Virgil in this introduction (though, hopefully, not into *inferno*), the chapters to follow serve as the outstretching hand of Beatrice, hoping to ascend from Purgatory towards Paradise. At the end of the book, this guide, too, will have to be left behind. Hopefully, Saint Bernard is awaiting in other work.[1]

According to a well-known anecdote, Martin Heidegger was once asked which term in the title of his opus magnum *Being and Time* was most important. His impish response was 'and'. Metaxology is in some ways similar to Heidegger's playful response, as its focus is first on intermediation. Metaxology is Greek-English, a *logos* or speaking from the *metaxu* or between. But when one says the word 'between', one is immediately asked: between what and what? Like Heidegger, Desmond is not primarily interested in the two or more terms to which a relationship should be coordinated (although these surely play a role of importance), but with the very idea of relationality itself. The between is an openness or porosity, a space of passing and communication. In one place, Desmond defines it as "an ontological milieu that is overdeterminate: both indeterminate and determinate, taking form in a plurivocal interplay between otherness and sameness, openness and definition, and yet excessive to final fixation" (EB 1).

What does it mean to philosophize from the between, from this space where different views, ideas and passions transverse? This means that one is attentive to the singular identity of any idea but also the dialectical, even non-dialectical, relationality of things. Philosophy has taken some time to come to think of relationality on a par with identity. In the beginning of philosophy, and even still today in some circles, much of philosophy has fancied its binary oppositions: being and non-being, intelligible and unintelligible, good and evil, and so on. Desmond opposes such easy binary opposition as, borrowing a phrase from Blaise Pascal, an overindulgence in *esprit de géométrie* rather than the subtleness of *esprit de finesse*. This is unsurprising because Desmond's initial fame came as a student of Hegel,

---

[1] Next to the voluminous monographs written by Desmond himself, I would recommend the following resources: Kelly (2007), Simpson (2009) and Griffioen (2010). A recent anthology puts Desmond in dialogue with some of the more prominent theologians of the past and today: Simpson and Sammon (2017). In previous work, I have made humble attempts at outlining Desmond's philosophy: Vanden Auweele (2013a, b).

who was renowned for his search to overcome binary opposition. Hegel's one-time philosophical compatriot Schelling would even point out that the "main weakness of all modern philosophy" was that it "lacks an intermediate concept" which results in that "everything that does not *have being* is nothing, and everything that is not spiritual in the highest sense is material in the crudest sense, and everything that is not morally free is mechanical, and everything that is not intelligent is uncomprehending" (2000, p. 64 [286]). To think of reality in terms of simple opposition is simplistic. There is a constant going-over and going-under, a dialectical back and forth between abstract oppositions. All things exceed simple determination in pre-established systems of rationalist intelligibility. With and after Kant, philosophy started to stress relationality and dialectics over simple, univocal determinacy.

Metaxology takes its cues initially from dialectical philosophy, but as one repays a teacher poorly by remaining ever faithful—or so Nietzsche says in *Thus spoke Zarathustra*[2]—so Desmond has said his farewells to Hegel after taking his inheritance. He senses there to be something amiss with dialectical thought à la Hegel. The stress is there on dialectical self-determination, which leads easily towards a higher sense of determinate univocity, not fully true to the challenge of thinking otherness as otherness. This is Desmond's main qualm with Hegel even before *Hegel's God: A Counterfeit Double?*[3] where God, as the capitalized Other, is turned into the developmental progress of historical self-determination through spirit (*Geist*). Hegel might have thought that he overcame Kantian dualism by rethinking and revamping the absolute in terms of world history but, in truth, while Hegel might have believed this to be a step forwards, it is not progress. Something of the other as other is lost here, which leaves open the door for a potentially tyrannical appropriation of otherness by means of an over-reaching of dialectical self-mediation. One might even ask if the theodicy of Hegel's God is one that justifies all on the slaughter bench of history.

This is not the only sense of dialectical philosophy to be sure, as, for instance, the Socratic or Platonic practice of dialogue is more apt to escape potential tyranny. Hegelian dialectics had then a good point of departure, but it did not make it to the finish line unscathed. It is time then perhaps

---

[2] "One repays a teacher badly if one always remains a pupil only. And why would you not want to pluck at my wreath?" (Nietzsche 2006, p. 59).

[3] This issue was already at stake in Desire, Dialectic and Otherness (DDO).

for Hegel, Schelling and even Nietzsche to pass the relay stick to different ways of thinking about the community of being, being good and absolute being. This would have to be a way of thinking that is mindful of (absolute) difference, but open to infinite mediation and revelation. There is intimacy and familiarity in the between, but also mind-boggling strangeness. All of this is to be accounted for as intelligently as possible. In one place, such an approach is described thus: "It lives between peril and crux. As a figuring of the primal ethos, it divines the nature of the togetherness, the absolved relativity, with heed to the difference, and without forgetting the transcendence of the divine and its reserves. We need a finessed, transdialectical *logos* of the *metaxu*" (GB 117). In order to come to such a rethinking, we are in need foremost of two things: a phenomenologically robust account of wonder, astonishment and perplexity and a community between philosophy, religion and art.

In a number of places, Desmond outlines what could be called his philosophical method. This is not alike to a methodology that navigates from research question to results—as one is forced to write in 'research projects' these days. Instead, this is a method that is wary of the fact that the outcomes might not answer the questions fully, and so invite a return to the question. In *Perplexity and Ultimacy*, Desmond even praises the "nobility of philosophical thought" in terms of its "willingness to risk questions it may not be able to answer definitively" (PU 167).

Philosophy starts in wonder at profound questions about being, being good and divine being. These are three major questions of metaphysics, but they have gone out of fashion. There are numerous reasons for their untimeliness, such as excessive reliance on positivist truth, a watering down of transcendence in favour of autonomy or even a simple uneasiness with regard to questions that forestall final resolution. Such hesitations lull the human mind into a sleep of mere immanent finitude, where questions of more ultimate concern do not arise easily. In opposition to the temptation of excessive reductionism, one is to take up such questions again and again, *da capo*. When one then reflects on these topics, there are different responses that might emerge: marvel, familiarity, perplexity and astonishment (see, e.g., GB 118–121). The human condition is not entirely marvel and estrangement, but there is equally comfortable familiarity. We participate in the marvel of being before we are able to be reflective of that marvel.

Modern thought does not always take kindly to such a dwelling with marvel. In general, modern philosophy sought to think of perplexity in uniquely negative terms, namely as a challenge to be overcome. This is what Desmond calls a move from indeterminacy to determinacy, where the strange is made into the familiar. And indeed, many a thing can be rendered intelligible, but never without a certain reserve in excess to determinability. The perplexity is never merely negative; it is something constitutive of the subject matter. We can never exhaust metaphysical questions; there is never a way to settle things once and for all. But when one emphasizes such relatively univocal frames of thought, then one might beget answers to metaphysical questions. But these answers risk being shallow reactions to profound experiences.

One way to illustrate such a methodology is by what Desmond calls the hyperboles of being (GB 122–158). These attempt to navigate from the human condition towards absolute being: how does one think of God in the between? Most think then of the proofs of God, and they do have their role to play. These proofs were famously assaulted by Heidegger and others as unappreciative of the constitutive difference between beings and Being. In other words, the proofs of God are thought of as attempts to fill up a gap, they are signs of a lack in the between that is filled by absolute being. In doings so, one would miss the constitutive difference between immanent reason and transcendent poetry, so says Heidegger. Indeed, it is a perennial danger for any metaphysics to put God and being on a continuum that obviates the distinctness between these two. This was Hegel's mistake, but there are different ways of thinking from the between to God. Rather than univocal directions, these are indirections that propel or throw (*ballein*) one beyond (*hyper*) oneself. It is abundance that propels thought, not emptiness. The mere appearance of good, beauty and communal being makes one stagger. If contemplated sincerely, they occasion of themselves a move beyond finitude. Metaphysics must then not be abandoned as many would advocate today, but it only has to be returned to its source of inspiration: the overabundant plenitude of dwelling in the primal ethos of the between.

Thought is propelled by an excess to determinability. Whether or not philosophy can stay, by its means alone, faithful to such an excess is questionable. Philosophy is driven by a desire for understanding, an *eros* that seeks determination. At its best, philosophy allows itself to end up in *aporia*, like many of Plato's dialogues, but at times philosophy was an unfaithful friend of wisdom. When a desire for self-determination clogs up a porosity towards things in excess of determination, philosophy falls into the trap of homogeneity. One remedy to this challenge is to keep philosophy open to its others, most importantly art and religion: "Art and religion are ways of dealing affirmatively with the surplus equivocity; they are not defects from a univocity whose fastness allows us only to condemn equivocity. They offer forms of porosity, filled with finesse, to what is communicated in the saturated equivocity" (IU 171).

Taking its initial cues from Hegelian dialectic, metaxology realizes that one cannot divorce philosophy—as the attempt to *think* the absolute—from religion and art as respectively ways of symbolizing and representing the absolute. In Hegelian thought, this ultimately works out to the benefit of philosophy since it is most capable of thinking the absolute. In other words, Hegel recognizes the unique contribution of religion and art but ultimately mitigates that uniqueness by sublating their identity into philosophy. Metaxology is an attempt to think the community of art, religion and philosophy in a more robust way that recognizes at once the uniqueness and absolved relativity of these practices.

The first three chapters of Desmond's latest monograph, *The Intimate Universal* (2016), discuss respectively how religion, art and philosophy deal with the reality of an intimate universal in different but similar ways. The intimate universal is the revelation of being, goodness and divine being that is intimate and particular to one individual, but also universal to humanity. Philosophy, art and religion all have similar ways of dealing with such a thing, but their ways of interacting retain a constitutive difference. In each of these chapters, the emphasis is on thinking the intimate universal between the universalism that is associated with Enlightenment thought and the particularity of postmodern philosophy. This means that being religious is not merely a matter of personal belief or conviction but neither is there one cosmopolitan religion. Likewise, art is not merely the sensible representation or imitation of abstract thought but neither is it absolutely spontaneous self-creation. And this means that philosophy is not merely an abstract, universal theory or a personal practice of thinking. This is what makes art, religion and philosophy similar as these are all attempts to dwell in wonder and astonishment of the absolute but, at the same time, trying to find ways to revamp the absolute strangeness of such events.

This means that Desmond is, as no other, attentive to the importance of keeping an open line between art, religion and philosophy as attempts to accomplish similar ends. There are two ways in which this could go amiss. First, one could think of art, religion and philosophy as absolutely separate domains of human experience. In this case, philosophy proceeds as divorced from poetic revelation and becomes unresponsive to religious themes (which is perhaps the case in mainstream philosophy today); religion would then divorce itself from philosophical self-reflection and the power of poetic truth; art would be a practice for its own sake alone (*l'art pour l'art*) that does not deal with matters of ultimate concern or at any point becomes self-reflective of the role it has to play. Second, one could think of art, religion and philosophy as ultimately concentrated with one unit in this triad only. Generally, this has meant that art and religion were subsumed in a philosophical project. Very overtly, we see this in how, on the one hand, Kant subsumes religion and art in the project of practical philosophy and, on the other hand, Hegel dialectically sublates the identity of art and religion as part of the philosophical project of spirit.

To treat properly of art, religion and philosophy is not only a matter of fairness, but also one of truthfulness. Truthfulness is the capacity to keep an openness to the revelation of excess that disrupts or even traumatizes the way we have accustomed ourselves to think. Truthfulness means to deal with things both in their own identity as well as in their relationality. This has always been the task of philosophy, but it is a task that can never be complete. Philosophy must be a searching always, following its own directions and desires (*eros*), while remaining attentive to what is given and exceeds its immanent frame (*agape*).

Even though metaxology requires us to think of the community between art, religion and philosophy, the pragmatics of life must give way to a more compartmentalized approach. The chapters in this book are divided into five parts, which deal respectively with metaphysical issues of knowing and being; philosophical-theological questions of absolute being; moral matters of autonomy and porosity; Desmond's view of Hegel, wholeness and pantheism; and the embodiment and beauty of created being. While attempts were made to keep these different topics more or less self-confined, due to the nature of the matter, they tended to spill over into other domains. The volume opens with a contribution by John Milbank, who reflects on the modern attempts to rethink mathematics in terms of logics. In his view, a revision of this could support the 'third way' of a theistic metaphysics, which must, after Erich Przywara and William Desmond, be a metaphysics of the analogy of being or metaxology. Next to holding a chair at KU Leuven, Desmond has been a professor of philosophy at the University of Villanova. In his contribution, D.C. Schindler reminds us that the motto of Villanova consists of three terms: *Unitas, Caritas* and *Veritas*. Postmodern philosophy is keen to malign good

Veritas as an exercise in oppression, something which must be avoided if we truly want to reach universal care and unity. In opposition to this trend, Schindler illustrates how Desmond's philosophy is capable of giving truth its dues against the assaults of Vattimo and others, but also and more importantly that truth serves as foundational for unity and care. Building from Desmond's *Intimate Universal*, Schindler illustrates how care and unity need an ontological grounding in truth in order to be more than merely superficial. Daniel Minch gives a theological dimension to this issue, placing the importance of Desmond's philosophy within twentieth-century Catholic theology. Such theology recognized the impoverished states of a thinking about the created versus the creator in dualistic terms. Building on Schillebeeckx's hermeneutic interpretation of Christian faith, he stages new ways—building, in turn, on Desmond's fourfold sense of being—of thinking the relationship between immanent nature and transcendence beyond modernity's postulatory finitism. In her chapter, Sandra Lehmann continues on this point of the ontological grounding of truth by comparing Desmond's metaxology to the revival of metaphysics in the New Realism of Quentin Meillassoux. While noting the superficial similarities between these philosophical projects, Lehmann clarifies that metaxology provides a more robust alternative to the anti-metaphysical philosophies of finitude of the twentieth century. Particularly prominent in her argument is that Meillassoux's discussion of the ground of being does not allow him to escape the shadow of Heidegger's critique of metaphysics, which is something more ably accomplished by metaxology.

Questions of being and the ground of being have traditionally invited speculation about absolute being or God. Metaphysics is the life-blood of theology, and metaxology has been a spectacular instrument for contemporary theologians to escape the clutches of deconstructive and other anti-metaphysical ways of thinking (see, also, Simpson and Sammon 2017). In that spirit, reflection on this aspect of metaxology opens with a contribution by Brendan Sammon, who points out the similarities between Desmond's philosophical theology and the Divine Name tradition of Dionysius the Areopagite. These names have a tendency to name and un-name at the same time, appreciating the constitutive difference between God and creation. Continuing on this task of thinking God, Mark Novak advances the idea that the approaches by William Desmond and his long-standing travelling companion Richard Kearney are closely intertwined. Both are interested in thinking, not only about God but also on doing so from the between, a middle space of porosity that does not settle in advance on *eros* or *agape*, existence or possibility. While differences in emphasis emerge in discussion between them, Desmond and Kearney are largely of one mind on how to proceed, and Novak points out that both are involved in a process of theopoetics, namely the imaginative and poetical representation of God. Finally, Patrick Cooper offers a sustained reflection on the Augustinian adage that one ought to move from the exterior inwards and the inferior to the superior. Desmond had signalled early on that this is a central metaphor for metaxology, and Cooper traces its importance throughout mystics such as Pierre Scheuer, Joseph Maréchal and Jan van Ruusbroec.

To think of being inclines metaxological philosophy to ponder the goodness of being. In his contribution, Cyril O'Regan engages the various notes on evil throughout metaxological philosophy. His argument is that Desmond's view of evil comes close to Ricoeur in *The Symbolism of Evil*, where symbols of evil give philosophy to think about the excessive nature of evil. Such moral questions are obviously not uniquely abstract, but must be applied in the world. What does the metaxological rethinking of the community and goodness imply for discussions in bioethics? Roberto Dell'Oro argues that contemporary bioethics would benefit from a metaxological re-appreciation of the goodness of being, and especially the value of givenness. Continuing on the value of givenness, Dennis Vanden Auweele argues that a modern project for absolutized autonomy cannot do but dread silence, which signals a hiccup or momentary lapse in the project of *logos*. And yet, Vanden Auweele shows that silence can be a convalescence that renders human beings receptive to something in excess of finite determination, which can in turn inspire self-determination to new heights. In his contribution, Philip Gonzales stages a dialogue between two seemingly antithetical thinkers, Desmond and Agamben. Gonzales argues that Desmond provides a reconstructed Christian metaphysics against the profaning thought of Agamben. Agamben is incapable of thinking the Sabbath or rest of God beyond the terms of retreat while metaxology provides the resources to think the Sabbath of God as part of the creatureliness of human beings.

Metaxology proposes its own, unique sense of theism (for lack of a better term), seeking to avoid the pitfalls of, on the one hand, a pantheism that confuses the created and the creator and, on the other hand, a deism that radically disjoints God from creation. In this, Desmond has repeatedly expressed hesitations with regard to the way Hegel conceives of the relationship between God, religion and world. In his contribution, Sander

Griffioen traces these reservations throughout Desmond's oeuvre, from *Hegel's God* to *The Intimate Universal*. He helpfully distinguishes between three different uses of the term 'counterfeit', and the way these relate to 'perplexity', in order to get to the bottom of Desmond's discomfort with Hegel. Discussions on this topic of relating God to the world have been a mainstay in philosophical theology, for instance between the Russian authors Shestov and Solov'ëv. In discussion with Desmond's discussion of these authors in *Is there a Sabbath for Thought?* Josephien van Kessel proposes that there is far greater similarity between the Sophiology of Solov'ëv (and Bulgakov) and Desmond's metaxology. Philip Gottschalk carries this discussion one step further, engaging similar authors, but adding the dimension of Desmond's 'clash' with other, slightly more pious, Hegelians.

The final set of chapters discusses the contribution of metaxology to philosophizing about embodied, aesthetic being. Continuing his long-term voyage with Desmond, Richard Kearney takes up a number of paragraphs from Desmond's work so as to show how creation can be thought of in more dynamic, embodied and lively terms than as mere abstraction. Renée Kohler-Ryan, in turn, uses metaxology to understand better the failure of soliloquy in Shakespeare's Macbeth, and its success in Augustine. A conversation with our own, embodied self, which is in communication with other selves but also with itself, must always happen with a third element, a capitalized Other. In the last contribution, Alexandra Romanyshyn discusses the deprivation of value from the natural environment and traces through metaxology some of its sources. She suggests that metaxology can provide more holistic and moral perspective with regard to dealing with nature as other than the predominant instrumentalizing ways of modern thought. The volume ends with a short response by William Desmond to all individual contributions.

Bibliography

Dostoyevsky, Fyodor. 1918. Notes from the Underground. In *White Nights, and Other Stories*. Trans. Constance Garnett. New York: Macmillan.

Griffioen, Sander. 2010. Towards a Philosophy of God: A Study in William Desmond's Thought. *Philosophia Reformata* 75: 117–140.

Kelly, Thomas, ed. 2007. *Between System and Poetics: William Desmond and Philosophy After Dialectic*. Aldershot: Ashgate Press.

Nietzsche, F.W. 2006. *Thus Spoke Zarathustra*. Trans. Adrian Del Caro and Robert Pippin. Cambridge: Cambridge University Press.

Schelling, F.W.J. 2000. *The Ages of the World*. Trans. Jason Wirth. New York: SUNY Press.

Simpson, Chris. 2009. *Religion, Metaphysics, and the Postmodern: William Desmond and John D. Caputo*. Indianapolis, IN: Indiana University Press.

Simpson, Chris, and Brendan Sammon, eds. 2017. *William Desmond and Contemporary Theology*. Indiana: University of Notre Dame Press.

Vanden Auweele, Dennis. 2013a. Metaxological 'Yes' and Existential 'No': William Desmond and Atheism. *Sophia: International Journal of Philosophy and Traditions* 52: 637–655.

———. 2013b. The Poverty of Philosophy: Desmond's Hyperbolic Gifts and Caputo's Events. *American Catholic Philosophical Quarterly* 87: 411–432.

PART I

Being, Knowing and Intimacy

CHAPTER 2

Number and the Between

John Milbank

One could argue that there are three tendencies at work within current philosophy. There is still, and overwhelmingly, the dominance of post-Kantian 'critical' epistemology, whether this takes the form of phenomenology or of analysis. Then there is a sometimes explicitly anti-Kantian turn back to metaphysics, which often takes anti-humanist and nihilistic forms. In the third place, there is a revival of a theistic metaphysics, in various guises. William Desmond's work is here pre-eminently outstanding.

It pivots, above all, upon a reworking of analogy (see, especially, EB). Ontologized, analogy can appropriately be dubbed by Desmond the Platonic *metaxu*, or 'the between'. If the ultimate ingredients of reality are univocal and identical, then they are, in a way, self-explanatory. We may wonder, but the impulse to know does not compel us to look any further. If, on the other hand, they are endlessly heterogeneous, then ultimate reality may consist in a random, vital, though not holistic, heterogeneous flux. Alternatively, again, it may consist in a dialectical oscillation between a static sameness and a dynamic difference—whether this be governed by determinate negation after Hegel or a positive tensional assertion and counter-assertion after Schelling and his many postmodern avatars.

J. Milbank (✉)
University of Nottingham, Nottingham, UK
e-mail: John.Milbank@nottingham.ac.uk

In all three cases, the immanent all is self-explanatory, even if we cannot quite reach its meaning, or there is no 'meaning' in quite our sense to be reached. However, if diverse things are not altogether diverse and not altogether the same, then they exhibit an ineffable resemblance. This noetic affinity can reasonably be regarded as at one with their real connectedness, with what actually holds them together: an occult glue of which, if we read them unswervingly, the Neoplatonists expounded, Aristotle anticipated and Aquinas more cautiously upheld.

It is hard to account for this hermetic *convenientia*, as the medievals, including Aquinas, described it. What is more, it does not seem to be an absolute, self-sustaining principle, like univocity, which is a thing being itself and not its opposite, nor the equivocal creativity of flux which is its own wild, natural divinity, nor that variant upon the same which is modern dialectics. To discern the immanent ultimacy of the between is rather to discern the ultimacy of a positive, sophianic gap that remains nonetheless an obscure interval. If its mediation is indeed such, it cannot itself be erected into an absolute driving initiative: rather, it holds in true balance the same and the different. And not through the Schellingian game of their polar conflict, which renders *agon* the gnostic immanent reality. Instead, if this balance is positive, nutritive and congenial (and fallen distortion of this only contingent), nothing finite is after all ultimate: not the fixed nor the moving, not substance nor process, rather their interplay, which cannot be reduced to a rule standing over against the play and its poles—neither to warfare, nor to *eros* if this be understood as an impersonal all-consuming magnetism. Rather, we glimpse in the real a proto-personalism—the I and the thou and the complex linkage and birthing through linkage of rock and star and crystal, of seed and flower, field and forest, animal and humanity, man and woman, human and human, locality and nation, home and abroad (see, again, EB).

Everything here is fragment, though connected—and the mere connection is not the absolute. In this way, Desmond shows, with a unique perspicacity, how horizontal connectedness or analogy suggests also a vertical analogy. Since nothing is ultimate here below—not firm items, nor variable process, nor their agonistic or erotic linkage—then all is suspended from above. If anything rules here below at all, it is agapeic love, however constantly interrupted and contaminated. But love is not an earthly sway, it is not a covert domination. It only governs by obscure indication, by pointing away from itself, by revealing itself to be a mere indication of a transcendent plenitude just as much as all the partial things and dynamics which it, here, connects and constitutes.

Counting the Between

A question can then arise as to whether the analogical or the metaxological must also be regarded as strongly paradoxical, if it hovers always between identity and difference and is not partly one and partly the other, but somehow simultaneously both at once, which surely implies their (non-dialectical coincidence)?

This question can be linked to the rebuttal of the dominantly univocal or equivocal, whose alternative rationalism is, as Desmond and others have shown, strongly linked to the reign of the mathematical and the quantitative in the modern epoch (BB 47–130). The new questioning of the Kantian and anthropocentric in our own day has thrown this circumstance once more into relief. Kant is accused of actually *subverting* the real Copernican turn which situates man within nature, as Schelling already alleged against him, and of trying to hide from the disconcerting realist naturalism which this opens to view (Schelling 2004; see: Grant 2008). This allegation, from the Romantic period to our own day, goes along with a linkage of nature to number, with the latter being often regarded as the main route of access to a disclosure of nature's secrets (see Rosenstock 2017, pp. 1–41).

What is more, ever since Cusa and Bruno's nature has been infinitized, in a way that threatens to immanentize the divine. But here also mathematics has kept pace, by newly claiming to be able, in various ways (as with the Calculus itself) to calculate even the infinite. In the face of this new, double reckoning with the infinite, the Kantian claim to be holding knowledge within critical 'finite' bounds looks but debatably modern after all. If it is modern, then it represents only an alternative answer to a modern, post-theological dilemma: whether to consecrate human limits on the one hand or the limit of the whole of immanent natural reality on the other.

Nevertheless, as was realized by F.H. Jacobi, these two tendencies are still in collusion. In some hidden sense, Spinoza and Kant say the same thing (Jacobi 1994, pp. 173–251 and 339–378). The former thinks that human geometrized reasoning within its own bounds can reach the infinite ultimate, which is of itself 'nothing'. The latter thinks that human reasoning within anthropocentric, transcendental and 'non-mathematical' bounds must stop short of the nullity of a theoretically unknowable real.

It is for this reason that Kant was readily reversible into 'Spinoza' after his death. To get rid of the Kantian epistemological nullity, all one needs to do is to hypostasize and ontologize the boundaries of human knowledge, asserting that their very limits can either register as real resistance (Fichte)[1] or dialectically encompass the unlimited, even if this reasoning requires a long historical development, as for Schelling and Hegel. Then human beings can grasp the ultimate and infinite ontological nullity, however divinized, from which all else is taken to arise.

Indeed, this story looks clearer if we focus on *Naturphilosophie*, from which arguably later 'idealism' beyond Fichte was an offshoot. In seeking to show how all derived from nothing, Lorenz Oken and others tried to derive energy and life mathematically. In anticipation of Alain Badiou in our own day (and indeed like a kind of fusion of Badiou with Gilles Deleuze), Oken saw positive things as combinations and settings of nullity, rendering them like secondary nullities, whose positivity was an imposture, concealing the more primary nothingness which always eventually prevails as decay, destruction and warfare, which Oken regarded as darkly equivalent to the deepest human understanding (Rosenstock, *loc. cit*; Grant 2012, pp. 287–321).

Is the alternative then to Kantian humanism this sort of gnostic nihilism, to which Desmond accurately sees Hegelian dialectics as ultimately approximating (see HG)? The example of Oken, and the way it has in effect been taken up again in our own day, suggests that the question of number is not at all a marginal one for modern philosophy. For there is a modern mathematical prehistory to the kind of ontology of zero that Oken erected, which I shall invoke later. This prehistory itself endeavours to have a clear univocal and finite grasp of number and the infinite, in abandonment of the more perennial Western mathematical tradition.

It is surely right to be suspicious, like Schelling, of Kant's failure to give any account of how human mind lies within nature. It is also right to take account of modern scientific and mathematical discoveries. But is the modern mode of construal of quantity, and not *just* the modern bias towards quantity, altogether metaphysically and theologically neutral? Or is it itself already committed (as with Descartes) to a Faustian elevation of the finite human grasp as able univocally to sound the infinite depths? Does the third theistic metaphysical alternative in our own day have to ignore or fly in the face of a mathematized physics? Or is it possible to

---

[1] This is why Fichte's doctrine, with his notion of the positing mind's confrontation with a limiting *anstoss* could be readily inverted into realism by Novalis and Friedrich Schlegel. By comparison, the incorporation of the objective as a moment within dialectical, or else 'artistic' reasoning, by Hegel and Schelling is, paradoxically, more purely idealist.

understand mathematics and its relation to material being itself in a different way which already requires attention to the metaxological?

Moreover, as Nicolas of Cusa already averred, may it not be the case that if one returns analogy to what was after all (for the Pythagoreans and the Platonists) its original mathematical home, one sees there most starkly that the analogical is also the paradoxical (see Milbank 2017a, pp. 143–169). If the qualitative reminds the quantitative that something like sheer analogical resemblance appears even within the quantitative in terms of (for older mathematical tradition) the irreducible difference of the geometric and the arithmetic, and the mysteriously singular proportionate properties of every number that seems to transcend their mere aggregation (Rosenstock 2017, p. 53), then the quantitative reminds the qualitative that at the borders of ultimate individuation (only allowed by quantified, 'designated' matter according to Aquinas), analogy is shown to partake of the stark mystery of the paradoxical and the dialectic. This linkage of number to the metaphysics of the between that I try to establish in what follows.

Plato, Thing and Number

What is the difference between logic and mathematics? Western logic effectively began with Aristotle as a theory about the predication of words in terms of the consistent implications of ascriptions of identity and non-identity. That gave us the theory of the syllogism, which always belonged to philosophy. Only in the nineteenth century, with the work of the self-educated Lincolnshire man George Boole, did logic get transferred from words to algebraic signs through his invention of logical symbols, and so from philosophy to mathematics (Boole 1847). Once this had happened, an ironic consequence ensued: people tried to make logic the *foundation* of mathematics, and so, in a way, to verbalize number, or at any rate to algebraicize it, in the long-term wake of François Vieta and René Descartes (Vieta 1992, pp. 315–335; Klein 1992, pp. 150–224; Descartes 2003; Lachtermann 2009, pp. 124–205).

But mathematics is *not* about the predication of identity and non-identity: the basic operation of addition is not affirmation, just as the operation of subtraction is not denial. Rather, it is confusingly both a *construction* of an organized and self-consistent abstract spatial and temporal reality, and an *intuition* of this reality as existing, although normally invisible. One makes what one measures and measures what one makes. Thus 'the true is the made': the old medieval and Thomist transcendental *verum* is also the new transcendental *factum*, as first Nicholas of Cusa and later Giambattista Vico put it, initially in the context of the latter's philosophy of mathematics, before he applied this principle to human history. (The notion that all knowing is creating and all creating is knowing may be ultimately derived from John Scotus Eriugena; for all three thinkers, this is grounded in a Trinitarian logic—the Father knows in generating the Son/*Logos*.) These two conjoined characteristics, of measuring and making, invoke a solid and substantial, yet in some sense constructed, world that is intuitively quite different from the world of logic: it seems, by comparison, to partake both of 'art' and of external reality (Vico 2010, Cap I [14–28], pp. 12–29).

It is for this reason that mathematics, all the way from Pythagoras to Quine, has often presented itself as a more plausible candidate for ontologization than has logic, although such ontologization, as in the case of Quine, is intimately bound up with the natural pragmatism of mathematical activity. Even in the case of Plato, there was already a certain link between the theoretical certainty and the evident practicability of mathematics—a link later emphasized by the theurgist Neoplatonist Proclus. As with all the ancient Greeks, as Jacob Klein pointed out, number or *arithmos* was, for Plato, the measure of a collection of 'somethings', and never exists in pure abstraction (Klein 1992, pp. 46–99). It therefore follows that Plato himself was not 'a mathematical Platonist' in the debased sense in which that term is used today. However, if number is considered reflexively (as opposed to abstractly), then, considering the pragmatic reality of all *arithmoi*, it followed for Plato that if numbers themselves can be numbered (as seems to be strikingly the case) that they themselves constitute a 'corporeal' collection of real 'thingy' entities, existing on their own elevated psychic plane—yet *not* outside this plane of awareness—to which only souls have access.

Nevertheless, the air at this height is very thin and rarefied because it does not reach up to the real glorious heaven of the 'intellectual' divinities which is thickly populated with the plenitudinous *eidē* or 'forms'—the super-numbers—which are the archetypes of real physical entities. But as with the forms, so also with *arithmoi*, Plato's belief in their eternal character is not to do with a hypostatization of abstraction or empty universality but the very opposite: a broad ontological latitude that insists on the concrete character also of the ideal and of the eternal reality of the concretely manifest and identifiable content of all appearing entities. Just *because* of his conjoined realism and pragmatism concerning numbers, yet his sense of their abiding truth as disclosed by their perfect reflexivity, Plato arrived at his own authentic 'Platonism', for which number—and more particularly geometric shape—was the key to entering the philosophical academy, though it did not provide the whole content of the doctrine that one learnt within its portals.

For once inside them, one had to consider the shape of the key as a clue rather than a directly effective instrument: it pointed towards the abiding forms, but their fuller disclosure was less apodeictic than mathematical procedure, and involved the endless detours of both negative dialectical refutations of falsity and the positively poetic, rhetorical, mythical and ritual confirmations of truth through the reading of temporal, physical and cultural signs.

The richer truth of the forms in balmy celestial climes was nonetheless less evident than the bare but complete truth of number, directly accessible on the alpine heights by a purely alpine climb, since in the mathematical field ontological content and gnoseological method are purely at one. The fact that this is not the case for the higher and completer truth of the *eidē*, in whose truth even the truth of number merely participates (as the ineliminable mathematical *aporiae* tend to reveal) and constitutes what has well been called 'the ancient dilemma', whereby the further off and less accessible is truer, but the more completely at hand is deceptively clearer and more apparent (see Trimpi 1962, pp. 87–129).

One should not therefore take the immediacy, integrity and entirety of number for the final and complete truth, evading the need for a hermeneutic of obscure signs that always point away from themselves in lack of a completely realized integrity. But on the other hand, it is just because the forms do not, like numbers, offer themselves to an immediate vision and constitution, that this path of conjoined dialectical and grammatical method has to be trodden, and the guiding thread of this path remains that of number, since it leads the self-negation of the sign away from itself towards the super-integrity of the forms. It is just this logic that informed the medieval educational ascent by way of the 'liberal arts' from the *trivium* of the sign-disciplines through the *quadrivium* of the number disciplines (including music and astronomy) to the heights of philosophy (metaphysics, ethics and rational theology) and revealed theology concerned with the pure formal-intellectual existences of God and the angels, besides the hybrid formality of the created material world which participates in and is governed by the celestial realm (see McLuhan 2005; Lafleur 1994, pp. 45–65; Milbank 2017b, pp. 46–73).

If Ludwig Wittgenstein had been aware of all this, then surely he would have realized that his own intriguing anxiety concerning the modern 'forgetting' of simple mathematical processes of counting and so forth was a Platonic anxiety after all. This anxiety is, for example, expressed in his statement, with regard to Georg Cantor's diagonalisation proof, that "the *concept* 'real number'", that is, all the numbers on a modern number line, including fractions and irrationals, may have "much less real analogy with the concept 'cardinal number' than we, being misled by certain analogies, are inclined to believe" (Wittgenstein 1981, II § 22). I shall eventually revert to his attitude in this respect.

From Platonic to Modern Mathematics

For the moment, in relation to his remark, it should be noted here that traditional, Pythagorean and Platonic-influenced mathematics did not allow that fractions, decimal and negative numbers had the full status of *arithmos*, while zero quantity was not seen as a number at all, but rather as its specific absence. Many, like Jacob Klein, have supposed that this rendered ancient mathematics incapable of resolving the *aporiae* posed by irrationals, and so of approaching the modern 'solutions' proposed by calculus and other modes of probability theory, which depend upon the admission to full ontological status of all so-called real numbers (Klein 1992, pp. 117–224). But the Warwick University mathematician D.H. Fowler has shown that it is perfectly coherent to argue, after Plato, that any division is more primarily a multiplication, such that, for example, a divided loaf can only be perceived as such because, with phenomenological priority, division has resulted in the new appearance of two pieces of bread (Fowler 1987, pp. 108–117). With equal coherence, one can add, subtraction is more primarily, for Plato, an addition: there is only a remainder of three if you take two from five because you are still glimpsing the actuality of the banished two out of the corner of your eye, even if your action pretends otherwise.

In this way, on a Platonic view, the cumulative number series—1,2,3,4,5,6 and so on—holds logically and ontologically a pre-eminence, while the possibility of variant arithmetic operations of subtraction, division, multiplication and so forth has to do with the fact that the number one is not exactly a mere *arithmos*, but a reality transcendent to the entire arithmetic field, which allows it to exist at all. The tension between any ordinary *arithmos* and the number one, or the fact that, for example, the number five must be a complete unity in order to be 'five' and yet is not a pure single unity after all, is exactly what permits the methodical permutations on addition. Thus the number five, because it both is and is not a unity, can be further multiplied, removed from and divided. By contrast, these processes *cannot*, strictly speaking, be applied to the number one at all. When they are applied, for example, to the number five, it does not cease to be a unified five, since this starting point is the required presupposition for the operation of the processes. But when they are applied to the number one, then it has already ceased to be the number one and has become many, such that progress can only be here made by belying the reality of the starting point, that is, by cancelling its presupposition. Arithmetic is then primarily constructive, yet the possibility of this process rests transcendentally on a deconstructed ultimate foundation in unicity.

It is because these basic arithmetical situations and operations are already for Plato aporetic, involving a problematic diminution of thinly unified reality, on a psychic plane already less than the replete noetic reality of the forms, that he does not really have a problem with the aporias posed by the existence of incommensurability and irrational quantities (such as Pi).[2] For Plato, in *The Sophist*, and according to the record of his oral teaching, the Dyad was co-primary with the One, if of lower status. Accordingly (in line with the aporetic logic just described), the inherently indeterminate Two, problematically in conflict with the very unity that it also expresses, was ingredient in the ultimate reality known to us (see Kramer 1990).

By comparison, the early modern invention of 'the number line', or the acceptance of the full numerical reality of negatives, fractions, decimals, irrationals and zero, can be regarded as an attempt to evade the really non-avoidable *aporiae* consequent upon the problematic inter-involvement of the one with the many and of the indeterminate asymptotic approach to indeterminate quantities—which implies, in modern mathematical thought, a bizarrely measurable excess of a specifically indeterminate point over a specified indeterminate sequence. For now, the primary integral reality of the integers has been denied, along with the overarching transcendental character of numerical unity for the numerical field of pure multiples—abandoned by specifically Greek-hating Calvinists like Vieta in favour of an ultimately Hindu and Islamic-derived transcendentality of a blank Zero, which was now elevated beyond convenience (the Arabic

---

[2] In disagreement here with Heller-Roazen (2011).

numerals including the zero sign having been in Latin usage since around 1200), to be regarded not just as a fully fledged number, but as the very principle of number, replacing 'one' in this respect but with the very different transcendental implication of 'flattening' every other number to univocal equality with itself (Klein 1992, pp. 150–185). The new status of Zero as a proper number also implied a levelling of affirmation with negation and an insinuation of dubious conventions, such that the sum of two multiplied negations is a positive, as absolute and supposedly provable classroom truths.

In consequence of the epochal seventeenth-century shift, the number line approaches the condition of a *continuum*, or of a quasi-geometric indefinitely stretched, thread-like magnitude. In this way, after François Vieta and René Descartes, the difference between the arithmetic counting of a multitude of discrete items (reflexively the *arithmoi* themselves) and the geometric drawing of discrete magnitudes—which can, unlike arithmetic entities, be of any size, since their integrity is rather defined by their shape—is algebraically denied. Not only, as the esotericist René Guenon pointed out, does modern thought thereby undergo a quantification, it also loses a qualitative difference within the quantitative sphere itself (Guénon 2000, pp. 7–69).

Only recently has this suppression finally leaked through to ordinary linguistic usage itself; thus, the adjectival qualifier 'less' now serves to cover also 'fewer', to the screaming-point despair of people of my generation. But a serious *metaphysical* point lurks here: this suppression collapses both number and shape into, bizarrely, a quasi-linguistic because algebraic blur; just as inversely and tellingly, Vieta's Huguenot friend Pierre Ramus, who shared his hostility to the entire Greek legacy—to the extent of imagining a Biblical affinity to a conjectured truer, near-Eastern ancient science—collapses the linguistic sign into an exact measurable position on a grid of *mathesis* (see Pickstock 1998, pp. 49–57). In this way number and sign blend into each other, and thereby quantity and quality. In a really peculiar way, the quantification, which Guénon saw as the crucial mark of modernity, involves more deeply an unnatural qualifying of quantity, besides the quantification of quality. It is just this confusion which undergirds the modern claim, as with the calculus, to handle exactly the inexact.

For now the *continuum* can be divided *ad libitum*, and aporetic leaps can be putatively plastered over in terms of a precisely measurable consistent ratio of degrees of asymptotic approach to a transition that cannot really be made in any finitely specifiable series of steps. But the projected consistency of measure is supposed to be able to convey you safely and rationally over every quantitative abyss. One can note here that Wittgenstein's disquiet with non-finite number extended also to a certain unease even about the calculus of infinitesimals, precisely because he thought that, in a simple 'abacus' sense, "Mathematics is always a machine, a calculus. The calculus does not describe anything" (Wittgenstein 1979, p. 106).

One can claim that this modern geometrized and algebraicized arithmetic perspective suppresses *aporiae* since they would be an embarrassment for its finitized rationalism, whereas the older Platonic approach can readily confess them, within its hierarchy of metaphysical sense, which takes number as a guiding clue to the plenitude of the rational, the *logikos*, but not as its full actuality. And it is not, as Klein thought, inhibited from grasping 'solutions' like those of the differential calculus to the problem of the infinite 'fluxional' approach of the curve to the straight line because of its inability to see that fractions have the status of fully fledged numbers. For, as Fowler has shown, the mathematics of the Academy dealt with both fractions and asymptotic approaches in terms of *anthyphairesis*, which involves repeated positive process, whereby fractions can be reduced to the endless multiplicatory emergence of new whole numbers: so instead of one-half, two from one and so forth.[3]

This same approach, rather than claiming to isolate ever-new 'real' numbers, instead supplements strictly 'arithmetic' additive processes, whether pursued up or down the scale, with what the Greeks understood to be those of *logistike*, or of the ratios between numbers as exposed to a

---

[3] Fowler (1987, pp. 25–27, 31–66, 191–192 and 364–371). *Anthyphairesis*, a procedure also found in Euclid, literally means 'reciprocal subtraction' because the resultant remainder was then further reduced ad infinitum—again by multiplying fragmentation of a unity—by measure of the difference between the first remainder and the initially given unit. Repeated application of this process is also carried out by modern mathematics but in terms of pure division and divisors. But already Aristotle, in denying Plato's 'great' as well as 'small' infinite—arguing that in progress upwards we always transit by definite steps and do not encounter an infinitesimal interval that never arrives at nothing—removed the homology between infinite subtraction or division on the one hand and infinite addition on the other, and so opened the way for denying that the former can be 'reciprocally' conceived in a full sense as also a positive asymptotic progress. See Aristotle, *Physics*, III,6, 206b 3–206b 35. The *riposte* to Aristotle here would be to decide to treat the upwards infinite limit as an actuality of which zero (whose unattainable full stop Aristotle cannot deny) was but the echo. In the end, Aristotle himself has only decided against this outlook, not decisively argued against it.

more reflective consideration, such as is already involved for subtraction, multiplication and division. For a logistical perspective, it appears that the unity of three, for example, is really to do not just with the unproblematic counting of digits, but also with the mysteriously problematic proportion between 'three' and 'one', whereby the unity of three can nevertheless be recursively applied again to its threeness, to give three 'twice', and then indefinitely many other times. The other operations of subtraction, division and so forth can similarly be derived from this not exhaustively fathomable and tensional ratio (Klein 1992, pp. 17–25).[4]

Such a logistical approach to more complex arithmetic operations in terms of a consideration of proportions or ratios (or 'analogies') also implies a certain geometric dimension to arithmetic, since the repeated application of a ratio implies an indifference to exact multiple content, more characteristic of the geometric concern with integral magnitudes that can be of any size. Thus, in logistic, the operation of a rule of ratio involves the imagination of a certain quasi-spatial proportion rather than a completely specifiable quantity graspable by pure intellect as a series of cumulative temporal moments.

For this reason, as Klein showed, logistic tended to migrate in Neoplatonic thought, somewhat under the influence of the Pythagorean priority of arithmetic over geometry, to the side of mere pragmatic application of mathematical principles. But in the case of Plato himself, there remained a strict *logistikē theoretikē*, and this fact can be connected with both his privileging of geometry over arithmetic and his exaltation of the metaphysical dyad to near parity with the metaphysical monad. Logistic, in this way, formed a kind of hinterland between arithmetic and geometry, without ever losing the integral difference of the two processes (see Lachtermann 2009, pp. 124–205; Dimitri Nikulin 2002, pp. 63–68 and 210–260). This loss rather occurred in modern times, with Descartes and others, as we have just seen.

The invocation in Platonism and Neoplatonism of the principle of repeated application of proportionate operation allows that one might approach an inexpressible quantity in a consistently ordered way without abolishing the *aporia* of this advance, or invoking a kind of phantom exact quantity after the manner of Leibnizian or Newtonian calculus—a quan-

---

[4] The primacy of the actual and the positive in premodern western mathematics shows us how naturally Christian theological theses such as the privative theory of evil could be grafted onto what the student would have learnt in the *quadrivium*.

tity virtually present and entertained as a ghostly (non)possibility that is taken to command our conception of the mathematically actual.

Repeatability raises the issue of the infinite, but only with Plotinus and some of the Church Fathers did the unbounded as qualitative and simple, because beyond all quantitative bounds, emphatically become an attribute of the absolute, in a climate influenced by the general late antique exaltation of initiatory darkness and mystery.[5] It was this metaphysical development that made actual infinity respectable, and slowly it began to creep into the immanent sphere also.

The latter development was therefore plainly *not, contra* some accounts, at first a secularizing one. Thus, several of the scholastics already intimated the reality of transfinites because they observed, for example, that the infinite series of even numbers is equal in length to the infinite series of odd numbers, although the latter must be simultaneously of a seemingly greater size. Robert Grosseteste, the twelfth-century Bishop of Lincoln and Statesman, even constructed an ontology of light which construed it as mediating in a series of transfinite descents between the infinite God and finite creation (Grosseteste 1996, pp. 25–33). Nicholas of Cusa (followed later by Blaise Pascal) finally embraced the infinity of the universe, holding, with Giordano Bruno soon after, that it, too, was "an infinite sphere whose centre is everywhere and circumference nowhere".[6] But in the former case there was no blasphemy because Nicholas effectively saw this infinity as transfinite: it is extended or 'explicated' and not 'simple' or 'complicated', meaning 'infolded' in Cusan terminology.[7] There are, moreover, for him different degrees of infinity in, respectively, the intel-

---

[5] Plotinus, *Enneads* V.5.10: "[the Good's] being is not limited; what is there to set bounds to it? ... All its infinitude resides in its power: it does not change and will not fail; and in it all that is unfailing finds its duration"; V.5.11: "It is infinite also by right of being a pure unity with nothing towards which to direct any partial content"; VI, 9, 6: "We must ... take the Unity as infinite not in measureless extension or numerable quantity but in fathomless depths of power". [Stephen Mackenna's translation.]

[6] See Jorge Luis Borges, 'The Fearful Sphere of Pascal' in *Labyrinths* (London: Penguin, 1971), 189–192. But for a corrective of Borges, see Harries (1975, pp. 5–15). Harries rightly says that Cusa preceded Bruno—that early modern cosmology altered in the wake of this transference of metaphorical application rather than the reverse, and that the shift itself is not a secularizing cosmic appropriation of a divine attribute but rather a following through of the full cosmological implications of this attribute of an infinite creative God. As with Grosseteste, if God is infinite, then his productions, though finite, cannot themselves be finitely bounded. The closed universe was pagan, not uninflectedly religious.

[7] Nicholas of Cusa, *De Docta Ignorantia*, I, 12.33; 23; *De Visione Dei*, 13–15.

lectual, the psychic and the material spheres. In this way, we can see that the positive consideration of the actual infinite in Bruno and Spinoza is a *post*-Christian development.

But Bruno and Spinoza still left actual infinity as the presence of an immanent deity; it had not yet consistently invaded the domain of human mathematics as something that might be unproblematically dealt with. That began to happen after Descartes had algebraicized geometry, and Leibniz and Newton were then able to algebraicize and numerize in their 'Calculus' the 'fluxions' of curves as tending to straight lines or perfect circles, even though they do so by infinitesimal degrees.

We need however to note here that the link between the downgrading of geometric *construction* and the algebraic invocation of abstract infinity is not so obvious as some historians think. For in the case of Proclus, so influential on Cusa, the Neoplatonic gloss on Euclid held the abyssal mysteries and paradoxes of the metaphysical to be reflected in the *imagined* arithmetic one and the *drawn* point, line and circle, and in this fashion had already intimated the phenomena of *continuum* and calculus—as many Renaissance thinkers realized—yet still in entirely mystagogic, aporetic terms (Proclus 1992).[8] Even in early Enlightenment Naples, Giambattista Vico and Paulo Mattia Doria continued to be able to give Proclean renderings of the new incorporations of the infinite while *defending* the primacy of geometry over algebra and the primarily synthetic and physically constructed character of the former (Vico 2010, pp. 57–71; see Lachtermann 1985, pp. 47–97; Miner 2004, pp. 96–125). The *genuine* Platonic tradition in mathematics, because it believes, after Plato, that perceived mathematical realities only invoke the forms through dim recollection of a forgotten spiritual realm (*not* an a priori interior grasp) and therefore require the use of the senses, sustains the role both of intellectual intuition of numerical essence and ratio, or *theoremata*, and of concrete imaginary or physical construction, or *problemata*. This approximately accords with the way that there was, as we have seen, originally for Plato, but still more radically than for Neoplatonism, a 'theoretical logistic' or a reflexively operational 'theoretical application' to the material of *arithmoi* themselves.

[8] For the ontological role of *problema* in Proclus, see Part One, §§ 201, 243–244. His insistence on the essential initial role of problematic in producing the geometric field can be seen as consonant with his overall 'theurgic' perspective which, in contrast to Plotinus, stressed the full descent of the human soul into the human body and consequently the need for sensory and material mediation and the merciful descent of the gods to our realm, drawn down through and as myriad modes of ritual attraction.

The Cantorian Counter-Revolution

Partly because of the tension between a Cartesian formalist and pragmatic attitude to the calculus, and this more realist, ultimately Platonic metaphysical interpretation, there were heated debates in the eighteenth century about the 'infinitesimal' or an infinitely small number that is still more than zero (see Alexander 2015). These also correspond to the inevitable modern hesitation between the seeming opposites of mathematical conventionalism on the one hand, and a newly literal physicalization of mathematical truth consequent upon Descartes' attempted identification of arithmeticized geometric space with physical space itself, on the other. The formalist view was that the infinitesimal was a convenient fiction; the realist view was that the infinitesimals really exist. That view would effectively provide us with other examples of transfinites. This same spectre hovered over the new application of infinitesimal calculus to number theory in the nineteenth century by Bernhard Riemann and others (see Kaplan 2000, pp. 144–174; Seife 2000, pp. 131–156; Cajori 1919, pp. 367–447).

Riemann, much influenced by *Naturphilosophie*, also reconceived geometry in such a way as to think of manifest spatial relations as the productions of hidden forces, manifested by infinitesimal calculus as tensional and dynamic 'fluxions', which generated interrelated and co-varying functions constituting a particular determined 'manifold' (*Mannigfaltigkeit*), including, as but one example, three-dimensional space, which thereby loses its ontological or transcendental (Kant) normativity.[9] In an equivalent way, the equally post-Romantic Cantor saw any system of number as brought about by a 'generative principle' that constituted a manifold (which we now call a 'set') of items that can all be counted as of the same kind and so can be 'included' (Rosenstock 2017, pp. 45–47). In this way, the ontological or transcendental primacy of the finite ordinal number series was questioned. Cantor broke with the intuitive primacy of ordinal numbering in time by making spatial cardinality central: not the series 1, 2, 3 ... but, for example, the number 'three' standing alone and indicating in itself the single 'set' of all things (real or imagined) that contain three countable items (Cantor 1955).

---

[9] For this reason, he thought that binding gravity might be an intrinsic feature of three dimensionality, rendering space itself a vital force field. This seems to recover the Stoic conception of geometry as 'phoronomic' or more primarily concerned with moving than with static figures. Of course, it was his conception of the manifold that allowed him to think non-Euclidean geometries and to conjecture that our three dimensionality could itself be but the 'surface' of a concealed, more multidimensional 'sphericity'.

This new move has proved incredibly ambivalent. Was it about ending or rekindling mystery? It might seem to awaken certain Platonic and realist echoes, reinvoking the unique integrity of every *arithmos*.[10] But, conversely, the set can be construed, not as a reversion to *eidos* but rather as inviting a subordination of mathematics to a nominalistic logic, such that number becomes a sheerly conventional grouping of random singularities, brought together by a spatializing gesture to produce 'every three', 'every four' and so forth, according to a 'count as one', rather than being conceived as the unique result in due order of an inexorable process of addition. In that case, it is rather ordinality that would stand Platonic sentinel over the integrity of each unique linguistic arrival. By contrast, a nominalist conception of cardinality points to a formalism that encourages us to stop thinking of numbers as either artful construct or strange intuition of psychic essences, or else both at once.

Yet, on the other hand, Ludwig Wittgenstein complained in his notebooks that Cantor had invented sets precisely because he was a mystery-monger, in love with the pseudo-religious (as Wittgenstein debatably saw it) consolation of paradox.[11] How can this accusation be half-plausible? How can sets favour mystery as much as series? Or mystery lurk in space as much as time? How can sets prove to be just as primitive and indefinite and resistant to our conventional control as serial ordinals?

These strange circumstances arise because Cantor discovered three key contradictions. First, the set of all subsets contained within a set, the so-called power-set, is bigger than the original set. All the fractions of three are more than three; all the complexities of a seed exceed its visible oneness. We have already seen how the Platonic primacy of multiplication over division would, however, interpret this circumstance in terms of the aporetic relationship between the real transcendent numerical One and any purely finite unity. Cantor accepted this traditional solution because he cleaved to a Catholic sense of a true, absolute, simple infinite, though he newly linked this to the mystical resolution of emergent mathematical contradictions. He applied it also to the mystery of transfinite numbers, which he understood to be fully instantiated in reality.

For his second innovation was a new proof of transfinitude. If there exists a subset of all the numbers which do not count the number of the numbers in a series—as the final 4 counts the numbers in the series

[10] See Fowler (1987, p. 14): "A much more faithful impression of the very concrete sense of the Greek *arithmoi* is given by the sequence: *duet, trio, quartet, quintet*".
[11] For example, Wittgenstein (1981, II, §§ 18–38).

1,2,3,4—then a contradiction arises. How many numbers are there in this subset? If the number of these numbers is itself a member of the set, then it cannot be, since this number is now a number that counts all the numbers in the subset and so should be excluded. But if it is not a member of the subset, then by that very token it should be included within it after all. Therefore this aberrant number does not belong within the set of all natural, finite numbers. As unplaceable within their series, we have to consider it to be "transfinite" (Rosenstock 2017, p. 71n).

If there is a transfinite number 1, then it follows that there is an indefinite sequence of such numbers. However, at this level also, the perplexity of the power-set must intrude, in the form of the so-called Burali-Forti paradox (ibid., p. 70n and 71n). Once again, we have the problem that the ingredients of a supposed totality are greater than that totality. A number bigger than the totality must still belong to the series of ordinals, and yet it cannot do so, if it exceeds them all in size. In the case of the 'diagonalising out' of the power-set of the transfinites from their inclusive set, we seem to have to do with an impossible trans-transfinite. Once again, and indeed here especially, Cantor appealed, rather like Cusa, to the absolute infinity of God as lying beyond and yet 'including' all finite and finite/transfinite contradictions. God, for Cantor upheld without reduction, is the mystery of an ineffable and incomprehensible middle or 'between' that is somehow ingredient to all created being.

In the third place, Cantor vastly exacerbated the medieval examples of transfinitude by arguing that one transfinite can really be bigger than another. At least the series of all even and the series of all prime numbers are 'denumerable' in the sense that we can draw a series of 'bijecting' lines between each step of the two advancing series: 2,4,6,8,10,12 ad infinitum can be made in this way equivalent to 2,3,5,7,11,13 ad infintium, as we saw was observed by Grosseteste. So in one sense they are the same size after all, for they remain always strictly proportionate to each other.

But Cantor now showed that, in the case of infinite sets of real, decimalized numbers, all the endlessly diminishing or advancing horizontal series which we can display in a square diagram and which should be exhaustive, are always 'exceeded', since a diagonal series drawn across them will exhibit an alternatively ordered series to that of every instance of the horizontals by the simple device of changing in turn by one position the decimal place of the first number on the first line, then the second on the second line and so forth, a procedure which can go on indefinitely because decimal fractions are infinitely divisible. And this means that the infinite sum of all real numbers is greater than the infinite sum of all rational numbers, which can be exhaustively specified, even in the instance of their infinity, by the set contained in the square of their exhaustive succession.[12] Such a 'diagonal' excess can be equally seen as the excess of the power-set of the transfinites over the original one, or else indeed the 'transcendental' excess of that set itself over any possible subsettings—such that something always diagonally escapes any attempt as exhaustive sub-classification.

'Diagonalisation' is a geometric metaphor, and perhaps irreducibly so, to the point of real analogy. Such a geometrization of Cantor would be a Platonic, Proclean or Cusan move, as it would imply that his mathematical mystery is 'logistically' traversed within the real but contradictory structures of the geometric realm as finitely, physically embodied. By this same token, it would contend that his proof can after all also be performed with the infinitized positive multiples of prime numbers, omitting the initial decimal point, but now perhaps arranged in random, not regular, series, since regular series could not be modified. This presentation would be in accordance with the linked Platonic principles of the primacy of the positive and multiple over the negative and divisory, and of the determination of the infinite as equally 'great' and 'small'. But in that case the excess of the real over the rational infinite in the case of decimals is qualified: for it is only, after all, an instance of an excess pertaining also in the case of infinite primes, but with the additional Cantorian discovery—beyond Grosseteste—that this excess is no longer one of mere quantity, but also of measurable, denumerable ratio.

Alternatively, one could no doubt devise (or a computer could no doubt devise) a procedure whereby, even given regular horizontal series of whole numbers, the diagonal operator continuously altered the rule of succession for each line, giving an alternative logic to the succession achieved so far, since, in principle, this always remains possible: for example, 2, 2, 2, 2 might be completed by 4 if the rule has now become not 'repeat' but 'double at the fifth stage', while at the tenth it might be 'double' or it might be 'quadruple' and so on. It is always possible alternatively to complete a series by shifting the rule of composition and yet maintaining consistency.

---

[12] For a clear and simple summary of Cantor's diagonalisation proof and its immediate intellectual aftermath, see Seife (2000, pp. 147–153).

The obvious objection here is that these examples no longer sustain a single ordering principle throughout the series or only do so retrospectively and so can no longer be totalized. But precisely, if one adopts Cantor's mathematical realism, then one can allow that totalization is achieved by infinite actualization rather than by the indefinitely potential application of a rule. Hence, the transfinite series constructed through random or rule-varying sequence is still a totality and is still non-denumerable through bijection against other such series. But even were one to sustain that objection, one could still perform the proof with 'clumps' of integers within brackets, varying them in the same way as Cantor's decimals.

Whether in Cantor's terms, or these revised 'Platonic' ones, while one can indeed say that there is always 'one more' possible non-denumerable transfinite number outside the totalizing square, one might *equally* say (as perhaps Cantor did not indicate) that every time a 'further' denumeration lies ahead. Since the power-set not only is but also cannot be greater than the initial all-inclusive set, the excess over denumeration and so the sense in which one transfinite can be greater than another has surely to be indeterminable? There are and there are not differences in transfinite size, just as the infinite set of odd and the infinite set of even, or the infinite set of rabbits and of hares, both are and are not different from each other. In this sense, Cantor is not so far beyond Grosseteste after all.

In the case of the 'Platonic' version of Cantor's diagonal proof, an incommensurate and utterly paradoxical excess of infinite integers over the entire set of infinite integers is no longer simply an incommensurate excess of the real over the rational numbers, but rather of infinite natural numbers or integers over themselves. And since all calculations with real numbers can only use conventional permutations of the integers, one can argue that the instance of excess of the infinitesimals over the set of all rational numbers is secondary and parasitic. Looked at in this revised way, Cantor's discovery much more emphatically points, as he desired, to the *actuality* of transfinitude and the paradoxicality of the *real* limits of the world. Cantor might not have been averse to this development, precisely because as a devout Catholic he wished to read his transfinites as signs of the participation of the finite in the real, absolute simple infinite of God, enfolding all transfinites together in his ideas (see Dauben 1979; Perkert 2013; Newstead 2009, pp. 533–555).

Neither Wittgenstein nor Cantor would then turn out to be wholly right: the former's semi-finitism would have failed to allow for this new incommensurability (or even to admit Grosseteste's medieval paradox), but the latter would have apparently failed to see the primacy of the instance of the diagonal paradox in the series of mere infinite integers, given the imaginative, and so arguably transcendental primacy, of the ordinary countable number series, which Wittgenstein, curiously like the Platonic tradition, so much insisted upon. In that case, Cantor's argument assumes a much more immediately realist complexion. In saying that real numbers are only *analogous* to cardinal numbers, thereby affirming in some sense the latter's cognitive primacy, Wittgenstein was precisely gesturing towards realism in a Platonic fashion in a way that he did not, of course, suspect. However, he failed to allow that, even given such a primacy, Cantor's claim can still hold good, since it does *not*, once 'Platonically' revised, really depend upon the equally numerical character of infinitesimal fractions and decimals (along with zero and irrationals) along the modern 'real' number line.

Cantor and Wittgenstein

But do we really need to take Cantor seriously? Some of the intuitionists and constructivists, who favoured time, series and ordinality, thought not. These included Brouwer, Poincaré and Bergson, but also Wittgenstein, who heard Brouwer lecture, with approval (Marion 1998, pp. 18–19, 38–40, 84–85, 162–168 and 202–205). Wittgenstein, however, in order to reject the realism of Cantor and of Kurt Gödel, went to very extreme lengths. There is, for him, in the strong ontological sense, no potential infinite for mathematics, never mind any actual one (Wittgenstein 1981, II § 45; v § 14; Bosanquet et al. 1976, p. 255; Marion 1998, pp. 26–7, 181–188, 200–201).[13] Nor, once a theorem is constructed, is there any-

---

[13] Marion wrongly equates Wittgenstein's reduction of the potential infinite to the logical or grammatical rule to 'carry on', making it "the property of a law, not of its extension" (King and Lee 1980, p. 13) with Aristotle's denial that potential infinity would ever be actually realized, in the way that a potential statue can eventually come about [*Physics*, III, 6, 206a 18–20]. But for Aristotle, potential infinity still clearly denotes an indefinite power that is extensionally 'out there' in the world, something that can be ever further actualized, though never completed in its full actuality, which for him is impossible. Thus, time and human generation are both actually without limit, although this lack of limit "is not (like the statue potentialities of the bronze) all actualised at once but is in course of transit as long as it lasts" [*Physics* III, 6, 206a 22–24]. The same applies to division of a magnitude, except that in this case, the discarded parts remain to rebuke in their persisting actuality the infinitely destructive ambition of the divider and do not vanish down the abyss of the more successful destroyer, time [III, 6, 206a 30–206b 2]. Marion equally fails to see that for Aristotle *apeiron* is ontological chaos and not just heuristic instruction.

thing 'lurking' within the theorem waiting to be discovered, never mind the idea that the theorem itself was 'lurking' in the first place. This ultra anti-Platonism in the conventional modern sense—which rejects even 'a Platonism of the second phase' (or the fated logical implication of an arbitrarily willed foundation, as with Descartes) demands that 2 plus 1 = 3 in no way follows consistently from 1 plus 1 = 2, except by adopting the same merely conventionally transcendental rule of 'count one', which one has to keep reiterating at various stages of the counting process because every rule admits to some degree of ambiguity. Though we happen to build 2 plus 1 = 3, upon 1 plus 1 = 2, we might build something else incompatible with 2 plus 1 = 3 under another schoolmaster who might even keep changing the rule at every step.[14]

One can see why Alain Badiou today regards Wittgenstein as a sophist.[15] For surely, the integral *content* 1 plus 1 = 2 is already itself the patterned rule that leads next to 3, since 1 remains 1 as a transcendental reality in the older medieval sense with every arrival at a new unity. There is no duality of number and function, such as Wittgenstein appears to imply. Otherwise, we could not envisage '2' or '3' at all. Simply to make/envisage the number '1' is already to envisage that 1 plus 1 makes 2, 2 plus 1 makes 3 and so on. The endless sequences simply require an elaborative 'unfolding', and endlessly recursive reiteration, not just of a rule but of the logic of numerical unity, which is also, and uniquely, an ontologic.

---

[14] Waissmann (1979, p. 63): "In mathematics it is just as impossible to discover anything as it is in grammar" and p. 34: "What we find in books on mathematics is not a *description of something*, but the thing itself. We *make* mathematics". However, the real Platonic tradition concerning mathematics, which culminated in Cusa and Vico's Christian Trinitarian radicalisation, was able to regard making as also a seeing, also a describing. Wittgenstein is too conservative to be able to question this alternative. See also Wittgenstein (1981, § 5): "The Proposition: 'It is true that this follows from that' means simply 'this follows from that'". Here, the redundancy of the word 'true' redounds to the benefit of a convention that must be forever reiterated if it is to remain in force. In addition, see Wittgenstein (1978, § 185), where Wittgenstein argues that the instruction to 'add 2' to 1000 will not necessarily produce 1002, either according to rule-following or continuing to follow the rule in the same way. In either case, there remains a margin of interpretation which only brute imposition of the standard mode of reiteration can prevent. Finally, see Marion (1998, pp. 1–20) and on p. 22: "[Wittgenstein] insists that we *never* discover facts about structures that we have already set up: any new theorem is in fact a new extension of mathematics"; see also Klenk (1976, pp. 8–18).

[15] Badiou (2011, p. 75) and *passim*. The sophistic label is not meant to be entirely negative.

It is this same arbitrary transcendentalism (in a Kantian sense, now anarchized) about rules which disqualifies Wittgenstein's argument against a strong realist understanding of set-theory in general as, for example, it was espoused by Frank Ramsey, who defended the real instances of contradictory or 'impredicable' sets and the actual extension even of their infinite instances, with some anticipation of the contemporary dialetheism of Graham Priest (Wittgenstein 1981, II, §§ 21–22; Marion 1998, pp. 6, 187 and 200–201; Priest 1995). Wittgenstein thought that both Cantor and Ramsey had confused the deliberate 'intension' or meaning-input involved in constructing a set (as when one puts only recyclable items in the eco-green rather than the grey bin), with ad hoc extension (as when 101 random items go in the any-old grey bin in order to form the set that, without female supervision, might be our weekly unsorted planetarily-irresponsible male human rubbish). This, he considered, was to confuse a set made by the rule of ('arithmetic') intension with a set composed by ('geometric') extension which could then contain unknown infinite things which we have not really selected (Wittgenstein 1981, II, § 132; Marion 1998, pp. 12–13, 63–64, 181–189 and 200–201). The numbers in a set are only there for Wittgenstein because of the 'rule' of inclusion:

> A picture is conjured up which appears to fix the sense *unambiguously*. The actual use, compared with that suggested by the picture, seems somewhat muddied. Here again we get the same thing as in set theory. In the actual use of expressions we make detours, we go by sideroads. We see the straight highway before us, but of course we cannot use it, because it is permanently closed. (Wittgenstein 1978, § 426)

Wittgenstein here wishes to contrast what he takes to be a vicious dualism of set-theory between unambiguous meaning and impossibly infinite application with a pragmatist use of ad hoc initial definitions ceaselessly governed, yet ceaselessly qualified, by realistic rules that take us down the 'forking paths' which we can possibly take, while the 'dead end' which we cannot take is oxymoronically construed as sublime absolute openness.

Yet one could argue, just to the contrary, that while pragmatism still has a duality of rules such as 'go there' against the rhetorically anticipated, and then presently pictured content of 'where you can really, finitely get to', that set-theory—with a greater allegiance to the inherited ontology of number, for which content and rule, essence and method coincide—in its fully realist version implies no such duality. This is partly because the invoked or mentioned 'picture' is no less ambiguous and indeterminate than a rule for usage, as the paradoxes resultant from apparently clear definitions of numerical entities always expose. Some of these paradoxes result from recursion and not from infinitude, and so it is not manifestly the case that the problem is always the projection of a delimited sense upon an unlimited referent whose meaningful scope one can therefore never determine. To the contrary, the problem is often that one cannot readily fix the intensional sense, and that this cannot be done at all without ('geometrically and problematically') trying to determine its extent of referential relevance. A projected construction is inseparable, as for authentic Platonism, from an always obscurely (and so rhetorically or persuasively) envisaged end result.

In fact, set-theory does not really tolerate the duality of intension and extension that Wittgenstein imposes on it. Despite its initial logicist aspirations, it confirms that a number is more than a sign of a number, given that a sign is always a rule, like a signpost, that points away from itself to another content. For a number is rather itself a content that constitutes a rule: the number one, for example, has cardinal content, but also commands us ordinally to 'count one' in subtraction from the numerical pluriverse. Thus it is the very extension of number as a 'picture' which exposes—as for Neoplatonic, Cusan and Vichian geometry—the prospect of extension to the infinite, not the illegitimate breaking of the bounds of an arbitrary transcendental rule, as Wittgenstein in a Kantian lineage supposed. If, for example '1' denotes a single set of all unities, then this can legitimately be a set of an infinite number, while an ordinal series—for example, a series comprised by constant doubling—of itself must invoke infinity, and therefore point to the fact that the 'temporal' series is also an open-ended 'spatial' set. Otherwise it is *not* a series—defined for example by doubling, not by any limit of the items to be doubled—and there is no rule which derives from the setted content of seriality.[16]

So, while not all the paradoxes of number arise from the contagion of the infinite, it is nonetheless true that it is the very nature of numbers, not hubristic overreaching, that incites this contagion. *Only* quantification leads us to the unquantifiable, and without this approach we would not be

---

[16] As Jacques Lacan showed, even the sign-operation, in order to avoid anarchy, has to occur within certain loosely 'setted' parameters. In this way, number interferes with the field of sign, ensuring that it concerns always 'numbers of things' just as, in the case of number, sign and reality coincide, though in ontologically thin air. See Milbank (2009, pp. 118–120).

able to envisage the unconstrained power to quantify. We take the marked turnings one by one *because* we forever proceed up the open road. Moreover, the attempt to treat set-theory merely intensionally, as with Frege and Russell's use of logical quantifiers (Boole's 'or', 'and' and 'if', plus Frege's own 'for every' and 'there is a') lamentably failed to banish paradox, because it turned out that the ambitions of a neo-Leibnizian *mathesis universalis* (explicitly envisaged by Russell, as equally by Husserl with his 'phenomenology') which tries to extend logic into existential adjudication, cannot even deal comprehensively with the most abstract level of objective reality, which is the mathematical.

It is for this reason that, after Ernst Zermelo, set-theory has been ordered more randomly within the grey bins of extension according to ad hoc rules of empirical limitation designed to head-off paradox. Yet this, as Graham Priest argues, would appear to surrender both logical and mathematical consistency in the name of avoiding the inconsistencies that this very consistency tends to generate (Priest 1995).[17]

It is in fact most of all mathematics itself that should suggest to us (for reasons that we have already seen) that there is no warrant for any absolute intension/extension duality any more than there is for the almost identical dualities of sense and reference and mention and use, since here what we intend by making so exactly coincides with the ontological truth that we 'see'. In keeping with this mathematical paradigm of *verum-factum* (after Hobbes and Vico), one can suggest, indeed, after all, in concurrence with much of Wittgenstein's thinking, that we can only *refer* to what has a locatably different sense for us (Miner 2004, pp. 78–125). On the other hand, and also with Wittgenstein for much of the time, one can inversely and additionally suggest that the specific meanings of things out there in the world only disclose themselves to us in endlessly different *aspects* of real extension. The senses of 'evening-star' and 'morning-star' alone locate the referent Venus, but it is Venus *herself*, along with the entire cosmic order, who shows herself to us as the sense-referents 'evening-star' and 'morning-star' equally, though in diurnal perspectival oscillation (see Mulhall 1993).

However, it would seem that Wittgenstein did not entirely subordinate his account of 'rule' to his crucial account of 'aspects' (as rightly advertised by Stephen Mulhall), thereby risking an absolute, transcendentalist divide between rule and content. Herein is heard still an echo of the

---

[17] I am grateful to discussions with my son, Sebastian Milbank, on Priest and the ontological reality of paradox.

sense/reference divide which sustains the Fregean programme of logicist determination of the existential, genealogically derived in the long term (as with the Husserlian notion of what is 'intended') from the Scotist and neoscholastic isolation of a known 'object' (which may equally be possible or actual and eventually, for later Spanish Jesuit thought, equally a nullity as a reality) between the cognising subject and reality, independent of the act of judgement, in contrast to the Thomistic view that what we know *is* the known reality in a transmuted, ontologically 'intellectual' guise and that this reality as truth in the full sense is only ontologically present for *judging* and *living* mind (see Milbank 2013, pp. 31–34). The more they invoke knowledge as knowledge of 'aspects' of the real, the more both Husserl and Wittgenstein veer towards a kind of more relativistic and perspectival yet authentic construal of an Aristotelian-Thomist theory of understanding, but the more they qualify 'aspects' as tied to controlled, fully surveyable intention (Husserl) or as subordinate to an imposed transcendental rule (Wittgenstein), the more a neoscholastic perspective— ultimately traceable to the eighteenth-century Iberian peninsula via Austria and Bolzano, as Jacob Schmutz has now shown—remains to the fore (Schmutz 2010, pp. 603–615).

It is in terms of this latter perspective that, in his philosophy of mathematics, Wittgenstein exhibits a lingering Fregean and positivist conservatism *en dépit de tout*. For all his apparently drastic refusal of all mathematical formalization, and so all reduction of maths to logic, the retained intension/extension duality remains allied to such a programme. It is because of this retention, I would argue, that Wittgenstein erroneously tried to contradict Gödel's (perhaps authentically) Platonizing demonstration of mathematical incompleteness.[18] For this retention led him to deny in general (indeed in a disappointingly Anglo-Saxon-Lockean fashion) that there are any real ontological conundra, or openings for unavoidable speculation, as if ordinary language is after all well policed, and we must realize that there is no evading the ineluctable and so transcendental bounds of 'language games' and 'forms of life'.

For even if his 'rules' for language games other than those of mathematics are by no means so 'fixed' in distinction from the content, they govern, they still, as Conor Cunningham has argued, close themselves against speculation in a way that suggests an immanently controlling or

---

[18] The fact that Gödel did not see his demonstration of the undecidability of the continuum hypothesis as problematic for his Platonism might suggest its genuine character.

regulative boundary which, could it *be* identified, as Wittgenstein explicitly realizes, would thereby have been transgressed (Cunningham 1999, pp. 64–90). Yet, since Wittgenstein rightly insists that it cannot be finally or rigorously identified (precisely because 'knowing how to carry on' is given by prudential practice, not pre-given regulation), his nonetheless persisting supposition of a finite boundary to which we might appeal against illegitimately speculative, metaphysical and infinitizing uses of both sign and number remains itself speculative, and implausibly so, given the mathematical paradigm.

It then follows that Wittgenstein's entire tendency (early and late) to exile matters of ethics and religion to the sublime margins is questionable. For this assumes both that the infinite is non-mediable and that the aporetic involvement of the finite in the infinite can be evaded (Wittgenstein 1979, 1998). Yet, this involvement rather ensures that in fact there *is* no non-speculative human discourse, thereby rendering metaphysics a natural extension of ordinary language which has always been taking festive holiday time-off in order to do its job at all.

The paradoxical mysteries of mathematics are not then the preserve of pseudo-religion. Instead, Wittgenstein's failure to conjure them away at the very beginning and core of all his reflection on number, whose apparent surety he, as much as Plato, sees as the gateway to philosophy, reveals the spuriousness of trying to divide the existential mysteries of human life from the mysteries of reason and human practice from the speculative work of thought which fundamentally insists that, in order to engage with *the real*, we perforce have to try approximately to grasp its nature.

Conclusion

In trying to neutralize the mathematical and modern claims to reckon with the infinite, Wittgenstein returns us in a different way to Kant. But in consequence we are back with the prospect of an anthropomorphic scepticism, up against the absolutely null unknown which is only tempered by transcendental ethical gestures of an unhelpfully formal character.

Yet, the speculatively nihilistic alternative to this, of Badiou and others, does not merely recover 'Spinoza' in defiance of Kant. To the contrary, it remains within than Spinozan-Kantian collusion that Jacobi identified. For its conservative refusal to embrace with Cantor, the reality of paradox still really assumes the ultimacy of our human epistemological grasp. Rather than remain consistent with logic to the point of the breakdown of the law of identity, it prefers (as Graham Priest has argued) to stick with epistemological certainty through cobbled-together devices to ward off mathematical contradictions, like Russell's theory of types or the Zermelo-Fraenkel conventions concerning the 'well-made' set immune to paradoxical breakage. It is on only the basis of the latter, and not on the basis of Cantor, that it can be claimed that modern mathematics reveals the non-reality and impossibility of 'the all'. Thus the bias in Badiou runs arbitrarily in the direction of diagonalising escape, thereby supposedly revealing the 'originally' empty set as a substitute, pseudo-totality fostering anarchy throughout the secondary field of manifold, or setted being, whose every attempted sub-all must always be subject to illusion and futility. But if one sustains the paradoxical balance between escapage and non-escapage from transfinite totality, then one can allow for an ineffable inclusion beyond inclusion, outside the bounds of non-contradiction, as once proposed by Cusanus and so the existence of an immanent all, but only now (in the wake of Cantor) because it is supported by a transcendent absolute. Of course, this may be envisaged in more 'Hindu' terms as by Graham Priest, or in more Christian (or Jewish or Islamic) ones, but the latter would seem more clearly to escape the lure of the zero towards an original pole of plenitude.

In this way, even an alternative and revised classical mathematics and then a mathematicized physics also so conceived (and not here elaborated) could support the 'third way' of a theistic metaphysics, which must, after Erich Przywara and William Desmond, be a metaphysics of the analogy of being or of a metaxological reality. But the latter, beyond any orthodox Thomism, has to be construed as strongly paradoxical if it is to make any rigorously metacritical sense. Not only does the admission of such logical mystery beyond logic alone now permit us again to think the thought of God, it also permits us to salvage the appearances of ordinary, finite connectedness which we constantly intuit, rescuing them from the cognitive gulf into which they must otherwise inevitably tumble.

Bibliography

Alexander, Amir. 2015. *Infinitesimal: How a Dangerous Mathematical Idea Shaped the Modern World*. London: Oneworld.

Badiou, Alain. 2011. *Wittgenstein's Antiphilosophy*. Trans. Bruno Bosteels. London: Verso.

Boole, George. 1847. *The Mathematical Analysis of Logic: Being an Essay Towards a Calculus of Deductive Reasoning*. London: Macmillan, Barclay and Macmillan.

Borges, Jorge Luis. 1971. The Fearful Sphere of Pascal. In *Labyrinths*. London: Penguin.
Bosanquet, R., et al. 1976. *Wittgenstein's Lectures on the Foundations of Mathematics, Cambridge, 1939*. Ithaca, NY: Cornell University Press.
Cajori, Florian. 1919. *A History of Mathematics*. New York: Macmillan.
Cantor, Georg. 1955. *Contributions to the Founding of the Theory of Transfinite Numbers*. Trans. Philip E.B. Jourdain. New York: Dover.
Cunningham, Conor. 1999. Wittgenstein After Theology. In *Radical Orthodoxy: A New Theology*, ed. John Milbank, Catherine Pickstock, and Graham Ward. London: Routledge.
Dauben, Warren. 1979. *Georg Cantor: His Mathematics and Philosophy of the Infinite*. Cambridge, MA: Harvard University Press.
Descartes, René. 2003. *Geometry*. New York: Dover.
Fowler, D.H. 1987. *The Mathematics of Plato's Academy: A New Reconstruction*. New York: Oxford University Press.
Grant, Iain Hamilton. 2008. *Philosophies of Nature After Schelling*. London: Continuum.
———. 2012. Being and Slime: the Mathematics of Protoplasm in Lorenz Oken's "Physio-Philosophy". In *Collapse*, vol. IV, 287–321. Falmouth: Urbanomic.
Grosseteste, Robert. 1996. *De Luce*. Trans. Julian Lock in Iain M. Mackenzie, *The 'Obscurism' of Light*. Norwich: The Canterbury Press.
Guénon, René. 2000. *The Reign of Quantity and the Signs of the Times*. New Delhi: Mushiram.
Harries, Karsten. 1975. The Infinite Sphere: Comments on the History of a Metaphor. *Journal of the History of Philosophy* 13: 5–15.
Heller-Roazen, Daniel. 2011. *The Fifth Hammer: Pythagoras and the Disharmony of the World*. New York: Zone.
Jacobi, Friedrich Heinrich. 1994. Concerning the Doctrine of Spinoza in Letters to Herr Moses Mendelssohn (1787) and (1789). In *The Main Philosophical Writings*. Trans. George di Giovanni, 173–251, 339–378. Montreal/Kingston: McGill-Queens University Press.
Kaplan, Robert. 2000. *The Nothing That Is: A Natural History of Zero*. London: Penguin.
King, John, and Desmond Lee. 1980. *Wittgenstein's Lectures, Cambridge 1930–32*. Oxford: Blackwell.
Klein, Jacob. 1992. *Greek Mathematical Thought and the Origins of Algebra*. New York: Dover.
Klenk, Virginia H. 1976. *Wittgenstein's Philosophy of Mathematics*. The Hague: Martinus Nijhoff.
Kramer, Hans-Joachim. 1990. *Plato and the Foundations of Metaphysics*. Trans. John R. Catan. New York: SUNY.

Lachtermann, David Rapport. 1985. Mathematics and Nominalism in Vico's *Liber Metaphysicus* in *Sachkommentar zu Giambattisa Vico's* Liber Metaphysicus. Eds. S. Otto and H. Viechtbauer. Munich: Fink.
———. 2009. *The Ethics of Geometry*. London: Routledge.
Lafleur, Claude. 1994. *Scientia* et *ars* dans les introductions à la philosophie des maîtres dès arts de l'Université de Paris au XIIIe siècle. In *Scientia und ars im Hoch- und Spätmittelalter*, ed. Ingrid Craemer-Ruegenberg and Andreas Speer, 45–65. Berlin: Walter de Gruyter.
Marion, Matthieu. 1998. *Wittgenstein, Finitism and the Foundations of Mathematics*. Oxford: Oxford University Press.
McLuhan, Marshall. 2005. *The Classical Trivium: The Place of Thomas Nashe in the Learning of His Time*. Corte Madera, CA: Gingko.
Milbank, John. 2009. The Double Glory, or Paradox Versus Dialectics. In *The Monstrosity of Christ*, ed. Slavoj Žižek and John Milbank. Cambridge, MA: MIT Press.
———. 2013. *Beyond Secular Order*. Oxford: Blackwell.
———. 2017a. From *Mathesis to Mathexis:* Nicholas of Cusa's Post-Nominalist Realism. In *Participation et vision de Dieu chez Nicolas de Cues*, ed. Isabelle Moulin, 143–169. Paris: Vrin.
———. 2017b. Writing and the Order of Learning. *Philosophy, Theology and the Sciences* 4: 46–73.
Miner, Robert. 2004. *Truth in the Making: Creative Knowledge in Theology and Philosophy*. London: Routledge.
Mulhall, Stephen. 1993. *On Being in the World: Wittgenstein and Heidegger on Seeing Aspects*. London: Routledge.
Newstead, Anne. 2009. Cantor on Infinity in Nature, Number and the Divine Mind. *American Catholic Philosophical Quarterly* 83: 533–555.
Nikulin, Dimitri. 2002. *Matter, Imagination and Geometry: Ontology, Natural Philosophy and Mathematics in Plotinus, Proclus and Descartes*. Aldershot, Hants: Ashgate.
Perkert, Walter. 2013. *Georg Cantor 1845–1918*. Basel: Birkhäuser.
Pickstock, Catherine. 1998. *After Writing*. Oxford: Blackwell.
Priest, Graham. 1995. *Beyond the Limits of Thought*. Cambridge: Cambridge University Press.
Proclus. 1992. *A Commentary on the First Book of Euclid's Elements*. Trans. Glenn R. Morrow. Princeton: Princeton University Press.
Rosenstock, Bruce. 2017. *Transfinite Life: Oskar Goldberg and the Vitalist Imagination*. Indianapolis, IN: Indiana University Press.
Schelling, F.W.J. 2004. *First Outline of a System of the Philosophy of Nature*. New York: SUNY.

Schmutz, Jacob. 2010. Die Einfluss der böhomischen Jesuitphilosophie auf Bernard Bolzanos Wissenshaftlehre. In *Bohemia Jesuitica, 1556–2006*, ed. Petronilla Cemus et al. Würzburg: Echter.
Seife, Charles. 2000. *Zero: The Biography of a Dangerous Idea*. London: Souvenir.
Trimpi, Wesley. 1962. *Ben Jonson's Poems: A Study in the Plain Style*. Stanford, CA: Stanford University Press.
Vico, Giambattista. 2010. *On the Most Ancient Wisdom of the Italians*. Transl. Jason Taylor. New Haven, CN: Yale University Press.
Vieta, François. 1992. Introduction to the Analytic Art. In *Greek Mathematical Thought and the Origins of Algebra*, ed. Jacob Klein, 315–335. New York: Dover.
Waissmann, Friedrich. 1979. *Ludwig Wittgenstein and the Vienna Circle*. Oxford: Basil Blackwell.
Wittgenstein, Ludwig. 1978. *Philosophical Investigations*. Oxford: Blackwell.
———. 1979. *On Certainty*. Oxford: Basil Blackwell.
———. 1981. *Remarks on the Foundations of Mathematics*. Oxford: Blackwell.
———. 1998. *Culture and Value*. Oxford: Wiley-Blackwell.

CHAPTER 3

True Being and Being True: Metaxology and the Retrieval of Metaphysics

D. C. Schindler

William Desmond has held the David R. Cook Visiting Chair in Philosophy since 2005 at Villanova University, which was founded in 1842, exactly 175 years ago when this contribution was written. One of the only Augustinian universities in the world, Villanova chose as its motto a configuration of three themes, each of which plays a significant role in the thought of St. Augustine: *Veritas, Unitas, Caritas*. The juxtaposition of these words is powerful, since it suggests that there could be some profound connections between them, though what the connections might be is not immediately obvious, or at least not equally obvious in every age. Of the three words displayed on the motto, there is one that, in our current age, cannot pass our lips without a certain embarrassment, which we attempt to relieve by introducing a qualifier to neutralize it or by taking an ironic distance through scare quotes or a shrug of the eyebrows. We say 'unitas' with warmth, signaling the generosity of our hospitality, and 'caritas', with an even greater zeal to show effective kindness to those who may be otherwise left outside, without care. But *'veritas'*? *Truth*? As Nietzsche might have said, the word has come to represent something *indecent*. It has

---

D. C. Schindler (✉)
The John Paul II Institute, The Catholic University of America, Washington, DC, USA

© The Author(s) 2018
D. Vanden Auweele (ed.), *William Desmond's Philosophy between Metaphysics, Religion, Ethics, and Aesthetics*,
https://doi.org/10.1007/978-3-319-98992-1_3

become like the word 'mother' in Huxley's *Brave New World*, something that cannot be uttered in public without a snicker and a hot blush. Who in the twenty-first century has the stomach for such a thing as 'Truth', with a capital 'T'? Is it not—indeed, has it not *always* been—a thing indigestible, a rock that stands athwart the cultural streams of change? A rock presents an obstacle to our projects for improvement, or even more worryingly, a weapon to crush the heads of those we call our foes.

The anxiety regarding truth can go so far as to affirm not just a *tension* between it and the other two words on the motto, but an outright *opposition*. To insist on truth, it is commonly thought today, is to be exclusive, and thus to leave out all those who do not think as we do. Hence, *veritas* undermines *unitas*, or community. To insist on truth is likewise to prefer judgment to mercy; hence, *veritas* also threatens *caritas*. The Italian philosopher-politician Gianni Vattimo offers a sophisticated and literate expression of an extreme position on this score, but we may nevertheless take him simply to be spelling out more clearly and more boldly the implications of the general spirit of our postmodern age: Love, Vattimo argues, *demands* a relinquishing of truth claims (Vattimo 2007; Vattimo 2004). We need to withhold judgment in order to be able to affirm the other, and make a space for the other in our community: "Friendship can become the principle and factor of truth only if thought leaves behind any claim to an objective, universal, and apodictic foundation" (Vattimo 2007, p. 111). A desire for friendship, or *caritas*, requires that we reverse the traditional order of things, and so reconceive the very nature of truth: The Gospel's proclamation that "the truth shall make you free" ought to be interpreted as saying "only that which sets you free is truth, and thus, above all else, the 'discovery' that there are no ultimate foundations before which our freedom must come to a halt" (Vattimo 2004, p. xxv). It is not possible, of course, to empty our minds of fundamental beliefs, he admits, but a commitment to charity enables us more and more, as we train ourselves in this concern for others, to attain an ironic distance from our fundamental beliefs. What St. Paul said about marriage and property, Vattimo says about fundamental truth claims: We should make these claims *as if* we were not making them; our grasp should be an open-handed one, ready, the moment the need arises, to take hold of something else, something that may be altogether opposed to our initial beliefs (though of course to do so always with a similar reluctance to commit ourselves). While this irony might seem like a radical proposal, Vattimo claims it is nothing but the very essence of Christianity come to fruition: The highest act of charity, according to this ancient faith, is the death of the *Logos*, the Word or

Reason, that is, the crossing out of truth: "Conflict really escalates only when that dose of irony toward ourselves and our own claims to truth that Nietzsche described ... is missing. Perhaps, after all, this was just Nietzsche's 'secularized' way of expressing something far removed from any idea of will to power: what the Christian tradition taught us to call 'charity'" (ibid., p. 59). If *Logos* were to cling to itself as true, there would be no charity; the total self-emptying of *Logos*, to the point of its self-annihilation, is finally the supreme charity that can reach across any and all differences. The self-elimination of *veritas* thus creates the necessary conditions for the flourishing of *unitas* and *caritas*. Perhaps, if Vattimo is right, after 175 years, it is high time for Villanova to consider a change in the motto.

Now, it is not very difficult to show that the opposition between *veritas* and *caritas* that one finds in the work of Vattimo, but also in the popular imagination more generally, is self-undermining, and that the evacuation of truth will inevitably also imply the evacuation of charity, the transformation of charity into the most superficial of all sentiments, since it is accompanied by an absence of conviction (who wants to be loved *ironically?*), a mere feeling that quite literally does no one any genuine good. A traditional response to Vattimo would calmly point out that one needs to have a non-ironic, indeed, a non-negotiable conviction about the truth of love, the truth of human dignity, the truth of the ultimate goodness of reality and the claims that goodness implies, and indeed *all* such fundamental truths, if there is to be any genuine affirmation of the other and hospitable respect.[1] But it is reasonable to suggest that the traditional response needs to be deepened, or else it runs the risk of recreating and reinforcing the conditions that prompted Vattimo's reaction: What is it about truth, or at least the claims made about it, that might lead one to think that it is essentially oppressive, inimical to the respect we owe to the other, and at odds with the calling to love?

It seems to me that there is scarcely a philosopher alive today who could provide the resources to engage fruitfully with this particular problem of

---

[1] To be sure, Vattimo constantly cautions us not to allow the liberating 'death of God' to harden into a new 'truth' we can use to inflict violence on our enemies. Respect for everyone, according to him, requires, not a foundation, but a commitment to avoid violence. Much more would need to be said, here, to show the impotence of this commitment without a foundation (for a sustained discussion of this problem, see Schindler 2008, Chapter 1), but our concern here is not Vattimo himself, but the more general cultural drift he brings to expression.

truth and contemporary culture but William Desmond. At the heart of Desmond's philosophical project, as I have come to understand it, is a conception of reality that would resist falling into the either-or that frames the dilemma I have briefly presented: Either we affirm truth and compromise our ability to love, *or* we affirm love as the sole 'unconditional', and thereby sacrifice any serious devotion to truth. The resources for outwitting this dilemma become especially apparent in his most recent book, *The Intimate Universal*, which offers a profound and beautiful exposition of a notion that one frequently encounters in his work. There is no space in the present context to attempt to do justice to the subtle and rich argumentation of the book as a whole—and this is particularly regrettable in the present case since 'doing justice' is itself one of the many interesting themes of Desmond's book. But I hope in any event in the brief reflections offered here simply to indicate one of the themes, which I believe has special importance in relation to the problem posed by Vattimo. That theme is the book's recovery of the ontological, or better, the genuinely 'metaphysical', dimension of truth. In what follows, I offer a sketch of Desmond's notion of the 'intimate universal', explain how this notion transforms our understanding of truth, show how its foundations cannot but lie in the reality of being and, finally, suggest how a genuinely metaphysical conception of truth, such as Desmond has developed in his work, is essential for overcoming any putative opposition between truth and love.

To get at this, let us first consider what Desmond means by the 'intimate universal', the central and organizing notion of his book. We can enter into that notion by means of a simple question: Do we necessarily move away from ourselves, the closer we come to the other, and others, who lie in some sense beyond ourselves? Authentically religious thinking has generally recognized that this is not the case at least in the most original instance: The universal God is nevertheless more interior to me than I am to myself. Desmond might be interpreted as sounding out all the distinctly philosophical dimensions of this religious insight (in the broadest sense of philosophy). He thus brings us immediately beyond the impoverished thinking of our age, which swings between the equally unsatisfying alternatives of a hyper-rationalism that would allow the universal simply to eclipse the particularities of what is individual, and the nominalism that would take the universal to be essentially *nothing*—nothing but a *flatus vocis*, a sound that we take to be a name to be imposed on things that are irreducibly different in order to make our world intelligible. Given such a dualistic opposition, it is clear why an insistence on truth would seem to threaten with violence. If universal ideas do not reveal the meaning of the concrete things around us in the world, but *are* in fact merely imposed from the outside, taking such abstract ideals as a measure implies a neglect or abandonment of what things really are in themselves. Efforts have been made in the past to overcome this oppressive dualism, perhaps most notably Hegel's thought of the 'concrete universal', which intends to affirm a reciprocal dependence between the conceptual universal and the concrete particular in history, but Desmond argues convincingly that Hegel's notion is in the end *neither* concrete *nor* universal: It does not acknowledge the genuine transcendence of the universal, but binds it too closely to the immanent movements of history, and it fails to do justice to the genuine mystery of the concrete, which has an intimate life of its own beyond its function of realizing its governing concept (see IU 4–5). Desmond's intimate universal is an effort to do justice in a non-reductive way to all of these dimensions, from the interior mystery of the idiotic to the incarnate manifestness of the aesthetic, with all of the complexities of the love therein revealed as erotically agapeic and agapeically erotic.[2] His description of this complex reality offers a new way to think about an ancient question: What is Truth?

It seems to me that one of the things that allows him to hold together the extraordinarily rich array of features and dimensions in a unity that *is* and *remains* a unity even in the irreducible complexity, is his rooting of both unity and difference in *being*. Being itself is an expression, or indeed *the* expression, of intimate universality: "We love being in our being", he writes deep in the book, "and indeed in all being when we love. This is not neutral being—it is being as an intimate universal" (IU 401). Desmond's description of being here as an 'intimate universal' is reminiscent of Thomas Aquinas's characterization of being as simultaneously what is most intimate and most universal,[3] and his reflections on the implications of *forgetting* being under this aspect in the broad streams of modern and postmodern philosophical thought might be read as a contemporary retelling of Etienne Gilson's *The Unity of Philosophical Experience*, in a

---

[2] It is important to note that Desmond does not posit *eros* and *agape* as two separate kinds of love, but rather as different dimensions of one love, dimensions that always tend to share in themselves aspects of the other. In a similar way, the inwardness of the idiotic and the outward, expressiveness of the aesthetic are by no means opposed to each other.

[3] Aquinas, 1932, 3.7: "*Ipsum enim esse est communissimus effectus primus et intimior omnibus aliis effectibus*".

strikingly different idiom and with a broader reach into the cultural sphere.[4] Comparing Desmond's book to that of Gilson, one of the great defenders of metaphysics in the twentieth century, might initially provoke some protest. Until quite recently (and even now there are serious questions[5]), the word 'metaphysics' was also on the list of indecencies in polite philosophical conversation. William Desmond is nevertheless recognized as a thinker for his unabashed affirmation of metaphysics, even if he interprets the term with somewhat more finesse than one typically associates with the traditional technical sense, emphasizing instead the doubleness of the prefix 'meta' (which can mean both 'beyond' and 'in the midst of').[6] This affirmation of metaphysics, I wish to suggest, is the sine qua non of Desmond's outwitting of our dilemma. One might think, at first, that 'doing justice' to both truth and love, both the universal and the particular,[7] is finally just a matter of effecting the proper subjective disposition: Instead of condemning the other or holding a kind of hostile reserve toward him, we 'ought' to be kind, gentle, open, hospitable, gracious and generous. To be sure, as qualities of our disposition toward the other, all of these are to be recommended. But, what Desmond's book makes clear is that, if there is no ontological foundation for these qualities, if—let us use the word here—they are not grounded *in truth*, not only will they turn out to be superficial, they will also inevitably 'lock in' the very dualism they seek to overcome. Violence will thus not be eliminated, but simply rendered hidden, driven underground, where it can cause profound damage in secret, 'passive-aggressive' sorts of ways, and then explode onto the surface with

---

[4] Gilson (1999). Through a survey of monumental thinkers in the medieval and modern eras, Gilson shows the implications of the forgetting of the philosophy of being and its replacement by something else (e.g., theology or logic). Desmond engages more profoundly with late modern and postmodern thinkers, and explores the implications in concrete cultural realms such as the family, the experience of art, the shape of politics and so forth.

[5] The term 'metaphysics' has returned in contemporary philosophy, in particular, in the schools of 'speculative realism', 'object-oriented philosophy' and the like, but these movements are quite different from the traditional (and basically human-centered) sense of metaphysics as the study of being qua being.

[6] See 'Is there Metaphysics After Critique?', and 'Metaxological Metaphysics and the Equivocity of the Everyday', in ISB 89–119 and 155–184. Of course, this simply recovers the traditional sense. It is only in the modern period that metaphysics comes to mean 'beyond' in a straightforwardly dualistic way.

[7] This is not meant to imply a simple correlation between truth and universality, on the one hand, and love and the particular, on the other. Truth is of course *also* a matter of the particular, and love of course *also* has an essentially universal dimension.

a ferocity that is undiminished because the opposition at its source has continued silently to feed it.[8]

The point is subtle, but quite important: Vattimo does not have a sense of the intimately universal mystery of being that would unite the self and the other beyond but not in opposition to whatever it is that might differentiate them from one another. Because there is not some reality present that we can 'adhere to' in a positive way, we have to enact the essentially negative maneuver of ironic detachment from ourselves. To use Desmond's term, this is a 'counterfeit double' of transcendence. The problem with this negative maneuver is that it does not transform the terms, but tends to replace one problem with another, which turns out to be a reflection of the first. The dethronement of the rational sovereign ego widely advocated in postmodern thought, Desmond tells us, insofar as it only dethrones, inevitably *en*thrones some other power, equally sovereign:

> Postmodern thinking will perhaps deny a certain sovereignty, but one is tempted to think that it really is another form of erotic sovereignty, now in a frenzy of fragmentation or self-laceration, now in the orgy of a generalized *libido dominandi* that prefers to think of itself as a new libido, how bitter, now truculent, about the failure of its previous big ideas or grand narratives. (EB 343)

In the ironic detachment that Vattimo describes, the natural impulse of the mind to know and affirm has to be deliberately frustrated, which makes our relation to the other essentially *mindless*. But mindless means soulless and heartless; mindlessness is inevitably violent because it is essentially empty in its form. Desmond, by contrast, urges us always to be *mind-full*, which means among other things to act toward the other with intelligence intact. It is not an accident that the word 'mindful', beyond its literal sense, connotes for us a loving attention, a positive attitude of active receptivity. Desmond helpfully describes Vattimo's "weak thought" (*pensiero debole*) as a "debilitated mindfulness in the wake of the great foundationalisms of modern philosophy: deflationary finitism after a period of inflationary self-infinitizing thought" (IST 132n). This attempt at deflation presupposes a modern rationalistic and objectivistic—ultimately, Cartesian—sense of foundation, as if this were the only sort possible. But

---

[8] We might consider, in this regard, Vattimo's somewhat notorious support for the violence of Hamas.

there are deeper resources to draw on in response to modern rationalism, which do not allow modernity to set the terms.

To unfold these resources, let us explore a bit further what the mind is 'full' of, in the mindfulness Desmond both argues for and enacts in his own mode of thinking. What is the positive reality that carries us beyond opposition without compromising genuine and good difference? Overcoming the opposition between truth and love requires a recovery of the mystery of being, what Desmond refers elsewhere to as its 'intimate strangeness':

> The community of being as good comes to indeterminate mindfulness in the *innerness of selving* that is the mysterious coming to self in primal self-awakening to the 'to be'—a coming that is of the essence to singular self-hood and yet irreducibly communal, at once a relation to itself and a relation to what is other. It includes a relation to self given to itself, not by itself, but by the agape of the origin; and given to itself, not solely for itself, but in relation to all that is other. (ISB 171)

We note first of all that this 'fullness' of mind is not a wealth, a self-satisfied possessiveness, that would lord it over the needy. Because of the very nature of the *good being* that fills the mind, a being that does not belong to the ego as its exclusive property, an object under its sovereign control, this wealth is perfectly coincident with a radical poverty.[9] In this case, the more securely it is possessed, the more the self is genuinely open to what is other than the self, and in communion in principle with that other. The proper subjective disposition of 'being true', with all of the virtues of kindness and hospitality this disposition entails, thus 'arrives' as a response to the prior truth of being. Arguably, as a result of the forgetfulness of being, the sense of 'being true' has tended to survive in the modern era in the 'subjectivized', and thus impoverished, form that Rousseau granted it and Nietzsche celebrated: Truth as sincerity, a refusal to shift away from one's personal convictions: 'To thine own self be true'! Such a being true is ultimately indistinguishable from mere self-assertion, and Vattimo is right to want to overcome this one-sidedness. But without the truth of being, the only alternative to self-assertion is a kind of self-contempt. Freedom with respect to one's convictions can in this respect only be the negative

---

[9] For a fuller development of this particular sense of poverty in philosophy, see the essay entitled "Religion and the Poverty of Philosophy" in IST 105–133.

form, 'freedom from' my convictions, and indeed freedom from the truth's possession of me that takes place in those convictions. For Desmond, by contrast, there is a positive freedom that results from a deeper truth. His recovery of the mystery of being opens up a different sense of 'being true'. For him, it means a con-fidence, a fidelity that is *responsive* to a presence that precedes it.[10] As Desmond explains, "if faith is a confidence, something is confided to thought, and out of this confiding, thinking has confidence that its being is to be in relation to being as true" (IST 202). This confidence *is* a fidelity to myself, but contrary to the assumptions that drive nearly all the discussions in modern and postmodern thought, the recognition of the mystery of being reveals that my very own self is a participation in something greater than my self; the self-exceeds its own borders, and this excess is constitutive of its very being, its identity. I exist only as always-already a member of a community, originally from within the embrace of man and woman and the natural difference between them, as part of the community of a family, a neighborhood, a polis and so forth. I cannot be true to myself, understood in the light of the first truth of being, without simultaneously being true in all of these other ways. There is no opposition between self and other; they are rather reciprocally joined in the gift of being.

Heidegger has famously criticized the notion of truth as correctness, showing that correctness is possible only given a prior truth of being, which he interprets as an openness, a 'clearing', that enables a correspondence between the mind and particular things in any given instance. Desmond offers something similar, though his account does not eclipse the solidity, the certainty, of our coming to knowledge in the way that Heidegger's account arguably does. For Desmond, it is indeed the case that we can pose the 'what is' question and trust that we will be able to receive an answer to this question in any given case, indeed a clear answer that we can formulate in propositions. Whereas Heidegger tends to speak in a dark and largely negative language, Desmond is altogether affirmative, and this seems to be true because of the intimate universality of the truth that belongs to being. This truth, according to Desmond, *comes first*; it is prior, it is always already there before us. Its priority makes a claim on us, but it is a claim that liberates. In the conventional perspective (which we have been suggesting Vattimo concedes, perhaps in spite of himself), truth is nothing more than an attribute of our knowledge, and so of our claims.

[10] See 'The Confidence of Thought' in ISB 202–230.

To assert the truth of a proposition, in this case, is to grant a kind of absoluteness to the particular grasp that I, as an autonomous agent, have managed to achieve. As Vattimo explains, to make a truth claim is to isolate a single perspective from the infinity of possible perspectives and to accord that perspective a privilege that is denied to all the others.[11] This cannot but appear unjust, and indeed uncharitable. But this interpretation takes for granted that there is nothing beyond the infinity of perspectives, which is to say that truth is an adjective that can apply only to a subjective appropriation of a thing. It takes for granted that there is no truth of being as such.

The perspective changes radically, so to speak, when we recognize truth in its properly ontological or metaphysical sense. For William Desmond, to assert the truth of a proposition is to move in the opposite direction from what we described earlier—or better, to move in two directions at once. The lover of truth makes a claim, to be sure, but this claim is expressive of a more fundamental claim on me, a claim that enables my own claim. In confidently asserting the truth of a proposition, I am trusting not just myself, but myself only because I place my trust in something greater than myself. I am entrusting myself when I make a truth claim. Our autonomy as agents is not denied, but it is integrated in the more fundamental presence of the truth of being. As Desmond puts it, quite beautifully:

> there is a heteronomy at work here but it is no squashing otherness. It is releasing and enabling of the very search for truth, and this prior enabling is not determinate thought, nor determined through ourselves alone, hence it cannot be defined in the logic of autonomy. This prior enabling is just what allows us to be relatively autonomous at all. We would not be autonomous were not autonomy enabled by something prior to and other to autonomy. Self-determining thinking is released into its own freedom to think for itself by an enabling resource that is not itself, a source not to be captured in terms of this or that determinate thought, or by thought's determination by and for itself. There is more that allows thinking to be itself more than itself. (ISB 217)

To describe the radical shifting of perspective that occurs here, Desmond coins a phrase, inspired by a Wordsworth poem, a phrase that turns out

---

[11] Hence, the connection he draws between his version of hermeneutics, as opening up an infinity of interpretations, and (modern) democracy: see Chapter 8 of Vattimo (2004, pp. 90–101).

perspective, so to speak, around on itself: He speaks of a "beholding from", an admiring gaze that is not an intentional act that originates in a subject and terminates in an object. Instead, it is a beholding that originates from an already given unity, we might say, between the subject and object, so that *my act* of beholding sources beyond *my act*, and thus takes on the character of a participation in a beholding that is greater than just me alone. Desmond associates this "beholding from" with what he calls "astonishment".[12]

It is right here that we meet up with what I believe is one of Desmond's most powerful insights, and I would suggest that it is precisely this insight, even more perhaps than the notion of the 'between' that is most often associated with him, that gives his thought its most distinctive color and depth. This insight is what Desmond calls the 'passio essendi', the 'patience of being', which he reveals to be the more original root of the 'conatus essendi', so fundamental to the thought of Spinoza, and therefore to the whole modern world. For Spinoza, the conatus is a striving after self-preservation. But for Desmond, this striving is not what is most basic—to think that it is, is to miss the most fundamental meaning of being. To exist at all is to have been *given* being: "We do not first choose our being or freedom; both are first given to us; and being given, we begin to give ourselves to ourselves" (EB 368). This givenness of our being or our freedom is not simply an inert starting point, which we regrettably have no control over but which allows us, once we accept it, to have control over everything else. Instead, givenness abides as a genuine point of origin: "There is an ontological patience in our being received into being of which we always continue to be the recipients. Its mindful counterpart is astonishment and marvel at being at all, and marvel at the good of being" (IU 402). This grateful reception of what is given is the anchor, we might say, of truth: "There is a deeper level of fidelity and 'doing justice'" than simply being sure to carry out our theory in practice, Desmond explains: "This is the more primordial level of the patience of being, patience in being in true" (IU 144). Desmond makes clear that a recognition of this dimension eventually requires an openness to religion, or more specifically an openness to the God who is already gift in himself—which would explain why the dilemma we have been discussing would coincide with a marginalizing of religion, and why neither Vattimo's death of the *Logos* nor Heidegger's radically 'a-theistic' thinking suffices in the end to carry us beyond the dilemma. But this givenness is also necessarily mediated in and through the

---

[12] 'Ways of Wondering: Beyond the Barbarism of Reflection' in ISB 260–300, here: 266.

very concrete relationships with others that constitute our existence: By virtue of the intimate strangeness, the intimate universality, of being, we relate already to ourselves as other, but then of course to the others that constitute our family, the other members of our various communities and so forth. If Spinoza interprets the *conatus essendi* as an essentially non-analogous drive to self-preservation,[13] then Desmond, who reads this conatus as rooted in the prior *passio essendi*, is able, for his part, to bring out its etymological sense, echoing an insight from the French poet Paul Claudel[14]: conatus is a being-born-with, it is the self's discovery of itself as always-already intertwined in and with the other as a co-participant in the great mystery of being: "There is something in self-affirmation that relativizes self-affirmation. There is something in its self-affirmation communicating of its being given to be at all, something making it porous relative to what is other than itself, and porous not just as servile passivity" (IU 136).

What does all of this imply for the relation between truth and love? To reject metaphysics is to render inescapable an opposition between the two. In this case, we may wish to affirm love, but it cannot be a faithful love, cannot be *true*, and cannot do justice to the truth of love. The absolute self-sacrifice of such a love will turn out to be the flip side of an intractable narcissism because an unattainable other can make no real claim on me beyond what my sovereign ego wishes, ad libitum, to take upon itself. But the intimate universal reveals both that this claim cannot finally be reduced to a project of my own making, some form of idol or means of mere self-gratification or self-glorification, *and* at the same time that the claim of the other nevertheless *moves* me already from within, it remains a claim to what I have already begun to respond before any deliberate consent, as it were. This is why the response takes the form of *fidelity*, being true, doing justice, to what is already given. Being true is a response to a claim that both comes to me from without and addresses me from within, and so bears the same paradoxes of inwardness and self-transcendence that are inescapably a part of love. Because the claim arises from a place deeper than the self, whether mine or the other's, I am able in my response to draw on resources that exceed my inevitably all-too-narrow intentions, and able to touch the other intimately, to communicate in a profoundly effective way a goodness greater than myself. In this way, devotion to

---

[13] Robert Spaemann has shown the profound implications of Spinoza's removal of analogy from his interpretation of nature's tendency to self-preservation: See, for example, 'Nature' in Spaemann (2015, pp. 27–29) and 'Bourgeois Ethics and Non-Teleological Ontology' in Spaemann (2015, pp. 48–50).

[14] IU 135. Claudel develops his notion of 'co-naissance', 'being born with', in Claudel (1957, p. 1060 ff).

truth entails, not an oppressive imposition of my own ideas on the other, but a mysterious intertwining of the two of us, an intertwining that is captured with exquisite beauty in St. Augustine's description of the genuine act of teaching: In such an act, he says:

> the feeling of compassion [*compatientis affectus*] is so strong that, when our listeners are touched by us as we speak and we are touched by them as they learn, each of us comes to dwell in the other; and so they speak in us what they hear, while we in some way learn in them what we teach.[15]

In the place of autonomous agents acting *on* each other from the outside, forcing into the center their own inevitably partial conceptions of things, we have co-inhering actors, who dwell in each other because each arises from an intimate presence that transcends them both. William Desmond's intimate universal reveals, in a word, that *veritas* and *caritas* are not at odds but belong essentially together in a *unitas*, which is ultimately the unity of being.

Bibliography

Aquinas, Thomas. 1932. *Quaestiones disputatae De potentia dei*. Trans. English Dominicans. Westminster, MD: The Newman Press.
Augustine. 2017. *De catechizandis rudibus*. Unpublished Trans. Michael Camacho.
Claudel, Paul. 1957. L'art poétique. In *Oeuvre Poétique*. Paris: Gallimard.
Gilson, Etienne. 1999. *The Unity of Philosophical Experience: The Medieval Experiment, the Cartesian Experiment, the Modern Experiment*. San Francisco: Ignatius Press.
Schindler, D.C. 2008. *Plato's Critique of Impure Reason: On Goodness and Truth in the Republic*. Washington, DC: CUA Press.
Spaemann, Robert. 2015. *The Robert Spaemann Reader*. Oxford: Oxford University Press.
Vattimo, Gianni. 2004. *Nihilism and Emancipation: Ethics, Politics, and Law*. New York: Columbia University Press.
———. 2007. *After Christianity*. New York: Columbia University Press.

---

[15] Augustine (2017, 12.17). I am grateful to Michael Camacho for pointing this passage out to me; the translation is Michael's. I would also like more generally to acknowledge helpful suggestions by Dennis Vanden Auweele in preparing this chapter.

CHAPTER 4

Hermeneutical Selving as Metaxological Selving: Bridging the Perceived Gap Between Theological Hermeneutics and Metaphysics

Daniel Minch

One major impetus behind William Desmond's work has been crafting a suitable response to what he perceives to be problems, contradictions, and *aporiai* that have arisen in Western thought, and in post-Hegelian philosophy particularly. The reduction of the cosmos from a rich interplay of transcendent and immanent dimensions, to an objective immanent 'thereness', is a multifaceted historical phenomenon that goes by many names: the disenchantment of the world, secularization, demythologization, and, in Desmond's terms, 'postulatory finitism'. The philosophical trend of 'postulatory finitism' begins with the proposition that finite immanence is the whole of reality, and that there is no transcendence, at least not in the way that previous eras had spoken about such a concept in terms of a highest principle, ground of Being, or a creator-God. Desmond has referred to this ultimate form of transcendence as a power that is "original, creative possibilizing beyond determinate possibility, and 'real' beyond all

D. Minch (✉)
KU Leuven, Leuven, Belgium
e-mail: daniel.minchjr@kuleuven.be

© The Author(s) 2018
D. Vanden Auweele (ed.), *William Desmond's Philosophy between Metaphysics, Religion, Ethics, and Aesthetics*,
https://doi.org/10.1007/978-3-319-98992-1_4

determinate realization, beyond all self-determining self-realization".[1] As such, it is essentially a "*hyperbolic* sense of transcendence, bringing to mind the question of God beyond the immanence of transcendence in nature and human being" (GB 23).

Postulatory finitism precludes the possibility of an 'outside' or a beyond for humanity to reach for, and it is meant, at least in some cases, to redirect our focus to the historical reality in which humanity finds itself and to shape that in a better, more reasonable, or more humane way. It has other effects, however, including the reorientation of our view of the cosmos around a fundamentally anthropocentric model—one which ignores or re-narrates the struggles that humanity has always had with finitude. The enigma of finitude always lies in the unstable collision of the finite and the infinite and the concrete experience of being a historical being whose purpose in the universe is unclear. Desmond contends that philosophers of finitude, those who insist that immanent finitude is 'all there is', neither accurately understand nor describe finitude.[2] Instead, the "turn to ourselves, and to ourselves only", risks merely creating 'counterfeit doubles' of finitude (IST 43). The rejection of transcendence, and turn to immanentism, therefore leads to a misunderstanding of finitude, as well as a kind of forced silence in philosophy about God and of transcendence's nature and possibility.

When viewed historically, however, this contemporary silence about God and transcendence is "the anomaly rather than the rule" (Desmond 2010, p. 101).[3] Desmond's work presents a rehabilitation of the ideas of metaphysics and God in a way that takes the recent history of philosophical skepticism quite seriously; however, he does not shy away from contextualizing the critics of theistic metaphysics or from showing how isolated they are in the Western philosophical tradition. The problems with traditional metaphysics and transcendence have not been confined to philosophy alone. Theology has also had to contend with an ongoing 'crisis of metaphysics', caused in part by a problematic understanding of finitude inherited from neoscholasticism. In what follows, I examine

---

[1] Desmond terms this 'Third Transcendence', alongside the 'First Transcendence' (being as exterior other) and 'Second Transcendence' (being as self-transcendence) (HG 2–7 and GB 22).

[2] He ascribes this position to Nietzsche, Heidegger, Sartre, and the 'anti-metaphysical' traditions of the twentieth century. See Desmond (2011, pp. 130–133).

[3] See also DDO 11 where Desmond (rightly) regards 'ontotheology' as a bogeyman "conjured up to frighten philosophical thought away from origins."

the theological 'turn to experience' that occurred in Catholic theology following the Second Vatican Council as a way of correcting the theological and philosophical accounts of finitude in relation to transcendence. In particular, I draw upon the thought of the Flemish theologian Edward Schillebeeckx, whose work in the area of theological hermeneutics has proven particularly important and influential. Schillebeeckx recognized human *experience* as the precondition for religious faith, and so he applied hermeneutical principles to the experience of faith in the modern world. I then attempt to bridge the gap between hermeneutics and metaphysics by showing how Schillebeeckx's theological-anthropological structure corresponds to the process of human 'selving' as elaborated by William Desmond, especially in his programmatic volume *Being and the Between*. In that section, I also apply the fourfold sense of being as it corresponds to human experience. Essentially, a hermeneutics of experience presents the interplay between transcendence and immanence in a theological and metaphysical way without explicitly setting out to 'do metaphysics'. A hermeneutics of experience allows us to see the relation of the finite to the infinite in its different modes, opening up paths for dialogue between philosophy and theology in their respective modes of thought about God and humanity. By way of a conclusion, I point to the importance of hermeneutics for reconceiving 'metaphysics' as an empowering and dynamic structure rather than as a static and hierarchical order.

THE CRISIS OF METAPHYSICS IN THEOLOGY

The 'crisis of metaphysics' was, and remains, a slow-burning issue in Catholic theology that is intimately connected to the rise of postulatory finitism. It is a problem with thought and paradigms, but it is also a problem of *order*. This includes the difficulties that arose alongside secularization and industrialization, particularly in the heavily Hegelian tradition of German Liberal Protestantism. However, the issue is rooted further back than the eighteenth and nineteenth centuries. Both Edward Schillebeeckx and Henri de Lubac have traced the rise of secularization to the thirteenth century and the postulation of a 'natural law' between human conscience and the divine law (de Lubac 1998, pp. 32–52; Schillebeeckx 2014d, pp. 33–34 [56–58]).[4] Eventually, this led to the development of the theory

---

[4] All citations from Schillebeeckx's *Collected Works* series also include the pagination of the original English editions in square brackets.

of 'pure nature' such that humanity has both a natural and a supernatural end, effectively separating the realms of the divine from the worldly and thereby leading to a situation in which the world is understood as anthropocentric, or even anthropomorphic, and can be forced to conform to humanity's needs and wishes. The postulation of a 'gap' between God, as creator, and the creation that is given to itself to become itself is a development from the Augustinian 'vertical' ordering of the cosmos along a hierarchy of being (Schillebeeckx 2014d, pp. 33–35 [55–60]). The problem was that the theological postulate of a 'horizontal', immanent realm tended to be developed in two directions: either God was banished from the realm of immanence altogether, or God continued to remain a part of it as the highest rational principle, collapsing the infinite into the finite. God was gradually 'naturalized', and the latter model merged into the former in some cases. Enlightenment thinkers increasingly identified God with perfect reason, transmuting the creator into the universal substance of the cosmos, the idealized 'book of nature', or even the World-Spirit working out its own self-determination in history.

It may come as a surprise that, in Catholic theology, the 'modern' naturalizing tendency was carried to an extreme at the First Vatican Council, in which an anathema was proclaimed against anyone who denied that God could be known purely through created things or in the light of natural reason.[5] Here, the medieval vertical dimension had been fused closely with the horizontal: the cosmos was ordered hierarchically by divine fiat, and as a part of that hierarchy, human social relations needed to conform to specific medieval patterns in order to reflect the rational, objective reality of God's truth. The revival of the scholastic method in the nineteenth century was partly a theological reaction against the modern world, prompted in no small part by the spread of democratic reforms across Europe, as well as by the loss of the Papacy's temporal power and authority (Schoof 2008, pp. 30–32). The emergent neoscholastic synthesis was a departure from the historical and sacramental work of the Tübingen School and John Henry Newman, as well as a capitulation to the spirit of the age. As a method, it sought to be an analytic, objective, and an "apparently mathematical way of

---

[5] See (Pius IX 1870, Canon II.2) "*Si quis dixerit, Deum unum et verum, Creatorem et Dominum nostrum, per ea, quae facta sunt, naturali rationis humanae lumine certo cognosci non posse; anathema sit*". We must now interpret the truth of this doctrine apart from the hierarchical metaphysical structure that produced it. See also Schoof (2008, pp. 178–179).

dealing with an ever increasing number of more and more precisely defined concepts" (Schoof 2008, p. 34). It emphasized the intellectual and supremely rational aspect of faith and revelation, adopting the terminology of rational certainty from the historical and physical sciences of the time. This separated the experiential dimensions of human life in the world from the supernatural realm, which could be reached through reason and appeals to authority. In the short term, this provided the church with a rational defense against its perceived enemies, but in the long term, it helped to precipitate the crisis of metaphysics once the foundations of neoscholasticism were undermined by social change and by rigorous study of the sources of 'tradition' itself.

Liberal Protestantism also tended to identify revelation with social order, but with that of the modern nation state and its political ambitions, rather than with the *Ancien Régime*. Metaphysics, in both senses, was about *order*. Both of these visions came grinding to a halt when they collided with the reality of the First World War (Hall 1999). The Catholic synthesis emerged less badly damaged from the war, thanks in part to strict methodological limitations on theological inquiry. Eventually, however, theologians working within this framework began to return to the writings of medieval and patristic authors themselves rather than to the narrowly constructed manuals of doctrine and commentaries on those sources. It was, therefore, from *within* the neoscholastic school that the most significant cracks began to appear. This *Ressourcement* movement, coupled with the early successes of Catholic Action, the worker priest movement, and the massive social changes that occurred after the Second World War, further widened those cracks in the socio-metaphysical worldview (Schelkens et al. 2013, pp. 101–126). The situation only came to a head in 1962 with the opening of the Second Vatican Council, when the bishops and theologians gathered in Rome to find a new way forward and a renewed understanding of finite humanity's relation to God and to the world.

The Unfinished *Humanum* and the 'Secular' World

New approaches introduced in Catholic theology in the wake of Vatican II helped to break up the older, static models of natural philosophy and the reified structures of nature and grace which were closely associated with metaphysical 'order' (de Lubac 1998, pp. 32–36; Schillebeeckx 2014d, pp. 33–34 [56–58]). One of the most important factors was the Pastoral Constitution on the Church in the Modern World, *Gaudium et Spes*, which was finally approved after a lengthy and controversial debate at the Council's final session (O'Malley 2008, pp. 204-205 and 258-268). Edward Schillebeeckx had, in an unofficial capacity, influenced the formation of the document, and he was in turn influenced by it once it was officially promulgated (Bauer 2012; Borgman 2003, pp. 334-337 and 350-351; Minch 2018b). Schillebeeckx's early anthropological reflections on *Gaudium et Spes* set much of the tone for his later work. He recognized that humanity's self-understanding influences and reciprocally shapes human understanding of both God and the world.

Whether or not we consider the world to be a meaningless thereness, a preordained divine order, or a given realm of situated and historical freedom matters for what humanity is and becomes in the world. *Gaudium et Spes* affirms that the world is a *humanized world*, one which can be shaped to fit humanity's needs (Schillebeeckx 1973, p. 56). The 'natural' state of the world, as we find it, is not a preordained order that cannot be disturbed, just as human social relations are not divinely instituted. Furthermore, for Schillebeeckx, the human creation of a more livable world is itself 'natural' in the sense that it is an intrinsic ability of a humanity that experiences itself as "a being who makes history" (Schillebeeckx 1973, p. 81). This ability can and has been abused, but the fundamental image of humanity and world is now "basically a project for the future. Man's [*sic*] aim is to build a new world" (Schillebeeckx 1973, p. 81). From this it follows that the "definition of human existence is not a preexistent datum", as a historical being oriented toward the future (Schillebeeckx 1978a, p. 28). There are two reasons for this, from the perspective of a Christian anthropology: first, the human is "a being caught up in history", and as historical is fundamentally unfinished—an admixture of potentiality and actuality, partially determined by context and partially self-determining; second, the expectation of meaning and the process of self-realization is an eschatological reality (Schillebeeckx 1978a, p. 30). The meaning of the whole of reality is partially present, but is also hidden in the salvific future that is yet to come.

Humanity, therefore, is fundamentally unfinished in the sense of both the unfinished *humanum* as a whole and historical individuals who coexist in societies. There is no a priori normative definition of human nature, of what is humanly desirable, or what counts as 'salvation'. What we have instead are multiple historical images and descriptions that are often complementary, but are also, just as often, fragmentary and even contradictory (Schillebeeckx 2014e, p. 58 [65]). In the 1970s, Schillebeeckx articulated a set of seven 'anthropological constants' that provide a "kind of system of coordinates which focus on the human *person-identify* within *social culture*" (Schillebeeckx 1978a, p. 31). Elsewhere, I have worked out the importance of these constants in excavating the transcendental foundation upon which they have been built (Minch 2017). I argue that the phenomenological constants—such as embodiment, existence as co-existence, the space-time dimension of human life, the irreducible synthesis of all coordinates, and the resulting necessary pluralism of creation—all rely upon a more fundamental ontological point. Here, I more fully elaborate on this 'ontological constant' in order to connect it to Desmond's metaphysics of 'the between'. Schillebeeckx continues to be an important thinker in part because of his commitment to hermeneutics and his deep understanding and integration of Hans-Georg Gadamer's insistence that 'hermeneutics' is "*not proposing a method*; [it is] describing *what is the case*" (Gadamer 2004a, p. 512). In other words, the hermeneutical worldview taken over by Schillebeeckx from Gadamer and Heidegger, does not merely judge between competing interpretations of the world. It is a thoroughgoing examination of the very foundations of being itself, and therefore is an attempt to present an ontological position.

The most fundamental point from which Schillebeeckx works is what, in one of his last major works, he names 'the absolute limit' (*absolute grens*). This 'limit' does not describe limit situations, such as being unable to run very fast, or to read without one's glasses. It is rather, "an experience of an absolute limit *in* the constant experience of all our relative limits" (Schillebeeckx 2014b, p. 76 [78]). It is the experience of radical contingency or finitude that is present *in* all types of experience, through which we come to realize that we "are neither lords nor masters of ourselves, far less of nature and history" (Schillebeeckx 2014b, p. 76 [78]). The absolute limit is not a proof for God's existence, and is in fact recognized by atheistic philosophers as a fundamental element of human experience. The facticity of human finitude is not, however, an essential flaw that has to be overcome through technology, or a secularized eschatology of social acceleration—the realization of all human possibilities in one lifetime (see Rosa 2003). In fact, it could be argued that many of the problems that humanity has caused stem from the denial of this limit or from the hubristic assumption of a place of judgment and manipulation—acting as if we were in fact the lords and masters of ourselves and of history. The rejection of the absolute limit is in fact one *interpretation* of it. As Schillebeeckx recognized, the "real fact of this limit also compels us to interpret it" (Schillebeeckx 2014b, p. 77 [79]). This throws us back to the hermeneutical nature of human existence: the human subject as a whole comes up against its own existential limit in experience, which it is compelled to interpret. Experiences make up the various 'parts' of the larger whole of the self, and the subject becomes different in each experiential moment, both quantitatively (more experience) and qualitatively (differently experienced). Simply by existing in the world, the human subject is caught up in the interpretive movement between 'part' and 'whole' that constitutes all of experience. The subject experiences with a horizon of past experiences and stands in the stream of multiple traditions—these provide the subject the raw material of being: language. People are given language, and "no one is sovereign over his or her own speech. As a beginning, we can say that the speaker appeals to a language which he or she did not invent, but which was already given to the speaker" (Schillebeeckx 1983, p. 8).

Freedom in being, because it is historical, is not merely 'given'—it must be realized through active participation in the world in which we find ourselves; this involves using, exercising, and changing our language and self-understanding (Schillebeeckx 2014c, pp. 22–23 [24–25]). The realization of freedom and the process of becoming are therefore hermeneutical. In experience, which is an encounter with an other, human narratives can change. This occurs both with regard to the (re-)interpretation of the past and in the anticipation of the future. The type of historicity possessed by the finite human subject is essentially a *narrative historicity*. What allows for the back-and-forth movement of the self in experience, from the inside to the outside and back again, is the fact that it is finite to begin with. The absolute limit constitutes the border between self and other. It gives a point for us to 'make contact' with an other and it provides a basis for thinking the subject in terms of an original unity capable of being affected and *capable of experience*. The finitude of the human being is the ontological constant that grounds and makes possible all attempts at determining what it is to be a human being in the world. Because humans are finite, they can conceive of a whole 'self' while also recognizing otherness as that which is not the self.[6] Gadamer's understanding of a fore-conception of completeness is also the projection of the wholeness of beings in time and space: we hermeneutically perceive and complete partial perceptions as meaningful 'wholes' that are then open to possible revision, based on how they appear in experience (Gadamer 2004b, p. 364).

[6] Here, we have the interplay between Desmond's Transcendence 1 and 2. See GB 23–24.

This preconceived wholeness conditions the hermeneutical movement: the whole is expected and known from its parts, while the parts are reinterpreted in light of the whole (Schillebeeckx 1978b, p. 393). Hence, humanity is essentially *unfinished*—it is still becoming what it will be in history based on its own self-understanding and interpretation of the world in which it exists. The *humanum* as the eschatological manifestation of a collective humanity in its universal resurrected form is, in our continuing history, always partially hidden and obscured by our finite existence. It is also given shape and form at the absolute limit of human finitude (Schillebeeckx 2014a, pp. 830–834 [835–839]).

THE METAPHYSICAL BRIDGE AND THE CONSTRUCTION OF THE SELF

Hermeneutics, as proposed by Schillebeeckx, runs with the essential insight that limitation and historicity are *features* of being, not flaws. It is what makes the movement of beings possible. Following Gadamer, Schillebeeckx is not really proposing a method, although it was that as well, he is describing how beings are and become themselves. There is a metaphysical structure at work here, although it is something he would not have named as metaphysics, partially in order to distance himself from the neoscholastic framework of deduction from absolute principles, and wandering speculations about heaven, hell, purgatory, and the nature of the soul. In order to draw out what is really at stake here, I try to create a metaphysical 'bridge' from Schillebeeckx's hermeneutical ontology to William Desmond's explication and understanding of 'selving'. This includes the fourfold sense of being: the univocal, equivocal, dialectical, and the metaxological. Each of these plays a role in the overall construction of human subjects in being.

For Schillebeeckx, experience is far from the simple interaction of accidentally and extrinsically related objects. Beings are not merely self-enclosed by the absolute limit like monadic atoms where relations between them are nonessential to their own composition. This would portray beings as eternal and unchangeable essences instead of hermeneutical subjects. Rather, in the encounter with the unexpected—the 'revelatory'—and the other in experience, we encounter "what we ourselves had never thought of and never produced [which] occurs to us as a gift" (Schillebeeckx 2014b, p. 21 [22]). Because language is the medium and mediator of being, human subjects are all mutually implicated in one another's interpretative horizons at various levels. In Desmond's terminology, the human subject as finite is not self-grounding, pointing to both an asymmetry between finite being and its absolute ground, as well as allowing for the experience of otherness and 'genuine plurality' (DDO 200). In being itself, the subject comes up against that which is other in experience, and by encountering its own limit it is forced to recognize an 'outside' to the horizon of experience and interpretation possessed by the subject that had constituted its self-understanding and the source of its identity. This leads to "a new reinterpretation of our own identity", essentially a 'disintegration' and then a new "reintegration with a different orientation" (Schillebeeckx 2014b, p. 22 [22]).

What occurs in experience is essential to the active process of 'selving' as described by Desmond—becoming a determinate human subject. In coming up against the 'otherness' found in lived experience, the self as a determinate identity experiences an ecstatic motion away from itself, placing itself in a position of risk; the encounter with an other, at the absolute limit of finitude, always risks the disintegration of identity (see EB 327). But this movement, in a second, examined moment, shows that the determinate self is not only itself as a univocally determined element. Here I begin to use Desmond's language about the 'fourfold sense of being' to describe this movement. The encounter with the other in lived experience is always essentially contrastive: the self-same subject meets what is not itself and recoils back into itself to re-form with a new and different horizon of expectation and interpretation. There is a spectrum of experiences: this is barely noticeable in mundane experience, but in larger more 'revelatory' experiences, the contrastive nature becomes more exaggerated. From the subject's side, the self is revealed to itself as plural—what was a 'one' is doubled back on itself when it comes up against physical, mental, and phenomenological relative limits in the world which bring with them the imperative to interpret what occurs at the absolute limit. This equivocal moment of disintegration of determinate identity is both a hermeneutical moment and a movement: "the moment of understanding is the moment of interpretation is the moment of *application*" (Godzieba 2013, p. 92). The doubled self shows us that we are not yet ourselves, but we cannot seek ourselves without first being a self in some respect (BB 110–111). The self as self-transcending is doubled from within its own structure, and it is intrinsically linked with the other beings around it by provoking and mediating this movement. In other words, things are not only themselves because of themselves, but because of their relations with others, or their *mutual relativity* (BB 150).

The subject begins, therefore, in the univocal mode, centered in its own identity, but it is immediately de-centered through the mediation of itself in experience. There is no pure univocal or equivocal moment, because both are elements of an essentially dialectical *movement* between self and other, both *ad intra* and *ad extra*, and between the part and the whole. The structure of dialectic is rhythmic—it is immediately itself (univocal), but its self-relatedness reveals another depth dimension (equivocal), and other-relatedness returns it to itself, both changing and confirming the being as itself (dialectic). The self can give itself, but only because it is already given to itself to become itself (BB 153). Throughout this process, the identity of the subject remains. Barring some traumatic psychological or physical violence, the disintegration of the self in hermeneutical experience is always essentially constructive, and "self opposition serves the purpose of fuller self-becoming" (BB 286). Equivocal being is mediated through self-becoming into a more determinate self. What we do not yet have, however, is the metaxological sense of being. This movement could close in on itself and end with the dialectical as pure self-mediation. The ways in which Schillebeeckx and Desmond avoid this outcome approach the problem from different starting points, but they are essentially complementary.

While Desmond takes what might be called a 'transcendental-philosophical' approach, Schillebeeckx begins from the historical situatedness of humanity: human existence is always co-existence and, therefore, is also intrinsically related to historically contingent social and instructional structures (Schillebeeckx 1978a, pp. 34–35). That is not to say that Desmond disregards lived experience altogether, but it is neither his focus nor is it his primary starting point for reflection. Desmond's work is 'transcendental' in the sense that it begins from a reflection on at least quasi-universal structures that make up the conditions of possibility for experience. As he himself states, philosophical approaches are "always mediated to some degree by our historical situation" (DDO 11). In contrast to the contemporary anthropological model that is dominated by 'economic' relations between rational agents—*homo economicus*—Schillebeeckx observes that the "social dimension is not something that is added to our person-identity, it is a dimension of this very identity"

(Schillebeeckx 1978a, pp. 34–35).[7] The 'historical between' is a fact of human life and mixture of sense and non-sense, even to the point of absurd and inexplicable suffering. Any "pretension to take a stand outside the historical action and thought of man [*sic*] is a threat to real humanity" (Schillebeeckx 1978a, p. 36).

There cannot be any full closure of the self in its own dialectical movement, since it is produced from a social otherness; even one's best attempt to shut out the world or to instrumentalize others is still very much a reaction to the intrinsic relation that is already *given*. Schillebeeckx views the historical situatedness of humanity within the wider context of coming eschatological salvation. This does not mean that he appeals to an extra-historical ideological image of universal salvation; on the contrary, we only know something about salvation because of the historical fragments that have already been experienced and are passed on through traditions of experience. Moreover, the experiences of suffering and non-sense that are also an unavoidable part of human life, what he terms experiences of 'negative contrast', indicate to us the unfinished character of history and humanity itself—the total meaning of reality is present, yet unavailable; it can be glimpsed through its reverse-image in our appeals for change and our spontaneous resistance to inhumanity and suffering. Desmond has also pointed to this type of experience and given it ontological roots: the spontaneous recoil from suffering and ugliness as a response to our primordial expectation of the good (EB 166–177 and 206–209). Hence, we are beings that become ourselves in a hermeneutical between. We are between the beginning and the end, both of which are in excess of what can be grasped and transfigured into a univocal whole. Desmond's language about beings as 'open wholes' is an excellent description of creation and of beings as self-determining "without being completely determined in themselves" (BB 182).

The eschatological excess that characterizes the mystery of salvation points directly toward the 'overdetermined' origin as well. Beings are *promises*: they contain the promise of a surplus and, for Schillebeeckx, this is an eschatological surplus given by the God who *is* the future of humanity (BB 241; Schillebeeckx 1973, p. 86) The promise of being sends the self beyond itself in the first place, placing the agapeic excess prior to the attempt of an individual being to fill a gap in itself. There is a self-giving

---

[7] For the relation of the anthropological constants to economic anthropology, see Minch (2018a).

agapeic fullness that grounds and produces the precondition for the *ek-static* movement of the self toward the other beyond itself and gives the promise of becoming (BB 260).[8] Christianity places this fullness at both the beginning and at the end. Creation can only be fulfilled at the end because its fullness is also already present both now and in the beginning. In Desmond's words: "The giving of being is in excess of any closed 'for-self,' for if there were only such closed 'for-selves,' there would be no giving of otherness as other; there would only be a circle of self-giving, which is no real giving" (BB 185).

Beings, therefore, have a wholeness as for-themselves, but they are not closed in on themselves. The self is an open whole, dialectically mediated both interiorly and exteriorly. Open wholes are contained within a wider whole that is also open and unfinished. The process, or rhythm, is mirrored at a larger level. This is *metaxological* because what creation becomes is not contingent upon the origin, only upon how it becomes—the power of self-transcendence imparted to creation as its own particular infinitude, or the "open promise of creation even in its finitude" (BB 288–289). There is a hermeneutic circle in the movement of subjects that *become selves*, empowered by the potencies of being. The metaxological 'sense' of being allows and underwrites selving as a hermeneutic process, and it precludes a closure of beings in on themselves from the outset. The 'between' must, therefore, be thought of in terms of historicity since it is from history that we can begin to reflect on both origins and ends.

Conclusion: Metaphysics as Originating Process

The defining characteristic of such a hermeneutical-metaxological metaphysics is that it does not have to rely on conceptions of 'metaphysics' that have become implausible or were previously experienced as totalitarian and oppressive. Essentially, the stress is on the "forming rather than the form, on the structuring rather than on the structure" (BB 149). The rhythmic process of becoming yields insights into what is 'above' the physical world, but it does not provide us with recipes or a set of instructions for ordering the world in correspondence with the structure of being. The metaxological-hermeneutical concept of being is always in motion, as a

---

[8] Erotic desire and 'erotic selving' are predicated on a prior agapeic fullness. There is also a parallel here to the 'self as promise' that is affirmed by being fulfilled in 'second ethical selving'. See EB 256–260.

founding constitution, pattern, or an empowering process, and through this motion it enshrines the necessity of internal difference for beings in the world as a constant. Without the differentiating power of being, "the thing as identifiable would disappear into the resulting absence of distinction, and we would have the limiting case of the purely homogeneous—what in former ages was sometimes called *materia prima*" (DDO 102–103). By destroying the internal difference of things, all things end up the same. Internal differentiation is necessary to distinguish self from self, and ultimately self from other. Without this, reality collapses into immediate unity, which is only a step on the way to equivocal dissolution. Thus, the hermeneutical movement is necessary to maintain the unity of selves, who also have the space to become themselves through an encounter with otherness at the absolute limit.

The absolute limit that stands at the base of human experience is our own facticity: "We ourselves are this limit" (Schillebeeckx 2014b, p. 76 [79]). As Desmond says, "we do not draw this limit; it draws us" (DDO 154). This is a positive indeterminacy, "this limit is also an unlimit: instead of confining us, it fulfills and frees us, frees us to the enjoyment of irreducible otherness" (DDO 154) Finitude is actually a 'positive power', as finitude is not just exhausted by the opposition of subject and object, but the finite subject is empowered by the hermeneutical movement of becoming to both return to itself and return to the other in new and unexpected ways. Hence, the dynamic interaction of beings within such a structure gives each being access to a kind of infinite, albeit one still constrained by the creaturely and hermeneutical limitations of history. This is an 'intentional infinitude', or the interior infinitude of the subject within the ongoing hermeneutic circle of the self in its mediation of itself with others. Of course, this is an 'infinite' in a highly analogical form—it is inexhaustible and yet also finite, historically situated and experiential. Intentional finitude bears an analogical relationship with actual infinitude, or the inexhaustibility of the originary power of being. Both are intimately related, and actual infinitude acts as our sustainer and source. "In other words", Schillebeeckx argues, "if God exists, the boundary between God and the finite is not on God's side, but on the side of the finite" (Schillebeeckx 2014b, p. 77 [79]).

The limitation of finitude and its structure are not based on a lack of being, making beings deficient gradations of the 'perfect Being' at the head of a hierarchical order. To be finite in the empowering flux of being also means being 'secular' in the sense that what is secular is "that which is not godly" (Schillebeeckx 2014b, p. 231 [234]). To conceive of the world as fundamentally 'not-god' does not necessarily capitulate to postulatory finitism, because the autonomy of the world is a gift given from the absolute origin. It does, however, necessitate that we conceive of questions about salvation and the ultimate meaning of history quite differently from that of a determinate metaphysical order. As autonomous, the world and the human history that occurs within it bears some measure of responsibility for what it will be. At the same time, because we are 'not-god' we must also acknowledge that the final word on the meaning of history is not ours. All efforts at self-liberation have limits, codified in the absolute limit and seen in our concrete efforts at freely producing salvation and liberation in the world, all of which can only be partial, flawed, and contingent. "The history of freedom *remains* a history of human suffering", which should bring into sharp relief the nature of existence as both limited and an absolute gift (Schillebeeckx 2014a, p. 767 [769–770]).

This shift to 'movement' does not eliminate the possibility of ethics, or of ethical norms, but it should call our attention to the importance of history and context for ethical action. It also highlights the fact that all attempts to create meaning or to impose order are provisional and incomplete. Even the most emphatic and authoritative truth-statement is co-constituted by the context in which it arises. All teleology must, therefore, be de-totalized and relativized to a certain extent. What this ontological structure reveals to us is something other than the ancient and medieval cosmology that thought of 'the whole' of reality as finite and ordered or 'enveloped' by the divine (DDO 146) The eschatological expectation of fulfilled and renewed creation gives us a metaphysical perspective on present reality, but it does not absolve us from all responsibility for it. Schillebeeckx has argued that the eschatological nature of Christian expectation actually *radicalizes* Christian commitment to the world. The hope that comes from the recognition of a 'hermeneutical between' is, in fact:

> a hope against hope, a hope against all despair that comes from our human experience which continues to suggest that all our attempts to build a better world are in vain. The radical character of this Christian commitment and of the surrender to faith cannot be justified in the light of purely human experience. It is, of its very nature, a hoping in God (explicitly or implicitly) as the future for man [*sic*]. (Schillebeeckx 1973, p. 87)

A metaphysical view is necessary as a complement to historically situated or experiential-expressivist approaches. We must think the origin and the end as good, if what lies in between is also to have the potential to be good—there is an *ontological* basis for value itself in being. The process of selving points to the goodness of the origin, via the promise of the future. This can only be revealed by passing through the proving ground of present and past experience, suggesting to us that ontological, or more properly, *eschatological* hermeneutics is essentially metaxological.

Bibliography

Bauer, Christian. 2012. Heiligkeit Des Profanen: Spuren Der "école Chenu-Schillebeeckx" (H. de Lubac) Auf Dem Zweiten Vatikanum. In *Edward Schillebeeckx: Impulse Für Theologien Im 21. Jahrhundert/Impetus Towards Theologies in the 21st Century*, ed. Thomas Eggensperger, Ulrich Engel, and Angel F. Méndez Montoya, 67–83. Ostfildern: Grünewald.

Borgman, Erik. 2003. *Edward Schillebeeckx: A Theologian in His History*. Trans. John Bowden. London/New York: Continuum.

Desmond, William. 2010. On God and the Between. In *Between Philosophy and Theology: Contemporary Interpretations of Christianity*, ed. Lieven Boeve and Christophe Brabant, 99–125. Burlington, VT: Ashgate.

———. 2011. Between Finitude and Infinity: On Hegel's Sublationary Infinitism. In *Hegel & the Infinite: Religion, Politics, and Dialectic*, Insurrections, ed. Slavoj Žižek, Clayton Crockett, and Creston Davis, 115–140. New York: Columbia University Press.

Gadamer, Hans-Georg. 2004a. Hermeneutics and Historicism (1965). In *Truth and Method*. Transl Joel Weinsheimer and Donald G. Marshall, 2nd ed., 507–545. London/New York: Continuum.

———. 2004b. *Truth and Method*. Trans. Joel Weinsheimer and Donald G. Marshall, 2nd ed. London/New York: Continuum.

Godzieba, Anthony J. 2013. Ut Musica Christianitas: Christian History as a History of Performances. In *The Shaping of Tradition: Context and Normativity*, Annua Nuntia Lovaniensia, ed. Colby Dickinson, vol. 70, 91–99. Leuven/Paris/Walpole, MA: Peeters.

Hall, Douglas John. 1999. 'The Great War' and the Theologians. In *The Twentieth Century: A Theological Overview*, ed. Gregory Baum, 3–13. Maryknoll, NY: Orbis.

de Lubac, S.J. Henri. 1998. *The Mystery of the Supernatural*. Trans. Rosemary Sheed. New York: Herder and Herder/Crossroad.

Minch, Daniel. 2017. Re-Examining Edward Schillebeeckx's Anthropological Constants: An Ontological Perspective. In *Salvation in the World: The Crossroads of Public Theology*, T&T Clark Studies in Edward Schillebeeckx, ed. Stephan van Erp, Christopher Cimorelli, and Christiane Alpers, vol. 2, 113–130. London: Bloomsbury T&T Clark.

———. 2018a. Economic Theological Anthropology and Metaphysics of Money: The Challenge of Optimism for Active Christian Hope. In *Driven by Hope: Economics and Theology in Dialogue, Christian Perspectives on Leadership and Social Ethics*, ed. P. Nullens and S. van den Heuvel, vol. 6, 137–150. Leuven: Peeters Press.

———. 2018b. Eschatology and Theology of Hope: The Impact of Gaudium et Spes on the Thought of Edward Schillebeeckx: Eschatology and Theology of Hope. *The Heythrop Journal* 59: 273–285.

O'Malley, John. 2008. *What Happened at Vatican II*. Cambridge, MA: Belknap Press of Harvard University Press.

Pius IX. 1870. Constitutio dogmatica: Dei Filius. *Vatican Website*, 24 April. https://w2.vatican.va/content/pius-ix/la/documents/constitutio-dogmatica-dei-filius-24-aprilis-1870.html.

Rosa, Hartmut. 2003. Social Acceleration: Ethical and Political Consequences of a Desynchronized High-Speed Society. *Constellations* 10 (1): 1–33.

Schelkens, Karim, John A. Dick, and Jürgen Mettepeningen. 2013. *Aggiornamento?: Catholicism from Gregory XVI to Benedict XVI*, Brill's Series in Church History. Vol. 63. Leiden/Boston: Brill.

Schillebeeckx, Edward. 1973. Christian Faith and Man's Expectation for the Future on Earth. In *The Mission of the Church*. Trans. N.D. Smith, 51–89. New York: Seabury Press.

———. 1978a. Questions on Christian Salvation of and for Man. In *Toward Vatican III: The Work That Needs to Be Done*, ed. David Tracy, Hans Küng, and Johann Baptist Metz, 27–44. New York: Gill and Macmillan.

———. 1978b. Theologie der Erfahrung – Sackgasse oder Weg zum Glauben? *Herderkorrespondenz* 92: 391–397.

———. 1983. The Magisterium and Ideology. In *Authority in the Church*, Annua Nuntia Lovaniensia, ed. Piet F. Fransen, vol. 26, 5–17. Leuven: Leuven University Press.

———. 2014a. *Christ: The Christian Experience in the Modern World*, Collected Works of Edward Schillebeeckx. Trans. John Bowden, vol. 7. London: Bloomsbury T&T Clark.

———. 2014b. *Church: The Human Story of God*. Trans. John Bowden, Collected Works of Edward Schillebeeckx 10. London: Bloomsbury T&T Clark.

———. 2014c. Linguistic Criteria. In *The Understanding of Faith: Interpretation and Criticism*, Collected Works of Edward Schillebeeckx. Trans. N.D. Smith, vol. 5, 19–40. London: Bloomsbury T&T Clark.

———. 2014d. Secularization and Christian Belief in God. In *God the Future of Man*, Collected Works of Edward Schillebeeckx. Trans. N.D. Smith, vol. 3, 31–54. London: Bloomsbury T&T Clark.

———. 2014e. Theological Criteria. In *The Understanding of Faith*, Collected Works of Edward Schillebeeckx. Trans. N.D. Smith, vol. 5, 41–68. London: Bloomsbury T&T Clark.

Schoof, Ted Mark. 2008. *A Survey of Catholic Theology, 1800–1970*. Trans. N.D. Smith. Eugene, OR: Wipf and Stock.

CHAPTER 5

Metaxology and New Realist Philosophy

Sandra Lehmann

This chapter examines whether there is a relationship between William Desmond's metaxology and what I call new realist thought. By this term, I refer to several recent approaches such as speculative realism, Markus Gabriel's neutral realism, and certain types of new materialism such as Karen Barad's agential realism, to name only some of the most prominent examples. At first glance, there seems to be considerable agreement between Desmond's metaxology and new realist thinking concerning the basic character of theoretical philosophy. There are two main aspects to this: First, both lines of thought are critical of the Kantian and post-Kantian mainstream of modern philosophy. Second, they both re-establish the primacy of ontology over epistemology.

Concerning the first aspect, as Peter Gratton observes, despite all conceptual differences, new realist thinkers "seemingly agree on but one thing: that European philosophy since the time of Kant has stopped talking about reality, since it's stuck thinking about how we know reality" (Gratton 2014, p. 4). From a different perspective (and less bluntly), Desmond argues that the alleged overcoming of metaphysics related to thinkers such as Heidegger and Derrida appears "to lie along the line of [a] deflation of confidence in philosophical reason that we diversely

S. Lehmann (✉)
University of Vienna, Vienna, Austria
e-mail: sandra.lehmann@univie.ac.at

© The Author(s) 2018
D. Vanden Auweele (ed.), *William Desmond's Philosophy between Metaphysics, Religion, Ethics, and Aesthetics*,
https://doi.org/10.1007/978-3-319-98992-1_5

witnessed since Kant's critique of pure reason" (ISB xvi). By contrast, Desmond is "convinced that there is no overcoming of metaphysics as such" (ibid.). Concerning the second aspect, as Ricardo Martinelli correctly notes, the debate about new realism is not "whether one is realist or not about the external world"; rather, it is about "taking a position on ontology" (Martinelli 2015, p. 25). In Desmond's case, the ontological concern is more than obvious. Let me just recall that Desmond bases his advocacy for metaphysics on mindfulness for "the sourcing powers of 'to be'" (ISB xvi), and that the first volume of his great systematic trilogy on metaxology is entitled *Being and the Between*.

Does this mean that metaxology is new realism *avant la lettre*? In order to propose an answer to this question, in what follows, I discuss certain aspects of both metaxology and new realist thinking. At this point, and to roughly sketch the situation, it may suffice to note that there is a fundamental difference between both ways of thought, and that this is due to their different overall design. While Desmond is putting forward a metaphysical theism, the new realist authors generally emphasize the groundless character of the absolute. Nevertheless, there is something like a kinship between metaxology and the new realisms, and this kinship is a result of their shared ontological concern. As I argue, it is for this reason that metaxology can open another path for new realist thinking. Up until now, in my view, metaxology has achieved more than the new realists, especially in terms of plausibility. This is so because Desmond gives a more convincing account of the relation between the human access to, and understanding of, Being and Being itself. As we shall see, in identifying the dynamic, ever self-transcending character of this relation, metaxology is able to do theoretical justice to both poles without preferring one over the other in a reductionist way.

In order to examine the relationship between metaxology and new realist thinking, I refer to a chosen example of speculative realism, namely, to Quentin Meillassoux's 'speculative materialism', as he himself calls it. I make this choice because both programmatically and methodologically, I consider Meillassoux's approach as the key approach of new realist philosophy. In a paradigmatic manner, Meillassoux addresses the theoretical objectives of new realist thought, and against what it is directed. Furthermore, and to put it somewhat apodictically, he defines the fundamental methodological principle of any serious new realist approach. As must be added, however, he also exemplifies the shortcomings arising whenever ontological thought too soon abandons the reference to human experience.

In short, then, this is how I proceed: I first discuss the three key elements of Meillassoux's approach. They serve as a guideline for briefly addressing both speculative materialism's merits and its aporias. Afterward, I examine how Desmond's approach relates to this. In sum, I argue that in focusing on the surplus character of Being, Desmond can offer a metaxological realism that surpasses both Meillassoux's main counterpart, namely Martin Heidegger's *Seinsdenken*, and Meillassoux's own approach.

Speculative Materialism on Being

Meillassoux's approach has three key elements that are closely interrelated. There is, first, the so-called critique of correlationism; second, the notion of "the givenness of a being anterior to givenness" (Meillassoux 2008, p. 14), that is, "anterior to every form of human relation to the world" (ibid., p. 10); and, third, the basic methodological principle, namely, the principle of factiality (*le principe de factualité*). Allow me to briefly outline what these three elements are about.

The critique of correlationism essentially implies a revision of Kant's Copernican or critical turn. As Meillassoux argues convincingly, the critical turn has defined the basic premise of modern thought, namely, the assumption of the inescapable relation of thinking and Being. To quote from Meillassoux's seminal essay *After Finitude*:

> By 'correlation' we mean the idea according to which we only ever have access to the correlation between thinking and being, and never to either term considered apart from the other. We will henceforth call correlationism any current of thought which maintains the unsurpassable character of the correlation so defined. (ibid., p. 5)

Meillassoux distinguishes a weak and a strong form of correlationism. The paradigm of weak correlationism is Kant's critical philosophy. According to it, what is beyond the correlation, the thing-in-itself, "is unknowable", yet "it is *thinkable*" (ibid., p. 31). The "most rigorous, as well as most contemporary" (ibid., p. 31) form of correlationism, however, is the strong form. Its "emblematic representatives" (ibid., p. 41) are Heidegger as well as Wittgenstein. It "prohibit[s] all relation between thought and the absolute", maintaining "not only that it is illegitimate to claim that we can *know* the in-it-self, but also that it is illegitimate to claim that we can at least *think* it" (ibid., p. 35). Strong correlationism may also include approaches that emphasize the non-rational character of the human access to Being, as it is the case with, for example, Merleau-Ponty's phenomenology of corporality or other forms of body philosophy.[1]

Regarding all forms of correlationism, Meillassoux questions whether it is really true that the way in which we access, or disclose, Being defines the framework of what we can say about Being. In order to make his point, Meillassoux refers to the mathematics-based natural sciences. In this context, the second main element of Meillassoux's approach comes into play, namely, the notion of givenness anterior to givenness. It indicates formally what escapes correlational givenness. As Meillassoux argues, the natural sciences can provide information about the cosmos long before human beings existed, a reality that he calls 'ancestral'. If we understand givenness as the situation in which Being is correlatively given to human beings, then the natural sciences provide information about Being before there was givenness. There is, in other words, no givenness, and yet this does not mean that there is nothing. Rather, there is something given before there is correlational givenness.

Note that one must take care to understand the proper meaning of anteriority in Meillassoux's argument from the ancestral. In fact, his entry into the discussion is rather unfavorable, suggesting that anteriority had to do with the past. It certainly has temporal meaning. However, in this case, time is not related to the correlation, that is, for example, it is not a form of perception, as for Kant, or it is not related to the temporality of *Dasein*, as for Heidegger. Rather, anteriority indicates time before time, and that means that it indicates a time thoroughly independent of correlational time. One might wonder, then, what we can possibly say about this time anterior to time, or this givenness anterior to givenness, and whether the term anteriority only suggests a relation where, in fact, there is none. Precisely this constitutes the core of the new realist problem, as it is paradigmatically unfolded by Meillassoux: How can we arrive at a proper mode of thinking Being independent of the human access to Being? In other words: How can we reach beyond the correlation? How can we give an account of the absolute character of Being?

---

[1] For a thorough discussion of Merleau-Ponty's correlationism, see Sparrow (2014, pp. 43–50).

We come to the third key element. Meillassoux's answer to the new realist problem is what he calls the 'principle of factiality'. According to it, "it is not the correlation but the facticity of the correlation that constitutes the absolute" (ibid., p. 52). According to correlationism, the correlation of Being and the human access to Being is inescapable, yet, it is contingent. Therefore, correlationism (whether weak or strong) cannot exclude that Being could, or even, has already, come into being differently. It only prevents that we can say anything about this being-different. However, as Meillassoux argues, correlationism must regard Being's possibility-to-be-different as a real possibility. Otherwise, it would have to grant the correlation absolute status, and that would contradict its own claim that we cannot say anything about the beyond of the correlation, including that there is no such beyond. If the possibility-to-be-different is real, what makes it real?—the answer is: It is facticity, or that-it-is. Facticity is not constituted by the correlation; however, it must be presupposed to keep correlationism running. This also explains the absolute status of facticity. According to Meillassoux's minimal definition, the absolute is "a being whose *severance* [...] and whose separateness from thought is such that it presents itself to us as non-relative to us, and hence as capable of existing whether we exist or not" (ibid., p. 28). The facticity of the possibility-to-be-different, or, as Meillassoux has it, the "capacity-to-be-other" (ibid., p. 34) is, therefore, the absolute, and it also applies to the correlation because the correlation does not exist by necessity.

The significance of Meillassoux's approach lies in the way in which it relates the absolute and contingency to one another, establishing, so to speak, on the back side of the principle of factiality, the "principle of unreason" (*principe d'irraison*) (ibid., p. 60). As Meillassoux argues, there is no necessary entity, everything is contingent. As an objection (and indicative of the profoundly ontological character of this discussion), one might recall Thomas Aquinas' Third Way, that is, the argument for the existence of God from possibility and necessity. We can refer to Desmond's concise summary in *God and the Between*: Under the condition of contingency, "at some time, [...] the possibility of everything *not being* will be. If this possibility of *not being* is possible, then nothing could ever come to be; for nothing comes from nothing; hence nothing could *now* exist" (GB p. 132). Meillassoux anticipates this objection, however, in pointing out "that the facticity of everything cannot be [itself] thought as a fact" (Meillassoux 2008, p. 79) for then it would lose its absolute status. Therefore, everything could also not be, and there is no reason why it should be. However, there will always be facticity, or rather, to "describe the speculative essence of facticity", "factiality" (ibid., p. 79), even if it is the factiality of nothing. In other words, Being has no ground, yet as such it exists necessarily.[2]

Ultimately, however, Meillassoux's vision of a groundless absolute fails. Essentially unresolved, the aporias of total contingency reappear at another level, namely at the level of temporality. As noted, according to Meillassoux, the time of the absolute, or absolute time, is detached from the time of the correlation, or correlative time. This means that it lacks the consistency of correlative time. Rather, it is a "time without becoming" (this is also the title of a 2008 lecture of Meillassoux; see Meillassoux 2014). That is, "a time that would be capable of bringing forth or abolishing everything, [...] a time that cannot be conceived as having emerged or as being abolished except in time, which is to say, in itself" (Meillassoux 2008, p. 61). And some passages later: "It is a Time [sic] capable of destroying even becoming itself by bringing forth, perhaps forever, fixity, stasis, and death" (ibid., p. 64). The problem here is that this capacity of self-abolishing also affects the past of absolute time. The moment it abolishes itself, it has never existed and, therefore, it will never exist again. There might be timeless factiality, or timeless existence. Yet it has always already swallowed the capacity-to-be-other. Contingency will never be able to unfold. In effect, this means that totally contingent Being exists only virtually, forever encapsulated in pure factiality. In this sense, Meillassoux is correct, at least regarding his own approach, when he states that "*l'affaire de la philosophie n'est pas l'être, mais le peut-être*. Philosophy's main concern is not with being but with the may-be" (ibid., p. 27). Only that this passing over of being has the consequence that his approach never actually reaches Being; that it rather, strangely conflicting with its own realist claims, remains restricted to a mere possibilism.

Let me conclude this section in noting that the possibilist failure of Meillassoux's project also indicates that he has never set himself free from correlationism or, more precisely, from strong correlationism. Meillassoux does not only (as we have seen) develop his argument out of strong correlationism. Rather, he carries with him two of its basic premises: First, that the facticity of Being is contingent; second, that there is no ultimate ground. All sophisticated reasoning notwithstanding, in the final analysis,

---

[2] I agree with Meillassoux's notion of the non-factual character of factiality, even if his argument is a *petitio principii*, arguing for the absolute character of factiality on the basis that it is supposed to be absolute.

his approach boils down to the subtraction of the 'human factor' from the correlation. He therefore surpasses correlationism only in that he makes the correlationist condition absolute. There are contingency and groundlessness without a human subject, or any other subject for that matter.

METAXOLOGY AND HEIDEGGER'S STRONG CORRELATIONISM

Let me adopt Meillassoux's terminology. At first sight, Desmond's metaxology applies a correlational scheme. In fact, there seems to be a kinship to one of the declared fathers of strong correlationism, namely to Heidegger. Both Desmond's and Heidegger's approaches recognize the factual character of Being. However, they both connect it with the notion of openness, or opening, a notion that has correlationist character because it describes the relation between Being and human being. Thus, as Desmond tells us in *Being and the Between*, the ontological starting point is human mindfulness to Being. Mindfulness is "the opening to Being" (BB 4). Yet it is "given over [to Being] immediately and from the start" (BB 4), that is, it is always already involved in Being. There is a clear correspondence between the human opening to Being and the opening of Being itself. Heidegger's thinking of Being (*Seinsdenken*), for its part, reflects on 'the open' under different names such as, most prominently, *alētheia* (*Unverborgenheit*, unconcealment) or the clearing (*Lichtung*). One might think here of the almost classic formulation in the *Letter on Humanism*: "Man in his essence is ek-sistent into the openness of Being, into the open region that lights the 'between' within which a 'relation' of subject to object can 'be'" (Heidegger 1993a, p. 252).

It is crucial, however, to see the fundamental difference between both approaches concerning the question of the open, the space of the between. In fact, understanding this difference will also help clarify that Desmond is not only rather far from Heidegger, even if he acknowledges him as "a guardian of astonishment before the 'that it is' of all being" (AOO 229). What is more, Desmond's notion of the between will also show that the question of the real is only in the second place decided by the question of the correlation. Certainly, Meillassoux is correct when criticizing the one-sided emphasis on the human access to Being in Kantian and post-Kantian thought. It does not follow from this, however, that the human factor must be eliminated. As we can learn from Desmond, it suffices to remove the human being from the center of Being and to subordinate it to the far greater powers of Being itself.

The decisive point concerning the difference between Desmond and Heidegger is how they understand Being in its capacity to give itself over to beings in order to let them be. Both Desmond and Heidegger agree on the inexhaustibility of Being by beings. Yet, for Heidegger, the inexhaustibility of Being has a negative, even abysmal character. First, Being has a twofold structure. While unconcealing itself and letting beings be, it at the same time conceals itself. That is, Being is never fully present in beings. Even beings as a whole cannot exhaust it. Yet, and second, this concealment of Being conceals nothing. Being insofar as it gives itself over is the act of giving, on the one side (the side of unconcealment), and it is nothing, on the other (the side of concealment). In other words, while Being 'is' the giving of beings, it also 'is' the giving of nothing (i.e., of itself). According to Heidegger's notorious 1929 lecture *What is Metaphysics?*[3] "for human existence, the nothing makes possible the openedness of beings as such. The nothing does not merely serve as the counterconcept of beings; rather, it originally belongs to their essential unfolding as such. In the Being of beings the nihilation of the nothing occurs" (Heidegger 1993b, p. 104).

There are two reasons why Heidegger puts emphasis on the nothingness of Being. First, he wants to avoid onto-theology. That is, Being cannot be a being, not even the *ens realissimum*. Accordingly, if Being gives itself over, or if it lets beings be, it cannot be a 'giving something', but must be 'no-thing'—nothing. Second, and more importantly, according to Heidegger, Being can only be thought in finite terms. We can identify this as the correlationist aspect of his thinking. Indeed, one may wonder, with Desmond, "if a certain privileging of 'self' is never completely purged [in Heidegger]" (AOO 222). One would have to discuss in detail why this is so. Let me just say at this point that, in my view, the reason is ideological. Heidegger has taken the deliberate decision for a philosophy of finitude. This corresponds with some key elements of the phenomenological method (especially, the notion of intentionality). Yet, as the approaches of authors such as Michel Henry or Jean-Luc Marion show, it is not necessarily demanded by phenomenology.

---

[3] From a rather different, logical-positivist perspective (Desmond would call it univocal), Rudolf Carnap, in his 1932 essay *Overcoming of Metaphysics through Logical Translation of Language*, uses the notion of nothing of this lecture as an example for showing that all metaphysical claims are pseudo-statements.

For Heidegger, however, it is settled that the giving of Being must be structured in accordance with finitude. Therefore, the excessive character of Being, its inexhaustibility, is negative. It can only appear according to the conditions of finite *Dasein*, that is, where *Dasein* experiences both its own facticity, or that-it-is, and the limits of its existence, in anxiety, or, even more fundamentally, in anticipating the indefinite certainty of death. We can find this clearly formulated in *What is Metaphysics?*: "Being and nothing do belong together [...] because Being itself is essentially finite and reveals itself only in the transcendence of Dasein which is held out into the nothing" (Heidegger 1993b, p. 108). Yet also the late Heidegger understands the giving-itself-over of Being, that is, the event (*Ereignis*) of Being as "what lets the two matters [the Being of beings and time] belong together" (Heidegger 1972, p. 19), while "the sending source keeps itself back and, thus, withdraws from unconcealment" (ibid., p. 22).

In a discussion of Heidegger in *Art, Origins, Otherness*, Desmond notes that Heidegger did not distinguish well enough "between 'coming to be' and 'becoming'" (AOO 223). We can identify the awareness of this distinction as what is at the heart of Desmond's approach. As he continues, "the former [that is, coming to be] suggests something more radically originative than the latter [that is, becoming], and to which thinking in terms of time could not do justice, since the issue is just the coming to be of time itself" (AOO 223).

One might say that, for Desmond, the encounter with Being takes place within finitude, yet it leads beyond the finite order, or beyond negativity. While, similar to Heidegger, metaxological ontology starts with the awareness of the that-it-is of being "in the midst of beings", and that we have always "already begun" (BB 5), this awareness is "*doubly* mediated" (BB 6). On the one hand, it is characterized by the notion of something other than ourselves that we lack, because temporality prevents us from coinciding with it, whether it is the otherness of other beings, or the otherness of ourselves (one might recall Rimbaud's "I am an other"). Desmond calls this 'erotic'. On the other hand, however, there is the notion of the plenitude of Being that is prior to the notion of lack and that, in a sense, is its condition of possibility: "It is the original power of being in us, waking up to itself as mindful, and driven beyond itself to mindfulness of being other than itself. This anterior original power is an excess to lack" (BB 6). This plenitude Desmond calls 'agapeic'. It creates the "vector of transcendence" that runs through the between of Being (BB 5).

Metaxology traces this vector of transcendence. In order to set in perspective how Desmond understands the giving of Being, we need to notice that also for Desmond, Being is inexhaustible and, therefore, it is no thing. Yet in contrast to Heidegger, the non-objective character of Being is not abysmal, a matter of withdrawal into nothingness, but, rather, overdetermined and overflowing. It indicates a "superplus power" (AOO 251). Being gives itself in plenitude.

> For this power of origination [that is, the giving of beings, S.L.] is not nothing, though it be no thing; it is what makes the being of being be; not only possibilizing in the logical sense of formal possibility; but possibilizing in an ontological sense in which the creative power of the possible is at work: *posse* as power to bring to be. (AOO 251)

As Desmond underscores, this notion is not to be confused with "Heidegger's dictum that possibility is higher than actuality" (AOO 251). For Heidegger, possibility is the way in which Being comes to pass in finitude, and since finitude sets the limit of Being, possibility is the ultimate mode of Being. Being is always-ever-becoming in realizing possibilities. By contrast, Desmond links *posse* back to *esse*. That is, Being is not structured by possibility. Rather, possibility is a manifestation of Being. It is the giving-itself-over of Being that, however, and again, cannot exhaust Being. The possibilizing power of Being is always excessive. This is what distinguishes the coming to be of Being from Being's mere becoming. While coming to be, Being lets finite beings be. Yet, in doing so, it communicates its own abundance to them. It inscribes transcendence, the movement beyond themselves, into them.

The 'superplus' or surplus power of Being creates a lasting gap between Being and the human access to Being (i.e., mindfulness). In other words, it opens the correlation, and it changes its meaning. This is so because, as Desmond writes, the correlation, that is, "the between shows itself as a coming to be that communicates of its origin as other to the between itself" (AOO 249). There is Being, and there is the human access, or relation, to Being. Moreover, however, there is the possibilizing surplus power of Being coming to be, that is, of Being giving itself over in order to become the inexhaustible Being of beings. "The sense of the origin of both coming to be and what has come to be exceeds the happening of the between itself. It is [...] hyperbolically other to beings, other to the happening of finite beings" (AOO 249).

As surplus power, Being cannot be reduced to what is taking place in the between. Rather, what is taking place in the between could not do so without the giving of Being. It could not even exist. Accordingly, the between as well as what is taking place in it testify to the possibilizing power of Being. This relativizes the significance of the correlationist perspective, whether correlationism is weak or strong. The human access to Being is not at the center of the opening of Being, it does not make Being happen. Rather, it is a point of passage that formally (i.e., from the point of view of the coming to be of Being) has the same value as the "enigmatic thereness of things" (AOO 226). That does not mean, however, that according to metaxology, the human is to be regarded as thoroughly equivalent to things. It is important to find the right ontological balance here. From a material, or content, point of view, the human has singular status because of the way in which it delivers the surplus of Being to the between. By contrast to other beings, it does so explicitly, by means of the reflecting powers of reason. It articulates transcendence by the self-transcending of the mind. Again, however, as "articulate selfhood", the human is "an expression of the articulating energy of being" (AOO 224). It stands out by the articulating function. Yet, apart from that, it partakes in the excessive *dynamis* of Being just like all beings. The excess of Being creates them, and lets them be, and it does so in pointing them beyond themselves, in some way or other.

METAXOLOGICAL REALISM

Desmond does not only offer a strong alternative to Heidegger's philosophy of finitude. He also provides an answer to the new realist question of the absolute, or of Being beyond the human access to Being. In fact, his approach proves superior to Meillassoux's speculative materialism, in that it alone provides an appropriate interpretation of the absolute character of facticity, or that-it-is.

As we have seen, in the final analysis, Meillassoux gains theoretical access to the absoluteness of facticity by eliminating the human factor from strong correlationism. The result is that the contingency of Being is no longer restricted by the human expectation that Being, at least to a certain extent, might have consistency, and that we can give an account of it. Rather, there is nothing but the capacity-to-be-other. We may also look at this from another perspective and say that, while in Heidegger's strong correlationism, the ground of Being is withdrawn, in speculative materialism, it is thoroughly suspended. There is no reason at all why something is what it is.

It cannot be denied that the connection that Meillassoux establishes between the absolute and the utter groundlessness of Being is rather bold. Yet, ultimately, and as we have also seen, his approach results in aporia. Situating himself 'after finitude', unlike Heidegger, Meillassoux is aware of the difference between coming to be and becoming. Yet, according to him, becoming, or finite time, would have to emerge from a time without becoming. Time without becoming, however, could never have been. At best, it is ever-possible time.

In order to put Desmond's approach in perspective, it seems advisable, at this point, to make a small digression. For admittedly, and as the never-ending struggle of metaphysics demonstrates, there can be no final certainty regarding the ultimate character of Being. Therefore, at first glance, it might seem possible that Being is characterized by the groundless capacity-to-be-other, or by absolute contingency. Yet we can argue *ex negativo*. First, Meillassoux's account of the absolute obviously fails. Therefore, the dark backside of the principle of factiality, the principle of unreason, does not apply. Second, we cannot know whether, at some point in the future, Being comes to nothing. However, as already Parmenides observed, it does not make sense to speak of what 'is' Non-Being, or nothing. Accordingly, Desmond is right when he notes that "the absolute nothing [that is, Non-Being] is qualified by the gift of being" (BB 281). Nothing always ever appears in the horizon of Being; that means it appears as relative nothing. There is an overweight of Being over nothing. It implies that Being gives itself excessively, perpetually surpassing the negativity of relative nothingness. This also bears on the problem of time: If there is time, there is time beyond finite time. For we can address Being coming to be also in temporal terms as the coming to be of the absolute Now. While the absolute Now is coming to be in finite being, it is affected by the ruptures of finite negativity. Yet, in the course of finite time, the absolute Now creates a fluid presence, or ephemeral Now, that escapes negativity. As Desmond notes, "creation [that is, finite being] as continuing cannot be separated from discontinuity" (BB 294). Yet "the discontinuity and possible nothingness of the creation, as outcome, suggests the continuity of creation, as agapeic origination" (BB 270). In other words, to understand the genesis of finite time, we must draw on the notion of ever-abundant rather than ever-possible time.

Against this background, we can say that only Desmond fully develops the notion that 'the facticity of the correlation is the absolute'. Desmond starts from the surplus character of facticity and applies it to what is taking place in the between, that is, to the correlation. He has no need, therefore, to eliminate the correlation. Rather, he opens it from within. All beings originate in the plenitude of Being giving itself over. That is, they originate in "an 'overdetermined' whole [that] already is a surplus of being within itself" (BB 255). This means that all beings are amidst each other, and yet they are beyond each other. Accordingly, the human access cannot exhaust them. There can be a human account of beings, yet we must concede that beings are beyond our account. If facticity is the absolute, everything is inexhaustible.

In closing, let me return one last time to Meillassoux's key elements. We can observe that metaxology breathes real theoretical life into them—unlike speculative materialism itself. Thus, there is the principle of factiality, given with the mindful awareness that "we do not first produce being, or make it be as for us; originally it is given as an excess of otherness which arouses our astonishment that it is at all" (Desmond 2000, p. 5). In fact, we can identify the "last difference" (AOO 249), that is, the gap between Being as surplus power, on the one hand, and the correlation between Being and human mindfulness, on the other, as the opening into the absolute that the new realists are searching for. It is the gap of the inner transcendence of beings that results from the abundance of Being.

In addition, there is also givenness anterior to givenness in metaxology. For Being coming to be is precisely givenness anterior to givenness; givenness in the sense of a giving that continues to have always already taken place; givenness that, because of its excessive character cannot have resulted from the correlation, but rather originates independently from its own having always already being-there.

Consequently, at several points, Desmond alludes to the speculative character of his thinking. Most significantly maybe, in *God and the Between*, he refers to his approach as "speculative metaxology" that is not to be confused with "speculative dialectic in Hegel's sense" (GB 159). Both the productive distance to Hegel and the *hyperbole* by which this distance is created bear similarity to Meillassoux's approach, even if the direction of Desmond's *hyperbole* is diametrically opposed to the one of Meillassoux, pointing at the inexhaustible plenitude of Being rather than the empty facticity of what is thoroughly contingent.

Finally, in *Desire, Dialectic, and Otherness*, Desmond discusses the realist character of his approach, identifying it as "a metaxological 'realism' beyond idealism" (DDO xxi). This realism is based on the reflective awareness of both the transcendence and the precedence of the other. That means that since other beings originate in the surplus power of Being, they are neither a matter of identity (or the mental powers of the self) nor of difference (or pure multiplicity), nor of dialectical mediation. Rather, they are "metaxologically pluralized" (DDO 171).[4] That is, since they exist through the inner transcendence of Being, they cannot be reduced to the self (there is no absolute self). Yet, this does not mean that beings are totally other and escape any determination (Meillassoux's approach, in fact, is a radical version of this equivocal approach). Rather, in being understood, that is, in being determinate, they at the same time indicate that they are beyond determination. Because all beings originate in the excessive power of Being, they all equally elude the clutches of determination.

At the beginning, we asked whether Desmond's metaxology was new realism *avant la lettre*. We can now present our answer. If new realist thinking is based on the presupposition that the absolute is absolute groundless, that becoming, at best, is blind emergence, and that, therefore, the order of things is necessarily characterized by inconsistent multiplicity, metaxology certainly has very little in common with it. If, however, and by contrast, new realist thinking is seriously concerned with the question of the real, and if the courage for speculation also means being prepared to follow metaphysical ways (a possibility many new realists shortsightedly dismiss), metaxology—metaxological realism has much to offer. To begin with, it shows that understanding the real is intrinsically linked with understanding the excessive or surplus character of Being. Therefore, Being does neither manifest itself as the fateful interlocking of 'thrown projection' (*geworfener Entwurf*) and being-unto-death, as for Heidegger, nor by the reasonless, groundless capacity-to-be-other, as for Meillassoux. Rather, it bestows beings with the capacity to be beyond themselves amidst other beings.

---

[4] See also the broader discussion of metaxological realism in DDO 169–171. At this point, one might also introduce Desmond's distinction of the univocal, the equivocal, the dialectical, and the metaxological meaning of Being. However, due to lack of space, I decided to focus on what I regard to be the main ontological structure of metaxology, and that is the vector of transcendence, originating in the plenitude of Being itself.

Bibliography

Desmond, William. 2000. Being, Determination, and Dialectic: On the Sources of Metaphysical Thinking. In *Being and Dialectic: Metaphysics as a Cultural Presence*, ed. William Desmond and Joseph Grange, 3–36. Albany: State University of New York Press.

Gratton, Peter. 2014. *Speculative Realism: Problems and Prospects*. London: Continuum.

Heidegger, Martin. 1972. *On Time and Being*. Trans. Joan Stambaugh. New York: Harper & Row.

———. 1993a. Letter on Humanism. In *Basic Writings: From Being and Time (1927) to The Task of Thinking (1964)*, ed. David Farrell Krell, 213–266. London: Routledge.

———. 1993b. What Is Metaphysics? In *Basic Writings: From Being and Time (1927) to The Task of Thinking (1964)*, ed. David Farrell Krell, 89–110. London: Routledge.

Martinelli, Riccardo. 2015. Realism, Ontology, and the Concept of Reality. In *Moral Realism and Political Decisions: Practical Rationality in Contemporary Public Contexts*, ed. Gabriele de Anna and Riccardo Martinelli, 19–28. Bamberg: University of Bamberg Press.

Meillassoux, Quentin. 2008. *After Finitude: An Essay on the Necessity of Contingency*. Trans. R. Brassier. London: Continuum.

———. 2014. *Time Without Becoming*. Ed. Anna Longo. Hythe: Mimesis International.

Sparrow, Tom. 2014. *The End of Phenomenology: Metaphysics and the New Realism*. Edinburgh: Edinburgh University Press.

PART II

Absolute Being and Talking God

CHAPTER 6

The Metaxology of the Divine Names

Brendan Thomas Sammon

The work of William Desmond is only beginning to receive the attention that it more than merits. Since the 1990 publication of *Philosophy and Its Others*, and the 1995 publication of *Being and the Between*, arguably the two works that formally gave birth to the metaxological, there have been more than a few dissertations and monographs published on his metaphysics, most in his own field of philosophy (e.g., Simpson 2009; Shaw 2012; Kelly 2007), though some in other fields (e.g., Simpson and Sammon 2017). However, the work of translating his idiom for broader readership remains a challenge for those enthusiasts who are convinced, as I am, that his metaphysics not only offers something important but essential for properly diagnosing and effectively confronting the problems that beset human beings today.

A question that continually seems to arise whenever I present Desmond's thought to an audience concerns how a person unfamiliar with the complexities of metaxology might begin to 'crack his code' so to speak. To this question, there are a few responses. One way is to struggle in the shadow cast by the light of Desmond's work, patiently thinking and rethinking his thoughts with him until a moment of clarity offers itself, and some progress is made. Or one can familiarize oneself with the Western intellectual

B. T. Sammon (✉)
Saint Joseph's University, Philadelphia, PA, USA
e-mail: bsammon@sju.edu

tradition itself in order to better understand Desmond's place in this esteemed pantheon of thought. Still a third way presents itself: one can approach his thought comparatively, seeking to 'crack his code,' so to speak, by understanding his relation with his others. Such an approach follows what might be considered a dimension of the metaxological method: coming to knowledge of something by knowing the many and various relations that constitute it. This chapter follows this third avenue by examining how metaxology relates to the tradition of the divine names.

The thesis at the foundation of this chapter is this: there is a kinship between the tradition of the divine names and metaxology such that one provides significant resources for understanding the other. This thesis, then, moves along three interrelated vectors. The first concerns the particular content associated with the tradition of the divine names. Those already familiar with the various components of this tradition—for example, ancient Jewish thought, Platonism, late ancient Christian theology, Neoplatonic philosophy, and even scholasticism—may find a helpful avenue for entering more fully into the metaxological idiom, which in turn may open new vistas in the divine name tradition as well. The second vector concerns those already familiar with Desmond's thought. It is hoped that interest in his thought might also stimulate interest in this once esteemed divine name tradition so that one can better recognize in Desmond's thinking a creative retrieval (though no simple reprise) of a thought form that has shaped in a number of vital ways various intellectual traditions. The third vector concerns those who may have either limited or no familiarity with either the divine name tradition or metaxology. This third vector, although the most unstable in terms of outcome, is also where a heightened sense of both the divine names and metaxology present themselves. For not only does this third trajectory inhabit a 'space' between the first two trajectories, but it is also a trajectory that, free from any predetermined ideas of either, allows one to move more freely in the 'space between both' (so to speak). For although familiarity at the beginning of any inquiry provides certain benefits for the inquiry itself, there are also benefits that follow from the absence of such familiarity, the most important of which is that the inquiry proceeds with minimal risk of reduction to the familiar.

Bearing all this in mind, this chapter proceeds as follows. First, I present a brief account of the tradition of the divine names in somewhat broad strokes, with an eye toward two fundamental features that not only bear a significant degree of socio-cultural import, but that resonate with

Desmond's project: transcendence and community. I then examine how both the divine names and metaxology provide indelible resources for reflection upon and practices of transcendence. I follow this with an examination of the relationship between transcendence and community and argue that Desmond's project can be read as a creative retrieval of a divine name communivocity, that is, the way in which the divine names as metaxological phenomena voice themselves so as to help secure authentic community.

THE TRADITION OF THE DIVINE NAMES: A PROTOTYPICAL METAXOLOGY

Since I have done so elsewhere, and since space does not allow, I do not reproduce an exhaustive historical account of the tradition of the divine names here (see Sammon 2013, pp. 95–120). Rather, I lay out some of the more important dimensions of this tradition insofar as it concerns present purposes, more particularly the way it articulates a *metaxu*. This is an articulation that concerns the divine names tradition both in terms of what it is as a tradition and the content of what it communicates. The subtle argument being made here is that Desmond's metaxology provides a hermeneutical key for understanding this mysterious tradition and its influence on belief about existence, human nature, society, and the divine.

The metaxology of the divine names—as a tradition—can be discerned from two primary perspectives. The first concerns the way that this tradition emerges out of a 'middle' between the Biblical (Jewish and early Christian) tradition and Neoplatonism. Although one finds references to a divine name tradition in various late ancient sources, it is in the work of the enigmatic figure Dionysius the Areopagite where one finds the first and most systematic account. In the opening lines of his *On the Divine Names*, the allonymous author indicates that the tradition of the divine names precedes his own contribution: "To my fellow Presbyter Timothy, Dionysius the Presbyter. What is the purpose of the discourse, and the tradition regarding the divine names."[1] Yet the lack of historical treatises that might corroborate his claim makes it unclear exactly to what he is referring. Given his Neoplatonic pedigree, perhaps Dionysius is referring to a tradition of philosophical inquiry into language examined in such seminal texts as Plato's *Cratylus*, Aristotle's *Topics*, or *On Interpretation*,

---

[1] Dionysius the Areopagite, *On the Divine Names* [hereafter = DN] 1, 1 [585A]).

et al. However, the Areopagite's own treatise does not contain much in terms of a philosophy or theology of language, so even if such texts may have influenced his thinking, it seems unlikely that they constitute the tradition into which he claims to enter. In fact, overemphasizing the linguistic element that seems obvious in the divine name tradition risks anachronistically distorting a tradition that is much more of a metaphysics of being than a reflection upon language.

Perhaps the Areopagite's allegiance to the Biblical tradition indicates that his divine name tradition is a reference to the honored Jewish tradition of naming God. Throughout Jewish classical literature and practice, names rather than concepts serve as the primary referential mechanism. Although in Judaism, there are a multiplicity and variety of names appropriated to God (Leeman 2004, p. 104), it is the Tetragrammaton, the *Hashem*, often represented as YHWH, which occurs most frequently throughout Scripture—6828 times to be precise (Leeman 2004, p. 104). Many names are used throughout the Old Testament to identify God, but only YHWH identifies the personal name of God (Gieschen 2003, p. 121; Adler 2009, p. 266). This Biblical sense of naming, as evidenced in Exodus, entails a relationship of intimacy, love, and trust—such names are trans-discursive events rather than conceptual mechanisms. For this reason, they are best approached and understood through practicing them, that is, by pursuing them through repeated actions. Responding to Moses's request for a name to present to the Israelites, the author(s) of Exodus present a God who not only identifies himself as being/existence (YHWH, and Ehyeh asher Ehyeh), but also as the One who acts in history and who will endure into posterity: "Thus you shall say to the Israelites, '*HaShem*, the God of your ancestors, the God of Abraham, the God of Isaac, and the God of Jacob, has sent me to you': This is my name forever, and this is my title for all generations" (Ex. 3:15). In this sense, God's name is not a concept to be grasped within the limits of human thought, but a plenitude of existence that guides, teaches, and loves in fullness and abundance; the capacity 'to be whatever God wills to be.' And this is why a divine name in the Biblical tradition is a phenomenon that is practiced into being, one whose presence is made manifest in human action.

In either case, there does not seem to be enough textual evidence in the Dionysian corpus to conclude decisively for either divine name option. And although Dionysius himself claims a strict authoritative adherence to the Biblical tradition, Dionysian scholarship in the twentieth century has demonstrated that Neoplatonism at the very least assumes a grammatical authority. A metaxological approach encourages one to look between every dialectical coupling, which in this case enables one to justifiably resist the urge to prioritize either the Biblical or the Neoplatonic tradition of divine naming. Rather, a metaxological reading recognizes not only the mutual influence of both, but the way that each, insofar as they enter into the metaxological event of the divine name tradition, comes to constitute the other.

The second perspective that reveals the metaxology of the divine names concerns the locus of the treatise *On the Divine Names* in the overall Dionysian corpus. It is a locus that indicates how a divine name occupies a metaxological 'space,' which in turn communicates the way that a divine name identifies a metaxological 'form.' In the Dionysian project, the treatise *On the Divine Names* stands in between two lost treatises. On the one hand, *The Theological Outlines*, a treatise that, in Dionysius's own words "celebrates the principle affirmative expressions respecting God insofar as God is both one and three by considering unions and distinctions as they are in the divine itself, and which is neither possible to say or to conceive" (Dionyius, Mystical Theology, c. 3). On the other hand, *On Symbolic Theology* celebrates God through sensible symbols "transferred from objects of sense to things divine" (Dionyius, Mystical Theology, c. 3). So, on one end of the spectrum stands the *Theological Outlines*, a treatise that concerns the ineffable, unspeakable names of God, and on the other end stands *On Symbolic Theology*, which treats of those names derived from creatures. Situated between the ineffable, unspeakable names and those that are creaturely and therefore properly metaphorical are the divine names, which bears something of both: they are names sanctioned by Biblical revelation but that are also found in the formal constitution of creatures, making them thoroughly metaxological.

A divine name, then, can be said to identify a divine perfection that proceeds from the divine superessential plenitude to inhabit the formal constitution of creatures. Such names include the good, light, beauty, love, being, wisdom, and so on. As processions from the divine superessential plenitude, divine names are bearers of the divine substance without being identical to that substance. As some recent scholars have articulated it, the divine names are the presence of the divine in creaturely constitutions (O'Rourke 2005, p. 9; Jones 2008, pp. 157–162). Insofar as they inhabit the formal constitution of creatures, the divine names serve as vehicles by which the divine substance becomes available to finite conditions. And insofar as they are bearers of the divine substance, the divine names make this substance available to human thought and practice albeit in an 'overdetermined' way (to borrow Desmond's terminology). As overdetermined, that is, as bearers of content in excess of, though always hospitable to, finite determination, the divine names release a multiplicity of ways to God. But this multiplicity is held together by an always-arriving unity, making the divine names communivocal phenomena, or phenomena that require a community of voicings in order to do justice to the fullness of their intelligible content.

What the divine names communicate, then, is a prototypical metaxology that communivocally intermediates between God and the world. This way of configuring the divine names may seem to give them a revelatory status, but an important distinction is necessary. Indeed, the divine names do reveal the divine substance, but in a way that is perhaps best articulated by referring to them as the divine 'public identity.' This reference ought not be taken in opposition to some divine 'private identity,' which would not only privilege a certain modern dichotomy of public versus private, but also call to mind all sorts of gnostic problems. Rather, God's 'public identity' stands in contrast with the 'intimate,' or 'endemic' identity that various faith traditions believe God reveals. In other words, where God's revealed identity gives rise to an endemic and intimate relationship constituted by specific forms of faith, dogma, liturgical rites, and creedal confessions and practices, the divine names as God's public self-presentation give rise to more general, socio-cultural forms of these.

In this sense, the divine names can be said to communicate a metaxological form that performs a metaxological service to the broader sociocultural milieu: they serve as a locus of mediation between human and divine and so also provide a model for mediation as such. In the history of the Christian intellectual tradition, the divine names performed an indelible role in shaping how divine transcendence, and thus transcendence in itself, was understood by those communities that entered into this tradition. In the following section, I briefly lay out some of the contours of such transcendental shaping and gesture toward the ways in which metaxology creatively retrieves this shaping capacity.

Transcendence

The eclipse of transcendence in the modern world, as Charles Taylor has shown, is not merely a matter of personal preference among a certain elite echelon of academics but is constitutive of how a majority of persons today experiences the world (Taylor 2007, p. 307ff.). So much is this the case that one is inclined to agree with Taylor when he diagnoses a certain 'malaise of immanence' that has taken hold of the modern mind. Taylor identifies three forms this malaise may take: a fragility to our quest for meaning that quickens our urgency for some overarching significance, our shared impotence to ritualize those crucial moments of passage in our lives, and the 'flatness' or emptiness of the ordinary (Taylor 2007, p. 309). To the extent that Taylor is correct, a retrieval of an authentic account of transcendence is not only timely but urgent.

What do the divine names provide that might alleviate this 'malaise of the immanent'? What role do the divine names perform in the human understanding of transcendence as such, and divine transcendence in particular? It has already been established that they perform a communivocal intermediating role, but what does this role communicate about transcendence? I want to draw attention to three primary dimensions of transcendence that are communicated by the divine names, dimensions that are retrieved creatively by Desmond's metaxology: (1) the plenitude, or overdetermination, of the Origin (God); (2) the necessity of participation; and (3) ontologically constitutive otherness.

In the Dionysian *Denkform*, the divine names are a necessity. This is because the God of Dionysius, much like the God of metaxology, is a plenitude of substance, the overfull excess of being as such and thus even beyond being. Dionysius uses words like 'superessential' or 'supergood' to characterize the hyperbolic, or excessive, nature of the divine especially in relation to creatures. Reflecting a Pauline principle, a principle to which Dionysius's allegiance follows from the enigmatic author's choice of the allonym Dionysius the Areopagite (from Acts 17:34), the God of Dionysius is 'the one in whom we live, and move, and have our being.' In other words, because the divine being is never one among other beings, that is, never a mere presence in the world, knowledge of the divine being cannot occur by means of some detached, neutral observation. Inquiry into the divine substance can only happen dialectically, that is to say, founded upon a relation. However, in order to do justice to the divine plenitude, this relation must manifest itself in plural form, must be voiced communally rather than unilaterally, or univocally (cf. PO 6). The divine names are a communication of such a communal voicing, in that, even though they differ according to how they are understood by the human mind, they are all the same in terms of substance (as scholasticism would later emphasize, though in differing tones). Dionysius stresses, in other words, that such names should not be conceived as partial components of God. Rather, "all the God-becoming names of God are celebrated by the Oracles not in part, but as applied entirely, wholly, and completely to the full Godhead" (DN, 2, 1 [637A]). Dionysius even goes so far as to assert that it is blasphemy to consider one of these names as identifying only a part of God.

Insofar as the divine names serve as a communal voicing of the divine into our common and shared human practices, by creating a kind of 'buffer zone' between God and creation, they also perform the role of safeguarding the ineffable and unknowable divine transcendence. A common thread tying the Biblical and Neoplatonic traditions together is a shared sense of the utter and absolute transcendence of the divine above and beyond all. For Dionysius, the divine names point to this mode of divine transcendence precisely as images of it. As images of the Godhead, the divine names can never be identical with the Godhead, who remains always beyond in its ineffability and unknowability. However, as images of the Godhead, the divine names communicate the divine substance to God's finite others.

Part of this communication includes the way in which the absolute being-beyond of the divine transcendence relates to forms of transcendence in the world. As beyond, divine transcendence does not withhold transcendence as such. Rather it communicates transcendence albeit in different forms, all of which involve the divine names. Serving in this middle, the divine names, then, also communicate the way in which transcendence is itself an analogous phenomenon. To borrow a well-known Aristotelian phrasing, 'transcendence is spoken in many ways.' Such an analogy of transcendence is necessary not only to understand its finite iterations, but to preserve the unique mode of transcendence that belongs to the divine amidst those finite iterations.

In metaxology, the divine names, or at least variations on them, become the topics of inquiry both in terms of their being ways in which the Overdetermined, Agapeic Origin (God) communicates with the world and in terms of their being phenomena present in the natural order (see e.g., GB 176–190). Within the metaxological picture of these phenomena, a similar analogy of transcendence comes to light. This analogy of transcendence begins with what throughout his work Desmond refers to as "vectors of transcendence," a taxonomy of the diverse ways in which transcendence as such presents itself in the world.

Desmond identifies three such vectors of transcendence. Briefly put: first transcendence, T^1, identifies the exteriority of being as it is present in the otherness of extra-mental beings, that is, a world that is in becoming because it comes to be. It is the transcendence of creation itself as something given beyond any single self. Second transcendence, or T^2, identifies the transcendence of self-being, or simply self-transcendence. The emphasis in this mode of transcendence is interiority, but an interiority that Desmond argues is only fulfilled by what is other to itself. There is in this interiority, therefore, an otherness at play in the self, that is, a surplus of self that stands other to the 'becoming self,' testifying to the self's reliance upon otherness as such. Third transcendence, or T^3, identifies transcendence as such, that is, as the superior (rather than exterior or interior) other. It is a hyperbolic sense of transcendence serving as the original ground for all subsequent determinations (these three vectors appear throughout Desmond's work especially after Philosophy and Its Others). The enumeration of these ought not be taken to correspond to three discrete phenomena. Each vector is intertwined with the others, and each is a vital way in which being communicates itself. As Desmond explains, in tones similar to Dionysius above, "if we think any one of these (vectors of transcendence), or the One, we find ourselves also thinking of the others … because each is as communicative being, or a communication of being" (GB 107). To put it another way, these vectors of transcendence identify being in its communicative state, a happening of communication itself opening itself to participation. Similar to how the divine names identify communications from the superessential divine plenitude intending and inviting participation, so too does each vector for Desmond perform a similar role.

There is a sense in which Desmond reads these vectors and the ontological conditions they constitute and make possible, from the perspective of participation, or even celebration. Even though he at times uses both terms, we might look at what he says of the "indirections of transcendence in the between" (GB 122–128). For Desmond, being arises from an overdetermined surplus to which the word 'God' and others like it (the divine, the absolute, etc.) point. Such pointing can only ever be indirect, given the overdetermination of that to which they point, and Desmond foregrounds four primary forms of such indirection: metaphoric, analogic, symbolic, and hyperbolic. God is not a univocally reducible being, which makes such indirections vital methods for metaxology.

How are these indirections participatory, or celebratory? As Desmond explains, "[i]ndirections that are directions can be (pre)figurations of that to which they are directed. They can be figurings in and through the primal ethos of what in the between is intimated as ultimate" (GB 122). Indirections in other words involve a porous openness to what is given before any consequent act that determines the given, the giver, or the giving: "In all these figurings," explains Desmond, "mindfulness is patient to a communication of ultimacy we cannot either univocalize or dialectically sublate, even as we are in passage towards the hyperbole of the ultimate as the agapeic origin" (GB 122–123). These indirections reflect, then, the Dionysian senses of participation/celebration, in that they are ways of coming to share in the communication of the overdetermined origin insofar as they provoke a sharing in the very acts that constitute them.

The metaxological way of configuring transcendence reflects the Dionysian notion of divine presence in and with the formal inhabitation of creatures by the divine names. As if echoing the dynamic present in Dionsyius, Desmond, reflecting on the way that sacred naming relates to the hyperboles of being, asks: "How do the One and the many look here? There is some intimation of One beyond determination, as well as a sense of the indeterminate many ... the overdeterminate One and indeterminate manyness are more than merely univocal, because charged with the equivocity of sacred value" (GB 177). It is precisely this equivocity of sacred value where the *metaxu* opens itself as the space between excess and finite determination. It is also the between where the divine names inhabit human thought as a way to God that is then known and understood in the performance of that way. This between is porous to the excess beyond itself provoking more definite expressions of the sacred.

For Desmond, as for Dionysius, divine names are given but not given simply, or univocally. In both projects, transcendence is conceived as the activity first of the overfull, plenitude of being that marks the divine, which is why participation becomes vital for each iteration. For Dionysius, the divine transcendence is known primarily by virtue of revelation and the *metaxu* of the divine names. These latter communicate the divine substance through the formal properties of creatures, which means they are "bearers" so to speak of divine transcendence (T^3), as well as the otherness of creaturely transcendence (T^1). Participation in them secures human self-transcendence (T^2). In metaxology, the *metaxu* of the divine names undergoes an even more rigorous treatment, in which is discerned several other attributes and elements of this porous middle. "Plurivocal manifestation," Desmond explains, "has to do with the intertwining of selving and othering. Given the intertwining, does our naming the divine also show the divine naming itself—naming itself as entering into communication with us—endowing the open porosity of community" (GB 179)? And it is precisely by virtue of the configuration of transcendence released by this middle that community originates and is sustained more effectively.

Community

Can community exist without transcendence? Can anything be gathered without some power outside of those gathered things guiding and sustaining the very gathering that constitutes community? Even for the argument that there is only the power of immanence that erupts as a communifying force, could this eruption, taking plural form since it erupts from diverse agents, ever find a commonality without some transcendent force giving itself to each eruption as that common and shared condition for unity?

The concern of this final section is not so much directed toward particular communities, or the way that community arises through social construction. Rather, what is at stake here concerns the underlying givenness of community from a primordial, ontological origin. As the source of community, this primordial origin must be the fullness of being-as-community. This more primordial, ontological sense of community provides the conditions for the eventual communities that result from social construction. But it does not necessitate such construction in a univocal way, since the ontological givenness of community is itself a plurivocal phenomenon that announces itself and shapes itself with the diversity released from this plurivocity. There is, therefore, an urgency involved in thinking this primordial, ontological community as authentically as possible insofar as it will either be ratified or rejected at the level of social construction. The challenge is not to 'get it right' since this would wrongly fix community in a univocal way. Rather, the challenge is to think properly the ontological givenness of community in order to overcome problematic interpretations that renege on what is given plurivocally (at times, even a reneging on the plurivocity itself as seen in, e.g., regimes of totality and tyranny). Is it possible to honor and do justice to that plurality without properly thinking the phenomenon of transcendence? The claim here is that part of what is at stake in properly thinking the ontologically given community concerns the role of transcendence.

For Dionysius, community most effectively takes the form of hierarchy, but grounded only upon the recognition that God, the good, transcends all things. "It is characteristic of the universal Cause, of this goodness beyond all," writes the Areopagite, "to summon everything to communion with him."[2] It is on account of the divine transcendence that God is able to be present to all things at all times, not as some discrete being in competition with other beings, but as the very form of communion that Dionysius believes is the divine intention. God is, we might say, the ontological valence at the very foundation of all beings holding them together in their integrity and drawing them to each other in community.

For Dionysius, the communion of all creatures in God takes the form of a hierarchy, not as a system of unjustifiable superiority, or power maintenance (as it is often conceived today), but as a community of unity-in-plurality (see, e.g., Dionysius, DN 4, 10 [705 BC], and The Ecclesiastical Hierarchy 1, 1 [372B]). His vision, however, is much more than a social observation, but exposits a metaphysics of beauty by which all beings share their unique, integral ontological constitutions with other beings. In this sense, hierarchy is not an expression of a valuation system, but rather a dynamic (as opposed to static) intermediation of being and all its various modalities (the divine names) in and through the beings that constitute the hierarchy.

Given his Neoplatonic pedigree, it is not surprising to see hierarchy bound up with the dynamic of emanation. This means that the hierarchical community envisioned by Dionysius begins with God, who then emanates the divine names as the bonding agents, so to speak, through which beings are able to relate to one another. Dionysius provides the most explicit definition of hierarchy in the third chapter of his *Celestial Hierarchy* predicated on his notion of symbolism. Symbolism, for Dionysius, identifies a mode of being's power to distill the divine transcendent plenitude into more limited, or determined, forms. It therefore provides the foundation upon which the hierarchical activity can be understood as a 'symbolic' appearance, or 'theophany,' of the divine in and as the world.

At the very beginning of chapter three in the *Celestial Hierarchy*, Dionysius sets out his explanation of hierarchy by distinguishing it as a triad: (1) a sacred ordering, (2) a science or knowledge, and (3) an action/operation/energy. Given its place at the opening of his account of hierarchy, such distinctions suggest that hierarchy ought to be understood for the remainder of the text in terms of dynamic activity rather than static structure.

---

[2] Dionsyius, The Celestial Hierarchy [hereafter = CH], 4 [177C].

The remainder of this opening passage of the *Celestial Hierarchy*, indicating the purpose and goal, explains that hierarchical activity is "assimilated, as far as attainable, to the likeness of God, and conducted to the illuminations granted to it from God, according to its capacity, with a view to the Divine imitation" (CH 3, 1 [164D]). Hierarchy is an activity, an operation of sacred ordering, whose goal is divine union, and—through reception of divine light—divine imitation. For Dionysius, the cosmic order is designed in such a way that each created thing, expressing its unique relationship to its divine origin, bears its own inherent limitations (CH 3, 2 [165AB]). The hierarchical activity is designed so as to allow every participant to learn these limitations—limitations which, because they are hierarchically constituted, become more and more liberated by being's hierarchical activity. That is to say, they are limitations that do not remain stagnant in some spatial-temporal position but are continually being pushed further and further into the very excess they attempt to limit. But such liberation is not a freeing from the hierarchy itself. Rather, it is a liberation into a greater participation within the operation of sacred ordering that marks hierarchical community. Hierarchy is an activity, that is, an active unifying of difference and an active differentiation of unity, that teaches as it assimilates, allowing its practitioners to unify themselves with each other and God, as the image of divine beauty (CH 3, 2 [165B]). As being is distilled through hierarchical activity, the intentionality becomes apparent:

"The purpose, then, of hierarchy is the assimilation and union, as far as attainable, with God, having him leader of all religious science and operation, by looking unflinchingly to his most divine beauty, and copying, as far as possible, and by perfecting its own followers as divine images, mirrors most luminous and without flaw, receptive of the primal light and the supremely divine ray, and devoutly filled with the entrusted radiance, and again, spreading this radiance ungrudgingly to those after it, in accordance with the supremely divine regulations" (CH, 3, 2 [165A]).

When read through the metaxological distinction between *passio essendi*, that is, the patience of being or the reception of the given, and the *conatus essendi*, that is, the active effort to be, Dionysian community is both, though more a *passio essendi* than a *conatus essendi*, requiring the reception of being given first from its divine source, but then transferred through the (secondary causality of) other creatures. In its vertical reception, 'being' in this form is horizontally passed through members of the hierarchy to other members: being inhabits the *metaxu* between 'vertical' and 'horizontal.' This 'receiving' and 'passing on' occurs when each member vertically looks 'unflinchingly' at the divine beauty in order to imitate this beauty for every other member. Community, in this Dionysian vision, involves the ontological union of all things with each other in and as their differences from one another.

In the divine name tradition, however, God is both the names and beyond these names simultaneously, introducing a depth of between-ness not easily spoken or thought. It is this depth of between-ness where the ontologically primordial gathering power of being first erupts to become intelligible. Metaxology provides the grounds for a deepening recognition of this utter between-ness found in the divine name tradition. We see this in the way that Desmond articulates, for instance, the role of beauty and the aesthetic in the primordial togetherness of being and its subsequent communication. "Aesthetic happening," writes Desmond, "shows the enabling ethos as a togetherness of splendid beings. Beauty here is not something subjectivistic: aesthetic show communicates the beings themselves and their togetherness in terms of integral harmony and community with others" (GB 135). Here, beauty reveals how the good (the enabling ethos) is already a togetherness of beings that are in themselves splendid, or beautiful, albeit in an overdetermined unity. But beauty here does not indicate the subjective judgment of taste on the outward appearance of a being. It means, in ways similar to Dionysius, the very communication of a self as an outward manifestation in self-transcendence (T^2) as well as how the self relates to or is in togetherness with other beings (T^1) in terms of an integral harmony with the agapeic origin (T^3).

Community, therefore, derives from the communicative dimension of being, a dimension which is porous to the overdetermined agapeic origin. Desmond refers to being's porosity to its origin with the name 'open whole,' a name that, like the divine names, not only identifies the communication of the origin in and as being, but gestures toward the God beyond the whole. "The 'open whole' of communicative being suggests a God beyond the whole, where now communicative being entails the communication of being in a radical ontological sense. If the communicative being of the human being (T^2) and world (T^1) communicates opening to their other, is that other merely the recipient of that opening? But how could that be? For are not the human being and the world themselves given to be? If so, would not the original other be communicative being as 'over,' as in excess of what is given in finite transcendence? Were not this other a source of communicative being, hence a source of giving out beyond itself, the result would be the fixation of God in a frozen impassivity, and we would return to dualistic opposition. We would passionately transcend to this other, but we would speak with a wall. There would be no communication" (GB 108).

In metaxology, community is mined to a depth where being is itself communicative: community presupposes communication as much as communication presupposes community, both of which in turn presuppose a giving of being that is both an act of self-transcendence and a unity with others. The communicative nature of being, in turn, requires and therefore can be said to prove transcendence (T^3). What we find in metaxology, as well as in the divine name tradition is a sense of being as a "communicative togetherness" (GB 176). That is, there is a comradery, a togetherness, a solidarity, at the level of communicative intentionality—communication intends togetherness in some fashion. In the intention of all events of communication, there is a togetherness even prior to the event that reveals itself by means of the subsequent act of communication. Communication, in turn, manifests the conditions of community that provided the very conditions for the event of communication even as the event of communication now ratifies the primordial togetherness of community (or its neglect).

Community and communication bespeak the active presence of those phenomena identified as divine names—one could even go so far as to say communication and community are themselves divine names precisely because they depend on transcendence! God, it might be said, leaks into our every effort to communicate, in that every communicative effort presupposes a shared ethos (the good) by which the meaning of communication can be made intelligible (the true). Such a making intelligible takes many forms because the communicative dimension of being is itself plurivocal precisely as communicative. And so what we find in both metaxology and the divine name tradition is an account of being whose communicative intentionality announces in continual performance the divine presence; not, to be sure, as a univocal identity to be taken hold of, but as a presence always to be sought in and through community.

Conclusion

In similar ways, metaxology and the divine names provide resources for thinking and practicing transcendence and community, both in terms of how each engenders a habit of mind conscious of the porous nature of being in its relation to the overdetermined, agapeic origin, and for how each offers a more determinate account of what the origin releases in its transcendence communication. Also like the divine name tradition, metaxology imagines being as a community of the good, the true, the beautiful—in effect, as a community of metaphysical phenomena porously open to their origin while equally communicative of that origin to finite human thought. When considered in such a context, it becomes possible to see how both the divine name tradition and metaxology establish a sense of transcendence that is as beyond as it is intimate to the finite order. Only from within such a context of transcendence can community flourish because such flourishing depends on a coming together in unity of diverse agents without compromising either the unity or the diversity. Insofar as this sort of gathering is possible, it might be that it is only recognizable and communicable by means of a logos that is willing to stand utterly between. The divine names once provided both the context and the courage to stand in this between. It may be that one day a debt of gratitude will be owed to William Desmond for reawakening this vital sense of transcendence and community.

Bibliography

Adler, Amitai. 2009. What's in a Name? Reflections upon Divine Names and the Attraction of God to Israel. *Jewish Biblical Quarterly* 37: 265–269.

Dionysius the Areopagite. 1991. On the Divine Names: The Celestial Hierarchy, the Ecclesiastical Hierarchy, the Mystical Theology. In *Corpus Dionysiacum*, ed. Beate R. Suchla, G. Heil, and A.M. Ritter, vols. I–II. Berlin: De Gruyter, 1990.

Gieschen, Charles. 2003. The Divine Name in Ante-Nicene Christology. *Vigilae Christianae* 57: 115–158.

Jones, John D. 2008. (Mis?)-Reading the Divine Names as a Science: Aquinas's Interpretation of the Divine Names of (Pseudo) Dionysius the Areopagite. *St. Vladimir's Theological Quarterly* 52: 143–172.

Kelly, Thomas A.F., ed. 2007. *Between System and Poetics: William Desmond and Philosophy After Dialectics*. London: Routledge.

Leeman, Saul. 2004. The Names of God. *Jewish Biblical Quarterly* 32: 104–107.

O'Rourke, Fran. 2005. *Pseudo-Dionysius and the Metaphysics of Aquinas*. Notre Dame: NDU Press.

Sammon, Brendan. 2013. *The God Who Is Beauty: Beauty as a Divine Name in Thomas Aquinas and Dionysius the Areopagite*. Eugene: Pickwick.

Shaw, Christopher David. 2012. *On Exceeding Determination and the Ideal of Reason: Immanuel Kant, William Desmond, and the Noumenological Principle.* Newcastle: Cambridge Scholars Press.

Simpson, Christopher Ben. 2009. *Religion, Metaphysics, and the Postmodern: William Desmond and John D. Caputo.* Eugene: Wipf and Stock.

Simpson, Christopher Ben, and Brendan Sammon, eds. 2017. *William Desmond and Contemporary Theology.* South Bend: Notre Dame University Press.

Taylor, Charles. 2007. *A Secular Age.* London: Belknap Press.

CHAPTER 7

Metaxologizing Our God-Talk: Desmond, Kearney, and the Divine Between

Mark F. Novak

Contemporary philosophy of religion in recent decades has seen traditional metaphysical understandings of God slowly crumble apart. God is no longer generally understood as being omnipotent, omniscient, or omni-anything. In certain circles, God is perceived as weak and powerless, an event, and a call for justice (e.g., Derrida, Caputo). In other circles, God is relegated to the sublime, fully unknown and unrepresentable, in two divergent poles: revered and apophatic (e.g., Marion, Levinas), and horrific and monstrous (e.g., Žižek, Kristeva). While some of these moves seem helpful in our ongoing task of coming to understand who God is, others present changes that are either unhelpful or simply negative. Regarding all these new possibilities and manners of thinking about God, we must ask: Which ones are helpful? What aspects will lead us closer to a truer understanding of God?

Two of the main figures engaged in this area of rethinking and reimagining God are William Desmond and Richard Kearney. Their recent work pushes the boundaries of the ways that we think and talk about God, and they both share a common theme: a strong desire to work in the middle

M. F. Novak (✉)
McMaster University, Hamilton, ON, Canada
e-mail: novakm1@mcmaster.ca

© The Author(s) 2018
D. Vanden Auweele (ed.), *William Desmond's Philosophy between Metaphysics, Religion, Ethics, and Aesthetics*,
https://doi.org/10.1007/978-3-319-98992-1_7

spaces, in the in-betweens, *se metaxu*. Their own individual work over the years has been productive, as has the ongoing dialogue between them. How can we talk about God without creating dominating and totalizing views? How can we balance the hope for an *eschaton* with the weight of an *archē*? When is it appropriate to speak of God as *agape* and when as *eros*? I explore these questions by examining Desmond and Kearney's work, to see the ways in which they create more space to continue defining and imagining God via middle ways and in-betweens between polarizing views. Charting a course through actuality and possibility, eschatology and *archē*-ology, and *agape* and *eros* provides us with the most apt ways of talking about God based on our phenomenological and historical experiences of the world.

I examine these topics in four main sections: First I look at the work done by Desmond on the topics of Being and God with an ear to his notion of metaxology. Next, I look at the similar, and in many ways overlapping, work of Kearney, a thinker who also inhabits between spaces. Third, I examine some of their scholarly interaction, and how it has moved their thought forward. I turn lastly to theopoetics, showing that theopoetics and metaxology are apt partners for carrying forward our understanding of Being and God. As Heidegger saliently alerts us:

> Language is the house of Being. In its home man dwells. Those who think and those who create with words are the guardians of this home. Their guardianship accomplishes the manifestation of Being insofar as they bring the manifestation to language and maintain it in language through their speech. (1977, p. 193)

Since humans and Being both come to fruition in a linguistic milieu, it is our responsibility to continually be creative with our language about Being and God. By ever expanding and playing with our God-talk, and using different modes of imag(in)ing and conceptualizing God at different times, we can help prevent the ossification and idolization of those conceptions, thus allowing God to truly live.[1]

---

[1] Richard J. Colledge makes a similar comparison of Desmond and Kearney in a recent edited book on Kearney, though he does not pursue the theopoetic angle. Unfortunately, I did not have access to this volume before my piece was sent to the publisher. See Colledge (2018).

Desmond on the Overdeterminacy of the Agapeic God

Although I have invoked Heidegger's notion of the world-creating power of language, it must be noted that Desmond is, shall we say, allergic to much of what Heidegger has to say. While he agrees with Heidegger that there is a need to open ourselves up to the question of Being again, or to truly open ourselves up to questions of Being for the first time in a rigorous manner, Desmond finds that Heidegger has left us empty in many ways. In an interview with Kearney, Desmond wonders if Heidegger has not, in his questioning of Being, removed the Good from Being entirely (Kearney and Desmond 2012, p. 239). This is a move that Desmond takes to be unacceptable. The question of Being, and of the Divine in relation to questions of Being, must be: How do we think of Being and the Good together? How can we come to solutions, tenuous as they may be, that do not sacrifice one of these to the other? If we are unable to prevent the Good from being jettisoned in our ongoing discussions of Being and God, then we are doomed from the get-go. Like many working in continental philosophy since its post-structural and post-modern events, Desmond is cognizant of the need to move past traditional understandings of God and metaphysics; however, unlike many of these thinkers, he is not willing to abandon metaphysical thinking altogether. He is committed to finding new, fresh, and life-giving ways to think on these topics, and his manner of approaching this is to do so 'from the middle.'

Desmond's aim in thinking of Being is to think of Being and metaphysics in and from the middle. In his words: "I develop what I call the 'metaxological sense of being,' in contrast to the univocal, the equivocal, and the dialectical senses.... The metaxological sense of being is concerned with a *logos* of the *metaxu*, a discourse of the 'between,' the middle" (PU 10–11). He sees this middle way as a helpful corrective to extant ways of metaphysical thinking. According to Desmond, a univocal reading of Being is reductionistic, simplistic, and completely misses the complexities of life; an equivocal reading, however, swings the pendulum to the opposite side, providing a deconstructive reading that is also unhelpful, in many ways because it has given up on thinking through the ambiguities of Being (PU 12–13). While dialectical thinking allows the discourse between opposites, such as transcendence-immanence, self-other, unity-plurality, and even *agape-eros*, ultimately, this way of thinking collapses these poles, subsuming both into some new transcendence, what Desmond refers to as a 'dialectical univocity' (PU 14). Desmond's helpful move with metaphysical thinking is to make this collapse of the middle impossible (PU 12). He aims to achieve this state of tension with his novel idea 'metaxology.' While metaxology is not the antithesis of dialectical thinking, it takes a firm stance against any type of thinking that reduces otherness and intermediation (PU 14). Applying this approach to transcendence and the divine, Desmond writes: "How think of a God of the between, from the between, without reducing God to the between?" (2006, p. 58). Our best hope for understanding God and Being must take place in this middle space, where genuine dialogue and interaction with otherness can happen.

In addition to its commitment to honouring otherness and plurality in a non-reducible middle is the dual nature of metaxology. In his recent book *The Intimate Universal*, Desmond explains this dual nature with a nod to the Divine:

> While there is divine transcendence in excess to immanence, this transcendence is intimate with the being of the *metaxu*, the between. It involves a *meta*: both a 'beyond' and an 'in the midst,' both an outside and an inside, both making us at home and making us not at home. (IU 418)

If the transcendent Divine were either wholly outside or wholly inside our conceptual grasp, destruction and violence would ensue. Rather, metaxology calls us towards a faithful response to this doubleness. "*Outside*: all our idols come into question but this is a release toward the true God. *Inside*: agapeic love appeals to us, most intimately and most universally, in the beloved community where goodness gives us to ourselves, goodness that we can pass on to others" (IU 418). Metaxology, then, is a dialogue of the middle and in the middle that helps to stave off totalizing violence from either side, especially when it concerns our relation to the Divine. In its desire to speak about God, human discourse reaches its limit and so, as Desmond writes in *God and the Between*, "[g]iven our indirect direction to God via the hyperboles," metaxology becomes "an adventure in speculative metaxology" (GB 159). Rather than firm absolutes about God, Desmond describes the journey to plurivocity and naming God as "groping in darkness or feeling one's way in a fog" (GB 281).

Desmond's work here highlights something crucial: Metaxological thinking requires not *just* a stance of thinking about Being from the middle, but an explanation of *how* this thinking is to be done. Invoking words such as 'play,' 'prayer,' 'adventure,' 'poetics,' and 'mindfulness' in his writing, Desmond alerts us to the approach that we are to take towards life lived in the middle. His "interest is not with sheer indefiniteness, nor fixed determinacy, but with something of the play *between* the indeterminate and determinacy; and again not an interplay that leads to the determination or self-determination of the indeterminacy as indefinite" (IST 112). Desmond thus encourages a stance of continued openness to the divine that is found in the stance from and of the middle. In *Is There a Sabbath for Thought*, he writes that

> [p]rayer is awakening to the passing communication of the divine in the finite *metaxu*. We do not produce it; it is not the result of our determination or self-determination; we are 'determined,' or better, released into the middle where we can sink deeper into ontological sleep, or begin to awake more fully to what communicates us to be at all. (IST 130)

It is this being 'released into the middle' (a point that I return to in the final section on theopoetics) that is key to bear in mind, for "[m]etaxological metaphysics seeks to be mindfulness in an agapeic way" (IST 132).

KEARNEY ON THE EROTIC GOD OF POSSIBILITY

Kearney starts his *The God Who May Be* with the enticing claim "God neither is nor is not but may be" (2001, p. 1). This statement exemplifies his commitment to overcoming, or thinking through, traditional binary logical structures by looking for what lies between. Specifically, this statement begins his never-ending wager to overcome ontotheology, which he sees as a tradition that has "granted priority to being over the good" (2001, p. 19) and actuality over possibility (2001, p. 99). The connection or fusion of ontology and theology into ontotheology can be largely traced back, as he sees it, to the interpretative mishaps that led the *'ehyeh 'asher 'ehyeh* of Exodus 3:14—that mysterious name of God which has a plurality of possible, and ever-growing, meanings—to become "I AM that I AM." Greek translators translated the Hebrew verb *'ehyeh* as *einai*, and later Latin thinkers translated it as *esse*, as they assumed there to be no fundamental difference between the original Hebrew and the Greek translation (2001, p. 22). When read in the light of Greek philosophical categories, this translation encourages us to see no future or past in God, but instead to understand God's essence as synonymous with God's existence, and even with existence as such. When religious thinkers (especially in the scholastic period) interpreted God and scripture through Greek metaphysical categories, the "conflation of Yahweh with the supreme Being of the philosophers [was] sealed" (2001, p. 24). This can be seen, in a way, as the beginning of the death of God. The tempestuous and mercurial Yahweh is now the God of metaphysics, and, as Heidegger made clear (1960, p. 53), all ontology was now ontotheology, what Kearney calls "the conceptual capture of God as a category of substance" (2001, p. 24).

Kearney's specific approach to God derives from his general approach towards matters of divinity and hermeneutics. In *The God Who May Be*, Kearney discusses possible names—"methodological pseudonyms" (2001, p. 6)—for the kind of philosophical work that he is engaged in. He names three: *dynamatology*, for describing potency, possibility, and the 'logic of the dynamizing possibility'; *metaphorology*, for the ways that religious language can say something about the unsayable and can "transfer, transit, or carry across" (2001, p. 7) that which can be approximated, but never fully grasped; and, aptly, the middle of the three options that he suggests for his poetics of possibility is Desmond's metaxology, highlighting his and Desmond's "determination to choose a middle way (Greek, *metaxy*) between the extremes of absolutism and relativism" (2001, p. 6). Kearney writes that "this middle space, or as I prefer to call it *mi-lieu*, is chosen as an alternative to what I consider to be two polar opposites in contemporary thinking about God (which sometimes end up colluding with each other), namely: (a) the hyper-ascendant deity of mystical or negative theology; and (b) the consigning of the sacred to the domain of abyssal abjection" (2001, pp. 6–7). He argues that "[w]hile both positions push the notion of God to opposite extremes—to the highest of heights or lowest of depths—they share a common aversion to any mediating role for narrative imagination. For both, the divine remains utterly unthinkable, unnameable, unrepresentable—that is, unmediatable" (2001, p. 7). Coming from his strong background in, and methodological adherence to, hermeneutics, Kearney's approach to questions of religion and the Divine actively seeks out this mediating function, not least for its attention to otherness. This early work on metaxology is picked up by Kearney in his 2010 book *Anatheism*, where he explores a new way of understanding God after God. Similar to how Desmond understands metaxology, Kearney describes anatheism as neither a univocal or equivocal reading of God or religion, nor as the synthesis of these produced via sublation of a dialectic; rather, anatheism "is a movement—not a state—that refuses all absolute talk about the absolute, negative or positive" (2010, p. 16).

Kearney, then, like Desmond, operates in the between spaces and the beyond places of philosophy, religion, and hermeneutics, and seeks a God who neither is nor is not—that is, neither ontological (and so surely not onto-theo-logical) nor eschatological—but who may be, that is, onto-eschatological. Kearney's proposed third way approaches God "neither as non-being nor as being but as the possibility-to-be" (2001, p. 8). He finds support for this view from Nicholas of Cusa, the fifteenth-century mystic and philosophical theologian, who suggested that we think of God as *possest*. This coinage combines, but really seeks to chart a path between, *posse* and *esse* (or *est*). According to Kearney, this possibilizing middle way is where we "encounter the nuptial nexus where divine and human desires overlap" (2001, p. 8). The middle way highlights a stance of co-possibility for humanity and divinity. He suggests that, in reference to Exodus 3:14, "God's 'I shall be' appears to need Moses' response 'Here I am' in order to enter history and blaze the path towards the Kingdom" (2001, p. 26). God can then be thought of as beyond Being, or between Being and non-Being, requiring us to answer a call to allow God to be. Kearney explicates that God may or may not be, and so that God is not required to be. But if God is not required to be, if God is a may-be (*peut-être*) God, what are the conditions upon which God moves from may-Being to Being proper? Kearney responds that it is the affirming response of humans that continually brings God into Being. In Kearney's poetics of a possible God, God possibilizes humans who in turn possibilize God. This relation is not a one-way street, then, but a back and forth, a dance of lovers. And good dances, eschatological dances, take two (2001, p. 110).

Desmond and Kearney Together: Finding the Middle Ground

Having looked at Desmond and Kearney on metaxology and the Divine, it is quite apparent that there are many similarities in their thinking. The most important of these similarities are their adherence to thinking from the middle, and the use of play and poetics in their musings on Being and the Divine. In this section, I examine the productive interchanges that have taken place between them. As we have seen, both thinkers are engaged in rethinking our understanding of metaphysics, and do so in a way that takes a stance against univocity, equivocity, and dialecticism. However, even though metaxological thinking is antithetical to dialectical thinking, because of its attempts to overcome otherness, both Desmond and Kearney seemingly take a preference to one side of certain dialectics over the other. That is, though they are adamant about being in the middle, they are not adrift in the flux completely, but choose to align themselves with a specific shoreline. The main dialectics, at least as I read them, are actuality and possibility, eschatology and ontology, and *agape* and *eros*. As both thinkers are content to live in the tension of the metaxological space, neither of them are tied down to an entrenched and dogmatic position. Rather, we can detect a movement in their views of God and Being, due in no small part to their ongoing relationship, dialogue, and kindred critique of each other.

Kearney's attempt at re-conceiving God focuses on the importance of eschatology and God as loving-possibilizing, rather than a position that sees God purely as actuality and *fait accompli*. Commenting on Kearney's preferred futural stance, Desmond writes: "I have learned from his stress on eschatological possibility, for my own work tends more to stress a certain 'archaeology.' My conviction is that we cannot think last things without first thinking first things, there being no re-creation and eschatology without first creation" (2006, p. 56). We can see here that, though Desmond is antithetical to how dialectical thinking fully sublates two differing positions, he is comfortable with leaning closer to one side. So, while he has learnt from Kearney, Desmond's concern is that Kearney's eschatological possibilizing may fall into certain temptations and ignore that for God to possibilize anything, God must first *be* in actuality. As Desmond points out, in *The God Who May Be*, Kearney writes that "*possest* may now be seen as advent rather than *archē*, as *eschaton* rather than *principium*" (2006, p. 67; referring to Kearney 2001, pp. 110–111). Desmond is right to question Kearney on this, for if the eschatological takes complete precedence, then to what extent is God *onto*-eschatological, and in what sense is this God still seen metaxologically? Kearney does make clear, though, that his understanding of God is *onto*-eschatological, that *possest* contains both *posse* and *esse* primordially. This position of onto-eschatology is one that, though it can lean one way or the other, tries to honour the best of what metaxology is aiming for, and though Kearney leans more towards eschatological possibility, and Desmond more towards *archē*-ological actuality, both are willing to live and move in this tension.

When it comes to the love of God, Desmond and Kearney again find themselves leaning towards one type of love over the other. Desmond sees *agape* as the type of love that should be primary, for its self-sacrificial and service-oriented stance, whereas Kearney puts primacy on *eros*, for the sensuous, passionate, and desiring nature of God. Since the Bible attests to God revealing Godself in both these manners of love, neither Desmond's nor Kearney's case is without warrant. Because of the dual nature of *eros*—heavenly (*eros uranios*) and tyrannical (*eros turannos*)—and that the former is too easily tempted by the latter, Desmond is adamant that, though there is an erotic expression to the love of God, ultimately the surplus of agapeic love must be primary. Kearney takes the opposite stance: While there are dimensions of *agape* in God, it is the erotic and desiring that are primary. So there seems to be a bit of a standoff: Each thinker critiques the other's preference for how best to understand God's love. However, Kearney has responded to Desmond by saying that his understanding of God as *eros* is not operating out of lack.

According to the most common interpretation of desire, something or someone is sought out by desire—and usually objectified in the process—to meet a need, or fill a lack in the seeker. Aware of this general view, and avoiding its pitfalls, Kearney avers that the God of loving-possibilizing desires out of excess. From this standpoint, God's desire is not from less to more, but from more to less (2007, p. 193).[2] Kearney suggests another move to further align his and Desmond's views. In response to Desmond's critique, Kearney writes that

> we should try to avoid both extreme positions—of reducing agape to eros (as he thinks I suggest) or of reducing eros to agape (as I think he suggests)—and that we should do so by speaking instead of a very specific modality of eros, agapeic eros, which would be suitable to God, capturing both the sense of unconditional agape and conditional dependency on history for this love to be realized as the 'more' (of surplus and excess) moving towards the 'less' (of human frailty and flesh). (2007, p. 195)

---

[2] See also Kearney (2001, p. 64): "But this elevation of desire towards the Most-High does not imply (as one might think) a Platonic elevation to a transcendental hinterworld. On the contrary, the experience of height arises, once again, *in the midst of* my relation to the concrete living other. The good *beyond* finds itself inscribed *between* one and another. Desire here again reveals itself not as deficiency but as positivity. Not as *manque-à-être* but as grace and gratuity, gift and surplus. Less as insufficiency than as the bursting forth of the 'more' in the 'less'."

Kearney's sense of 'agapeic eros' (and should we not also have an 'erotic agape'?) seems to answer Desmond's concerns, and more, it seems to operate more truly from out of the metaxological space. That is, it strongly resists reducing aspects of love to one of its modalities, and so affirms continually living in the space between them.

How has Desmond responded to Kearney's idea of speaking of this specific modality of 'agapeic eros'? In *The Intimate Universal*—which came out in 2016, nine years after the chapter containing Kearney's suggestion—Desmond seemingly provides an answer:

> The excellences of immanence need not be negated by the agapeics of the intimate universal. Nor is it a question of dualistic opposition of erotics and agapeics, of immanent excellence and transcendent good. It is not a question of one side determining the other, or of one side dialectically sublating the other into a self-determining totality.... The agapeics is not a dialectical sublation (or sublimation) of the erotics. (IU 390)

And a few pages later, he writes: "[O]nce again there is no need dualistically to oppose the erotics and the agapeics. There can be differences without dualistic oppositions, for these latter easily turn into antagonisms and so return us to a dialectic of sovereignty and servility" (IU 394). In both these passages, Desmond makes clear that *agape* and *eros* should be on equal footing. Neither type of love should be primary and reduce other forms of love to it, thereby attempting to create a self-determined or self-mediated totality. In this way, he has greatly complicated their relation to one another or, rather, allowed this always-existing complex relation to come to the fore. However, it still seems that he gives preference to or sees *agape* as more originary.

The last four chapters of *The Intimate Universal*, for example, go from the idiotics, to the aesthetics, to the erotics, and lastly to the agapeics of the intimate universal, this being the pattern that he follows in the 'selving' of human beings in *Being and the Between* (BB 377–415). So, while the erotic and agapeic are related non-oppositionally, there is still an asymmetry present wherein *agape* is higher than *eros*. While this might be true, it misses another layer of complexity that Desmond sees when it comes to these tiers of 'selving,' or the 'potencies of being,' and thus to the place of *eros* and *agape*. The potencies of being should not be thought of as ascending rungs of a ladder, but as co-existing. From this stance, *agape* is a type of 'factor' or secret companion that is present in all four of the aspects which come to full fruition in the final, agapeic level. Desmond highlights this view when he writes that "[a]gapeic being is itself idiotic" (BB 415). Though Desmond here complicates the relation between *eros* and *agape*, his bias towards *agape* is still clear: *Agape* is the silent partner and the culminating position; it thus guides and allows the 'potencies of being' to be.

At the end of this look at Desmond and Kearney's influence on each other, we can see that there has been a greater alignment of their viewpoints. Nevertheless, it seems that in their quest to understand God from the middle, both Desmond and Kearney lean towards other sides of the middle: Desmond more towards *agape*, *archē*, and actuality, and Kearney more towards *eros*, *eschaton*, and possibility. Commenting on this, and how we should understand God and the middle, Desmond writes that

> otherness and transcendence is a great problem.... I would say it is not a matter of finding a middle between these, as thinking about the meaning of middles, and of the God of the between that possibilizes the between without being reduced to it, whose otherness as creative is also a name for its being in communication with what it brings to be. (2006, p. 59)

It is Desmond's invocation of this creative 'God of the between' that brings us to our final section.

THEOPOETICS AS METAXOLOGY'S FUTURE

In this last section, I want to look at the ways in which theopoetics may be a vehicle for metaxology, a way of expressing, espousing, and even creating the divine from within the milieu of the between. This is because theopoetics is a way of living in the middle, and of eschewing final and totalizing answers and discourse. Indeed, theopoetics is as much—if not more—concerned with *how* it conveys what it conveys, than in *what* it conveys. This is to say that the form of theopoetics *is* what it is trying to convey. Rather than just a way of writing, theopoetics is an embodied way of being-in-the-world that includes writing, speaking, acting, experiencing, and thinking, but ultimately, it is a way of being-in-the-middle. The function of questions in theopoetics is not to lead one to hard and fast answers, or to answers at all, but rather to have one's questions deepened. The mystery of God and life (are they not the same?) is expanded, then, and not contracted. This is because theopoetics is not merely another way of thinking, another metaphysical jumping through the hoops; rather, it is a way of being-in-the-world. And as a discourse native to being-in-the-world, theopoetics attempts to "speak at the intersection of spiritual and material reality without compromising either side" (Krabbe 2016, pp. 13–14).

In his recent book on theopoetics—*A Beautiful Bricolage: Theopoetics as God-Talk for Our Time*—Silas Krabbe discusses the history and development of theopoetics, from its origins in people like Gabriel Vahanian, Rubem Alves, and Amos Wilder, to figures like Catherine Keller, John D. Caputo, and Kearney who are engaging with it today. When discussing theopoetics' relation to God and how we talk about God, Krabbe writes that "[i]nsofar as God *lives*, propositional language will continue to fail to correlate directly to God, or fully correspond to humanity that lives anew in the resurrection life" (2016, p. 108). By living in this middle space, and at the intersection of spiritual and material realities, theopoetics finds that the best way for humans to express God is not through propositional language, but through the poetic. However, to be clear, theopoetics is not a discourse *against* theology, or against systematic thinking, nor is it just poetry added to systemic thinking. It should rather be understood as what comes before system, and so what guides and allows systematic thinking to be. Again, it is a form of enactment, a way of being. Further, and in a way that echoes Desmond, theopoetics is concerned with releasing, or 'letting be,' both humans and God into the middle space. Krabbe writes that "theopoetics can be understood as humanity's way of returning the favor and extending *Gelassenheit* to God. For in theopoetics, there is intentional space for the interpreter, the new, the novel, and the possible—all spaces in which God can play and resist the ossification of the grave" (2016, p. 108). This aspect of theopoetics aligns with Kearney's emphasis on the co-possibilizing powers for God and humans. When system ignores its poetic origins, it becomes stale, static, and ultimately destructive towards God and humans. Tuned in to this realization, both Desmond and Kearney's work uses theopoetics as a discourse for understanding and expressing God.

In *Beyond Hegel and Dialectic*, Desmond writes, in a way, of the importance of a theopoetic way of thinking and writing. He highlights a key feature of theopoetics, namely, that poetic thinking is prior to systematic thinking:

> The fact that I have to tell a story to make a philosophical point is relevant to the metaxological mode of naming the happening of evil.[3] As philosophers, we cannot escape from the truth of the story in its representational

---

[3] Though referring specifically to evil, the point he makes is relevant to all discourse.

particularity into the impersonal universal. The story keeps us mindful of the intimate truth of particularity that the philosophical concept is tempted to subordinate or supersede or forget. Metaxological naming must be both imagistic and conceptual to do justice to the mindfulness required by the matter at issue. And there is no speculative *Aufhebung* of the story into the concept. Rather the naming of the philosopher must be plurivocal. Our very concepts must themselves try to maintain in themselves the memory of the truth that the story tells. The concept must bear in itself the traces of its own origin in its other, the originating story. (BHD 233–234)

What Desmond draws to the fore here is that the originating story must always lead and direct our conceptualizations of it. Though our naming and wording of anything, but especially the divine, involves both imaging and concepts, both stories and systems, to live life in the between one must always be open to the guiding of images and stories. Desmond is clear that metaxological thinking is *both* imagistic and conceptual, but that the latter is impotent without the former.

This commitment to living and thinking from the middle of the systematic and poetic has been with Desmond throughout his career. Desmond fleshes out further his reasoning for this in his essay "Between System and Poetics: On the Practices of Philosophy." He makes salient that philosophizing requires systematic thinking; however, since poetic thinking is more primary, and closer to the givenness of Being, there cannot be honest systematic thinking without poetics (2007, pp. 20–21). On this view, Desmond writes that "without the poetics of coming to be, for us there is no systematics of being at all. Poetics deals with a bringing or coming to be; systematics finds interconnections in what has come to be" (2007, p. 21). When discussing what poetics means to him, Desmond elucidates that it is more than just adding poetry to systematic thinking. Describing his own practice, he writes that poetics

> is not a matter of giving to thought a kind of 'feel'; not simply a kind of evocation, though it can be both; not just a rhetorical embellishment that otherwise puts drapery over the sturdy drab furniture of thinking. It has more to do with *enactment*: the very concreteness of thinking itself as performed in fitting words. The words are not just a matter of 'talk about' a something, but are uttered or written somehow to bring to pass a happening, to enact it mindfully. (2007, p. 26)

Theopoetics, then, is a way of enacting and performing Being—a way of bringing it into existence. It is, Desmond writes, "like a *poiesis*: a coming or bringing to be; an emergence as if from a kind of nothing, but then also a becoming in terms of a forming" (2007, p. 26). Before looking further at *poiesis*, and its relation to language, I turn now to Kearney's engagement with theopoetics.

Kearney's commitment to a poetic and narrative way of thinking has been a key element of his career. And, according to him, this way of thinking is closely tied to metaxology. He writes that the *metaxu* is "a frontier zone where narratives flourish and abound. It is a place where stories, songs, parables, and prophecies resound as human imaginations try to say the unsayable and think the unthinkable" (2001, p. 8). Rather than making firm declarations on who or what the Divine is, these poetic and narrative musings native to the middle space hint towards, point at, and even lure us in the direction of the transcendent, all without reducing or idolizing it. In our ongoing efforts to understand God, this poetic type of thinking is necessary: "[W]ithout some poetic release into a free variation of possibles, the return to a God beyond God is virtually impossible" (2010, p. 15). Kearney, like Desmond, does not want to merely use poetics, story, and parable to describe the transcendent. Rather, there is a constructive aspect at the heart of this type of thinking, which has led Kearney further towards theopoetics in recent years. In the essay "God Making: An Essay in Theopoetic Imagination," he says that "[t]heopoetics names how the divine (*theos*) manifests itself as making (*poiesis*). The term ... mean[s] both the making human of the divine and the making divine of humanity" (2017, p. 31). Tying this idea of theopoetics or theopoiesis to his anatheism, Kearney writes: "*Theopoiesis* is about coming back again (*ana*)—creating again time after time. In a word: *ana-poiesis*. Theopoetics is anapoetics" (2017, p. 35). For Kearney, both anatheism and metaxology's discourse on the Divine is a discourse that continually brings the Divine into Being.

The creative and forming powers of *poiesis* are important themes in the writings of both Desmond and Kearney. It is this formative aspect that leads us to language, and the linguistic capabilities of human beings. Referring back to the Heidegger passage, we are reminded that through our words (i.e., thinking, speaking, and writing), we create the "house of Being." Commenting on these ideas, and their relation to the *metaxu*, Desmond writes in *God and the Between*: "Word brings a world to be, word communicates a world, lets it issue into a space of sharing with others. Wording the between (*logos* of the *metaxu*): not thought thinking itself, not even thought thinking its other, but thought singing the other. Wording the between: a sung world" (GB 253). In 'God Making,' Kearney also highlights the creative powers of language and their relation to God.

He writes, affirming Genesis and Proverbs, that "God is a relation. Not a self-subsisting remote substance but a relationship between two—Yahweh and Sophia, Elohim and Adam—through the medium of a third (the breath of language)" (2017, p. 33). As we can see, for Kearney, God is intimately tied to language. God, though not reduced to language, is expressed as a relation in and through language. Connecting to thoughts that we have seen him express in *The God Who May Be*, he writes in 'God Making' that "poetics is the first bridge between word and flesh.... [T]he real work of theopoetics [is]: us 'making' God as God makes us. When it comes to divinity *poiesis*, not *theoria*, has the last word. Orthopoiesis trumps orthodoxy" (2017, pp. 41–42).

One of the pioneers of theopoetics, Gabriel Vahanian, thought that, like Heidegger, our world only occurs through the word and that it is impotent without it (2009, p. 56). On the connection of language to God, Vahanian writes in *No Other God: Wording the World and Worlding the Word* that God's "reality is given with 'the actualization of language,' with the fact of existence, even the empirical irreducibility of the human phenomenon" (2009, pp. 57–58). God, then, is indelibly tied to humans, and specifically to ways in which humans speak, write, and even sing the Divine. "*God is a word*," Vahanian writes,

> the word that our words do not speak unless they are shocked both out of their literal and out of their symbolic meaning. Through the metaphor the word of man shows that this is possible. And this cannot be possible unless its reality is given with its possibility, unless the Word of God is given with the occurrence of that reality. (2009, p. 61)[4]

Our words, then, can only accurately speak (about) God when they are released to the middle between the literal and the symbolic.

In their ongoing desire to understand the Divine, to say something about the unsayable, to describe the indescribable, both William Desmond and Richard Kearney continue to show that the most fruitful manner of doing this is via the artistic, imagistic, and poetic. Although philosophical and theological conceptions and systematic formulations of God have their place, they must ultimately be led, informed, and created by the poetic. Because our being-in-the-world is a being-in-the-middle, and because this middle that our being finds itself in is a linguistic and poetic

---

[4] See also Martin Heidegger, "Hölderlin and the Essence of Poetry," trans. Douglas Scott, in *Existence and Being*, (Chicago, IL: Henry Regnery Company, 1949), 279.

milieu, our mode of God-talk is most appropriately theopoetic, a mode of "contemplating, discussing, and speaking the divine" (Krabbe 2016, p. 4) that opens us up to the depth of the mystery at the heart of life. Our human response to the awareness of this way of being is to continually metaxologize our God-talk.

Bibliography

Colledge, Richard J. 2018. Kin and Stranger: Kearney and Desmond on God. In *Richard Kearney's Anatheistic Wager: Philosophy, Theology, Poetics*, ed. Chris Doude van Troostwijk and Matthew Clemente, 125–141. Bloomington: Indiana University Press.

Desmond, William. 2006. Maybe, Maybe Not: Richard Kearney and God. In *After God: Richard Kearney and the Religious Turn in Continental Philosophy*, ed. John Panteleimon Manoussakis, 55–77. New York: Fordham University Press.

———. 2007. Between System and Poetics: On the Practices of Philosophy. In *Between System and Poetics: William Desmond and Philosophy After Dialectic*, ed. Thomas A.F. Kelly, 13–36. Burlington: Ashgate Publishing Company.

Heidegger, Martin. 1949. Hölderlin and the Essence of Poetry. Trans. Douglas Scott. In *Existence and Being*, 270–291. Chicago: Henry Regnery Company.

———. 1960. *Essays in Metaphysics: Identity and Difference*. Trans. Kurt F. Leidecker. New York: Philosophical Library Inc.

———. 1977. Letter on Humanism. In *Basic Writings*, ed. David Farrell Krell, 189–242. New York: Harper & Row, Publishers.

Kearney, Richard. 2001. *The God Who May Be: A Hermeneutics of Religion*. Bloomington: Indiana University Press.

———. 2007. Maybe Not, Maybe: William Desmond on God. In *Between System and Poetics: William Desmond and Philosophy After Dialectic*, ed. Thomas A.F. Kelly, 191–200. Burlington: Ashgate Publishing Company.

———. 2010. *Anatheism: Returning to God After God*. New York: Columbia University Press.

———. 2017. God Making: An Essay in Theopoetic Imagination. *Journal of Aesthetics and Phenomenology* 4 (1): 31–44.

Kearney, Richard, and William Desmond. 2012. Two Thinks at a Distance: An Interview by Richard Kearney on 9 January 2011. In *The William Desmond Reader*, ed. Christopher Ben Simpson, 229–244. Albany: State University of New York Press.

Krabbe, Silas C. 2016. *A Beautiful Bricolage: Theopoetics as God-Talk for Our Time*. Eugene: Wipf and Stock Publishers.

Vahanian, Gabriel. 2009. *No Other God: Wording the World and Worlding the Word*. Eugene: Wipf and Stock Publishers.

CHAPTER 8

Espousing Intimacies: Mystics and the Metaxological

Patrick Ryan Cooper

The following aims to explore the porosity between metaphysics and mysticism that animates William Desmond's metaxology. It does so by tracing the general contours of Desmond's metaxological Augustinianism and, in particular, the simultaneity of Augustine's philosophical and theological itinerary to the mystery of God and man alike, *ab exterioribus ad interiora, ab inferioribus ad superiora*, a double vision that both informs and is at the root of Desmond's own unique thinking of the 'between' that characterizes his metaxological *finesse*. Secondly, as a critical interlude, consideration is paid to certain other modern Augustinian reconfigurations of the metaphysical and mystical by exploring the Blondelian influence upon earlier influential Leuven Jesuit *inside-outsiders*, Pierre Scheuer and Joseph Maréchal, for whom the quest for identity and immediacy of 'presence' within metaphysics and mysticism was both profoundly influential and yet of marked contrast with Desmond's otherwise similar appeals to the idiotics of experience. Finally, this chapter concludes with a certain metaxological reconfiguration of the mystical that renews our attention to the very mystery of mediation, with special attention paid to the late-medieval

---

P. R. Cooper (✉)
Saint Martin's University, Lacey, WA, USA
e-mail: PCooper@stmartin.edu

© The Author(s) 2018
D. Vanden Auweele (ed.), *William Desmond's Philosophy between Metaphysics, Religion, Ethics, and Aesthetics*,
https://doi.org/10.1007/978-3-319-98992-1_8

Brabantine mystic Jan van Ruusbroec (1293–1381) and the Augustinian inflections of his view of the common life [*ghemeyne leven*].

Desmond's thought converges with the mystical in several respects, including his unique contributions toward the intimate universal and the intimacy of the idiotics (PO 361n), both of which are crucial for mystical theology. Preserving metaxological dynamism is key for Desmond, who frequently reminds us that the 'meta' is both *above* and *in the midst*. Such dynamism similarly characterizes his approach to mysticism, as itself exemplary of the intimate universal (Desmond 2012, pp. 25–44) characterized by the porosity and 'open whole' of the metaxological and thus distinct from forms of realism, nominalism and the Hegelian universal as concrete. The intimate universal becomes manifestly concerned with preserving the doubleness of an irreducible intimacy that cannot but remain open and communicable to the others (religion, aesthetics, politics, etc.) by its own universal promise. Preserving such dialogical openness from otherwise closure requires *finesse*, at once so characteristic of Desmond's approach between poetics and systematics, and is not merely an aesthetic artifice; rather, it is Augustinian in its core, by its approach to the very inseparability of the double beyond reduction and collapse that in turn portrays more than a simple family resemblance to the history of mysticism.

In his early writings, Desmond shows a compellingly nuanced regard for mysticism, not as something entirely gratuitous, extraordinary and infused, and instead veers decisively toward more the naturally acquired and habitual dimensions of contemplation and mindfulness, stating: "Mysticism ... has nothing to do with a leap into some other world but is merely the proper mindfulness of an otherness that is right now present to one, proper mindfulness of what is and what one is" (PO 237). In his later writings, Desmond will greatly expand upon this basic orientation, most notably in the pronounced equivocities of the "woo of the mystic" from *God and the Between* (GB 259–278). However, I want to suggest that the intimate universal itself substantiates this compelling intuition with an overall philosophical idiom that legitimates the distinctive hermeneutical character of mystical theological texts and their robust, metaphysical inheritance of 'proper mindfulness' of transcendent otherness as given and mediated between others and self without reductively relegating them as escapist, other-worldly vagaries of what Desmond calls a 'cartoonish' Platonism. Instead, the intimate espousal between metaphysics and mysticism renewed by Desmond's metaxology aims to cultivate anew a proper mindfulness toward this very mystery of mediation that renders greater intensity of togetherness, difference and unity within overlapping vectors of relationality: the ever-greater *interior intimo meo* that confers an idiotic intimacy of selves not by way of isolation of identity that is self-referential and reductively autonomous, yet is safeguarded by the bridging of the togetherness of others and selves within what he calls 'agapeic community'.

Desmond's approach is indeed highly fruitful for theologians concerned with the mystical theological canon, as he retains a high regard for interiority and its erotic ascending, all the while attentive to the very real dangers that emerge from within the porosity of the superabundant—or in his terms, the 'overdeterminate'. Approaching intimacy and interiority in terms of the idiotics of being redeems the promise of a gratuitous, descending agapeics by simultaneously opening such idiotic interiority of the self into its communal/ecclesial and public relevance and prophetic engagement. Idiocy is here understood as affirming the very prior givenness and gratuitousness of being and thus the very contingency and fragility *that it is* at once prior to the vectors of becoming. Contemplative mindfulness of such idiotic givenness thus keeps one daily awake to such givenness and veers one away from what Desmond calls the 'familiar middle' whereby the asymmetry and fragility of being's idiotic giftedness becomes demoted into that which is 'taken for granted', assumed and thus manipulable. Herein the idiocy of being converges with the ethics of that it is and, inseparably, that it is good, as the idiocy of being is as much about the unsurpassable givenness of being and its created origins as much as it likewise concerns the very receptivity and porosity toward such givenness of metaxological being. Such receptivity, beyond reductive passivity, is of central significance to the mystical, as it likewise is for Desmond (Cooper 2017, pp. 1–24). For receptivity recognizes the mediatory power and ontological worth of the porosity of being, the *passio essendi*, that is at once inseparable with and yet non-identical to the absolute origin, the *semper maior* of God's transcendence that makes possible the erotic strivings of the *connatus essendi*.

Finesse for this inseparability, of idiotic givenness and intimate receptivity that opens onto communicability and otherness with the 'intimate universal' thus allows one to speak of the idiocy of the mystic, an approach that occludes both the subjective antinomies of modernism and the ever-reappearing phantom of quietism and autotheism that has otherwise stalked the mystical tradition. Rather, by keeping with Desmond's distinct Augustinian ethos, such finesse returns us to the very crux of the experiential that is at once both idiotic in its singular intimacy and public in the porosity of its communicable address. The complex togetherness of the metaphysical and the mystical that Desmond elicits returns us to the idiocy of experience that likewise informs the *ressourcement* of theological sources by approaching anew the power of metaphor and analogical similitude, the ontological symbol and the excess of hyperbole (BB 207–222) that earlier nominated mysticism the 'crown of metaphysics'. By its speaking from the between of ontological difference and the superabundance of its givenness, this 'crown' gives voice to the very eros of impossibility as a "hunger unstilled [....] Man cannot leave it, nor grasp it; he cannot do without it, nor can he obtain it; he cannot speak about it, nor can he be silent about it [...]" (Ruusbroec 1991, ll. 554, 555–557).

Desmond's Metaxological Augustinianism

Early in *Desire, Dialectic and Otherness*, Desmond describes the root dynamism of the metaxological as his "Augustinian odyssey after Hegel" (DDO xxii), citing Augustine's well-known statement from his Exposition on Psalm 145 *ab exterioribus ad interiora, ab inferioribus ad superiora* as encapsulating the Augustinian way to the ever-greater mystery of God and man alike. Desmond reads Augustine's itinerary as a double movement characteristic of our 'ineluctable desiring', that is, both our natural desire for transcendence and its dynamic happening within the middle that inexorably leads through the abyss of man—*grande profundum est ipse homo*—all of which are appropriately forecasted in his first published article, *Augustine's Confessions: On Desire, Conversion and Reflection*. Here, human desire is seen as bridging the gap between speculative and experiential approaches—what he would later on term as between system and poetics'—to the question of God that entails both individual and universal description. Metaxological mediation thereby rightfully turns upon desire, for "when reflection turns to desire", Desmond reminds us, "it cannot rest with an abstract knowledge alone. Any way to God [...] must pass through him as an infinite desire to this desire's end" (Desmond 1980, p. 25) while placing the metaxological firmly beyond any and all anthropological reduction.

In *Philosophy and Its Others*, reference to this Augustinian itinerary is conjoined by roundly undermining any depiction of a closed, non-porous approach to interiority that obfuscates such "inward otherness" beyond the determinacy of self-mastery, in addition to the "closed circle of the 'metaphysics of presence'". "We cannot master our own otherness", Desmond adds, "much less God's" (PO 362n). Such assertions show the seminal parameters of what Desmond would later on give greater elaboration upon—such as idiocy, the erotics and agapeics—as earlier indicative of his treatment of religious inwardness as "not a domination of otherness, but a living of metaxological openness in selfhood itself [...] deeper than the domination of self-mediation of secular modernity, the self can live and safeguard in inwardness a metaxological respect for being in otherness.... [a] perplexed openness to, patient readiness before the absolute original as the radical other" (PO 114).

With *Perplexity and Ultimacy*, Desmond provides a full-fledged commentary upon this itinerary by explicitly framing his continued interest and increasing finesse for the giftedness and overdeterminacy of agapeic being as offering an admirable resistance to the wayward, tyrannical erotics of the mystical under its Hegelian influence that too easily regards otherness as provisional in its ascent to a unity of sameness and identity. Desmond thus regards Augustine's first movement—from exterior to interior—as the waking of our interiority within the "middle of things—the exteriors" (PU 11), while marking our interiority as both erotic in its self-transcending and agapeically porous. The second movement—from inferior to superior—foregrounds this porosity within these interior erotics as an opening onto an other, "more ultimate than ourselves" (ibid.). For Desmond, it is utterly crucial to recognize that while we identify with these interior erotics, so too do we recognize an insurmountable superiority that is both "irreducible to us and mediates with us—the inferior—through the agapeic excess of its own unequalizable plentitude" (ibid.). Here, Desmond's long-standing interest in correcting a largely philosophical silence toward agapeic love is keyed within this attention to an irreducible otherness, such that our desires are intimately defining as much as they are othering with a plentitude and giftedness that exceeds and is superior to ourselves.

Both the intimacy and otherness of desire unveil in us a capacity for such unfolding that extends well beyond psychological description. This native capacity for an irreducible otherness refreshes and renews the task of metaphysics as the never-ending occasion to think and be mindful of this very givenness, plurality and overdeterminacy of such desires that not only refuses determinacy yet likewise illumines the "polyphony of being" (DDO 169) and subsequently, the plurivocal constitution of metaphysics itself. "The paradox of human identity is that, because its origin is linked with desire, it is also nonidentity—that is, the space where the sense of difference enters the world" (DDO 26). The activity of desire is the necessary movement, not only from the external to the internal, yet by mediating this between, this active mediatory power of desire opens onto the agapeic porosity of the overdeterminate that is at once beyond mere privation. Desire's fundamental paradox—that lack proceeds only from a greater, replete and inexhaustible fullness—becomes itself doubled as emerging from the difference of the self and its native orientation to that which is ever greater.

Such movements are signified by what Desmond terms as the "open whole", wherein the irruption of porosity and difference becomes poised between the dialectical tension of the infinitude of desires and the ever-persistent, wayward temptation toward erotic closure, the "absorbing god" (DDO 34–40) of the whole, which is keyed principally in critical response to closure and self-mediation of Hegelian dialectic. Considering his early Hegelian studies, Desmond shows a rich sensitivity for the concealed workings of such dialectical closure that is immensely relevant and constructive for mysticism. The monstrosity of this 'absorbing god' regularly reemerges throughout the history of mysticism as the dialectical consummation of difference into the erotic self-mediation of the whole, from the secret of the gnostic self; the pantheistic collapse of difference; and the ascetic and quietistic abnegation of desire and likewise, the blurring of distinction between the *civitas Dei* and the *civitas terrain*. Desire, after all, is inescapably wed to a "commensurate telos with corresponding absoluteness" (DDO 35), which in the case of desire's infinitude, apart from ascribing such a telos to a repeated activity that would amount to a bad infinity of the same, an object is thereby sought. And this telos-object, as we see at various junctions of gnosticism and quietism, the absorbing god of the erotic self-mediated wholeness sufficiently lacks the plurivocal interruptions of the community and the Church as much as the "end is the utter abnegation of desire as such, no distinction being made between worthwhile and worthless desire" (DDO 35). Subsequently, as much as our desires excavate and plumb our interiority, so too do they distinguish and particularize our identities, whereas the quietistic abnegation of desires in view of the totalizing whole of the absorbing god distinctly entails the likewise abnegation of self as distinct (DDO 38).

Desmond completely reorients this familiar apophatic dilemma by approaching the inseparability of the mystery of God and the mystery of man, both of which "stops short in silence before an enigma it refuses to reduce, a silence not empty but full" (Desmond 1980, p. 25). Desmond's remark on this distinct form of philosophical silence as overdeterminate is highly suggestive in contrast with the privative silence of limits (as will be seen in Scheuer and Maréchal) that issues from such plentitudes. For Desmond, the fullness of silence to which his metaxology is responsive is characterized not by a halting of finitude yet by an approach to a limit that is fundamentally porous. Hence, the mystery of such porous limits of the open whole is not something "lamentable", but instead "evokes celebration of the mystery beyond present comprehension" (Desmond 1980, p. 32). The silent limit is thus a reckoning of our creaturliness—*ab inferioribus*—that is both humble and poor beyond privation and thus relishes in its finitude. The communicable address of this distinct, philosophical silence both engages the dialectic of presence and absence and transcends this opposition that fuels the very dynamism of desire within the metaxological. Moreover, the communicable overdeterminacy of silence and of desire are not merely analogous to one another, yet they appear to both draw upon hidden reservoirs of secretive plentitude that animate the very *commercium* between God and man, wherein *in the midst* of that which is *superior, commercium* with the '*inferioribus*' is exalted by its very being reduced to the humility of a porous between—again, not a poverty of privation and enclosure, yet the poverty of an idiocy that cannot but open onto communicability with others.

Critical Interlude: Leuven Philosophical Inside-Outsiders—Scheuer and Maréchal

Recalling Desmond characterizing his first significant foray into an explicit metaxological direction as none other than his "Augustinian odyssey, embarked on in the wake of Hegel", nearly thirty years later, Desmond revisits this earlier preferential remark and the central significance of *ab exterioribus ad interiora, ab inferioribus ad superiora*, stating:

> I felt that modern philosophy with its turn to the subject represented a version of the first move [i.e., from exterior to interior], but that the second move had become problematic, not least because the turn to the self left in equivocity the essential nature of our relation to otherness. (DDO xxii)

In this following interlude, I would like to show the literal veracity of this assertion, over and above the accuracy of its general description, which is altogether stunning, when we view the slight, yet crucial distortion of its citation by Blondel in furthering his own philosophy of immanence, this time however after the wake of Kant:

> Ab exterioribus ad interiora, *ab interioribus* ad superiora. But if, of these *three* terms which Saint Augustine indicates, one suppresses the intermediary, the bridge is broken, and one has only incommunicable entities present to each other. From objective knowledge to the reality of the subject, there is no direct route by means of theory or abstract logic. One cannot attain or define the transcendent except by the role of immanence, exteriority except by interiority. (Blondel 1906, p. 237)

Here, by this literal misquotation, Blondel neglects Augustine's '*inferioribus*', while substituting instead the interiority of immanence—the self-determinacy of the subject—who alone bridges the external and the transcendent, while keeping at bay what would otherwise fly away into the equivocal night as "only incommunicable entities" of absolutized difference. By way of sharp relief, Blondel's appeal to immanence presents a drastic difference from Desmond's *metaxological Augustinianism* by reducing the metaxological 'fourth' and its "internal overdeterminacy, preventing the exhaustive definition of each in terms of any binary opposition" (DDO xix). Instead, Blondel approaches the Augustinian itinerary by counting to 'three', with the immanent subject holding together and bridging these equivocal binaries of externality and transcendence in a self-determining manner. Herein, Augustinian interiority is strongly invoked within a milieu of philosophical immanence that initially counts to three and ends up with one, "the one initially indeterminate, now at the end, the absolutely self-determining one" (DDO xix).

The influence of Blondel is indeed complex and thoroughly resists any mere simplistic dismissal. However, appeals to such immanence would come to be readily detected in the Jesuit Scholasticate in Leuven and its own, more dialogical approach to Thomas Aquinas in view of the Kantian turn to the subject. The major figures of this philosophical Leuven school, among others, are Pierre Scheuer (1872–1957) and Joseph Maréchal (1878–1944), both of whom were in their own respects not unlike the 'outsider-insider' of William Desmond yet more so 'inside-outsiders'. Though certainly lesser known today than Maréchal, Scheuer exerted a considerable internal influence in Leuven, especially among the Jesuit scholastics in the early to mid-twentieth century. For Scheuer, the immanent interiority and rigor of metaphysics was itself never alien to 'philosophy's others', especially in its altogether openness to spiritual and mystical proclivities whereby the transcendental orientation of mind is ultimately one of *esse ad Deum* and the Platonism of participation fully realized in the truths of faith, to which philosophically we can only know negatively by way of a reverential silence. This metaphysical grounding in the identity of immanence would prove decisive indeed in shaping not only the trajectory of the latter Transcendental Thomism of Rahner and Lonergan, but furthermore, and more to our specific focus, upon the mystical itself as tethered to such thinking of identity.

Interestingly enough, in Scheuer, as in Blondel, we see the same abridged attribution to Augustine that foregoes the *inferioribus* and instead regards interiority as a bridge of transcendental affirmation and identity between thought and being. "St. Augustine has an apt phrase" Scheuer writes, "which sums up our position: *Ab exterioribus ad interiora, per interiora ad superiora*" (Scheuer 1966, p. 167). For Scheuer, Blondelian immanence is expanded upon against this abridged Augustinian formula, which *from four to three,*

> expresses the three degrees of being which are our indissoluble data. The human Ego is first exterior to itself; as Ego-object it is the body with its relations, the Ego is identified with the material element. Second movement: the Ego enters into itself and knows itself as such, as Ego. Third moment: in knowing itself, it knows immediately the necessary identity of the real and the intelligible, because the Ego itself is such an affirmation, and transcends itself. (Ibid., p. 167)

There is an amazing contrast in appeals to Augustinian interiority as either one of self-same identity and affirmation (Blondel/Scheuer) or the *inferioribus* of a porous otherness that leads both inward and outward (Desmond). For Scheuer, the metaphysical quest, from the exterior indeterminacy of material being, as both composite and related, to the interior determinacy and identity between thought and being, evinces the workings of univocity within a polarized field of sameness and difference. Metaphysics, as the first science of being *qua* being, is here regarded as a creaturely undertaking, which for man is thus rooted in the Thomistic composite of *essentia* and *esse* and thereby knowing is mediated as once sensual and rational, whereas the intuitive mindfulness of immediacy is denied as exclusively angelic. This familiar Scholastic division reverberates within the reduction of the Augustinian itinerary, from the irreducible doubleness of the fourth to the resolved singularity of a third that dialectically emerges from the dualism of creaturely knowing, mediated and immediate, man and angel alike.

A casualty of this abridged Augustinian itinerary is none other than the *diminished mystery of mediation itself*, as the irreducible *inter* from within and beyond the between loses much of its initial allure and fascination. For such mediation concerns a porosity of otherness that turns upon the *inferioribus*. Otherness is irreducible to any immanent wholeness that thereby in turn keeps open the plurality of the *inter* such that the one is inseparable to the other. Whereas in the purview of the abridged third, mediation is seen as once removed, as a stepping stone, the rung of a ladder of ascents, as composite and mixed to the purity of the immediate to which it is at once denied. Within such a configuration, there is a certain transgressive allure of limits that takes over in the cry and appeal of the immediate, heeding the unmixed and pure which swells and affixes the eros of our self-surpassing. Subsequently, the allure of immediacy as the self-transgression of limits possesses significant consequences in how we frame the mystical itself. As a creaturely venture, the *adequatio* of transcendental affirmation of being and thought, from exterior to interior and the closure of porous otherness, thus hinges upon the very *inadequatio* of erotic transcending, from the second to the third, which remains ever superior and hence, equivocally negative.

Herein we arrive at the familiarity of the apophatic in modernity, as the apophatic as *inadequatio* is principally self-referential and construed as a limit of our finite strivings. The *adequatio* of identity, the univocal determinability of thought and being in which God is inescapably affirmed—the 'proving' of God by way of transcendental affirmation—is likewise inseparable from the very 'disproving' of God, as the *inadequatio* of indeterminacy is inseparable from human affirmation of God. In other words, it is just as easy to affirm God in such a transcendental scheme as it is to disavow him. Within the transcendental affirmation of being and thought, the *adequatio* of being as equal and "coextensive with the intelligible" (ibid., p. 163) whereby God too is affirmed in thought itself holds primary importance as none other than the principle of identity itself. This abridged Augustinian itinerary roots itself in the *adequatio* of identity, as the movement from the first to the second. Whereas the *inadequatio*, from the second to the third, becomes taken up by the analogy of proportionality whereby the dissimilitude of equivocal difference haunts as its interminable shadow. Herein, the apophatic becomes itself "identical with the knowledge of the *inadequatio* of the real and finite; therefore it is a negative knowledge" (ibid., p. 168). In the erotic self-surpassing from second to third, our knowledge of God becomes inseparable from the indeterminacy of the *inadequatio* itself, "that void which remains in us, through that drive of ours towards the intelligible which, finding only the finite, is almost entirely frustrated" (ibid., p. 168). The apophatics of the limit thus become inseparable from the pursuit of determinacy within the principle of identity itself. Scheuer himself recognizes this polarity, noting that the apophatic "satisfies at one and the same time both the principle of analogy and the principle of homology" (ibid., p. 169).

The dialectics of this abridged Augustinian itinerary similarly rears its head in the transgressive eros amid the designation of the mystical itself. As an erotic transcending of opposites, between the initial *adequatio* of thought itself and the *inadequatio* of its finite strivings, a resolved mysticism of identity and unity emerges whereby the mystery of identity becomes a source of renewed wonder. Scheuer elicits this allure in his influential course notes for Metaphysics: "How does it happen that the intellect, while assimilating the objects according to *its own laws* reaches nevertheless the being *in itself* of these objects? Nay, that the objectivity of its knowledge increases with its immanence", whereby amid this progression from exterior indeterminacy to interior determinacy, the "real and the intelligible are *absolutely identical*" and that amid such self-same identity, the "Ego ... discovers himself as the active identity of the real and the intelligible, as an infinity which compromises *suo modo omnia* (everything in its own way)" (ibid., pp. 341–342). Scheuer accounts for this resolved absolute identity within a metaphysics of participation such that "it is God Himself, present at the core of our intellects ... who moves us and is the *middle term* between being and thought" (ibid., p. 170). Here, the terminus of a metaphysics of identity, twinned by a mysticism of unmediated presence, is fully unveiled as navigating the polarities of the *adequatio* and *inadequatio*, of sameness and difference, such that

> metaphysics turns out to be more than a simple system of abstract truths. It is, in our created being, that last and hidden point at which, through a distant participation, something lives of the *Thought which thinks itself*. This explains why, discouraged by the scantiness of notional concepts, every metaphysics worthy of its name endeavors to transcend them to achieve itself in the profound silence of mystical introversion. (Scheuer 1957, p. 342)

The rapturous allure of such identity and 'mystical introversion' is amplified by the direct linkage between Scheuer and Maréchal, who only a few years later in 1927 first published his highly influential *Studies in the Psychology of the Mystics*. For Maréchal, he too considers mysticism as the "crown of metaphysics" [*le couronnement de la métaphysique*] (Maréchal 1927, p. v), and in direct continuity with Blondelian immanence and the interior metaphysics of Scheuer, he recognizes the "striking analogy" between human psychology and mystical ascent that none other than follows the same, abridged Augustinianism. Maréchal assuredly recognizes that the issue of the mystical at once begs for the competencies of the philosopher and theologian alike, and yet he explicitly judges the phenomenological description of psychology as warranting less suspicion than that of the metaphysical. Thus, as a further development of the silence and 'mystical introversion' of unity beyond opposites that we find in Scheuer, in the hands of Maréchal, the mystical becomes inescapably defined within the self-referentiality of consciousness itself and the question over the immediacy of 'presence'. Maréchal, who was indeed a sympathetic reader of the mystical canon, comes to translate his own critical realism, transcendental Thomism and thinking of identity into the very core of the mystical tradition itself, defining it as the "feeling of the immediate presence of a Transcendent Being" (Maréchal 1927, p. 103). The rich hyperboles of mystical experience become instead enveloped within a thinking of identity and immediacy that becomes inescapably self-referential.

And yet, recalling our earlier discussions of the equivocities between the *adequatio* and *inadequatio*, any supposed deconstruction of this "metaphysics of presence" in favor of such a resolved apophatic is at best a redundancy. The radical *inadequatio* of Scheuer returns in Maréchal as a two-fold play between the "immediate assimilation of Being in an intuition" as well as the negative surplus of our created, "radical capacity for embracing being .... All our psychology is contained in this natural *inadequatio* of the fundamental tendency and the possible realization" (Maréchal 1927, pp. 196–197). Maréchal thus calls the *inadequatio* of equivocal difference the very analogical "connecting-link of supernatural grace in human nature" (Maréchal 1927, p. 197). This radical *inadequatio* is then immediately translated back to Thomas' *desiderium naturale* and man's obidiential potency as *esse ad Deum*, such that these natural erotic strivings become inseparable to the limits of finitude, of *esse ad inadequatio* that ultimately facilitates a reading of grace, nature and the very paradox of man that both directly influenced and anticipated de Lubac et al. and the project of *Ressourcement*.

For Maréchal, the very silence and mystical introversion resulting from the *inadequatio* between immediate transcendental affirmation and our created capacity for absolute Being is the residue of our "obscure desire [that] hurls itself against the barriers of quantity and falls powerless; it grasps of Being only an image refracted in sense perception, and all its efforts has to be limited to refining symbol" (Maréchal 1927, p. 197). The eros and apophatics of the limits of finitude, the limits of the *inadequatio* and the limits of mediation, all become reduplicated, that is, from a silence of deficiency and lack to that of the silence as a hyperbolic response, as grace itself "completes and crowns nature by transforming into an end ... what was only the *superior* and inaccessible *limit* of a radical tendency" (Maréchal 1927, p. 198). In the end, the very negotiations of *limits* retrench the very equivocities of analogy between the *adequatio* and *inadequatio*, though at the same time, by way of turning to Thomas' *desiderium naturale*, we see in figures such as Scheuer and Maréchal a clear attempt to position equivocal difference beyond philosophical and theological dualism. Such attempts similarly explain in part their renewed interest in mysticism. Herein, the mystical comes to represent the very transgression of limits of equivocal difference. Yet so long as this abridged Augustinianism remained tethered to a thinking of identity, with immanence as bridging these very equivocities from otherwise flying interminably away from one another within the autonomous ethos of modernity, the transgressions of the mystical would irresistibly become reinscribed within the dialectical affirmation of the mystical as self-mediating this whole of which God becomes immanently confined as the middle term.

To conclude this brief interlude on Scheuer and Maréchal, once more we see a forceful argument of Desmond's own assessment of modern philosophy's turn to the subject as at once following yet problematizing the Augustinian itinerary, as it "leaves in equivocity the essential nature of our relation to otherness". Regarding the Blondelian legacy of the Leuven Jesuits Scheuer and Maréchal, Desmond's reading is stunning, wherein the *adequatio* of identity inescapably finds its terminus in the equivocities of the apophatic as limit, while a mysticism of interiority and unity becomes the terminus of every metaphysics "worthy of such a name" in its interior reconciliation of these opposites and finds its theological corollary in the appeals of the immediate and unmediated mystical experience as one of interiority.

The difference that Desmond's metaxology revivifies in these respects is profoundly contrasted by the irreducible double within Augustine, which leads, as in the language of the intimate universal, not between "poles of opposition but between partners in espousal"(Desmond 2012, p. 25). In the mystical canon, appeals to interiority and immediacy are of themselves central and yet, appeals 'beyond' mediation are always hyperbolic in their own overdeterminacy such that they do not depart from forms of mediation. Such appeals rather intensify them, as ascents subsequently become descents, as is eminently seen in terms of what Ruusbroec calls the "common life" [*ghemeyne leven*], whereby such commons witness to the very flourishing of the fourth as an irreducible doubleness beyond dualism. Whereas, by way of the abridged third that steers away from the intermediation of otherness, regarding instead polarized difference as the occasion of erotic ascent and the transgression of limits, mediation becomes reduced to the novitiate and the pious many, the first rung on the ascending ladder, while appeals for greater immediacy and purity become increasingly static in their gnostic rendering of the secret among the selfsame few—a recurrence that is of itself, ever ancient, ever new.

Metaxological Mysticism: The Intimate Espousal of Analogy

This third and final section will now briefly indicate certain contours of metaxology specifically in the direction of the mystical. In doing so, let us recall Desmond's compelling intuition of mysticism's double mindfulness, that is, mindfulness of an "otherness that is right now present to one" as well as a mindfulness of "what is and what one is". Mysticism's double mindfulness of otherness intermediating both *what is* and *what one is* necessarily turns upon the very defining of our desires. The history of the Christian mystical tradition and its reception history possess a substantial wealth in this regard, which in the West largely amounts to tracing the enormous Augustinian influence on its own distinctive erotics as much as it at various times has (un)wittingly colluded with such forms of erotic selving and autonomy such that the heavenly and tyrannical forms of erotic closure become excessively blurred. Ruusbroec for one eminently displays this Augustinian influence as well as a profound suppleness in his erotics. In a pivotal passage from his masterpiece *The Spiritual Espousals*, not only does Ruusbroec synthesize the doubling of exterior-interior and inferior-superior with that of Augustinian immanence of *interior intimo meo*, but furthermore, he characterizes the desiring of this dynamic middle not simply as 'autistic', nor statically polarized, yet doubled in espousal:

Out of this unity where the spirit is united with God without intermediary, flow grace and all gifts .... Thus grace falls into us in the unity of our superior faculties and of our spirit, from which, by the power of grace, the higher faculties flow out actively in all virtues and into which same (unity) they return again in the bond of love [*minnen*] .... Now the grace of God which flows out of God is an inward impulse or prodding of the Holy Spirit, Who impels our spirit from within and stokes it towards all virtue. This grace flows from within, not from without. For God is more inwards to us than we are to ourselves, and His inward impulse, or working, within us, naturally or supernaturally, is nearer and more inner to us than our own work. And therefore God works from in us outwards [*van binnen uutweert*], and all creatures from outward inwards [*van buten inwert*]. And this is why grace and all divine gifts and God's interior speech come from within, in the unity of our spirit, not from without, in the imagination, by sensory images. (Ruusbroec 1988, b, ll. 107–108, 115–118, 128–137)

As this specific passage makes evident, Ruusbroec's writings continuously navigate both sameness and difference, however never at the expense of the rich porosity and intimacy of the idiotics. When affirming the reciprocal degrees of the *admirabile commercium* between God and the human person as the mystical tradition invariably does, accusations of pantheistic absorption are often raised—of which Desmond is all too familiar and similarly shares at times such cautious reserve—as the Parisian Chancellor Jean Gerson (1363–1429) famously charged Book Three of Ruusbroec's *Espousals*. However, Ruusbroec's writings, even when hyperbolically pushing the limits of identity and difference, never lose sight of God's evergreater otherness and dissimilitude, which far from being an ill or something to overcome is rather encountered endlessly as the central Christian mystery and the "greatest of goods", as von Balthasar acclaimed (CDF 1989, n. 14). For the strong erotics that Ruusbroec's writings evince are but a release of the asymmetrical promise of the agapeics themselves and the porosity of its plentitude, an anteriority of given superabundance that enflames an insatiable degree of indebtedness that remains impossible to reciprocate. Desires become intimately defining, as *inferioribus*, as much as their gifted plentitude, as *superiora*, exceeds self-identity by the sheer superiority of their excess.

As Desmond has repeatedly claimed, it is often in such texts that the magnitude and the intensity of the intimate universal and the need for a far greater, dynamized or 'reformed' analogy, which the metaxological responds to, becomes most evident. Otherwise, the invasive ingression of a more traditional analogy of equivocal limits in safeguarding ultimate transcendence from a reduction to erotic selving becomes so predominant and overbearing that it risks becoming a "fixed polarity", which Desmond repeatedly argues becomes nothing other than an "implicit mathematization of the univocal" (BB 212). The univocal can here be clearly seen in this static, ossified relation, as the thinking of the beyond is regarded as a clearly delineated limit, a demarcation that in fact says far less about the beyond itself and more about the constraint of the immanent self-transcendence of the creature and the allure of its transgressive drama, as seen in Scheuer and Maréchal.

Subsequently, the dynamism of Desmond's metaxology strongly contrasts the mathesis of such a static analogy of proportion, wherein the former retains the complex intermediation of the between as we have seen previously in his explicit recourse to Augustine (ISB 231–259). The double mediation of both the erotics of creaturely immanence as a self-mediation that is fundamentally open and porous and the agapeics that is itself "other-related with respect to an interplay with what is not itself" critically destabilizes the stasis and mathematical univocity of analogy specifically by way of this complex intermediation of the erotic and agapeic hyperboles of being.

Likewise, insofar as Ruusbroec regards union with God—with means, without means and without difference or distinction (Ruusbroec 1981, ll. 34–41)—as corresponding to the fullness of creaturely being, the thinking of such plurality and intermediation thus aligns him well within a certain metaxological milieu. To argue as much is to firmly counter various commentators, all of whom—and not without good reason—overwhelmingly viewed mysticism as a discourse of identity and thereby in turn regarded some of the late-medieval canonical masters, such as Ruusbroec—in addition to Eckhart, Suso and Tauler, the earlier Cistercians such as Bernard and William of St. Thierry and the Spanish Carmelite tradition, to name but the common canonical list of figures—as thoroughly dialectical in their negotiation of difference (active life); sameness (interior life) and its self-mediated whole (contemplative/super-essential). However, this dialectical portrait largely obfuscates both the strong erotic and ecstatic dimensions of the tradition, and in particular that of Ruusbroec's thought, seen especially in view of mutual indwelling that rightly characterizes him not in the least as a thinker of dualistic opposition between transcendence and immanence, but instead as a thinker of doubleness that regards relationality as superabundant and the truthfulness of its loving encounter and union as minne-love, which is seen as intrinsically double (Ruusbroec 2006, bk. 4, ll. 1687–1709), as *fully ours* and *fully God's*—a *common love*. "This minne-love that is God is common to us all and to each one in particular and (belongs) totally to those who love" (Ruusbroec 2000, bk. 2b, ll. 662–664). Secondly, such dialectical portraits are interminably wrapped up in the ever-recurring drama of gnostic quietism, autotheism and the self-mediated collapse into the totality of the whole which Ruusbroec regarded among the then currents of the Free Spirit movement as unequivocally heterodox that leads to an idol [*afgod*] of the self. And yet, in providing an antidote to this counterfeiting, never once did Ruusbroec temper his thinking by insisting upon a more cautious traditionalism absent the otherwise provocative and speculative assertions of superessential union and the ecstatic erotics of minne-love. Instead, the antidote repeatedly consisted in the very plurality of the common life, which synthesizes the otherwise traditional three ways of knowing and loving God only to the extent that this plurality is maintained, as one-in-the-other, and lived within a milieu of ecclesial service to others in the world.

COMMON IS THE COMMON LIFE: RETURNING TO THE MYSTERY OF MEDIATION

Proper mindfulness of *that which is* interminably turns upon the astounding wonder *that it is at all*, which subsequently keys us to the fragility and contingency of being and therefore, its goodness in the *to be*. Such fragility and its attendant goodness largely escapes us unaware, while the agapeic promise of giftedness in this to be is none other than ceaselessly fulfilled— *creatio continua*—by way of the excess of the ontological secret whereby otherness is given to be for itself as a continual calling out amid the silent givenness of things and others. Mindfulness of this ceaseless fulfilling beyond the inertness of simple thereness holds out the ecstatic promise that patiently ushers us toward the indeterminable absolute origin of that which is prior. That is, a leading not away from yet into the coming to be, offering but a *prayer of all things* that "go to God by way of things" (Charles 1964, p. 1) as both intimately singular and universally communicable. Such affirmation by way of its superabundant origins requires a certain 'unclogging' of the porosity, as Desmond often states, that is none other than a fruition of the *inferioribus* that restores wonder at the agapeic 'for itself' that characterizes proper mindfulness of both "what is and what one is".

However, we may likewise say that this double vision and the contemplative affirmation of the for-itself is at the same time redoubled in this double vision and is thereby startled from an otherwise restful closure of presence such that by its sheer givenness that we can never be fully at home with being (PU 19). The double vision of the metaxological affords the promise that refreshes us to the very freshest of things given, a freshness that emerges anew daily as an 'open whole' of possibility and by the dynamism that we are in, but not of the world, which intensifies and charges, rather than mistaking the *common is* from the commonplace. As Desmond writes: "But the very elemental presence of being ought to subvert every form of simplemindedness and challenge us to the highest sophistication and deepest openness. The commonness of the 'is' indicates its significance …. We have our metaxological being in this commonality; we participate in, draw on, exhibit its communicating energy" (DDO 168). Such an ecstatic commons of metaxological being—both in its lowliness by which its sheer dailyness anonymously refracts attention away from its given plentitude and in its sheer relationality as the conjoining and bridging of being in community—finds a companion and concretion in one of the most pregnant notions from Ruusbroec's corpus, namely, the *common life*.

For Ruusbroec, the common life is none other than the Brabantine's addition of a *fourth*—and thereby implicitly a tensed double to which his characteristic erotics of minne-love aptly express—to that of the traditional *triptych* within mystical literature of purgation, interior union and illumination. The fourth of Ruusbroec's common life inverts the ladder of traditional ascent to God as equally one of descent. Here, the dialectical tensions so ripe and continuous within the spiritual tradition between the *vita activa* and *vita contemplativa* arguably are not so much resolved dialectically into a final third as much as they are reaffirmed as a *continuous life* from which the plurality of the fourth releases. The going up as much as the going down, in their singular and ecclesial communal expression, are tensely held together in the common life. Such a life of participative commercium and reciprocity is of itself refreshed and renewed daily, vivified by an indebtedness that can never be repaid amid the going up into rest and enjoyment, and the going down into the suffering outpouring of self in recognition that highness cannot but persist in lowliness (Ruusbroec 2001, ll. 567–570). Hence, it is by recognizing the inexhaustibility of a prior debt of givenness that cannot be reciprocated, yet spurns one forward anew from its plenitidinous origins and plurality of responses, that one finds a unique concretion of the energy and ethos of the metaxological by way of Ruusbroec's common life. This vivifying commercium of highness persisting in lowliness in Ruusbroec's common life seeks not to appropriate and consume difference and otherness, such as an erotic quest for possession proceeds solely from lack to wholeness. However, the excessive goodness of being arises in plentitude from which the moral and the ontological are neither dualistically opposed, nor that of the singular individual from that of the community's tense mediation of difference and relation from which self-identity emerges from the varying inflections of such a commons.

From these convergences, the porous exchange of a metaxological mysticism cultivates anew the very mystery of mediation, the mystery of the open commons. Such an intimate espousal of mysticism metaxologically finessed is seen decisively in contrast to the legacy of the transcendental turn to the subject, its thinking of identity and psychological self-reference of consciousness in pursuit of a metaphysics of presence and transcendent immediacy, whereby such a particular reconstructed ethos largely degrades the very allure of mediation itself. Mediation, so construed, was something to be transgressively overcome, especially in view of 'religious experience' and the mystical tradition. Whereas the espoused intimacy of the metaphysical and the mystical that we see in Desmond is in part anchored in the Augustinian view of the fluid penetration of the theological and philosophical and thus of grace and nature such that our ways to God are neither reducible too, nor inseparable from, the abyssal depths of the human person wherein fresh appeal is made to a philosophical capacity whereby transcendence exceeds and thereby mediates diversely within life that calls upon our ability to cultivate a proper mindfulness to better reflect upon this plural mediation.

Bibliography

Blondel, Maurice. 1906. Le Point de Départ de la Recherche Philosophique. *Annales de Philosophie Chrétienne* 152: 225–250.

Charles, Pierre. 1964. *The Prayer of All Things*. New York: Herder and Herder.

Congregation of the Doctrine of the Faith. 1989. *On Some Aspects of Christian Meditation*. Vatican: Holy See.

Cooper, Patrick. 2017. The Virginal Middle: Towards a Marian Metaxology. *Medieval Mystical Theology* 25: 1–24.

Desmond, William. 1980. Augustine's Confessions: On Desire, Conversion and Reflection. *Irish Theological Quarterly* 1: 24–33.

———. 2012. Mysticism and the Intimate Universal: Philosophical Reflections on the Arnhem Mystical Sermons and Sri Aurobindo. In *Mystical Anthropology: Cross-Religious Perspectives and Interdisciplinary Reflections on the Arnhem Mystical Sermons and Sri Aurobindo*, ed. Ineke Cornet, Rob Faesen, and Martin Sebastian Kallungal, 25–44. Leuven: Peeters.

Maréchal, Joseph. 1927. *Studies in the Psychology of the Mystics*. Trans. Algar Thorold. New York: Benzinger Brothers Press.

Ruusbroec, Jan van. 1981. *Boecsken der verclaringhe*. Trans. Ph. Crowley and H. Rolfson. Tielt: Lannoo, Leiden: Brill.

———. 1988. *Die Geestelike Brulocht*. Trans. H. Rolfson. Tielt: Lannoo, Turnhout: Brepols.

———. 1991. *Vanden Blinkenden Steen*. Trans. A. Lefevere. Tielt: Lannoo, Turnhout: Brepols.

———. 2000. *Vanden XII Beghinen Text and Apparatus*. Trans. H. Rolfson. Tielt: Lannoo, Turnhout: Brepols.

———. 2001. *Spieghel der eeuwigher salicheit*. Trans. A. Lefevere. Tielt: Lannoo, Turnhout: Brepols.

———. 2006. *Van den Geesteliken Tabernakel*. Trans. H. Rolfson. Tielt: Lannoo, Turnhout: Brepols.

Scheuer, Pierre. 1957. Notes on Metaphysics. Trans. Joseph Donceel. *Cross Currents* 7: 337–346.

———. 1966. *An Interior Metaphysics: The Philosophical Synthesis of Pierre Scheuer S.J.* Trans. Daniel J. Shine S.J. Weston, MA: College Press.

PART III

Autonomy, Porosity, and Goodness

CHAPTER 9

Evil: From Phenomenology to Thought

Cyril O'Regan

William Desmond is a philosopher of enormous accomplishment who exhibits an encyclopedic grasp of the Western philosophical tradition and who has shown the ability in his celebrated trilogy of the 'Between' to keep it all in play as he charts his own unique phenomenological-metaphysical course in the wake of Hegel, who has betrayed phenomenology and discredited metaphysics, and also Hegel's postmodern tormenters content to embrace a nihilistic alternative.[1] If Desmond is a major critic of philosophical gluttony that insists on speculatively mastering the entire range and depth of the real, this should not disguise the fact that the refusal of system does not function to narrow, but rather open up multiple phenomenological-metaphysical vistas into individuals, communities, selves, desire, drive, receptivity, the nature of art, religion and philosophy, and the good, the true, and the beautiful to name but a few. If the theme of evil is just one of many in Desmond's ever-expanding oeuvre, nonetheless, here Desmond proves to be as intellectually penetrating as he is in his elaboration of the

---

[1] I have written articles on each of these major contributions to philosophy. See O'Regan (1997, 2002, 2008, 2012).

C. O'Regan (✉)
University of Notre Dame, Notre Dame, IN, USA
e-mail: Cyril.J.O'Regan.1@nd.edu

© The Author(s) 2018
D. Vanden Auweele (ed.), *William Desmond's Philosophy between Metaphysics, Religion, Ethics, and Aesthetics*,
https://doi.org/10.1007/978-3-319-98992-1_9

good and, it goes without saying, also as existentially and phenomenologically adroit as he refuses to position his phenomenology against metaphysics. Although the theme of evil recurs constantly throughout its oeuvre, as yet Desmond has not offered a monograph-sized account, nor for that matter have his interpreters felt it necessary to highlight the importance of the theme, present its outline, explore its ramifications, and discern how Desmond's views are in critical conversation with other views in the Western philosophical and theological traditions, and take on the responsibility of broadening and deepening the range of critical conversation.

The aim of this chapter is to attend in some modest way to all the above-named lacks. I propose to carry out this task in three main steps. In the first section, cutting across a wide swathe of texts from different periods of Desmond's literary production, I present (a) a *Gestalt* of Desmond's phenomenological but also metaphysical view of evil and (b) underscore Desmond's emphasis on the surd quality of evil that makes it resistant to explanation and rules out theodicy. In the second section in addition to pointing to philosophical figures and religious thinkers such as Augustine and Kant with whom Desmond is in actual discussion on the topic of evil, I develop a comparison with Paul Ricoeur, the contemporary philosopher who has offered the deepest and most ramified analysis of evil in a broadly phenomenological register which, similar to Desmond, pays as much attention to symbols and myths of evil as concepts of evil. In addition, both philosophers illustrate a high degree of openness to religion in general and a significant degree of elective affinity to Christianity without either essentially blurring the boundaries between philosophy and theology. In Section 'Principle of Reserve: Inverted Icon—Figure of Medusa,' having already underscored Desmond's tendency to approach evil sideways through literary figures in the previous section, I both thematize and supplement Desmond's reserve with regard to evil which essentially proscribes any form of tarrying with evil that might fold into obsession by proposing that the figure of Medusa haunts Desmond's discourse as the crisis and limit in focus that must be avoided should we successfully avoid becoming complicit with the evil that we would represent.

Phenomena of Evil and the Lure of Explanation

In the first section of this chapter I would like to do two different but related things. First, I would like to offer a sketch of the negative phenomena that appear within the metaxological milieu, tax it, deplete its energy, contract its joyousness, and perhaps take away its singing. Second, I would like to lay bare how Desmond, on the one hand, fully accepts that the phenomena of evil give themselves to thought and, on the other, that such phenomena resist it sufficiently that at the very least we have to give up on the lure of total explanation. The most elementary thing to say about the metaxological milieu, which is truly elemental, is that we are not in control of it: what appears is what appears, and one set of appearances are negative. From the perspective of experience, we can say that in significant respects appearances of evil are—to use the ugly Heideggerian locution—'equiprimordial' with the appearances of the good.[2] I will return to the implied caveat in due course when I speak to an implied narrative line of origin and end.

Although there is no single text of Desmond in which he provides an inventory of the phenomena of evil, and we can find instruction throughout his work, early or late, when he writes diversely of tragedy and courage, on particular philosophical figures such as Kant and Schopenhauer, or literary figures such as Shakespeare, I think on balance that we find the deepest and most ramified discussion on the phenomena of evil precisely in the text where we would expect to find it, that is, *Ethics and the Between*. Although Desmond understands his discussion of evil to be secondary with respect to his discussion of the good, importantly we are speaking of phenomena of evil rather than the phenomenon of evil. In the metaxological milieu we experience our own fragility and incoherence (EB 55) and the drift toward nothing (EB 44). This experience is not only a grasp of our mortality and deep vulnerability, but a deeper sense that our existence is without why, something grasped existentially by Augustine and expressed with slightly different accents in modern thought in Kierkegaard and Heidegger. For Desmond, the experience of evil certainly includes what happenings turn out to be unpropitious for human beings, whether these experiences are enveloped in chance or fate, but, as we might expect in a text which has 'ethics' in the title, human failure and evil intention are

---

[2] The locution of 'equiprimordial' (*gleichursprünglich*) is a key term of Heidegger's existential analysis of Dasein in *Sein und Zeit* (1927).

relatively prominent. There is the tendency toward construction and fabrication (EB 55), systemic displays of disordered forms of erotic sovereignty (EB 307 and 311) that run the gamut from lack of solicitude toward the other, to sheer malice and will to destruction, the perception of constitutive existential tension and dividedness (EB 296), and within the ligatures of the division at the root of the self-temptation as a presentiment of one's succumbing to what one would and presumably could avoid (EB 282–285).

This is hardly a full catalogue of human vulnerability and morally distorted agency provided by *Ethics and the Between*, not to mention other texts. Elsewhere death and physical suffering parse vulnerability, and throughout his oeuvre Desmond puts literature to work as a phenomenological resource to get at the appearances of jealousy (Othello), hatred or malice (Iago), nihilism (Iago, and Dostoyevsky's 'underground man'), and overweening ambition (many characters in Greek tragedy and also Lady Macbeth). Arguably, Desmond's underscoring of the systemic negative phenomenon of idolatry represents his homage to Platonic tradition, such modern versions of it laid out by Weil and Murdoch as well as the texts of the historical Plato.[3] The function of the idol is to project transcendence only insofar as it contributes to individual or communal self-affirmation and self-enhancement. The idol tends toward its reproduction and protects its generator or recycler against the inconvenience of testing the truth of their assumptions. In addition, the function of the idol is to neutralize the claim of the other beforehand by not recognizing her. The idol both reflects and induces a form of studied ignorance or regime of inattention. Still, even if there is a significant recall of Platonism in Desmond, when it comes to the appearances of evil and some of its more basic structures, it would be a mistake to think that this is the sole or perhaps even the dominant figuration.

What suggests that Platonism provides an important language of response to human evil, but neither the sole nor constitutive response, is Desmond's reflections in *Ethics and the Between* on 'sovereignty.' Sovereignty is both an old-fashioned word in that it is common to both Christian and legal thought, and suggests both negative and positive

---

[3] See O'Regan (2002) in which I articulate the relationship between the highly situated and enfleshed Platonism of Simone Weil and Iris Murdoch and the particular configuration to be found in Desmond's *Ethics and the Between*.

freedom, that is, freedom from and freedom to.[4] In the case of Christianity, sovereignty is a kind of transferred asset from the divine to human being who is commanded to exercise its gifts of intelligence and judgment responsibly and be mindful of its creatureliness. In the case of legal thought, sovereignty is applied to a corporate rather than individual subject. Sovereignty is supposed to enjoy respectful recognition from other corporate entities and perhaps also enjoin certain privileges vis-à-vis them. In both cases will, at the very least, seems to be as pertinent as reason. Of course, sovereignty is also a concept that circulates within postmodern discourses. If it is implied in Nietzsche, it is elevated in Bataille,[5] who in turn brings the tradition of Sade into the twentieth century, recycled in Agamben,[6] who has Carl Schmitt as a precursor. Here the voluntarist calibration is elevated. The best way to think of Desmond's excurses on 'erotic sovereignty' is to think of him bringing to our attention the tendency toward destructive self-assertion over others that is a common feature of human selving, which in turn should force us to think long and hard about the givenness of the other as other and our would-be Levinasian obsession with the other as other and our persecution by her.[7] If the latter is a given, then it necessarily must be archeological: if we experience the other as the singular categorical imperative, it is sometimes only in and through the haze of the other's construction and violation. Desmond provides his readers with good reasons that the general register of erotic sovereignty is Augustinian, even if not exclusively so. Clues are provided in his account of tension and division as constitutive of the self and of the tendency of human beings to construct and fabulate. But the clincher with regard to the Augustinian nature of the register is the violence always near to the surface of sovereignty. *Libido dominandi* is at its very heart. If not intrinsically willfully violent, on Desmond's account, erotic sovereignty exhibits a tendency to be so.

Now, at the very beginning of this section when I announced the 'equiprimordiality' of the phenomena of good and evil, I also suggested a caveat. Here it is: negative phenomena are ambiguously primary and sec-

---

[4] Here I recall Isaiah Berlin's famous distinction in his essay 'Two Concepts of Liberty,' originally published as a pamphlet by Clarendon Press in 1958 and included in Berlin (1969).

[5] For convenient English access to Bataille's reflection on sovereignty, see Bataille (1993).

[6] For Giorgio Agamben on the notion of sovereignty with a particularly deep engagement with the political philosophy and 'theology' of Carl Schmitt, see Agamben (1998, 2005, 2011).

[7] See Levinas (1969, 1981).

ondary. They are at once phenomena of interruption and thus endemic to the metaxological field. Yet, they might just as easily be cast as interruptive phenomena, which suggests a kind of secondness. I submit, then, that what Desmond attempts to do in *Ethics and the Between* and elsewhere is precisely to suggest a kind of secondness in the metaxological sphere despite the fact that in many respects the phenomena of evil are given just as the phenomena of the good are given. Now faithfulness to the originating experiences demands that one cannot have recourse to the kinds of metaphysical explanation of secondness provided by the Platonic tradition and taken up into Christianity: logically and ontologically evil always is inscribed in a hierarchy in which it is invariably second.[8] With this kind of explanation not a viable option, 'secondness' will necessarily be somewhat more phenomenological and more spectral, since at first blush the phenomena of evil give themselves to be every bit as primary as the phenomena of the good, care, solicitude, happy dependence, and so on. This spectrality deserves a far more detailed treatment than what I can provide here. Perhaps it might be sufficient to draw attention to one detail in Desmond's account of erotic sovereignty. Desmond is convinced that human beings reveal themselves as complex unities of agency and passion, exercise of will and vulnerability, or, putting it in the language of human unity provided by Leibniz, complex unities of *conatus essendi* and *passio essendi*.[9] Unlike Kant and Levinas, Desmond does not think that we are justified in excoriating the energy or drive of the self as given. In harmony

---

[8] While Desmond has profound sympathies with the classical philosophical tradition, given the phenomenological register of his metaphysical thought, he does not automatically buy into received notions in Catholic philosophy such as analogy or for that matter evil as the privation of being. These notions have to pass the phenomenological test. In *Being and the Between*, Desmond worried about the abstractness of the traditional doctrine of analogy and wondered whether in the last instance it sufficiently emphasized difference. In this sense metaxology is the counter. One could, however, see his recent work as evincing a greater hospitality to analogy. Similarly, although Desmond is shy about adopting a privatio boni view of evil for fear that the seriousness of evil is diluted, this does not mean that he would not be open to it as long as the metaphysics would not uncouple from the experience of evil in which the phenomenon is all too real.

[9] Desmond is in line with much of modern philosophy and theology in rejecting theodicy as a properly philosophical aspiration. While this rejection most certainly applies to Leibniz's *Theodicy* (1710), which has commonly come to be regarded as theodicy's laughable limit, this does not apply to Leibniz's metaphysics. Desmond's articulation of *conatus essendi* and *passio essendi* certainly recalls the metaphysics elaborated in Leibniz's *Monadology* (1714) and his earlier *Discourse on Metaphysics* (1686).

with the passion of the self, energy and drive can be affirmed. He underscores their mutual correction and enhancement: the passion for existence modifies the potential for aggression of the *conatus essendi*, just as *conatus essendi* gives energy and strength to the *passio essendi*. If expressions of good are to be powerful, then the energy of desire will have been harnessed, and if a good person is to be formed, then the *passio essendi* will have to be supplemented by energy and power. While Desmond hardly depends on precedent to make this point, it is interesting that two post-Leibnizians, Schelling and Nietzsche, spent considerable time making the point.[10] Now, if the *conatus essendi* is not intrinsically violent, it becomes so when separated from its complement that keeps it in check. Moral evil, then, comes into being when the desire for self-affirmation and self-enhancement separates from the givenness of the self and its porosity with respect to other selves and the world and comes to behave like a free radical. The relevant contrast thus is between a good that is an integral part of action and passion, and a fragment that terrorizes and rends the metaxological milieu. If in some sense the phenomena of evil are on the same phenomenal plane as the phenomena of the good, in another sense, there are at least penumbral hints of splitting and thus secondness. Of course, it should be pointed out, and here the analogy with Schelling in particular is relevant, Desmond thinks of good in two different ways: on the one hand, the elemental good of 'to be' in which the self has precipitated out the elemental field of becoming and lives in a certain innocence, and, on the other, a good that signals recognition of the phenomena of evil and one's capacity for complicity and repetition and a choice for good.

With this we turn to the second of my two tasks in the first section of the chapter that is the correlative of the first. I am speaking here of Desmond's insistence that we tarry with the phenomena of evil as long as possible and resist acquiescence to the lure of explanation. Although Desmond is an anti-theodicy thinker, this is not to say that theodicy is a focal subject of analysis. In his wide-ranging discourse of evil, there is no recourse to Bayle, Voltaire, or Hume. Nor are there any vatic pronouncements on the obscenity of theodicy, as occur fairly regularly in current philosophy of religion.[11] Nonetheless, it is obvious from his very earliest

---

[10] Schelling's famous *Freiheit* essay (1809) is illustrative here. For a recent translation, see Schelling (2007).

[11] Various forms of the 'moral obscenity' provided by Voltaire are offered in the more recent philosophical and theological literature that focuses on theodicy. Representative examples include Tilley (2000) and Pinnock (2002).

work that theodicy emerges as a problem because of the tendency of the experiencer of evil to contain the phenomena of evil that emerge within and to some extent rend the metaxological milieu. The primary form of containment that Desmond attends to is discursive, but in principle the containment might also take the form of ritual action or political response, and it is, arguably, the case that the third form of containment is just now appearing on the horizon of Desmond's work (see IU), although much of his work and all of his appreciation for Plato and Augustine have prepared for it. In terms of discursive response, Desmond is aware that the discourses of art, religion, and philosophy can all respond to the provocation of the phenomena of evil by enacting a program of containment in which the challenge of evil to meaning, truth, and goodness is met or at least significantly alleviated. *Art and the Absolute: A study of Hegel's Aesthetics* is an early text that provides a complex response, since aesthetic theory in Hegel is an elaboration of the principles of art within a governing philosophical matrix. In his chapter, 'Aesthetic Theodicy and the Transfiguration of the Ugly' (AA 150–159), Desmond challenges Hegel's preferred pattern of the concordance of discordance and concordance in which discordance is resolved. The tears in the fabric of sense are always stitched over in and through an aesthetic that reconciles opposites. This is perhaps clearest in Hegel's treatment of Greek tragedy. Despite the fact that Hegel chooses *Antigone*, in which there is irreconcilable conflict between the imperatives of family and state, he insists on tragedy as the epitome of all art and as providing a pattern of resolution that both religion and philosophy can imitate and philosophy can justify. Desmond's resistance to the symbolic and narrative domestication of the phenomenon of evil as elaborated in Hegel recalls both Adorno and Derrida without, however, giving credence to the negative dialectics of the former or the exaltation of the sublime of the other in which irresolution rules.[12]

---

[12] Adorno and Derrida are advocates of the postmodern sublime which radicalizes Kant's reflection. One can also certainly add Jean-Luc Nancy to the list. Among other things the sublime both establishes and is signaled by a separation between sign and signified. After Edward Jabès Derrida can associate this disconnection with Judaism and counterpose Judaism to the Western philosophical tradition with which Christianity is broadly and deeply imbricated. See Derrida (1978, 64–78, 1990). Originally published in French in 1974 this text is a takedown of Hegel's speculative system. See O'Regan (2013, 383–425). Looking for tropes that expose both the ontotheological and logocentric nature of the Western tradi-

As Desmond's work unfolds it gains amplitude regarding its resistance to over-explanation of the phenomena of evil while also adding nuance. In a very important chapter in *God and the Between* (GB Chap. 11) Desmond shows that all forms of pantheism, ancient or modern, represent attempts to elevate the universal at the cost of what is contingent, singular, and most relevantly here interruptive. While there is no listing of suspects, one can suppose that certain forms of Platonism, Christian or otherwise, would come under the general interdiction, as would certain forms of Romantic and Idealist thought, while it would not be clear whether so-called current panentheistic forms of Christian thought would be provided a clean bill of health. There is no intimation of whether Spinoza would come under the condemnation, although in any event the identity of Spinoza would have to be decided: either the naturalist that the eighteenth century made him out to be or the 'refined pantheist' he was assumed to be in German letters from Lessing on. Needless to say, judgment one way or the other is not essential to Desmond's claim that pantheism, whether in a more nearly religious or philosophical modality, is a discourse of containment. Nonetheless, in his other text on Hegel, *Hegel's God* (HG 143), Desmond does seem to suggest that Spinoza's pantheistic metaphysics is a discourse of containment. And Desmond essentially doubles down on German Romantic and Idealist insistence that Spinoza's discourse is a non-dialectical analogue of their more dialectical, more historical holistic discourse. Of course, Hegel's dialectical ontology represents the limit in explanatory ambition to comprehend evil. In his outstanding chapter on Hegelian theodicy (HG Chap. 6), Desmond focuses on the washing out of singularity in Hegel's discourse, laments the lack of attention to the victims of history who cry out against a mere historical judgment, and condemns the substitution for the agapeic Christian God of a God of erotic becoming for whom history is the arena of divine self-definition. Desmond grasps well that in Hegel the appearance of evil is, from a metaphysical point of view, a *felix culpa* that guarantees that the end exceeds origin. In Desmond's telling reading of Hegel's account of the Fall story in *Lectures on the Philosophy of Religion* and in his *Zusatz* to #24 of the *Encyclopaedia of Philosophical Sciences* (HG 158), unenlightened egoism and the turn to objectification are dialectically positive insofar as in the long run they serve as vehicles toward total knowing, mastering the earth,

---

tion, Derrida also types the sublime as Egyptian. See his famous essay—again directed at Hegel—Derrida (1982, 69–108).

and creating community. Yes, there will be a price to be paid. Desmond sees the relationship between his reading of Hegel and that of Bataille,[13] whose reflection on *Aufhebung* in Hegel operates in terms of the metaphor of labor and the yielding of profit. However, although Desmond denies what Bataille denies, he does not affirm what Bataille affirms. He does not yield to Bataille's an-economic alternative of excess, which positively comes to involve ecstatic, unknowing forms of knowledge within the alternate matrix of sovereignty and transgression. Desmond believes in innocence, in childlikeness which involves a return move to the plenitude of origin, and does not think that the participation so desired is to be granted by maddening logic and escape from mere knowledge verified only through outrage. This is at once the road of Sade and Nietzsche. By the same token, Desmond does not refuse Derrida's diagnosis of Hegel's discourse as being constitutively theodicy oriented in nature, and rightly so since the main contours of Derrida's critique are set down by Bataille. In his Hegel book he takes advantage in the way that Derrida does in *Glas* of Hegel's organic metaphors,[14] especially the alimentary. In Hegel's case singularity and evil are not appearances that refuse assimilation; rather, they are the conditions of assimilation's operation. In Hegelian logic, precisely as a theo-onto-logic, nothing can resist the assimilating power of Spirit except nothing which cannot make an appearance.

As is obvious from the subtitle of his second Hegel book, Desmond does not think that Hegelian thought presents an adequate translation of the rendering in Christian symbols and narrative of the emergence and perduring of the appearances of evil. It is not simply that there is considerable distortion. It is also the case that the contingency of the emergence of evil as well as the gratuity of origin and end, which are both fundament to the sense of the Christian story, are erased (HG 158). Christianity is provoked by evil and responds to it in thought, liturgy, and in church, while recognizing all the time its contingency as well as its power. While it is true that he demonstrates Derrida's adage that it is extraordinarily difficult for

---

[13] In addition to narrating the history of transgression and using his novels as explorations of transgression that uncover sovereign subjectivity, Bataille was a relentless critic of Hegelian dialectic which not only issued in the closed circuit of self-knowledge, but also justified itself in that all negation yielded a profit. With respect to the former, see Bataille (2001). With respect to the economy (of sacrifice), see Bataille (1989).

[14] The generalization of the image of digestion from its local site in Hegel's *Philosophy of Nature* to characterize dialectic as such is prominent in *Glas*.

a philosopher not to keep returning to Hegel,[15] Desmond is not Hegel obsessed. There are forms of religious thought in the Western tradition not so philosophically adroit as Hegelianism that also suggest a solution to the 'nightmare' of embodiment, time, and history. As he describes the phenomenon in *God and the Between*, Gnosticism constitutes an important exemplar of a mentality that makes knowledge itself crucial for deliverance (GB Chap. 10),[16] even if the range of deliverance is considerably more restricted in scope than that advanced by Hegel by insisting on disembodied existence. Moreover, Desmond's commitment to embodiment is such that it is not evident that he can entirely avoid charting a distance between his own thought and a certain Plato who figured knowledge and memory sufficient for liberation from accident, opinion or ideology, and the brutality of power.

A second objection to Gnosticism can serve as a bridge to qualms expressed by Desmond regarding the explanatory quotients in other modern discourses that intentionally are anti-theodicy in form. In his wonderful chapter on Gnosticism in *God and the Between*, it is not only Gnostic therapy that is an object of critique, but the suggestion of a quasi-demonic origin of a material temporal world that will show only evidence of necessity and none of providence. Here contingency is removed and the enigma mastered. One might say that Desmond's response here is patterned after Augustine's response to Manichaeism which holds an analogous view of the necessity of the phenomena of evil and the peculiar consolations provided to the knowing subject that there is no way out or only impossible ways out. How to determine Nietzsche's aesthetic philosophy? Granted its consistently anti-rationalist complexion, the question arises—is this sufficient to guarantee that his discourse is anti-theodicy? Desmond's reflection on Nietzsche throughout his oeuvre forces the question, even if he does not explicitly answer it. Perhaps, given Nietzsche's styles, his contradictions, and his double takes, it is difficult to construct a univocal answer. But if life is the seething cauldron depicted in *The Birth of Tragedy* that goes under the figure of Dionysus, then the world is locked in a necessity that the genuine thinker must accept and recognize. If the appearances of evil are questionable, they are only notionally so, since, as is the case in Spinoza, and perhaps also in Heraclitus, whose ontological agonism

---

[15] For Derrida's avowal of the inescapability of Hegel, see Derrida (1981, 43–44).
[16] I have discussed this particular chapter which is explicitly on ancient Gnosticism as well as modern candidates for Gnostic ascription in O'Regan (2017, 239–268).

Nietzsche venerates, the answer precedes the question. Nietzsche's aesthetic philosophy then, which is absolutely disposed against theodicy explanations thrown up by the Western tradition, whether Platonic, Christian, or modern bourgeois, can be understood to be a theodicy discourse by other means.

THE RICOEURIAN TEMPLATE

While the title of the chapter may accidentally recall Heidegger (Richardson 1963), it is calculated to evoke Paul Ricoeur, whose reflections on evil begin with the phenomenon or phenomena of evil as these are embedded in symbols and narratives and invite—if not compel—reflection. Without suggesting that Desmond's exploration of the phenomena of evil or his analyses of the symbols and narratives of evil is anywhere near as focused and systematic, and again without implying that in his reflections and analyses Desmond is genetically dependent on Ricoeur, it is evident that there is a significant measure of repetition on both the substantive and methodological levels. In texts such as *The Symbolism of Evil* and *Fallible Man*, Ricoeur sets the essential terms of an analysis of evil in a phenomenological register (Ricoeur 1969, 1986). Arguably, the three most important of these are (a) the complexity and ambiguity in the experience of evil, (b) plurality in the experience of evil, and (c) the reference always implied in the symbols and narratives of evil to evil's overcoming.

The experience of evil is complex in that it concerns the origin as well as the nature of evil, and ambiguous in that the phenomenon of evil does not give itself to univocal identification. Evil gives itself as simply being the order of things, or origin as simply being there from the foundation of the world, thus as *moira* or fate; or evil gives itself as divinely directed envy of mortals who are presumptuously divine in their ambition. Or again as the upsurge of chaos that can never be reduced to naught. Or evil gives itself as arising from finite and vulnerable human being who is the chiasmus between the voluntary and the involuntary.[17] As with origin, nature is not without a fundamental measure of ambiguity. Evil gives itself as chance

---

[17] *The Symbolism of Evil* is basically divided into two parts. The first deals with the different forms of experience indicated in the symbols of 'defilement,' 'sin,' and 'guilt.' The second deals with the four main narratives or myths of evil, in order (a) the drama of creation (theogonic account); (b) the myth of the jealous God; (c) Genesis Adamic myth; (d) myth of the fall of the soul; they are the focus of the second part of the text.

that makes human intention incoherent, as affliction, that is, a reduction of the vulnerable human subject to some form of abjection or alternatively as uncontrolled and violent self-insistence. As well as being complex and ambiguous, the experience of evil is plural. This is already suggested by the complexity in the experience of evil. Ricoeur speaks eloquently of temptation,[18] the phenomena of sin and guilt,[19] the struggle within the self not so much of body and soul, but of fundamental orientation best captured, perhaps, in Paul and annotated in the Western tradition of reflective thought by Augustine and Pascal,[20] and finally in and as the enigmas of divine forces and cosmic misrule. Third, for Ricoeur every archeology of evil implies an eschatology in which the specific phenomenon or phenomena of evil are overcome. Usually, but not always, this means that human beings either revert back to or move forward to their normative state in which the negative features of individual and corporate human existence are done away with, harmony achieved with the cosmos, and reconciliation achieved with non-human forces beyond human control.

Now, as Ricoeur outlines the matrices of a phenomenological account of evil he sets very definite strictures regarding the conceptualization of evil. First, it is no accident that the phenomena of evil are mediated primarily through symbols and narratives rather than concepts, even if there has been much conceptualization of evil in the Western philosophical tradition from Plato to Hegel, Nietzsche, and Heidegger. The appeal of symbols and narratives is obvious: relative to concepts, symbols and narratives under-interpret rather than over-interpret the phenomena of evil, thereby being more faithful to the originating experiences and more responsive to

---

[18] When contrasted with Hegel's reductive account of the Fall of Adam, Ricoeur's account in 1969, 232–278 tarries with the text. A particular result of this is an analysis of temptation of Adam by the serpent (252–260), which is a detailing of the phenomenon which centrally involves incentives for transgression coming at once from inside and outside the self. Of course, unlike Hegel, Ricoeur thinks that the temptation is destructive to the self.

[19] It should be noted that while in *The Symbolism of Evil* Ricoeur generally keeps philosophers and theologians out of the picture, when it comes to the fall or what he calls the 'ethical view' of evil, he does not fail to notice, on the one hand, Saint Paul (1969, 332–335), and Augustine (83, 84, 89, 90, 91), on the other.

[20] Augustine and Pascal are two major exemplars of the existential rather than ontological duality of the self that Ricoeur thinks is phenomenologically verifiable and at the same time the properly biblical view. While this contrast was not a theme in *The Symbolism of Evil*, it is implied in the contrast between the Adamic myth and Orphic myth of the fall of the soul. If Plato is the second-order philosophical reflector of the latter, Augustine is the second-order reflector of the former.

the irreducible density, complexity, and ambiguity of the phenomena of evil and their enigmatic corona. Yes, 'the symbol gives rise to thought,'[21] yet equally it continues to exceed the thought it calls forth. And, as is well known, for Ricoeur the narratives of evil cannot be exhaustively translated into a conceptual idiom. Just as with regard to individual symbols and nexuses of symbols, narratives of evil invite interpretation, indeed, multiple interpretations, and it is presumed no final interpretation. No conceptualization is likely to be fully adequate to the phenomena and derivatively to their symbolic and narrative expressions, since while conceptualizations bring increased clarity and focus on the phenomena of evil, they also reduce the measure of complexity, ambiguity, plurality, and self-involvement evident at the symbolic and narrative level. Second, and relatedly, Ricoeur's phenomenological program is consistently anti-theodicy in its fundamental orientation. Attempts to rationalize the phenomenon of evil by appeal to the aesthetic contrast of dark and light—a canard generated in Neoplatonism, taken up by Augustine, and ready at hand in the bouquet of arguments in modern attempts to defend the accused divine— are dismissed. So also are dialectical accounts of evil, as well as other non-dialectical views of evil such as the metaphysical view of the best of possible worlds in which fault is aligned with the finitude of creation.

Third, an associated feature of his recurrence to symbol and narrative when it comes to registering the phenomena of evil is Ricoeur's general elevation of religion vis-à-vis philosophy. With regard to the symbolizations and narratives of evil in religions, Ricoeur lacks the range of the great phenomenologist of religion Mercea Eliade: one will not find in Ricoeur an analogue of Eliade's account of the upsurge of evil present in the myth of the aborigines in Australia, the accounts of shamans in Siberia, or that of the native-American Indians of the Plains. Nor do we have accounts of the Meso-American myths of evil of either the Incas and Aztecs and the peoples they displaced, nor again accounts of Asian world religions. Yet one can find in Ricoeur's discussions of the symbols and narratives of evil of the ancient Near East, Greek mystery religions such as Orphism and Pythagoreanism, as well, of course, of Judaism and Christianity.[22] Philosophically tinted religions such as Gnosticism and Manichaeism, and

---

[21] This phrase is nothing less than the guiding principle of Ricoeur's interpretation of evil in *The Symbolism of Evil*.

[22] For explicit connections between the Orphic myth of the fall of the soul and subsequent Platonic and Neoplatonic philosophy, see Ricoeur (1969, 279–281, 286 and 289).

religiously inflected forms of philosophy such as Neoplatonism (Ricoeur 1979a, 264–286), also come in for attention, even if much of the attention is somewhat negative, since the etiological quotient is deemed to be too dominant. Fourth, and finally, Christianity is the religion that is privileged by Ricoeur. It is a matter of fundamental importance to Ricoeur how its symbols and narratives in general are interpreted and how its symbols and narratives of evil and its overcoming are interpreted in particular. In terms of reception, the Patristic connoisseur of evil, that is, Augustine, is a prominent focus. Throughout Ricoeur's work there is a complicated to and fro between embrace and rejection. Embraced is Augustine's reading of the Fall story as the exercise of a fundamental option that has no ground, but which admits of being characterized relationally by rebellion and offense, psychologically as pride, and consequentially as alienation.[23] Refused is an Augustine who repeats the aesthetic theodicy of Platonism, as well as an Augustine whose dark eschatology in which the emphasis falls on damnation as a default. Ricoeur sides with Julian, Augustine's Pelagian adversary, who characterizes Augustine's eschatology as Manichaean,[24] thus the return of the repressed after his discovery of the Bible and his appropriation of Neoplatonic philosophy as a means to critique Manichaean mythological mystification.

I want to suggest that in his phenomenological account of the phenomena of evil at the level of both substance and method, Desmond operates broadly speaking within the parameters laid down by Ricoeur. With an eye turned toward the material presented in Section 'Phenomena of Evil and the Lure of Explanation,' it seems safe to say that for Desmond the appearances of evil are complex, ambiguous, and plural and that no less than for Ricoeur imagined ends of evil are invariably tied to the symbols and narratives of the origin of evil. Moreover, there is also considerable overlap when it comes to details. The overlap in terms of method is—if anything—more striking. Desmond is a great believer in the irreducibility of symbol and

---

[23] Despite reservations, Ricoeur does think that historically Augustine contributed significantly to the 'ethical' or freedom view of the origin of evil. He makes this clear in his essay on 'Original Sin' but also provides the basis of a cure from a literalization of symbols in Ricoeur (1979b, 287–314).

[24] On the basis of his own reading rather than a thorough grounding in the secondary literature, Ricoeur suggests that in his anti-Pelagian texts Augustine tends to construct or reconstruct a form of the Manichaean dualism that he had repented of almost 30 years earlier. This is not an uncommon accusation against Augustine made in the secondary literature and first made by his Pelagian opponent, Julian of Eclanum.

narrative to concept and is open eyed regarding the danger of the originating experiences becoming lost in translation and hostage to the impossible claim of total explanation. Desmond also favors religion over philosophy when it comes to preserving the grain and texture of the phenomena of evil and in turns favors Judaism and Christianity over other major world religions and over all other philosophical religions and religious philosophies. Even if the choice for Christianity in Desmond's work occurs largely out of sight, it seems likely that were Desmond asked to supply warrants, he would argue that it is Christianity that best uncovers the tensional constitution of human being that serves as the background for the experiences of evil being acquiesced in or willed. On the methodological side, Augustine can be regarded as a quintessential Christian figure to the degree to which his interpretations of the Christian symbols of evil and the enframing narrative do not leave behind the precipitating experiences.

Needless to say, neither at the level of substance nor method is Desmond's repetition of Ricoeur exact. Beginning with departures in terms of substance, I would like to draw attention to four in particular. (a) Relative to Ricoeur in Desmond's work the tension within the self, constitutive of self, is more hyperbolic. Although both Ricoeur and Desmond advance Pascal as an important thinker of the middle, it is only Desmond who is prepared to borrow the language of 'monster,' even if this language of self is more proximally recycled through Dostoyevsky's reflection on the doubleness and contradiction at the core of the self. (b) Of the two thinkers Desmond is the more focused on the nature rather than origin of evil. He is much less reluctant to produce malice as an appearance of evil, more eager to expose the tragic knots between persons, and less inclined to admit that temptation is only a psychic state. Desmond seems to allow with Ricoeur the structural ambiguity in representing temptation between interiority and exteriority,[25] but is more like Dostoyevsky in keeping the persona of the tempter in play. (c) Desmond is more given to figurations of evil: not only Adam, Eve, the serpent, and Job but also Iago, Lady Macbeth, Othello, and the correlative demonic figures in Dostoyevsky's hall of mirrors. For Desmond, figuration helps us to pick out forms of evil that otherwise would go unnoticed, which picking out in turn allows us to see more perspicuously the various shapes of the end. (d) Finally, Desmond

---

[25] For the phenomenological analysis of the tempting of Adam, see Ricoeur (1969, 252–260).

not only more forcefully insists on the secondness of the phenomena of evil, he essentially performs this secondness not only by pluralizing and ramifying it into phenomena but also—and essentially—by providing the thickest possible account of human being in the middle in which self-insistence is balanced by porosity with others, and self-determination and *conatus essendi* are offset by vulnerability and *passio essendi*. In general, in his account of the emergence of evil from the finite subject, Ricoeur seems to function more or less in the manner of the Kant of *Religion within the Boundaries of Reason Alone*[26]: both the character and the field of innocent humanity before the appearance of evil are presupposed rather than thickly illustrated. Desmond's genius goes in the opposite direction: the goodness of 'to be' is elemental, and a sphere of enjoyment and innocence, of which Kant, so focused on knowledge and responsibility, has no inkling, is rendered thickly throughout his trilogy, but with special force in *Ethics and the Between*.

Nor is there anything like a pure repetition of Ricoeur's dealing with evil at the formal or methodological level. For one thing, while in the movement from experience to thought Desmond insists, as Ricoeur does, on epistemic reserve, there is a noticeably different accent. While both can approve the 'dialectical' argumentative Job, unlike Kant from whom Ricoeur borrows his particular inflection of Job,[27] Desmond's Job has not been wrung through the epistemological strainer. Desmond points rather to an ethos of reserve that serves as the horizon for the symbolization, narratization, and figuration of evil. For another thing, Desmond elevates literary symbolization, narratization, and figuration of evil far beyond what they are granted in Ricoeur's discursive economy. If he privileges Greek tragedy, Sophocles in particular, Shakespeare, and Dostoyevsky, he refers to many others. Moreover, the openness to the deliverances of literature with respect to the phenomena of evil suggests the prospects for significant expansion. Perhaps more Dante but also Bernanos and Gide who give very different accounts of the violation of innocence.[28] Perhaps

---

[26] For a good English translation of this text, see Kant (1996, 41–215).

[27] Ricoeur makes an appeal to Job as a block against complete explanation of evil as early as *The Symbolism of Evil* (Ricoeur 1969, 314 ff.). Before Ricoeur Kant had used the figure of Job as a refutation not only of all actual but all possible theodicies. See his famous essay 'On the Miscarriage of All Philosophical Trials in Theodicy,' in Kant (1996, 19–31). For Ricoeur, see Ricoeur (1995, 249–261).

[28] Georges Bernanos and André Gide come at good and evil from very different points of view. Gide tends to think that 'good' is a mere conventional descriptor and that true human

adding to Dostoyevsky, other Russians such as the poet Anna Akhmatova and the novelist Alexander Solzhenitsyn. Perhaps adding William Golding, maybe the Irish novelist John Banville.

These are but two of the more important differences on the level of method. There are others. Christianity is favored by both religiously oriented philosophers, but there are salient differences with regard to the content and level of depiction of the end of evil and the healing that might take place in the between given the appearance of evil. With regard to the former, Desmond's protology suggests a far richer profile of what the end might look like in terms of converted selves, genuine community, and non-expropriative relations to the physical world. In contrast, when it comes to both the lived world that is ruptured by evil and the reintegrated world that is its end, Ricoeur tends to be more or less stipulative. Desmond is far more declarative about the prospects of healing, at once suggesting that the original milieu is not so spoiled as not to be in some respects a vehicle of the good—the hyperbolic good—and the generosity of reality granted at the foundation of the world. And finally, there are subtle but manifest differences when it comes to the interpretation of Augustine. Desmond is not quite as willing as Ricoeur to dismiss as retrograde any and all relation of Augustine to Platonism. For Desmond, both Weil and Murdoch have shown the genius of Platonism when it comes to unmasking inattentiveness and the complacency of insistence as two major forms of evil, which in turn are conditions of the possibility of the decay of community. In addition, while Desmond would grant Ricoeur's right to question certain elements in Augustine's reflection on evil, for example, his recurrence to an aesthetic theodicy, there are also real opportunities that he ignores. Ricoeur's ethical bias gets in the way of being instructed by an Augustine who embraces beauty as more fundamental than ugliness as well as being a possible source of healing. And Desmond is far more alive to the doxological Augustine who recites and comments on the Psalms as he gives glory back to God in gratitude which is the normative stance of the creature and who only in this modality of praise and gratitude is the glory of God.

---

development demands flouting convention. Transgression of value norms is a good that completes the self and refines the consciousness. One may consider *L'Immoraliste* (1902) as both an example and a manifesto of this attitude in which the innocent are merely ignorant. In contrast, Bernanos' world, whether it is the country priest Joan of Arc or other heroines under the charge of a delinquent cleric or lay, ratifies innocence and shows the depths of malice in the attempt to corrupt it.

Principle of Reserve: Inverted Icon—Figure of Medusa

In Desmond's oeuvre, reserve with regard to evil is exhibited—even produced—by two strategies: first, by a refusal to be loquacious or obsessive about the phenomenon of evil which, as we have seen, is really more nearly a compact or cluster of phenomena; second, by what Desmond actually says about evil, including its plurality of forms, its secondness regarding the truly primitive given of to be and the good of to be, as well as evil's intrinsic recalcitrance to analysis. 'Kakophany' is also a *mysterium tremendum et fascinans* and its excess can 'kill' which, following *Exodus* 3, means to undo the self that would pretend familiarity and intimacy with the phenomena of evil and think that he can perceive or conceive evil in the way it can perceive or conceive ordinary facts or objects in the world and do so without consequence. To apprehend evil is to remember, recall, perhaps over and over again, the insouciance of chance that explodes expectation and intention, the reality of broken bodies and vulnerable psyches, and the maiming of spirit that happens in environments of inattention or malice. To attempt to comprehend evil is to attempt more than to apprehend, and presents even more danger: it is to vet singly and together the unaccountable happenings of human failure and malice, to cut against the grain of evil's refusal of sense in accounting for and rhyming the stories of atrocities committed in the name of an idol or ideology, and pay insufficient attention to the reality of unaccountable apathy regarding humans in the most unaccommodated state, the shattering of all fidelity, empathy, and trust, and the pornographies of violence and torture and the desecrations of sexual bodies.

For Desmond, the attempt to comprehend the phenomenon of evil brings one to a threshold, an unholy ground, in which one should shake with fear comparable to the holy fear which is the appropriate response to the Holy: the fear is that one becomes what one sees. Perhaps literature provides the best examples of bringing the perception of evil to the dangerous threshold in which there is effected a decision to succumb or to resist. It is difficult not to consider the work of Georges Bataille, the novels which detail rituals of transgression (*Le Bleu de ciel; L'Abée C*); his cold but interested analysis of sensational murderers (*Gilles de Rais*) and violators (de Sade); his representation of the history of cruelty, including Chinese torture (*l'Histoire de l'oeil*); and his enunciations and even annunciations on sovereignty (*Une liberté souveraine*) as providing an example of writing succumbing to what it lays bare. And perhaps Bataille speaks for a French canon of the literature of transgression which has its origin and guide in Sade in which there is expressed the desire to reduce human subjects to things, to excrement, and perhaps not even that, since it too can be consumed (coprophagy).

A more approachable example of succumbing, however, is to be found in the work of the Polish-American novelist Jerzy Kosińksi, who is a survivor of the holocaust. In his searing novel of the coming of age of a young Jewish boy on the run from the gas chambers (partly autobiographical), *The Painted Bird* (Kosiński 1982), atrocity is impossibly piled on atrocity (betrayal, killing, rape) in the manner of *Candide*, except in this case the protagonist all too easily adapts and is constructed as a sociopath. The novel hangs on the razor's edge, at once a chronicle of how history and circumstance corrupt, thus a moral tale without a happy ending, and an exercise in sheer nihilism in which not only this world but any possible world is without empathy, connection, accountability, where all feeling is anaesthetized, and which in an not too subtle way prescribes predation. One way of thinking of the authorship of Kosińksi as a whole is the way that subsequent novels such as *Blind Date* and others display a measure of desensitization in representing human action that is on a par with the acts themselves which operate in a world beyond good and evil (Kosiński 1998).[29] The curiosity in presenting a history of suffering and producing fabula leads to the paradox of rhetorical distance from and psychic proximity to the 'realities' described.

An alternative writing on evil at the threshold of succumbing and resistance is that of the American novelist, Cormac McCarthy, who resists whereas Kosiński and Bataille succumb. In its chronicle of unremitting violence between the colonizing whites and Indians in the American West under an unforgiving and godless desert sky, McCarthy's classic *Blood Meridian* matches Kosinki's *The Painted Bird* (McCarthy 1990).[30] It

---

[29] Whereas as in *The Painted Bird* one can track the construction of a young sociopath from the horrors experienced in the Shoah, in the case of *Blind Date*, the tone and style of the novel conspire to make it difficult to determine whether the protagonist who perpetrated rape in the beginning is being condemned or applauded because he avoids special pleading in his own case.

[30] This is McCarthy's masterpiece in which he excavates the violence and counter-violence that is the expression of the wounded psyches of both whites and Indians in the West and thereby indelibly written into the American psyche as such. The evening redness of the Western desert sky recalls bloodletting but also a kind of nihilistic overcoming. Interestingly,

would not exaggerate to say that violence is not only the theme of the novel, but the subject of the novel in that it is the measureless measure of everything in the world of death, scalping, rape, and bloodlust. The blinding clarity with which McCarthy renders violence creates an ambiguity: he can equally be read as being in league with the violence he represents and thus an extension of it, or he can be read to expose the violence that constitutes the American Southwest with a view to getting rid of illusion. As in the case of Kosiński, McCarthy's later work disambiguates. Low-flying ethical measures do appear in the so-called Border trilogy, and especially in *All the Pretty Horses* (McCarthy 1993, 1994, 1998), which if filled with unanticipated violence, also has moments of loyalty and recognition of the rule of violence, which itself is a check on its absolutism. Allowing the Border trilogy to interpret *Blood Meridian* allows the analogy between McCarthy and Homer, at least the Homer of the *Iliad* as seen through the genius of Simone Weil, to come into view. Weil made a number of points in her great essay 'The *Iliad* as poem of Might.'[31] The most famous, however, is that the persona of the poem is war itself and the reproduction of violence in which the Greeks and Trojans trade places in that both seem equally incapable of transcending violence and unveiling real subjectivities, that is, subjectivities that are not a function of war and violence. This epical stance in which the interests of the particular groups are suspended in taking a look at war as a whole is I think repeated in the contagion of violence depicted by McCarthy in *Blood Meridian*. The other feature isolated by Weil is the appearance in the poem of might of a measure and thus an alternative to the violence which is the blind logos of the poem. This measure is provided by Achilles' best friend, that is, Patroclus, who is perhaps the only truly reflective man in the battle and the offset to the heroes (Achilles) and pseudo-heroes (Hector) alike. There is, as far as I can see, no such hero in *Blood Meridian* and thus no such critical measure. But such heroes are to be found in McCarthy's later novels which disambiguate in the direction of such a measure. In *No Country for Old Men* (McCarthy 2002), the sheriff, who has seen much evil in his life, nonetheless, believes it has limits or at least ought to have. But he also is the ethical measure of the sociopathy in which cruelty lives by rules all the more powerful because arbitrary, thereby confirming that the world is a world

---

one of the epigraphs is from the German apocalyptic mystic, Jacob Boehme (1575–1624), although Boehme spoke of *Aurora* or 'morning redness'.

[31] See Weil (1986, 162–195). See also O'Regan (2004, 182–186).

without value, where 'good' does not qualify the 'to be.' Perhaps the zenith in terms of the transparence of the moral measure is offered in the post-apocalyptic novel, *The Road* (McCarthy 2006),[32] in which the love of a father for his son shines out with impossible radiance in a world without light, a perpetual winter in which individuals are regarded as food either to be harvested or eaten in an orgy of rage. This small apocalypse of love represents a residual faith in humanity as well as a fragile hope for the future. At the end of the novel, as he is in his death throes from cancer, the father yields to the hope that the Trinity of humans he comes across, father, mother, daughter, will not consume his son and thus constitute him as another sign in the desecrated and defecated sacrament of violence that is the world.

As far as I am aware Desmond tarries with none of the above authors, who represent the phenomenon of evil so broadly and deeply as to come to the threshold, and in fact other than Bataille, does not mention them. Nonetheless, one can think of his reserve as being responsive to the problematic which defines each of the three authors' musings on evil. Curiosity, even curiosity which thinks of itself as an ethical necessity, brings one to the threshold where you run the danger of becoming what you see or, as theorists of the power of imagination such as Paracelsus and Boehme suggested,[33] becoming what you imagine. Desmond understands as well as any of these authors, including McCarthy with whom he appears to have most in common, that to stare too long at the phenomena of evil is to risk being petrified. Medusa is the symbol of the fate of the connoisseur of evil who presumes to transcend it. The mandate is not to look. Yet after significant exposure it might prove impossible to carry out. Still, the hideous aliveness of Medusa, with heads as trophies, hair-like serpents, and coiling limbs making resistance to her overwhelming chthonic force impossible, suggests that those who get too close blend with the chaos

---

[32] This post-apocalyptic book might be regarded as something of an answer to the apocalyptic of *Blood Meridian*, which concerns violence in the form of proctology as this text concerns violence in the form of eschatology. The ferocious love of a father for his son is the counterpoint to this violence and the sign of hope or hope against hope in a world in which violence is an essential part of the fabric of things. Counters to violence and the nihilism which is its source and its consequence can be found also in *No Country for Old Men* and in *All the Pretty Horses*.

[33] The German theosophical mystic (1575–1624), whose thought recalls both the Kabbalah and alchemy, in *Aurora* (1611), finds evil everywhere. Later in the texts of 1619–1624, however, it is not just the ubiquity of evil but its structural connection to the divine that is to the fore. For a focus yet comprehensive account of evil in the thought of Boehme, see the dissertation by Defoort (2012).

and disorder of the phenomena of evil that they would bring to our attention and defeat. If Pandora is the symbol of what happens when curiosity insists on an answer, and Bluebeard's Castle the symbol of a death wish, Medusa is the symbol of the writer who comes too close, even as she looks at a slant, looks too long and too keenly, and can never rid her mind of the images of violation.

I have thus far left out the most important thing about Medusa, that is, her gaze back or stare back that undoes the writer's gaze, whether the writer is a novelist, a theologian, or a philosopher. Desmond is rightly afraid of Medusa. While he glances, and he does often enough, as I have demonstrated, he also has the scruple of averting his gaze. I think we can get at Desmond's reserve by means of his fear of petrification, which will undo his singing of the real original of the 'to be' by another less imagistic reflection that can, however, also be interpreted as a kind of phenomenological translation of the Medusa figure. Recall in an early text by Jean-Luc Marion the famous distinction between 'icon' and 'idol' in which the latter mode of knowing is reflective of the limits of desire that involves self-affirmation and self-enhancement, whereas in contrast the icon is the phenomenon that is not only not captured by desire, but undoes it, by appearing to have an irreducible agency.[34] Although Marion, given his Patristic preoccupations, undoubtedly, has the iconodules or iconophiles as models for this, that Cusanus is the ultimate model is clear when Marion speaks of the icon as not only escaping our gaze, but which in its perceived looking back deconstitutes and reconstitutes the aim of our desire. Of course, the icon in the early Marion functions as the hyperousiological ultimate plenitude of Christian Neoplatonism, precisely the Good beyond determinate good that is the ground and apex of Desmond's figuration of transcendence.

One can easily imagine the superdeterminate reality of the Desmond of the trilogy and especially of *Ethics and the Between* being cast in the iconic terms of Cusa and Marion of that early text. But what if the phenomenon was not that of superessential being or the superessential good (coextensive), but of its phenomenological opposite? Can this be threaded through the

---

[34] See Marion (2001) in which the idol is as the limit of the human gaze the projection of human desire. In contrast, the icon as the limit of the human gaze is coming to be seen rather than seeing. Although Cusanus is not mentioned in this text, the reversal of flow from seeing to being seen finds its classical expression in De Visione Dei in which through the monks looking at an icon of Christ in a semi-circle each judges Christ's gaze to be uniquely on them. This receives full recognition in Marion (2016, 305–331).

language of icon and cast light on Desmond's reserve with respect to the phenomenon of evil which, if related to the strategies of excessive naming and silence, seems different in kind since it indicates a cessation rather than a stretching forward? I want to suggest that the phenomenon of evil functions iconically to the degree to which it stares back and in so doing deconstitutes and reconstitutes desire. Kakophany, however, stares back otherwise than theophany: it arrests or explodes the gazer's seeing and her subjectivity and comes to enlist it in its own culture of counter-seeing. It draws the seer into an economy of death and chaos, while confirming that eros can never be insistent enough, can never refuse transcendence enough, can never affirm its constructions and productions sufficiently enough. Ironically, as icon, kakophany confirms the idol and declares that it has no beyond. The phenomenon of evil is not the icon as such; it is the inverted icon.

AMEN

In this chapter I have barely scratched the surface of Desmond's exploration of the problem of evil, since not only would I have had to be far more ramified and subtle in my treatment of the experience, the discourses that try to express it, and its impenetrable mysteries, but to be faithful to the problem, I should have, as Ricoeur insisted throughout his career, linked evil to its eschatological overcoming, and to be faithful to Desmond, I should have brought out more aggressively the priority of the protological given which is the good of 'to be.' Still, the three features I have presented and explored in the chapter—(a) the phenomenological uncovering of evil; (b) the comparison with the work of Paul Ricoeur, who is not as friendly toward myth as Desmond and if Augustinian a different kind of Augustinian; and (c) finally my treatment of the conundrum of whether with respect to the phenomenon of evil silence as well as speech is necessarily part of a complex response—suggest at least the richness of Desmond's talk on this topic and invite us to think with him and even think further. This chapter is in the mode of amen and thank you, where the amen is simply an echo of ample amen of epic lyricism of Desmond's work and my thank you but a reverberation of the great thank you that is his work. In this work, in a register that is hospitable to Judaism and Christianity in a way that Heidegger's thought is not, thinking (*Denken*) is a thanking (*Danken*) directed at a person who hovers over the abyss and is not of it, to whom we direct our praise and hopes, and in the night of suffering, direct our complaints, which are counted on.

Bibliography

Agamben, Giorgio. 1998. *Homo Sacer: Sovereign Power and Bare Life*. Trans. Daniel Heller-Roazen. Stanford, CA: Stanford University Press.
———. 2005. *The State of Exception*. Trans. Kevin Attell. Chicago: University of Chicago Press.
———. 2011. *The Kingdom and the Glory: For a Theological Genealogy of Government*. Trans. Lorenzo Chiesa with Matteo Mandarini. Stanford: Stanford University Press.
Bataille, George. 1989. *Theory of Religion*. Trans. Robert Hurley. New York: Zone Books.
———. 1993. *The Accursed Share, Vols. 2 and 3: The History of Sexuality and Sovereignty*. Trans. Robert Hurley. Boson: Zone Books.
———. 2001. *The Unfinished System of Nonknowledge*. Trans. Michelle Kendall and Stuart Kendall. Minneapolis and London: University of Minnesota Press.
Berlin, Isaiah. 1969. *Four Essays on Liberty*. Oxford: Oxford University Press.
Defoort, Filips. 2012. *Imagination and Evil in Jacob Boehme's Mystical Anthropology*. Dissertation, Leuven.
Derrida, Jacques. 1978. Edmond Jabès and the Question of the Book. In *Writing and Difference*. Trans. with Intro Alan Bass. Chicago: University of Chicago Press.
———. 1981. *Positions*. Trans. Alan Bass. Chicago: University of Chicago Press.
———. 1982. The Pit and the Pyramid. In *Margins of Philosophy*. Trans. Alan Bass. Chicago: University of Chicago Press.
———. 1990. *Glas*. Trans. John P. Leavey Jr. Lincoln: University of Nebraska Press.
Kant, Immanuel. 1996. *Religion and Rational Theology*. Trans. and Ed. Allen Wood and George di Giovanni. New York: Cambridge University Press.
Kosiński, Jerzy. 1982. *The Painted Bird*. Essex: Arrow Press.
———. 1998. *Blind Date*. New York: Grove Press.
Levinas, Emmanuel. 1969. *Totality and Infinity: An Essay on Exteriority*. Trans. Alphonso Lingis. Pittsburgh, PA: Duquesne University Press.
———. 1981. *Otherwise Than Being or Beyond Essence*. Trans. Alphonso Lingis. The Hague: Martinus Nijhoff.
Marion, Jean-Luc. 2001. *Idol and Distance: Five Studies*. Trans. with Intro Thomas Carlson. New York: Fordham University Press.
———. 2016. Nicholas of Cusa's Contribution in *De Visione Dei*. *Journal of Religion* 96: 305–331.
McCarthy, Cormac. 1990. *Blood Meridian, or the Evening Redness in the West*. London: Picador.
———. 1993. *All the Pretty Horses (Volume 1)*. New York: Vintage Books.
———. 1994. *The Crossing (Volume 2)*. New York: Alfred A. Knopf.

———. 1998. *Cities of the Plains (Volume 3)*. New York: Alfred A. Knopf.
———. 2002. *No Country for Old Men*. New York: Vintage Books.
———. 2006. *The Road*. New York: Vintage Books.
O'Regan, Cyril. 1997. Metaphysics and the Metaxological Space of the Tradition. *Tijdschrift voor Filosofie* 59: 531–549.
———. 2002. The Poetics of Ethos: William Desmond and Poetic Redemption of Platonic Archeology. *Ethical Perspectives* 8: 272–302.
———. 2004. Counter-Mimesis and Simone Weil's Christian Platonic Hints for Overcoming the Glamor of Evil. In *The Christian Platonism of Simone Weil*, ed. Jane E. Doering and Eric Springsted. Notre Dame: University of Notre Dame Press.
———. 2008. What Theology Can Learn from A Philosophy Daring to Speak the Unspeakable. *Irish Theological Quarterly* 73: 243–262.
———. 2012. Naming God in *God and the Between*. *Louvain Studies* 36: 282–301.
———. 2013. Hegel, Sade, and Gnostic Infinities. *Radical Orthodoxy: Journal of Theology, Philosophy, and Politics* 3: 383–425.
———. 2017. The Impatience of Gnosis. In *William Desmond and Contemporary Theology*, ed. Christopher Ben Simpson and Brendan Thomas Sammon. Notre Dame, IN: University of Notre Dame Press.
Pinnock, Sarah Katherine. 2002. *Beyond Theodicy: Jewish and Christian Continental Thinkers Respond to the Holocaust*. Albany, NY: SUNY Press.
Richardson, William. 1963. *Through Phenomenology to Thought*. The Hague: Martinus Nijhoff.
Ricoeur, Paul. 1969. *The Symbolism of Evil*. Trans. Emerson Buchanan. Boston: Beacon Press.
———. 1979a. Original Sin: A Study in Meaning. In *The Conflict of Interpretations*, ed. D. Ihde. Evanston, IL: Northwestern University Press.
———. 1979b. The Hermeneutics of Symbols and Their Philosophical Reflection. In *The Conflict of Interpretations*, ed. D. Ihde. Evanston, IL: Northwestern University Press.
———. 1986. *Fallible Man*. Trans. Charles A. Kelbley, into. Walter Lowe. New York: Fordham University Press.
———. 1995. Evil, a Challenge to Philosophy and Theology. In *Figuring the Sacred*. Trans. David Pellauer and Mark L. Wallace. Minneapolis: Fortress Press.
Schelling, F.W.J. 2007. *Philosophical Investigations into the Essence of Human Freedom*. Trans. Jeff Love and Johannes Schmidt. Albany, NY: SUNY Press.
Tilley, Terrence W. 2000. *The Evils of Theodicy*. Eugene, OR: Wipf and Stock.
Weil, Simone. 1986. The *Iliad* or the Poem of Might. In *Simone Weil: An Anthology*, ed. Sian Miles. New York: Weidenfeld and Nicholson.

CHAPTER 10

Retrieving the Primal Ethos of Life: (Bio)Ethics in the Love of Being

Roberto Dell'Oro

I want to reflect in this chapter on love of being, or being as love, as the condition for the retrieval, in the field of bioethics, of what William Desmond calls the primal ethos of life. Such retrieval has been hindered, in the medical context, by the limited vision of positivist natural sciences, a recurring temptation of medicine. In ethics, the loss of the intimate universal is connected with a methodology that tends to reduce the contribution of ethics to the reconstruction of the conditions for moral consensus in society at large. My chapter comprises three parts. In the first, I make general claims about the predicament of contemporary bioethics with respect to what I call the *oblivion* of the intimate universal. In my second part, I reflect more specifically on the cases of assisted reproductive technologies and so-called aid in dying, showing how the ethical reflection on both practices reflects a distancing from the call of intimate universality, and thus warrants a task of retrieval. Finally, I offer a reconstructive attempt, in light of *The Intimate Universal*, of an ethics defined by love of being and the porosity that is bound up with the generosity of the agapeics.

R. Dell'Oro (✉)
Loyola Marymount University, Los Angeles, CA, USA
e-mail: Roberto.Dell'Oro@lmu.edu

© The Author(s) 2018
D. Vanden Auweele (ed.), *William Desmond's Philosophy between Metaphysics, Religion, Ethics, and Aesthetics*,
https://doi.org/10.1007/978-3-319-98992-1_10

The Wasteland of Medical Ethics and the Oblivion of the Intimate Universal

Some time ago, Warren Reich suggested that the problem of the search for meaning in medical ethics might be illustrated by the metaphor of the stethoscope. Richard Baron, in a famous article for the *Annals of Internal Medicine*, tells the story: "It happened the other morning on rounds, as it often does, that while I was carefully auscultating a patient's chest, he began to ask me a question. 'Quiet' I said. I can't hear you while I'm listening" (Baron 1985, p. 606). The stethoscope metaphor is emblematic of the inattention to meaning ('not hearing') brought about by the reductionist focus (the mode of restricted 'listening') in the methodologies of both modern scientific medicine and contemporary ethical theory (Reich and Dell'Oro 1996; Zaner 1988).

To start with, the mind-set created by modern scientific medicine has required for medicine *to be inattentive*, that is, not to hear the sick person's experience of illness. Influenced by a positivist framework, nineteenth-century medical scientists popularized the notion that *practical* clinical medicine should be viewed as a form of applied *theoretical* medicine. In the United States, the reformation of medical studies introduced by the medical educator Abraham Flexner, in the first part of the twentieth century, completed the picture. Moreover, this happened as a result of modernity's understanding of scientific knowledge, which Hans Georg Gadamer poignantly describes as a capacity to produce effects. In the *modern* version of scientific knowledge, the mathematical-quantitative isolation of laws of the natural order provides human action with the identification of specific contexts of cause and effects, together with new possibilities for intervention (Gadamer 1996, p. 35). In relation to clinical medicine, such an idealization entails a tendency to reduce the *praxis* of medicine, with its matrix of subjective components and contextual features, to the detached 'objectivity' of theoretical knowledge, and to interpret the healing process itself as a production of effects (Wartofsky 1997).

Of course, one cannot in principle question the application of scientific reasoning to medicine. In trying to identify and explain the cause of symptoms, medicine employs probabilistic laws and rules, theories and principles, of the biomedical sciences. Concepts of normal and abnormal, for an example, are statistically derived concepts, based on scientifically validated norms of human biological functioning. In the attempt to classify symptoms as the manifestation of particular disease entities, medicine relies upon hypothetic-deductive and inductive reasoning. Moreover, in order to determine what can be done to remove or alleviate the cause of particular diseases, medicine appeals to prognostic knowledge about the course of the diagnosed disease, as well as efficacy and toxicity of relevant therapeutic possibilities.

And yet, in spite of its undisputable scientific basis, medicine cannot be entirely equated with science. The goal of medicine is not to reduce different segments of scientific explanations into a unified theory; rather, the specific goal of medicine consists in bringing together, in a synthetic action, which is theoretical *and* practical at the same time, an understanding of illness with a specific medical decision on behalf of the patient (Pellegrino 1979; Pellegrino 1983). Unlike the patho-physiology of disease, the phenomenon of illness cannot be observed, analyzed, and explained *noumenically*, that is, "in itself" (Dell'Oro 2005). As Gadamer suggests, it can be fully understood only *hermeneutically*, that is, through an act of interpretation that takes place within the sociological, cultural, and ideological matrix of a defined life-world. For this reason, medicine represents a peculiar unity of theoretical *and* practical knowledge within the domain of the modern sciences, "a peculiar kind of practical science for which modern thought no longer possesses an adequate concept" (Gadamer 1996, p. 39).

For sure, careful scientific attention to the patho-physiology of disease, together with ever more extensive biotechnological applications, has doubtlessly yielded marvelous advances in modern medicine (Kass 2002, pp. 29–53). Yet, its positivistic reduction has also created a mind-set that brackets questions of meaning, themselves highly significant to human well-being and to the ethical aspects of medicine. Perhaps, the judgment of Edmund Husserl in his *Crisis of the European Sciences*, while summarizing the development of modern sciences, offers at the same time a prophetic anticipation of the predicament of contemporary medicine:

> The exclusiveness with which the total world-view of modern man lets itself be determined by the positive sciences and be blinded by the "prosperity" they produced, meant an indifferent turning away from the questions which are decisive for genuine humanity. Fact-minded science excludes in principle precisely the questions which man finds the most burning: questions of the meaning or meaninglessness of the whole of human existence. (Husserl 1970, pp. 5–6)

The central task of ethics in medicine is to foster an *anamnesis* of the meaning of the very questions medicine seems to suspend: the significance of illness and disease, of our human condition as embodied, of birth, suffering, and death, and of the service to the ethos of generosity that sustains the healing professions (Dell'Oro 2016; Kass 2002, pp. 55–76; Meilaender 1995).

I could rephrase the issue in terms that are closer to Desmond's language: we fashion for ourselves a *second* ethos that bears no connection with the primal ethos of life:

> We are rooted in nature, but we risk denaturing ourselves in claiming to make ourselves according to a second nature. The second nature is not a second 'yes', a redoubled 'yes' to the first 'yes' at work in the *poiesis* of naturing and our *passio*. More often, it is a 'yes' to a *conatus* that has deviated from the subtle insinuations of the now sunken matrix of fecundity. (IU 327)

I want to show this in relation to two issues that are on the forefront of our public ethical discussion today: one concerns the morality of artificial reproductive technologies, the other the ethics of a good death.

The Discussion on Assisted Reproduction and the Exploitation of the Body

A look at the cultural context in which artificial reproductive technologies have developed shows quite clearly that their evolution has led to nothing less than a *deconstruction* of procreation. From an integral experience of human relationality, endowed with specific phenomenological characteristics, *procreation* has now been reduced to *reproduction*, a process of technical making, guided by the logic of calculative rationality. Such a deconstruction, subtle as it may be, entails also a redefinition: not only of parenthood, but of human identity *tout court*. Though originally born of a commitment to the alleviation of infertility, artificial reproductive technologies have progressively surpassed, if not abandoned, their original *therapeutic* intent, taking on, rather, unquestionable *eugenic* features. The search for a remedy to pathological conditions in both women and men has morphed into the search for the *perfect* progeny, a development in line with the logic of neutralizing commodification pursued by the market: like things, gametes, embryos, the wombs of women, and so children also, have now a price, rather than a dignity. In the end, artificial reproductive technologies have revolutionized the dynamics driving the appropriation of personal identity, the bond between generations, and the meaning of the historical links that tie them together.

The discussion about artificial reproductive technologies is not taking place without being nourished by recessive premises. Consider, among others, the question of embodiment, a topic that hardly surfaces as relevant in contemporary bioethics. The focus on normative dimensions, further exacerbated by the pragmatic concern for a public policy based on so-called common morality, tends to push to the side premises of a deeper philosophical nature, unquestionably central to any ethical reflection (Taylor and Dell'Oro 2006; Evans 2002). Thus, what one encounters as serious suggestions for policy proposals on artificial reproductive technologies do fly in the face of elementary considerations about our embodied condition; as such, they hardly withstand even the lowest bar of philosophical justification.

Take as an example the case recently publicized in the American news, concerning the Food and Drug Administration (FDA) approval of an in vitro fertilization technique, which uses DNA from three people in an attempt to prevent certain illnesses, like muscular dystrophy and respiratory problems (Tingley 2014). The United Kingdom's fertility regulator, the *Human Fertilization and Embryo Authority*, already changed its own laws, in December 2016, to permit the procedure. And last January, the announcement came from Ukraine, that a child had been successfully produced with such mitochondrial transfer technique.

Most commentators, especially scientists and doctors, welcome the advent of yet another technological fix to a congenital predisposition with an attitude of unquestionable awe. On the other hand, the more critically minded, among them ethicists, are willing to grant that some moral problems for this 'three parent baby' solution do exist after all: doubts about safety are raised, together with the fear of unforeseen eugenic slippery slopes. Strangely passed over in silence, though, remains the most obvious question, 'whose child will this baby be?'

Of course, experts are quick to rebut this preoccupation as scientifically naïve, if not totally unfounded: they reassure the concerned public that because the female donor of healthy mitochondrial DNA to the defective biological mother provides, in the end, a very negligible genetic contribution, she should not be described appropriately as 'a parent'. However, when considered from another angle, namely, that of the *personal* identity of a child thus produced, the question 'whose child will this baby be?' comes to the fore as actually very serious.

This is so because personal identity is now imperiled by what I would call 'an ambiguity of belonging': for the child so produced, the embodied matrix of traceable biological debts represents more an opportunity for doubt than a condition for self-identification. Lack of evidence about one's *distinct* genetic lineage may turn the trust in the source that gives to be, under normal circumstances, the syngamy of two genomes into puzzlement about one's *own* origin and identity. Examples could be multiplied ad infinitum. Like others, the one I mentioned cannot fail to raise concerns. At stake are recessive premises about the body, embodiment, and the "embodied self" that drive these technologies in the first place and, more in general, our understanding of medicine's goals (Thiel 2013).

There is no denying the paradoxical situation within which artificial reproductive technologies have developed. As William Desmond suggests: "On the one hand, we block fertility, and, on the other hand, never have such extraordinary and emergency techniques been available and used to promote unblocked fertility" (IU 327). In his work, Desmond provides a genealogical interpretation, stemming from the recognition that the development of artificial reproductive technologies, especially in their most extreme expressions, stands squarely within the legacy of a dualistic anthropology, itself resting upon a broader attitude toward being as such. Anthropology always reflects a specific view of metaphysics, of what it means 'to be', and the mechanization of the body brought about by modernity can be properly understood when seen within the horizon of a more general neutralization of reality (EB 17–47; GB 17–30; Guardini 1951). The world, now become 'objective', stands also empty of meaning before a 'subject' that constitutes the only presence of value. As neutral, the natural order has no language of its own, no deeper message to convey to an observer willing to see or to listen. This is so because a deep perplexity has now replaced the ancient wonder (*thaumazein*) about the inherent value of being, more, about the inherent goodness of being.

In this view, the subject becomes also the *only* source of value in an ethical sense: the good is not, as in the classical definition, 'what everyone wants' (*bonum est quod omnes appetunt*); rather, what we want, we call the good (so Hobbes and his contemporary "contractualist" versions). Whether responding to the necessity of a rational ordering of duty, as in the Kantian version of autonomy, or the maximization of value in a network of effective powers, as in the calculative prudence of utilitarian rationality, the moral self of modernity emerges as 'radically self-assertive'. Moreover, the moral self stands before the good as a *dis-embodied self*, 'auto-nomous' because it is separated not only from what it sees as the heteronomy of nature, including that of the body, but also from the heteronomy of larger claims to social solidarity, as in the various versions of individual liberalism. The modern self, as Alasdair McIntyre and Charles Taylor have so eloquently highlighted, is, in the end, the *unencumbered self*, an atomistic individuality that fails to recognize the embodied nature of communal and historically defined ties. In his latest encyclical letter, *Laudato Si'*, Pope Francis has reminded us that the problems inherent in the modern paradigm cannot be denied any longer, for example, in the face of the current ecological crisis.

And yet, it is not only an explicitly Christian-inspired anthropology what raises doubts about our current predicament. The debate within feminist theories on the ethics of artificial reproductive technologies, among others, suggests something of the tensions intrinsic to the modern understanding of body, procreation, and parenthood as neutral practices, as such entirely open to endless manipulation (Lauritzen 1993). For sure, *pro-interventionist* feminist thinkers tend to welcome developments in reproductive technologies as positive. They promise to control nature, and to redefine the meaning of gender constructions, relative especially to the distinction between male and female. In this view, invasive procedures that break women's links to biology, birth, and maternal nurturing can only further a feminist agenda of self-sufficiency and control. On the other hand, *non-interventionist* feminist thinkers see reproductive technologies differently: a strengthening of arrogant human control over nature and thus over women as part of the 'nature' that is to be controlled. They see new reproductive technologies as an imposition upon women who look at themselves as failure, if they cannot become pregnant. They insist that technological progress, requiring the invasion and manipulation of women's bodies, must always be critically scrutinized with a kind of 'hermeneutics of suspicion', especially when the market becomes the ultimate mechanism for the exploitation of the body (Duden 1993; Haker 2011). It is hard to miss the marketing and advertisement strategies associated with fertility clinics and service providers, which, understandably, are eager to do what any business does best: sell to prospective customers and this in the language of products and commodities. As Desmond puts it:

The danger is that the bodies of the couple and the child—now conceived as a product—are seen too much under the light of serviceable disposability. Indeed embryos are disposable if they are not serviceable. It is manipulation, not participation, but also manipulation through a kind of participation: the exploitation of life is beneficiary to the gift of life that forgets the giftedness it exploits. These manipulations are ominous with respect to the deeper participation of the human being in energies of fecundity that come to it from beyond itself and that take it, help it partake of what is, beyond itself. (IU 327)

Indeed, there is more to body, procreation, and parenthood than our technical rationality assumes. There is an irreducible *otherness* to them that reflects the personal presence of the embodied person, an ontological incommunicability that resists any *constructive* pretense. Moreover, to recognize the embodied condition of our being-in-the-world, to grant its radical otherness, is to abide by the symbolic reminder of our *being given to be*. In the flesh that nourishes our joy and suffering, pain and pleasure, lies the trace of the *source* that releases us into being, the subtle allusion, most often forgotten, at times denied, of the *gift* that we are, not from ourselves, but from another.

The Debate on the 'Good Death': Striving to Be or Letting Go

The debate on the ethics of a good death provides a second example. What is at stake in the conversation is the problem of articulating the conditions for a *good death*—and more specifically, for a good death when faced with the vulnerability of old age, terminal disease, and unbearable suffering. Such a task remains quite formidable both in relation to its philosophical foundations, as well as with reference to the analysis of specific ethical quandaries. Drawing on William Desmond's distinction between *conatus* and *passio essendi* (IU and Desmond 2006), I focus on two 'existential modalities' of confronting death, and delineate some ethical implications with regard to these.

Conatus essendi is a way of standing before things defined by the endeavor, the effort, the strife to be. Here one is dealing with a position based on distance from reality, in which the subject determines the conditions for the appearing of things, whose certainty, if not truth, will entirely be defined by relation to a subjectivity that posits and determines. Being *is* insofar as it responds to the (transcendental) forms of its apperception on the part of a subjectivity that measures and rules its phenomenic presence.

Such a position has, first of all, an epistemological meaning. On the premise defined by the ambiguity of the appearing of things—thus the doubt pertaining to them—the *cogito* tries to recover an irrefutable certainty, no longer starting from the promise of meaning that inhabits reality, but from the subjective certainty that defines the very act of thinking, an act that must necessarily presuppose—and beyond all doubt no less—at least the existence of the *cogito* who thinks. In this way, however, one sees a shift, a 'Copernican revolution' in the way of conceiving of the relation between subject and object, and, moreover, of the priority of the former over the latter. Without entering here into the details of this 'anthropological turn', let us consider some of the important cultural consequences it entails. The scientific revolution, which affects medicine as well, is one of the significant consequences of this anthropological shift, wherein the relationship with nature is no longer 'undergone', so to speak, but shaped by precise heuristic models that reduce the complexity of nature to a univocal parameter. Nature is subjected to the mathematical hypothesis that will allow for it to be described and verified empirically. If true reality is only that which can be described mathematically, then we ought to bring the unverifiable *pathos* of reality back to the dianoetical precision of the formula. This holds true also for the subject, whose emotional complexity will have to be reduced, now, to the act of 'thinking clearly and distinctly'. In the words of Spinoza, *neque lugere, nec ridere, sed intelligere.*

What about the ethical implications of such an epistemological position? The subject who fashions reality is also he who grants it value. This is so because the neutralization of being, with respect to the object, entails something like a rebound effect, a kind of 'contraction of value'—especially with Kant—in favor of the subject. Only the person possesses an intrinsic value, is a good in itself, never to be treated as a means, only as an end. Unlike nature, understood now as a phenomenal field open to endless manipulation, the person is not neutral; rather, being the source of absolute meaning, she is the condition for the very possibility of meaning's attribution:

> Here is the sting. The subject cannot live with this devaluation of otherness, and even less with the devaluing of its own valuing. It will not be passive to this. It will be active. The subjectification of value inevitably leads to the

primacy of self-activity that impresses itself on the other. ... We witness the recoil of the subject on itself out of the hiding of neutrality it had schemed for itself. There is no escape from itself, but now when it awakens again to itself, it has been transformed into a more *radically self-assertive subjectivity.* (EB 29)

One might say that the good death is the *humanized* death, that is to say, death lived not as something man undergoes or endures; rather, as something man chooses to the extent that he determines it, in the same way in which he chooses and determines the theoretical models for his access to reality as such. If man is the 'measure of all things', death cannot be greater than man. Death can and should indeed be neutralized, if not in its inevitability of a fact that inexorably happens, at least, in its dramatic quality of an experience that can be endured (Scheffczyk 1992, p. 271). The effort to be, the *conatus essendi*, is a struggle against death, the attempt to indefinitely postpone it, or else to anticipate it rationally, as in the case of euthanasia or assisted suicide. Absolute passivity is not worthy of man.

This position is not without important emphases. The efforts to humanize death, for an example, the tasks of health care and scientific research aiming at the treatment and management of pain, are essential dimensions to our relationship with death. An inhumane and dehumanizing death cannot be good. Yet, if the good death represents the fulfillment of a good life, there is the risk of thinking about death according to the logic of scientific-technological control and neutralizing planning that, in the paradigm of modernity, renders a life worth living. The most we can do is to prolong life, eliminating from it all pain and suffering, but we have not yet succeeded in 'managing death'. Death will always come, now as an unexpected surprise, an expression of the heteronomy of nature that is even more striking, because it seems to contradict the autonomy with which we attempt to completely define ourselves.

Again, the separation, the dualism of person and nature, if it constitutes the condition of possibility for controlling death, can also lead to conflicting results: a technological effort that depersonalizes nature, or a will to power that denaturalizes the person to the level of a self-determining rationality, as in the cases of euthanasia and assisted suicide. For Desmond, the *conatus essendi* does not represent the ultimate (in the sense of the German *ursprünglich*) existential modality: the effort to be rests on a primal porosity, an attitude of more radical openness toward being. In wonder, man takes up his residence in the between, attuned to the saturation of meaning that dwells in things, in *their* value, and in whose midst he is called to make himself a world (Desmond 1995, pp. 3–46). Thus, the *conatus essendi* can only be a derivation, of course possible and legitimate, of a more original *passio essendi*, of an 'undergoing' (*passio*) being that also becomes a 'passion' for being.

The *passio essendi* entails the recognition that man is not the origin of meaning, only insofar as he is originated; he can and must attribute meaning to things. But man can do this only on the condition of a previous attunement to the promise of meaning that already dwells in reality. In this perspective, there is no separation between being and value, fact and meaning, for being is, intrinsically, promising and valid, good and beautiful. Of course, man produces and makes, searches, and fashions, yet he does all this far from the presupposition of a neutralization of nature, rather, on the basis of an activity that perfects nature, as it acknowledges in being a reserve of meaning to make his own and bring to fulfillment. The receptivity in question is clearly not a form of passivity either, for it is, nevertheless, to a consciousness and to its active intentionality that the meaning of things discloses itself. And yet the activity of consciousness rests on the presupposition of the inexhaustible depths of the mystery of things, of their endless and never to be reduced profundity, which makes itself known because it opens itself up, because it reveals itself. Man lives a relationship with reality in an attitude of trust, not of doubt or distancing suspicion. The task of freedom is to do and to build, to fashion the world only because, prior to this, the world was 'let be'. The task of freedom is a response, a responsibility, and one beyond the autonomy that is exercised in the will to power, seized at another's expense: a freedom that leaves things be in the generosity of love and gift. This inevitably entails a demystification of the modern ideal of autonomy, the recognition that, in the long run, Kantian autonomy degenerates into will to power (EB 17–47; Guardini 1951; De Lubac 1945).

The relationship with death unfolds within this context and according to the same logic. The humanization of death will be possible on the condition that death be accepted and not suppressed or censured. Death is, after all, part of the human experience, an event whose significance cannot be anticipated, in fact, a disclosure, a total revelation of meaning, both promising and significant (Scheler 1974; Sölle 1973; Demmer 1987). The 'passivity' implied by death is, thus, the final expression of the more general receptivity of life:

> There is a passivity without which man could not be man. Part of the reason for this is the fact we were born, we were given-birth-to. Here there follows the fact that we are loved. So, too, is the fact that we die. (Jüngel 1975, p. 85)

Yet, to accept death also implies an activity, an act of preparation that opens up a space of creativity. We all die, yet we face death *differently*; not unlike life, requiring its own special art, one that is accomplished daily in silence, and in the cultivation of virtues, so, too, does death require a kind of art, the *ars moriendi*, shared along a passage wherein one is not alone, in what Norbert Elias calls "the solitude of the dying person" (Elias 2001; Reich 1996). Death is a threshold toward which we journey together, as if in pilgrimage, comforted by prayer. In a Christian framework, death is, at bottom, an eschatological event, one which belongs to the personal narrative of each and every human being, yet also points to a transhistorical fulfillment, to definitive communion with God beyond the limits of history: "Birth and death are thresholds and transitions, and as the radical transition of birth is creation, the radical transition of death may not be nothing, but resurrection" (IU 363).

Bio(Ethics) in the Love of Being

Desmond's work offers several important insights into the predicament of contemporary bioethical thinking, and not only in relation to the issues highlighted above. Ethical conclusions stand or fall on the fundamental metaphysical imperative to retrieve the *intrinsic* value of being as loveable, and to recognize that the discovery of moral truth rests on the premise (or promise) of a *just* rapport with the good. To be *on a par* with the claim the good makes is to be more profoundly attuned to the generosity of its self-giving (*bonum diffusivum sui*), attentive to an offering of grace that is born (or reborn) of a porous opening. In it, the disposition to receive subtends any endeavor to be, mindfulness of the *cum* already companions the *conatus*, and this in terms of relativity to both the deeper theological and metaphysical (*onto-theological?*) sources of being, as well as the daily demands of merely *ontic* otherness: from those more *intimate*, implicated in the proximity of family and friends, to those awaken by a more *universal* generosity: to the unknown stranger, the lonely widow, the immigrant foreigner.

The reconstructed ethos of contemporary bioethics is blind to the sources of value that nourish the primal ethos of life. Phenomenologists speak of *Wertblindheit* (von Hildebrand 1953; Schmucker-Von Koch

1992), and perhaps this is an appropriate, if somewhat technical, way to put it: blindness to the sheer, I should say idiotic, givenness of being as good, now reduced to neutral thereness available for endless manipulation. Being springs from an origin that gives without boundaries, out of a love that is *agapeic* because unconditional, a love that lets be in a pluralized creation saturated with aesthetic worth. I speak of creation here, not to immediately qualify the issue as *theological*. One should resist the attempt to recolonize public discourse in the name of a *political* use of theology, born of resentment toward a secular bioethics that has marginalized religious voices. A metaxological metaphysics sees the issue as more deeply *philosophical* in nature: the task of a theologically mindful bioethics may not be achieved without unclogging the resistances to "think beyond", recognizing the hyperbolic signs at the heart of being itself. But this requires philosophical *finesse* more than proselytizing ardor. As von Balthasar suggests, "in order to be a serious theologian, one must also, indeed, first, be a philosopher; one must—precisely also in light of revelation—have immersed oneself in the mysterious structures of creaturely being" (Balthasar 2000, p. 8; Demmer 1989, pp. 119–178). *The Intimate Universal* puts the matter in terms of the porosity that we *are*: both in relation to what we have received, and in terms of our *own* openness beyond ourselves:

> We are porosity because we are first received in being: given to be, before we are self-surpassing, or porous in a derived sense to what is beyond ourselves. We are in being as idiotic singulars, but at the heart of the idiotic selving is this intimate porosity that is the mark of our being creatures: emergent as what we are from no-thing—created from nothing. (IU 211–212)

Recovering a sense of the worth of beings entails more than an articulation of respect on our part. This too is necessary, if not that, *qua* human expression, respect remains ambiguous, even contradictory: in the language of the National Bioethics Advisory Commission that drafted the first document on embryo experimentation for the purposes of stem cell extraction, respect for the embryo could still coexist with the intention to destroy and use it. The matter then, is deeper. At stake is not only an *ethical* attitude, but an *ontological* love, love of being as worthy to be and to be affirmed.

That we exist and live in the opening of such love, in the *passio essendi* that generates our ontological *complacentia* toward being, orients all our endeavors, the striving of our *conatus*, in the direction of an affirmation of otherness. Porosity beyond the atomistic individuality of 'unencumbered selfhood' is more than an exercise in autonomous self-determination. The question of what limits the latter is very much at stake in the tension between liberalism and communitarianism, which defines much of contemporary ethical discourse. For sure, the world endorsed in the communitarian social model appears to be in tension with the individualist mind-set of liberal thinkers. Individualists even claim that communitarians express little more than nostalgia for a simpler, premodern past. I believe the 'communitarian' model does not necessarily stand in opposition to the 'liberal' model. The recognition of individual freedoms, such as freedom of speech, religion, association, and privacy are unquestionable values for any contemporary rendition of the relation between self and society. A society is a good society when it sustains freedom through the mutual respect its members show in their interaction with one another. This goes, first of all, to the realization that aiming at the good of society entails protecting, rather than eroding, a space for moral pluralism, hospitable to an interaction across differences, on the presupposition that the *public realm* is not just the neutral space to be conquered or won over, and that the members of an 'open society' are not to be faced as enemies but as partners: dialogue among moral agents, whether 'strangers' or 'friends', to use the distinction *in vogue*, can only function on the presumption that any claim to meaning and truth is, at the same time, an attestation of freedom and respect for the other. To that extent, liberalism and communitarianism not only stress two different dimensions of the same reality, but grow one on top of the cultural achievements of the other. As Charles Taylor recognizes, free individuals with their own goals and aspirations are themselves only possible within a certain kind of civilization. It took a long development of certain institutions and practices, of the rule of law, of rules of equal respect, of habits of common deliberations, of cultural self-development, and so on, to produce the modern individual. Without these, the very sense of oneself as an individual would atrophy (Taylor 1989).

This is true. However, the agapeics of the intimate universal go even deeper, beyond the recognition of the potential accommodation of two reciprocally implicated social models. If what is at stake is ultimately the full extent of the porosity as an ontological condition, then the question is not only retrieving the relativity of autonomy to otherness, but 'to open up' autonomy, even the autonomy of social intermediation, beyond itself, toward a more generous freedom that responds to the worth of the other in its unconditional worth. Such freedom is irreducible to the erotics of serviceable disposability, whether predicated on contractarian interest or utilitarian maximization of social value: "The agapeics transforms the social space of our between-being, consecrates it into a neighborhood of love wherein neighboring, as a 'being beside', is neither simply passive nor simply active ... We receive and do ourselves in the agapeic neighborhood" (IU 411). Can such a freedom beyond autonomy be recognized without reference to an agapeic God, a source of endowing freedom that is also an enabling of social intermediation? Desmond speaks of the 'antinomy of autonomy and transcendence' and seems to offer a negative response, for the God of autonomy is only a practical postulate, not an endowing source. But to be bound to an agapeic God is not to be in bondage:

> The enabling of social power is given but now understood as gifted by a surplus generosity, ultimate in itself and calling human beings to imitate and to enact this generosity in finite life. This is not a matter of our erotic self-transcendence, it is a communication of transcendence itself into the midst of our transcending, which now no longer can just circle around itself. (IU 417)

Will contemporary ethical discourse heed the call to such a freedom, breaking the spell that has bewitched its reasoning into the vicious circularity of will to power, affirming only itself, only to destroy itself? I suggest that the opening can be occasioned by porosity to a theological contribution, itself sustained by a robust metaphysics, which calls public discussions on moral questions to the suspension of preconceived judgments and dogmatisms of any kind, opening our eyes to a deeper vision of what is good for us, because worthy to be affirmed in itself.

Bibliography

Balthasar, Hans Urs von. 2000. *Theo-Logic: Theological Logical Theory, Volume I/ Truth of the World*. Trans. A.J. Walker. San Francisco, CA: Ignatius Press.
Baron, Richard. 1985. An Introduction to Medical Phenomenology: I Can't Hear You While I'm Listening. *Annals of Internal Medicine* 103: 606.
De Lubac, Henri. 1945. *Le drame de l'humanisme athée*. Paris: Éditions Spes.
Dell'Oro, Roberto. 2005. Interpreting Clinical Judgment: Epistemological Notes on the Praxis of Medicine. In *Clinical Bioethics: A Search for the Foundations*, ed. Corrado Viafora, 155–167. Dordrecht: Springer.
———. 2016. Why Clinical Ethics? Experience, Discernment, and the Anamnesis of Meaning at the Bedside. *Persona y Bioetica* 20: 86–99.

Demmer, Klaus. 1987. *Leben in Menschenhand: Grudlagen des bioethischen Gesprächs*. Freiburg: Herder Verlag.
———. 1989. *Moraltheologische Methodenlehre*. Freiburg: Herder Verlag.
Desmond, William. 1995. *Being and the Between*. Albany, NY: SUNY Press.
———. 2001. *Ethics and the Between*. Albany, NY: SUNY Press.
———. 2006. Pluralism, Truthfulness, and the Patience of Being. In *Health and Human Flourishing: Religion, Medicine, and Moral Anthropology*, ed. Carol Taylor and Roberto Dell'Oro, 53–68. Washington, DC: Georgetown University Press.
———. 2008. *God and the Between*. Malden, MA: Blackwell.
———. 2016. *The Intimate Universal: The Hidden Porosity Among Religion, Art, Philosophy, and Politics*. New York: Columbia University Press.
Duden, Barbara. 1993. *Disembodying Women: Perspectives on Pregnancy and the Unborn*. Trans. Lee Hoinacki. Cambridge, MA: Harvard University Press.
Elias, Norbert. 2001. *The Loneliness of the Dying*. New York: Continuum.
Evans, John H. 2002. *Playing God? Human Genetic Engineering and the Rationalization of Public Bioethical Debate*. Chicago: University of Chicago Press.
Gadamer, Hans Georg. 1996. *The Enigma of Health: The Art of Healing in a Scientific Age*. Trans. J. Geiger and N. Walker. Stanford, CA: Stanford University Press.
Guardini, Romano. 1951. *Das Ende der Neuzeit: Ein Versuch zur Orientierung*. Würzburg: Werkbund Verlag.
Haker, Hille. 2011. *Haupsache gesund? Ethische Fragen der Pränatal- und Präimplantationsdiagnostik*. München: Kösel Verlag.
von Hildebrand, Dietrich. 1953. *Christian Ethics*. New York: David McKay Co.
Husserl, Edmund. 1970. *The Crisis of European Sciences*. Trans. D. Carr. Evanston, IL: Northwestern University Press.
Jüngel, Eberhard. 1975. *Death: The Riddle and the Mystery*. Trans. Iain and Ute Nicol. Edinburgh: The Saint Andrew Press.
Kass, Leon. 2002. *Life, Liberty and the Defense of Dignity: The Challenge for Bioethics*. San Francisco, CA: Encounter Books.
Lauritzen, Paul. 1993. *Pursuing Parenthood: Ethical Issues in Assisted Reproduction*. Bloomington: Indiana University Press.
Meilaender, Gilbert C. 1995. *Body, Soul, and Bioethics*. Notre Dame, IN: University of Notre Dame Press.
Pellegrino, Edmund. 1979. The Anatomy of Clinical Judgment: Some Notes on Right Reason and Right Action. In *Clinical Judgment: A Critical Appraisal*, ed. Tristram Engelhardt et al., 169–194. Dordrecht: D. Reidel Publishing Company.

———. 1983. The Healing Relationship: The Architectonics of Clinical Medicine. In *The Clinical Encounter: The Moral Fabric of the Patient-Physician Relationship*, ed. E. Shelp, 153–172. Dordrecht: D. Reidel Publishing Company.

Reich, Warren T. 1996. L'arte del prendersi cura del morente. *Itinerarium* 4: 31–43.

Reich, Warren T., and Roberto Dell'Oro. 1996. A New Era for Bioethics: The Search for Meaning in Moral Experience. In *Religion and Medical Ethics: Looking Back, Looking Forward*, ed. Allen Verhey, 96–119. Grand Rapids, MI: Eerdmans.

Scheffczyk, Leo. 1992. Die Phänomenologie des Todes bei Dietrich von Hildebrand und die neuere Eschatologie. In *Truth and Value: The Philosophy of Dietrich von Hildebrand*, ed. J. Seifert, 265–278. Bern: Peter Lang.

Scheler, Max. 1974. The Meaning of Suffering. In *Max Scheler (1874–1928): Centennial Essays*, ed. Manfred S. Frings, 121–163. The Hague: Martinus Nijhof.

Schmucker-Von Koch, Josef. 1992. Wertblindheit als Signatur der Moderne: Zum Verhältnis von Recht und Sittlichkeit bei Dietrich von Hildebrand. In *Truth and Value: The Philosophy of Dietrich von Hildebrand*, ed. J. Seifert, 141–152. Bern: Peter Lang.

Sölle, Dorothee. 1973. *Leiden*. Stuttgart: Kreuz Verlag.

Taylor, Charles. 1989. *Sources of the Self: The Making of Modern Identity*. Cambridge, MA: Harvard University Press.

Taylor, Carol, and Roberto Dell'Oro. 2006. *Health and Human Flourishing: Religion, Medicine, and Moral Anthropology*. Washington, DC: Georgetown University Press.

Thiel, Marie-Jo. 2013. La corporéité face à la maladie et la mort. In *Exploring the Boundaries of Bodyliness: Theological and Interdisciplinary Approaches to the Human Condition*, ed. Sigrid Müller, 1–13. Göttingen: Vienna University Press.

Tingley, Kim. 2014. The Brave New World of Three-Parent I.V.F. *The New York Times*, June 27.

Wartofsky, Marx W. 1997. What Can the Epistemologists Learn from the Endocrinologists? Or Is the Philosophy of Medicine Based on a Mistake? In *Philosophy of Medicine and Bioethics: A Twenty Years Retrospective and Critical Appraisal*, ed. Ronald A. Carson and Chester R. Burns, 55–68. Dordrecht: Kluwer Academic Publishers.

Zaner, Richard. 1988. *Ethics and the Clinical Encounter*. Englewood Cliffs, NJ: Prentice Hall.

CHAPTER 11

Silence, Excess, and Autonomy

Dennis Vanden Auweele

Letting go of his hopes for a miracle, Alyosha Karamazov, one of the protagonists of Fyodor Dostoyevsky's *The Brother Karamazov* (1880), comes to silence. Silence is in itself equivocal: there is a silence of impotence, consideration, trepidation, snide, and many more, but silence can also be a convalescence, a moment of repose that allows distance from one thing and the advance of something else. When his spiritual mentor, Father (*Starets*) Zosima, died, Alyosha hoped that some sort of miracle would signal his holiness, a miracle preferably accompanied by the angelic and vociferous blare of trumpets. The Heavens were silent, though, and this silence brought Alyosha to a crisis of faith. Another moment of silence, narrated masterfully by Dostoyevsky, brought Alyosha to renewed hope and faith:

> Alyosha gazed for half a minute at the coffin, at the covered, motionless dead man that lay in the coffin, with the ikon on his breast and the peaked cap with the octangular cross, on his head. He had only just been hearing his voice, and that voice was still ringing in his ears. He was listening, still expecting other words, but suddenly he turned sharply and went out of the cell. He did not stop on the steps either, but went quickly down; his soul,

D. Vanden Auweele (✉)
KU Leuven (University of Leuven), Leuven, Belgium
e-mail: Dennis.Vandenauweele@kuleuven.be

© The Author(s) 2018
D. Vanden Auweele (ed.), *William Desmond's Philosophy between Metaphysics, Religion, Ethics, and Aesthetics*,
https://doi.org/10.1007/978-3-319-98992-1_11

overflowing with rapture, yearned for freedom, space, openness. The vault of heaven, full of soft, shining stars, stretched vast and fathomless above him. The Milky Way ran in two pale streams from the zenith to the horizon. The fresh, motionless, still night enfolded the earth. The white towers and golden domes of the church gleamed out against the sapphire sky. The autumn flowers, in the garden, were slumbering. The silence of earth seemed to melt into the silence of the heavens. The mystery of earth was one with the mystery of the starts. (2007, p. 418)

Silence as a convalescence—can this be a resource for philosophical theology and ethics? Is silence, the intentional halting of autonomous thought and speech, of use when thinking about God, goodness, and autonomy? Or do we determine, *must* we determine, always the goodness of things? Are we legislators or subjects in the life of morality? Kant famously suggested in his final formulation of the categorical imperative that we are to think of ourselves *as if* we are both. But Kant's view emerged against the backdrop of a specific rhetoric about thinking God, ethics, and most importantly autonomy, one that is simply lacking in finesse in the grand pageant of the overdeterminacy of ethical life. In order to advance beyond this, that backdrop has to come to silence, and only then can silence and heteronomy serve again as a way of creating space for appreciating givenness (heteronomy) without dismantling self-determination (autonomy).

No better resource exists to make such a point than the metaxological philosophy of William Desmond. In his trilogy on 'the between' (dealing respectively with being, being good, and absolute being), Desmond consistently provides a sort of genealogy of our contemporary hesitations about speaking about being as such, the goodness of being and God as absolute being. A certain way of speaking has come to silence. His reflections on the porosity between philosophy and religion in *Is there a Sabbath for Thought?* is prefaced by a suggestive reflection on such silence:

> I remember a time when to mention God or religion in the company of advanced intellectuals was like mentioning sex in a prudish Victorian drawing room. An icy silence would descend, and the silence communicated more than the argument possibly could: we do not now talk of these things. (IST xi)

Such a silence can be deafening and is generally unhelpful for appreciating the goodness of receptivity. Many would read Desmond's work as reactionary against such silence, boldly advancing toward the glory of a

Christian, metaphysical theism. I think there are many people, Christian and otherwise, who advance forward despite silence, but this method simplifies matters as philosophy ought to be more appreciative of different sorts of silences. Indeed, one can learn from such silence that a certain way of speaking was inappropriate and thereby come to new insight and move toward more finessed ways of speaking. But also, one can take the moment of silence, of Sabbath, as occasion to get a good fill of those things in excess (overdeterminate) to human determination. Many philosophers and theologians today recognize the latter, but what sets Desmond apart is that such silence can give way to a new way of speaking, which leaves for a constitutive ambiguity of the *chiaroscuro* of thinking and living in 'the between'.[1]

SILENCE AND EXCESS

Much of postmodern philosophy is keen on heckling traditional philosophy. For one, it likes to point out that the tradition has done a poor task of coming to terms with thinking those things that are in excess of finite self-determination, most importantly God. They believe that traditional attempts to think God have been overly univocalizing and leveling; they have turned God into a being among beings that could be understood through immanent rationality. Heidegger might say that this approach misses the constitutive and infinite distance between immanent forms of rational thought and the poetry of transcendence: one should not speak of God in the way that one speaks of tables, germs, and potatoes. Indeed, there has been a long and lamentable tradition of turning God as transcendence into a counterfeit double of himself, to use Desmond's term (see HG and GB), where God is not transcendence thought of as absolute transcendence, but as the reversal of human finitude, the sum total of immanent being or even the world-historical process itself. This problem was perhaps most emphatically signaled by Jean-Luc Marion when he gives voice to the need to remove ourselves urgently from metaphysics, at least if we hope to think of God appropriately:

---

[1] In earlier work, I have taken up a similar topic where, at that point, I argued that metaxological porosity to divinity and a Nietzschean existentialist rejection of God are equally justified responses to the issue of religion and ethics (Vanden Auweele 2013, pp. 637–655). I consider the present account of the matter to be the more refined and nuanced.

> Nonidolatrous thought of God, which alone releases 'God' from his quotation marks by disengaging his apprehension from the conditions posed by onto-theo-logy, one would have to manage to think God outside of metaphysics insofar as metaphysics infallibility leads, by way of blasphemy (proof), to the twilight of the idols (conceptual atheism) [...] the step back out of metaphysics seems an urgent task. (2012, p. 37)

Postmodern philosophers very loudly call for silence when it comes to philosophical, and particularly metaphysical, accounts of God. Perhaps this can be a well-deserved respite from the clamoring of rationalist philosophy as an overexposure of thought to rationalism, reason, knowledge, and metaphysics has problematic consequences: too much talk makes for little understanding. In order for human beings to live and flourish, metaphysics has then to die; in order for humanity to prosper, we ought to come to silence about God. But is such philosophical silence about God and the step back from metaphysics the final move in the long and laudable history of philosophy? Is silence where philosophy comes to die? Or is there thought after silence?

If this were possible, this would have to be a thinking that takes the silence seriously. It cannot be the case that our newly developed poetry of God simply slides back into old patterns and rightly criticized ways of thinking: *No new wine in old barrels.* This is a mistake that ought to be avoided at all costs: simple repetition. In his recent *In Praise of Heteronomy*, Merold Westphal argues that those postmodern theologies that most vociferously want to get away from modern claims to universal reason are usually the ones that repeat similar mistakes:

> Certain postmodern theologies are only partly different from the modern theologies from which they seek to distance themselves. [...]. They have taken the hermeneutical turn and do not profess to speak as the voice of some universal view from nowhere. But if their understanding of reason is postmodern in this sense, they give it the same hegemony as their Enlightenment predecessors over the special revelation on which the 'religions of the book' seek to ground themselves. [...] Just as some postmodern thinkers have not abandoned the Enlightenment ideal of epistemic and social critique, so some have not abandoned the project of religion within the limits of reason alone. It should be noted that their faith in the resultant religions can be just as strong and (epistemically) intolerant as the faiths that seek to ground themselves on special revelation. But they are faiths, nevertheless—rival faiths. (2017, p. 214)

The silence about God can then not be a brief stammer in an otherwise fluent speech, a brief hiccup in a self-same plan. For most, this means that the silence kills metaphysics. Is there another way? This would mean that a speech emerges out of this silence, a speech invigorated and wounded by the silence at the same time.

Let us take silence seriously for a moment. When do we tend toward silence? Most profoundly, we are silent when we recognize that words do not do justice to what is happening. Better then to soak it all in than to render shallow those events of profundity. In *Perplexity and Ultimacy*, William Desmond discusses this form of silence, strangely illustrated by the 'howl' of Shakespeare's King Lear: a primal roar is tantamount to silence as words escape us. Entering the stage bearing Cordelia's dead body, Shakespeare's King Lear is tragically at loss and without words; at best, he utters a howl to give voice to his agony. About the tragic, one cannot speak philosophically: "We cannot, we will not speak about this Howl. We will be silent about heaven" (PU 28). But that voice of tragic howling, so continues Desmond, is itself being silenced by philosophy because it upsets, perhaps incapacitates, the philosophical project of determinate and systematic completeness: "It threatens, not because it will not hear the other, but rather from excess of hearing, from excess of exposure to an otherness that destroys every human self-sufficiency" (PU 28). What philosophical words of comfort could be offered to poor King Lear? At the high point of their personal tragedy, what logical argument might have wrested the danger from Romeo and Julia's hands? What use are arguments when we are being threatened in our very capacity for self-determination and self-understanding?

How must philosophy cope with this call to silence and reverence? Kant recognized something of this in the exaltation of the moral law, for which we must stand still and show reverence (*Achtung*). There is an honesty in Kant, who recognized the limits of the reach of philosophical talk. Very generally, philosophical thought comes to a breakdown when it vividly realizes that there is a gap between what can be determined and what is in excess of reasonable determination. This is not something that philosophy is at ease with since it is "driven by the conviction, should we say faith, that being is not ultimately tragic. True reason will never be at a loss; true reason will be the intelligent *finding* of the deep logical intelligibility that is inherent in the nature of things" (PU 30–31). Traditionally, much of philosophy has kept talking through the silence, insisting upon *logos* when it was not appropriate. In response, there is a trend in most postmodern philosophy, especially its deconstructive line of thought, to emphasize that such excess invites philosophy and metaphysics to silence: of which one cannot speak, one ought to be silent. This seems like defeatism to me and, with Desmond, I would ask whether "philosophical mind [can] break through to a deeper metaphysical thinking even in this breakdown?" (PU 29). This is not to say that all silence can inaugurate a new being. Silence is said (or not said!) in many ways:

> There is the empty silence of meaninglessness. There is the silence of an acknowledging, full of reverent respect before the other. There is a silence of despair. There is a silence of peace beyond measure. There is a tragic silence: this is a transconceptual silence that rends the silence, all silences, the conceptless silence of Lear's Howl. (PU 36)

Our focus further is only on this sense of tragic silence that brings philosophy's project to a standstill. How do we react to a givenness in excess of determinate thought? Is autonomous self-determination or heteronomous submission the answer? Or is this a false binary?

The Equivocity of Autonomy

In Plato's dialogue *Euthydemus*, Socrates gives us an image, one that is supposed to describe what it is like to do philosophy. The cover of this volume tries to communicate something similarly. Despite the seriousness of philosophical dialectics, Socrates there describes doing philosophy as children clumsily running after birds: "We were really quite ridiculous—just like children after crested larks; we kept thinking we were about to catch each one of the knowledges, but they always got away" (Plato 1997, p. 728 [291 b]). This wonderful image calls to mind something of the task of philosophy, namely to aspire to as much determination as humanly possible without thereby reducing the phenomena. The children are autonomously running after the larks, but when they reach out to catch one, their grip cannot be overly tight. If it would, then *bye bye birdy*. The same thing goes for dealing with those things in excess of determinate thought: when one grasps them too tight, one kills their vital energies. Plato knew well that such things as a carefulness out of truthfulness are hard to convey to readers yearning for determination. Because of this, as Desmond points, out Plato leaves us with an image when thinking about his own moment of tragedy, the death of Socrates:

This is not logic; this is not system; this is not the abstract universal. All of this is an image, a philosophical icon. At one level the image says: Philosophy must go on. But at another level it cautions: It can only go on if it is honest about loss, if it keeps before its thinking the image of death, the memory of the dead. (PU 44)

Moral goodness is one of these things that we risk grabbing too tight. What is the good, how is it determined, and where does it come from? From us or God? There is a view of the history of ethics that moves ethics from absolute heteronomy toward absolute autonomy, as for instance from the theory of moral obligation as a divine command toward the Kantian morality of autonomy. Most would see this move as an improvement, where the moral good is now determined relative to our autonomous giving the law to ourselves. But even in authors most famously associated with such a view, the matters remains equivocal. According to Kant, the sole moral good is the "good will" (1996, p. 49 [4:393]), which is a will that is free as "efficient independently of alien causes *determining* it" and as "being a law to itself" (ibid., p. 94 [4:446–447]). A morally good person has a will that determines itself according to certain universal and immutable laws. But what exactly does it mean to be a lawgiver to oneself? For Kant, this signals that the human will dictates to itself, from a source entirely a priori, certain basic principles:

> Here philosophy is to manifest its purity as sustainer of its own laws, not as herald of laws than an implanted sense of who knows what tutelary nature whispers to it, all of which—though they may always be better than nothing at all—can still never yield basic principles that reason dictates and that must have their source entirely and completely a priori. (1996, p. 77 [4:426])

The source of the dictates of morality lies in a priori reason, and the motivation to act in accordance with these principles, in turn, rests in respect for these principles. These principles, so Kant continues, "must have their commanding authority from this: that they expect nothing from the inclination of human beings but everything from the supremacy of the law and the respect owed to it, failing this, condemn the human being to contempt for himself and inner abhorrence" (ibid.).

Despite a whole, very lucrative, business of Kantian apologetics attempting explicitly to reconstruct and validate Kant's thoughts, this way of thinking about autonomy must strike our contemporary ears as awkward:

Kant turns autonomy into obedience! In *Daybreak*, Nietzsche berates this German proclivity, namely to find its own excellence in its capacity for obedience. There, he writes of German morality that "man has to have something which he can *obey unconditionally*" (1997, p. 129 [207]). Kant himself was not oblivious to the issue. In what is sometimes called the 'antinomy of duty', he calls moral duty the "*necessitation* (constraint) of free choice through the law" (1996, p. 512 [6:379]). When under a moral duty, human beings necessarily see themselves as both a sensible being and an intelligible being (1996, pp. 534–544 [6:418]). The intelligible aspect of the human being determines then the sensible aspect of the human being. This sort of panicky dualist metaphysics fails to do the trick anymore. In fact, Kantian autonomy has all semblance of heteronomy.

The equivocity in Kantian ethics is this: the moral law supposedly derives from our own lawgiving, but it lifts human beings to the level of universality. Kantian ethics, so says Desmond, tries to mediate dialectically between '*being given the law* and *giving oneself the law*" (EB 133). In Kantian ethics "we find ourselves under the moral law" (EB 136), but where exactly that moral law comes from remains unclear. Traditionally, one would point to a universal and absolute source of moral goodness, such as God, but Kant is averse to that:

> While Kant, at some decisive points, lets God peep ambiguously through the thick curtains of the critical system, he does not always want to draw attention to the fact. Why? Because his view of theological ethics entails a heteronomy that for him is undignified for us: we risk submission to the commands of a tyrannical master and are turned into abject dependents. (EB 136–137)

So for Kant, things remain ambiguous, but Kant's contemporary offspring evacuates any leftover dogmatism and heteronomy from his moral philosophy. Autonomy as self-law, autonomous decision—whether rational or not—is what bestows moral worth on behavior. Autonomy can then only be successful insofar as it succeeds in relativizing and mitigating any other source of moral value: "Autonomy functions only by relativizing this other source; and the more radically we insist on this autonomy, the more this relativizing must be completed" (EB 137). For the sake of absolute autonomy, the absoluteness of any other source of morality must be denied: "The antinomy: absolutize autonomy, and you relativize the good as other, or more than our self-determination; absolutize the good as other, and you must relativize autonomy" (EB 137–138).

This situation, and its equivocity, is even more apparent in Nietzsche's ethical imperatives, even though he refuses to call them as such. In Nietzsche, "the self-legislation of Kantian morality is transformed into an autonomy that is *not under* any moral law, since it claims itself to be the source of the law" (EB 152). Human beings are will to power and give expression—either strongly or weakly—to their will. Anything that could count as good in Nietzschean morality is to be understood in terms of human self-transcending, the capacity to overcome certain stagnant perspectives of the self. The case is similar in Nietzsche as in Kant: for the sake of their autonomy, they must deny absolute, heteronomous value. But this trapped Nietzsche in the nihilism he so hoped to overcome:

> Nietzsche so wanted to avoid inherent value that he was trapped in [...] nihilism, despite his excess of rhetoric about overcoming nihilism. And he wanted to avoid inherent value, because he wanted to avoid God, just as Kant wanted to put God in epoche to cling to the sacred cow of his own autonomy. (EB 154–155)

In *The Gay Science*, Nietzsche presents what most would take to be his prime ethical imperative: to give style to one's character. By this, he means the practice of those "who survey all the strengths and weaknesses that their nature has to offer and then fit them into an artistic plan until each appears as art and reason and even weaknesses delight the eye" (2001, p. 163 [290]). What is meant by this is that a self-styled person is someone who takes the myriad aspects of his personhood and molds these into something that adheres to a singular taste or style: "In the end, when the work is complete, it becomes clear how it was the force of a single taste that ruled and shaped everything great and small—whether the taste was good or bad means less than one may think; it's enough that it was one taste!" (2001, p. 164 [290]). Nietzsche's main dislike of much of his contemporary culture is that it is a motley patchwork of different tastes and styles, incapable of discerning finesse.

Nietzsche then follows Kant's lead in thinking about ethics in a sense of aestheticized autonomy: we create ourselves according to a style. But Nietzsche does not lack the intellectual honesty to recognize that submission to style reeks of subjection. How does one cope with submitting oneself to a singular style? Nietzsche believes that weak individuals can only respond slavishly, grudgingly following the imperatives (and allowing themselves occasional, small deviances). Strong natures, however, will adopt style as their fate, and move to love their fate: "It will be the strong and domineering natures who experience their most exquisite pleasure under such coercion, in being bound by but also perfected under their own law" (ibid.). Only this can make a human being bearable sight to behold, as he becomes self-satisfied through obedience to style: "For one thing is needful: that a human being should *attain* satisfaction with himself—be it through this or that poetry or art; only then is a human being at all tolerable to behold!" (ibid.).

Kantian and Nietzschean attempts at formulating a morality of autonomy inevitably wind up entangled with the heteronomy they so desire to avoid. Some sort of obedience cannot be avoided, if only obedience to some ambiguous sense of self (see EB 159–162). The Kantian moral law and Nietzschean love of fate, both of these are shimmers of heteronomy intent upon saving their respective moralities from the threat of nihilism. Autonomy is the wall we have set up to ward off nihilism. Perhaps rightly so, they fear together with Pascal that the silence of their own autonomy will make the silence of these infinites space dreadful. But then again, perhaps it is silence that can here be the savior?

The Silence of Autonomy

The moral project of autonomy operates under the conviction that the good is determined teleologically only. For instance, the generic answer to the question what the value is of such thing as being born white or black, Catholic or Muslim, man or woman, is simple: what you determine it to be. The good of something is what we determine it to be. But as we grow and develop autonomously into formidable individuals, we cannot help but ponder our roots. Does not absolute autonomy require us to belittle, even reject, the potential good of our origin? What does it matter that I was born a man if I desire to be a woman? Why can I not turn Buddhist overnight? Or why could I not transition to a new race, if that is what I desire? These are the views of a radical existentialism à la Sartre, which has crept in to what counts for moral decency today. Each determines at every moment what the value is of an origin, a given, a heritage, a thought, a belief, an orientation. But who or what is then doing the determining? What self are we obeying now? What supports this project of autonomous self-(re)creation? What solid ground is there to be who I want to be, if what I want to accomplish is to destroy all foundations?

There is a suspicion of otherness that creeps into these ways of thinking, an overemphasis on self-insistence when faced with otherness in favor of acceptance. There are other ways of handling this, evidenced by metaxology: "This concerns our being in the between insofar as our self-surpassing goes beyond itself from more than lack, and beyond erotic self-determination. There is a release towards the other for the sake of the other" (EB 161). When it comes to properly engaging the other, it is often the case that speech and reason stand in between us and the possibility for authentic engagement, even if the other is our self. Too much talk does not allow for intimacy. I know of no better illustration of this than the scene at the close of part III of *Thus spoke Zarathustra*. Here, Nietzsche paints a picture of a frustrated protagonist, unnerved by the elusiveness of his object of desire: Life. Dancing around and avoiding Zarathustra's grasp, Life as the ultimate other eludes Zarathustra. Zarathustra responds in anger and indignation, taking the whip to Life: "You witch, if I have so far sung for you, now *you* for me will—yell! To the beat of my whip you will dance so and yell so! But did I forget the whip?—Oh no!" (2006, p. 182). Life's response? Squeamishly she covers her ears and answers: "Oh Zarathustra! Please do not crack your whip so fearfully! Surely you know: noise murders thoughts—and just now the most tender thoughts are coming to me" (ibid.).

Nietzsche realizes he has come to a stalemate: insisting upon autonomy is possible, but it would have to take the whip to life. And as anyone ever in love will tell you, when you try to force reciprocity, then true love is gone. Life's elusiveness is what makes her enticing, rich, and fertile; a whipped life would be like a Platonic squeezed lark: empty of life. This kills what is excessive to determination, which is the fuel and life-blood of living. But is then Zarathustra, and so also we, supposed to submit to Life's desires and currents if this means relinquishing autonomy? Are we then condemned to silence and heteronomy? And how does one answer such a question when speaking and reason themselves make for the problem? Nietzsche's solution, brilliant in its rhetorical and imaginative potential, is thus: "'Yes,' I answered hesitating. 'But you also know—' And I said something in her ear, right in between her tangled yellow, foolish shaggy locks" (2006, p. 183). Nietzsche's final answer is a whisper, a secret kept between Life and himself. Whatever way this might be interpreted in the narrative structure of *Thus spoke Zarathustra*, it is telling that

Nietzsche's final word to Life borderlines silence. True intimacy requires one to drop the volume, to be willing to mitigate autonomy and keep open a release of self for the sake of the other.

This is what Desmond calls an "archeology of the good" (EB 163–165), which sees the good as developing from an origin (*arché*) prior to being able to progress toward an end (*telos*). Recognizing that there is something good at work in what is given in being, the good of the to be as such, is initially a matter for silent wonder. Such a given can arise in many ways: the goodness of being as such, the goodness of given beauty, the goodness of regularity, the goodness of becoming, the goodness of the gift, the transcendent good as other (EB 170–220). When the worth of such things is only dependent upon autonomous choice, one does not recognize that such autonomous choice, and its capacity for discernment, is itself derivative from a more original source, endowing it with goodness. Autonomy is then always relativized autonomy, never absolute, as dependent upon numerous sources of inspiration.

How does this end? With autonomy coming to silent reverence for the good of the given? On no account: the given goodness of being endows autonomy and reason with its own goodness; as inspired now by the intimacy of the goodness of being, autonomy is invigorated. In silence, there can be an intimation of a more primal passivity which impassions the pursuit of ever higher and more good. This is, I believe, what Desmond tries to signal with *passio essendi* being more primal than *conatus essendi*: a passion or patience for being that is more original than any endeavor to be. Such a patient and passionate silence is only to be feared if we remain in the project for an absolutized sense of autonomy. Then, all silence is dreadful. When we are willing to relativize autonomy and opening up charitably to the given, then silence can be an occasion for convalescence. Silence can then be itself an overcoming, an overcoming of an absolutized sense of selfhood in favor of a more community-based, open-dialectical entanglement with the world. Excess calls us to silence; silence brings us to new and more appropriate speech.

Conclusion

Silence can be a calling, evidenced by many religious people who take upon themselves a vow of silence. Silence can allow for superior listening, capable of recognizing the merit and goodness of otherness. And yet, silence is often dreaded, and we rush to fill in the silence with idle talk. In this contribution, I aimed to show that not all silence is to be feared as it can allow for an authentic openness to those things in excess of finite and autonomous determination. The modern project for an absolutized sense of autonomy runs into its own ambiguities, but it can be pushed beyond its own capacity. Then, the good is what we determine it to be, but we have no grounds to determine anything as being good, no community from which to receive our value as originators of value. For some, there is something offensive about being touched, or called to silence, by something other, something elevated over ourselves. Nietzsche quipped at one point that there could be no gods, because otherwise he could not stand, not to be a god. There are many reservations in modernity against those things that hamper our autonomous speech. And yet, silence, like Platonic madness, brings so much that is good.

Bibliography

Dostoyevsky, Fyodor. 2007. *The Brothers Karamazov*. Trans. Constance Garnett. New York: Signett Classics.

Kant, Immanuel. 1996. *Practical Philosophy. The Cambridge Edition of the Works of Immanuel Kant*. Ed. Paul Guyer and Allen Wood. Cambridge: Cambridge University Press.

Marion, Jean-Luc. 2012. *God Without Being*. Trans. Thomas Carlson. Chicago and London: University of Chicago Press.

Nietzsche, Friedrich. 1997. *Daybreak*. Ed. Maudemarie Clark and Brian Leiter. Cambridge: Cambridge University Press.

———. 2001. *The Gay Science*. Ed. Bernard Williams. Cambridge: Cambridge University Press.

———. 2006. *Thus Spoke Zarathustra*. Ed. Adrian Del Caro and Robert Pippin. Cambridge: Cambridge University Press.

Plato. 1997. Euthydemus. In *Plato: Collected Works*. Ed. John Cooper and Trans. Rosamond Kent Sprague. Indianapolis: Hackett Publishing.

Vanden Auweele, Dennis. 2013. Metaxological 'Yes' and Existential 'No': William Desmond and Atheism. *Sophia: International Journal of Philosophy and Traditions* 52: 637–655.

Westphal, Merold. 2017. *In Praise of Heteronomy. Making Room for Revelation*. Indianapolis: Indiana University Press.

CHAPTER 12

Reactivating Christian Metaphysical Glory in the Wake of Its Eclipse: William Desmond Contra Giorgio Agamben

Philip John Paul Gonzales

Contemporary Continental discourse is everywhere riddled with religious themes and symbols, especially of a Christian variety. This legacy of Christianity is significantly manifested in a reopening of the 'eschatological bureau,' which has clearly reemerged, in a non-identical way, since Ernst Troeltsch made his famous statement about its closure within Christianity in 1925. Indeed, the reason for this reactivation is largely due to the Hegelo-Kojèvian thematic of the end of history, the Nietzschean cry of the 'death of God' which has loosed the earth from the sun and the fateful emergence of *Ereignis* which the Heideggerian master narrative has appended to the end of the history of Being, understood as being's own history. This reopening, in the dimmed lighting of these three intellectual/metaphysical events of closure, has rightfully provoked a rethinking of messianic, eschatological and apocalyptic themes, a turn to the religious and, indeed, a thinking of a weakened and formless simulacrum of Christianity. The former is seen, most famously, in the work of Emmanuel

---

P. J. P. Gonzales (✉)
University of Dallas, Irving, TX, USA
e-mail: pgonzales@udallas.edu

Levinas and Jacques Derrida, while the latter is seen in the work of Mark C. Taylor, Gianni Vattimo, Richard Kearney and John Caputo, to name some of the most prominent.[1]

Beyond the first layer of this formless and nebulous reactivation of messianic, eschatological, apocalyptic and Christian themes must be added a second layer of reengagement with such themes within contemporary Continental discourse. This time, however, this reengagement is marked by a more substantial, serious and robust engagement with the Christian theological tradition which sees philosophy's reengagement with Christianity to be indispensable for thought today. This second wave can, in turn, be divided into two groups. The first consists in the theologically inclined yet profaning modes of philosophizing, exemplified in Žižek, Badiou and Agamben, while the second consists in expressly Christian philosophically inclined modes of *theo*logy exhibited in John Milbank, David Bentley Hart and Cyril O'Regan, alongside the theologically inclined mode of Christian philosophizing of William Desmond.

Yet the question immediately becomes, from a serious Christian metaphysical perspective, what to make of this return of Christian symbols and themes, of this sourcing of Christian sources and how does one understand this in the wake of the previous intellectual/metaphysical events of closure? Should history be read in the wake of a theogonic development of god, or Spirit, becoming God on the altar of time, history and becoming? Or should history be read in the wake of the death of the Christian God, in the name of a revaluation which seeks to resurrect chthonic deities? Or perhaps history should be read in the wake of being's own history which is thought in one thinker's mystagogical thought which initiates thinking into the *Ereignis* and thus the thinking otherwise of being, counter to the Western metaphysical tradition and, especially, the Christian tradition? What figuration of being is to be thought in the aftermath of these events?

For the Christian metaphysician cannot simply ignore these three great master narratives (Hegelian/Nietzschean/Heideggerian), but nor can Christian thinking seek to entirely base itself within the dimmed light of

---

[1] René Girard and Benoît Chantre have rightfully spoken about the leaping of Levinas' thought into eschatology (Girard and Chantre 2009, p. 107). For more on the distinction between eschatology and apocalyptic in relation to Levinas' thought, in the context of a discussion of Girard's apocalyptic turn, see O'Regan (2012, pp. 123–124). For Derrida's apocalyptic turn see Derrida (1993, pp. 117–171).

these events, in a state of paralysis (e.g. Marion), which is unable to think the dynamism and pleromatic visionary truth of its own tradition and story. Rather, Christian thinking must read these metaphysical, yet aesthetic and visionary narratives, from a Christian apocalyptic point-of-view which sees that "it is the free thinking intellect that makes history and its deep decisions roll and echo down through the centuries. In this way history is the apocalypse (that is to say, the opening) of the decision of the intellect for or against God" (Balthasar 1989, p. 39). History, read in this Christian light, must read these three narratives as symptomatic of what von Balthasar prophetically diagnoses as the eclipse of glory in modernity and philosophical modernity, in particular.

Thus the question of which figuration of being must be thought today, from a Christian perspective, is a question of the figuration of Christian metaphysical glory, in response to this dramatic hour of Christian history. I thus propose, in agreement with von Balthasar, that the 'epic' style of the *summa* and the 'lyric' style of the spiritual treatises, understood as past figurations of Christian metaphysical glory, are no longer operable in light of the challenges of our intellectual and metaphysical history (Balthasar 1988, p. 42). To propose this is to claim three things: First, at stake in the reactivation of messianic, eschatological, apocalyptic and Christian themes is nothing less than the question of a profanation, disfiguration and, ultimately, a deactivation of the tradition of Christian metaphysical glory. Second, in the face of this possibility, what is needed today is a reimagining and reactivation of Christian metaphysical glory, on our twilight side of history. Third, if this reactivation is to occur viably, then the Christian metaphysical style needed would have to be: pleromatic, performative, rhetorical, aesthetic and dramatic.[2] Moreover, this metaphysics would likewise have to critically judge and gauge the return of Christian themes from its own standpoint and tradition, thereby seeking to uncover 'counterfeit doubles' (Desmond) or profanations of Christianity which seek to deactivate Christian metaphysical glory with deceitful surrogates.

---

[2] This need can be said to be the leitmotif of my *Reimagining the Analogia Entis* (Gonzales 2019).

Electing Desmond and Agamben

In order to argue for the proposed reactivation of Christian metaphysical glory, in the wake of its eclipse and the continual possibility of its deactivation in Continental thought, I elect to treat two figures who are representative of the two standpoints, of the second wave, spoken about above: William Desmond and Giorgio Agamben.

Prior to giving reasons for electing these two figures, a few words must be said on their drastically different philosophical approaches. On the surface, Desmond's and Agamben's narratives could not be more distinct. Desmond's is an avowed Christian and theistic metaphysician after the 'end of history,' the 'death of God,' and the 'death of metaphysics,' while Agamben is an a/theistic and profaning thinker who powerfully thinks the unavoidability of political theology, in connection to ontology, in the wake of the aforementioned events of closure. Desmond's metaphysical mindfulness critically calls into question the absoluteness of the 'linguistic turn,' while Agamben's thinking takes place within this very turn. Further, the intellectual figures that recur in their work could not be more different. In Desmond one continually encounters: Plato, Augustine, Hegel and Nietzsche, along with Shakespeare, Dostoevsky, Pascal and Shestov. In Agamben, recurring figures include: Heidegger, Benjamin, Schmitt, Foucault, Aristotle, Spinoza and Kafka. Nor could their styles and methods be more different. Desmond's style and method is deeply metaphysical, with phenomenological accents of a Marcelian and thus non-Husserlian sort. Desmond's thinking is a thinking between system and poetics. Which means it is intimately universal and storied.[3] A thinking which is an enactment of selving within the concrete givenness of the milieu of the between: a style between idiocy and communication, passing over into the rhapsodic with particularly Irish intonations, while Agamben's thinking is methodical and archeological, in a Foucauldian sense. Moreover, his method is guided by an intense attention to philological details expressed in a rare erudition schooled in ancient rhetoric and grammar. Yet, Agamben's philological erudition is not without its poetic element as seen in his indebtedness to the thinking—poetically—of Heidegger and Benjamin, hence, his engagement with Rilke, Hölderlin, and, perhaps in a most celebrated manner, Mallarmé.

---

[3] See IU and also my review of this work in *The American Catholic Philosophical Quarterly*, forthcoming.

What, then, is exemplary in the respective thinking of Desmond and Agamben, in relation to my concern for a reactivation/deactivation of Christian metaphysical glory, in contemporary Continental discourse? I begin with the least important and, by degrees, work up to the most important reasons for my election. First, both thinkers seek to rethink creatively, in a serious and nuanced manner, our relation to the history of Western metaphysics, in the wake of the three aforementioned intellectual events, in a manner which is more profound than the simplistic departure from the Western metaphysical heritage proposed by many a Continental thinker. Second, what separates Desmond and Agamben from other approaches is their robust engagement with the Western Christian theological tradition, as opposed to the weak approaches one finds in other Continental thinkers (Derrida, Mark C. Taylor, Vattimo, Kearney and Caputo). Third, in relation to the first part of the second wave mentioned above, Agamben's engagement with the Western Christian theological tradition is the deepest and most comprehensive in comparison to Badiou and Žižek, while Desmond, in relation to the second part of the second wave, is the only thinker mentioned whose mode of discourse takes place on a fully Christian metaphysical register, in distinction to the overtly *theo*logical approach of Milbank, Hart and O'Regan. In light of this fact it can be argued that *God and the Between* (2008) presents a speculative metaphysical theology the likes of which have not be seen since Erich Przywara's brilliant and magisterial work: *Analogia Entis* (1932).[4] Fourth, Desmond's and Agamben's, respectively, deep engagements with the Western theological tradition, in relation to the question of the current figuration of being, are centrally connected with the question of Christian glory.

In order to approach the hermeneutic key of glory, it is necessary to see how each thinker approaches the question of the Sabbath. For both thinkers a certain kind of sabbatical thinking is required in relation to being, in this historical hour. Indeed, both go so far as offering interpretations of being as inherently sabbatical and it is, I contend, in these respective sabbatical interpretations of being, that their drastically different views of Christian glory are uncovered. Desmond's interpretation, I argue, seeks a non-identical reactivation of Christian metaphysical glory which goes a long way in creatively developing the kind of style of Christian metaphysics which I am advocating in this time of Christian history, while Agamben's

---

[4] See Przywara (2014). For more on the relation between Przywara and Desmond, see Gonzales (forthcoming).

brilliantly provocative thought and his comprehensive engagement with the theological tradition, ultimately, seeks the muting and deactivation of Christian glory; a muting which I am concerned with diagnosing and challenging from a Christian metaphysical register.

Agamben's Deactivation of Christian Glory

Agamben's nine-volume *Homo Sacer* project, written over a twenty-five year period, is undoubtedly one of the most important intellectual events of our time. And, in my view, it is so for three primary reasons. First, Agamben has unmasked the fact that the violence of the 'state of exception' is inherently and continuously operative in the founding mythologeme of the modern liberal State. In so doing, Agamben shows the hidden contiguity and affinity of modern liberal democracy with totalitarianism via the Schmittian question of the Sovereign and the 'state of exception.' The end result is, when seen from a Christian theo-political perspective, an apocalyptic diagnosis (Agamben would say messianic and I will deal with this distinction in due course) of the all-pervasive bio-political situation or the "camp as the *nomos* of the earth," understood as the real legacy of the political project of modernity (Agamben 1998, pp. 166–180). Agamben, then, like no thinker writing today, sees the links linking the foundation of liberal democracies with present-day post-democratic totalitarian societies of the spectacle (Guy Debord) and their glorifying economizing of the political. The present-day manifestation of the bio-political order must then be seen as a "bloody mystification of a new planetary order" (Agamben 1998, p. 12). Moreover, Agamben's radical and uncompromising analysis of the current political situation of the West clearly shows that any proposed restoration of classical politics, à la Hannah Arendt and Leo Strauss, is naïve and impossible. There can be no conservative restoration of politics. Thus, Agamben's provocative view that "nowhere on earth today is a legitimate power to be found: even the powerful are convinced of their own illegitimacy" raises—or should raise—serious worries concerning the widespread Christian accommodation within, and to, the current bio-political and Capitalistic order (Agamben 2012, p. 40).[5]

---

[5] Agamben's radical claim about the illegitimate nature of all political power today, given at Notre Dame Cathedral in March of 2009, was by no means the first of its kind. For such a claim was first powerfully voiced, in a radically Christian register, in the 1937 prophetic essay of Erik Peterson, 'Witness to the Truth.' This time, however, the challenging of the

Agamben's radical critique of the power and violence unleashed by the planetary illegitimacy of the bio-political world order thus lends the Christian thinker tools to diagnose the increasingly apocalyptic and dramatic situation in which Christians now find themselves. In this, Agamben's work can be said to offer two services to an apocalyptic Christian theo-political vision.[6] First, it reinforces a Christian apocalyptic view of history as an ever-increasing intensification of evil and violence as laid out in related, but differing ways, in von Balthasar and Girard (Balthasar 1994, 1998; Girard and Chantre 2009). Second, it shows the need, in light of the ubiquity of illegitimate political power, for the Christian metaphysician and theo-political thinker to think through the need of a theo-political metaphysics of martyrdom which would Christianly refuse to participate in the violence of political power in the name of a theo-politics of loving service, rooted within a Trinitarian analogical metaphysics of kenotic love. This is to assert, with Peterson, that any true Christian politics needs to be rooted within Trinitarian doctrine and the cosmic nature of the liturgy, and the latter understood as the public practice of the *ekklēsía*, which thus has radically political ramifications (Peterson 2011, p. 68). Second, Agamben realizes in the wake of Schmitt that there are deep analogies between politics and the situation of metaphysics. Third, Agamben rightly realizes beyond the philhellenic purview of Heidegger, in the wake of the prophetic theo-political insights of Peterson (and in a different tonality von Balthasar), that in order to get to the heart of the real questions of Western politics and metaphysics one has to confront the legacy of Christian theology, concentrated in the question of glory, doxology and, ultimately, the Trinity.

In light of my critique, I concentrate on the ontological underpinnings of the *Homo Sacer* project, that is, Agamben's search for a form-of-life where *bios* and *zoē* coincide, without remainder. I primarily focus on *The Kingdom and the Glory* where the inoperativity of the self is used to deactivate Christian glory and the Christian apocalypse via a profaning praxis of sabbatism. In other words, I argue that the strategy of Agamben's

---

modern political order, and its illegitimacy, was done with radically Christian theo-political intentions in light of the political order's rejection of the sovereignty of the royal priesthood of the eschatological Lamb. See Peterson (2011, pp. 151–181).

[6] For more programmatic thoughts on the current place of a Christian apocalyptic theo-politics of the martyr, in relation to the Christian *analogia entis*, see the last chapter of Gonzales (2019).

deactivation of Christian glory is centered in an immanentizing of the Sabbath and the Christian *Parousia*, in a sabbatical self that is a secularized profanation of Christian glory.

The ontological underpinnings of the *Homo Sacer* project must be characterized as a post-Hegelo-Kojèvian and a post-Heideggerian endeavor. That is, it is an attempt to think sovereignty and metaphysics in the time of the fulfillment of human history and Western metaphysics. The essential nature of this endeavor is an attempt to think ontological difference no longer as a relation of Being to being. Or in more archaic metaphysical language, it is an attempt to think potentiality without the sovereignty of actuality and thus a figure of human existence where *bios* and *zoē* coincide. Agamben's move of reconfiguring human existence beyond the Western dualism of Being/being, actuality/potentiality is done with the intent of freeing man, and politics, from the tyranny of the metaphysico-political destiny of the West.

Up until this point Agamben's project and strategy is a largely Heideggerian one, politically inflected. However, the devious brilliance of Agamben is to no longer situate the historic destiny of the Occident within the forgetting of ontological difference in the withdrawing dispensation of Being which occurred in early Greek thinking, but rather, in the binary opposition of the immanent/economic Trinity which is the real determinative event of the West which must be overcome. This is to say, what must be overcome, yet strongly acknowledged, is that that history itself, and an historical interpretation of Being and the West, is only possible because of Christianity. Christianity, and the Trinity, not Hellenic impersonal Being, gives rise to the historical (Agamben 2011, p. 5).[7] It is this Christian legacy that must be overcome, not by pretending that it does not exist à la Heidegger, but by acknowledging it, so as to profane it by lifting the veil to see what lies underneath and beyond. This, for Agamben, will remove the apocalyptic '*obscura verba*' (this is how Augustine describes the enigmatic Pauline *katechon*: Augustine 2000, Book X, Chap. 19) of the *katechon* (Thessalonians 2:3–9). Which is to say that the Trinitarian binary split between being/praxis which prevents their coinherence, in human existence, and thus a return to the messianic time of concrete anarchic eschatology, as opposed to the Christian apocalyptic 'suspended time' of delay,

---

[7] See also Agamben (2017, p. 26) where he says, 'History as we know it is a Christian concept.' Here Agamben affirms what Heidegger knew but refused to admit, namely, his thinking is not Greek but a perverse parody of the Christian narrative.

on Agamben's interpretation enforces the Occidental Christian split, between being and acting, form and life (Agamben 2011, p. 8).[8] Thus, in my reading, the Christian Trinitarian split between being/praxis, and its continuation in the governmental machine of the Western politics, serves as the famed apocalyptic Pauline *katechon* which is restraining, not the Second Coming, but a parousic messianic self (form-of-life) where *bios* and *zoē* coincide, without remainder. Agamben must thus remove this Christian *katechon*, and its legacy in the governmental machine, in order for his messianic version of the self and politics to be enacted.

This messianic strategy is taken up in *The Kingdom and the Glory* in a theological key, with the purpose of answering the question of why power, in the West, assumes the form of economy. Agamben's turn to the theologoumenon of Christian mystery—the Trinity—seeks to show that not only is the modern economy a secular version of the Christian economy, but more importantly, that Christian theology is of its very nature economic and that the economic is inherently Christian. This strategy takes on a subtle and interrelated twofold nature, as announced in the first section of the work. First, Agamben, in alluding to the debate on secularization in Germany during the 1960s, seeks to show that the real question of this debate is not secularization, but rather a question of philosophy of history and the theological legacy underpinning it (Agamben 2011, pp. 4–5). Thus Lowith's thesis on secular eschatology and the conscious reopening of the theme of the economic Trinity in Hegel and Schelling is not possible

---

[8] Agamben's seeking to return to 'the time that remains' is a move that is greatly indebted to the profound influence that Walter Benjamin has had upon his thinking. However, one would be remiss to not make the striking comparison between Agamben's view of Christian apocalyptic being a paralysis of time, as opposed to the moving time of concrete eschatology which propels human action, with Buber's view of the Jewish prophetic tradition in distinction from Christian apocalypse, especially, as seen in its Johannine provenance. Buber sees the prophetic tradition provoking radical decision, action and dialogue between God and man which always involves the possibility of turning, change and a future. This dynamism is lost with the worn-out Christian apocalyptic view where time and history are growing old and tired. Christian apocalypticists thus desire to flee and escape history instead of facing the demand for decisions within the historic hour of history and its concrete happening. See Buber (1957, pp. 192–207). Buber's (and Agamben's) view of Christian apocalyptic as enfeebling action is greatly mistaken, at least on a Tyconian-Augustinian-Balthasarian apocalyptic view, which expels and denies the expectation of the reign of a thousand-year kingdom, thought in historical terms. Rather, this view sees every Christian age as living within and having a qualitative relation to the 'end times' which thus demands, all the more, the urgency of Christian dramatic action where the Mystical Body is continually under attack by the spirit of the antichristic lie.

if the nature of theology is not itself economic, as Agamben seeks to genealogically establish, in keeping with his thesis that history is itself a Christian category. In a word, at stake is the question of a theological interpretation of history and its bequeathing to modernity the task of thinking "at one and the same time, an infinite being and its finite history—and hence the figure of being that survives the economy—forms precisely the theological inheritance of modern philosophy" (Agamben 2011, p. 211). In other words, Agamben must first acknowledge the theological essence of Western history in order to think the profaning post-Christian messianic moment which will render the Christian economy and its glory voided.

The second aspect of Agamben's messianic strategy is to establish that the great debate between Schmitt and Peterson—both of whom he is contending with throughout the entire text—on the possibility of political theology is really a debate between two Catholic thinkers who are "apocalyptics of the counterrevolution," insofar as they share the same theology of history which seeks to restrain the coming of the Antichrist (Agamben 2011, p. 6).[9] (This restraint occurs in Peterson by the theological delay of the conversion of the Jews and Schmitt by Christian Empire and its secular continuance in the modern State). Hence both act as delaying inquisitional figures assuring that the *parousia* does not take place in time, thereby prohibiting a concrete messianic eschatology. That is, Agamben must establish, contra Schmitt and Peterson, that the figure of being which resides after the economy—after the removal of the Trinitarian *katechon*—is not a Catholic apocalyptic figuration of being, but rather a post-Christian messianic figuration of being or a sabbatism of praxis which deactivates Christian glory and its legacy in the economy of the governmental machine.

The two sides of this messianic strategy, as already noted, revolve around the question of the Trinity and glory, understood as the decisive event in the West, read as the location of the binary and dualistic nature that Christian thinking bequeathed to the governmental machine of Western politics. There are two Trinities, which are split: to the immanent Trinity belongs God's Being in himself and to the economic Trinity God's revelation. In this dualistic Trinity, Being and praxis are radically split.

---

[9] Agamben is here borrowing a phrase which Jacob Taubes applies to Carl Schmitt. However, Agamben in his bizarre reading of Peterson seeks to apply it equally to Peterson. I have far more sympathies with Agamben's critique of Schmitt than Peterson's. For a splendid defense of Peterson contra Agamben see Schmidt (2014, pp. 182–203). For Taubes ascription of this title to Schmitt, see Taubes (2013, pp. 1–18).

Enter glory as the way that Christian theology has attempted to reconcile the immanent/economic Trinity, theology/economy, being/praxis, Government/Kingdom. Glory thus becomes the most dialectical part of theology, as the mirroring and circulating place of the unity of opposites. Glory's ambiguous function is seen in two ways. First, in relation to the three divine Person's reciprocal glorification, Agamben thinks that the subordinationalist position is never done away with (Agamben 2011, p. 209).[10] Second, in relation to man and God, man glorifies God's Glory which has no need of man's glorification (Agamben 2011, pp. 216–218). It thus seems implied that in some way God's glory is increased by external and subjective glorification. Moreover, it is not insignificant that in Agamben's critique of the dialectical and circular nature of glory that he appeals to two protestant dialectical theologians to prove his point, namely, Moltmann and Barth (Agamben 2011, for references to Moltmann see, p. 208 and p. 210; for Barth see, pp. 211–212 and pp. 214–216). Agamben thus weakens an already weak critique by never addressing the Catholic analogical answer to glory found in Przywara and von Balthasar, which finds a non-identical refrain in Desmond's metaxology. In taking the dialectical position as normative of Christian thought, he flatly ignores the *analogia entis* (or metaxology) which enacts an analogization of being in its difference from God, thereby safeguarding the distinction between the immanent/economic Trinity and the distinction between God and creatures. Agamben's denial of the analogical interval allows him to read the Christian legacy bequeathing to Western thought the task of thinking an infinite being's finite history. However, when read analogically, *this question is mute* as the relation between God and creation and God and the economic story of salvation history is one of free loving exchange—*commercium*—between God and man which is the consequence of the real analogical distance of God's creative act of freeing creation into its otherness. Without this distance, love and exchange are impossible, the Christian *Deus semper maior* becomes dependent on its economic activity, and this is precisely what Agamben's dialectical reading desires.

On this view, then, "the economy glorifies being as being glorifies the economy," and it is in this insubstantial mirroring that the divine mystery lays hidden (Agamben 2011, p. 209). At the heart of the Trinitarian God of glory stands the unsayable void of the inoperativity of power. The theological legacy of the West, and its political continuance in the governmental

---

[10] For a fitting refutation of Agamben's belief that the Trinity and glory always harbor a subordinationalist position, see Balthasar (1994, pp. 319–328).

machine, is symbolized in the iconography of the empty throne (*hetoimasia tou thronou*) (Agamben 2011, p. 243). Which means that behind the Trinitarian split between being and praxis, held together by the circular apparatus of glory, lies the vacant and anarchic seat of power-as-possibility. The veil of Christian glory has been rent and lifted and what resides after the ruse of the dialectical history of glory and an infinite being's finite history (Being/praxis) is man's own inoperativity. The mystery of the divinity is profaned, because when man glorifies, it is not a glorification of God, but a "glorification in which human inoperativity celebrates its eternal Sabbath" (Agamben 2011, p. 245). At the heart of the Christian *oikonomia* lies not the Christian Trinitarian God of absolute loving surrender and abandon, but man: "The Sabbatical animal par excellence" (Agamben 2011, p. 246).

The figuration of being, after the Christian economy and its secular continuance in the governmental machine, is a post-Christian and therefore a post-Apocalyptic messianic figure of the self where *bios* and *zoē* coincide, without remainder. Here the fracture between being and praxis is healed. The Christian history of the Trinitarian *katechon* is removed and taken into a self that, in a Spinozistic and Heideggerian fashion, contemplates its own 'live-ability,' its own ability to live and act (Agamben 2011, 251, for reference to Spinoza p. 249). The inoperativity of the self's pure possibility-to-be is a profane figuration of the peaceful rest of God's eternal Sabbath, after the Christian economy of salvation is revealed to be empty. Christian Eternal life is immanentized, and a theology of history is replaced and deactivated by a parousic self that serves its own immanent messianic function. By claiming that man's contemplation of his inoperativity is what frees man from the apparatus of the governmental machine, Agamben thinks he is freeing man from the Catholic legacy of the apocalyptic belief that the *parousia* occurs at the end of history, a belief which paralyzes concrete messianic eschatology. History after Christian glory and the apocalypse that never was is the messianic time that remains where, in the words of Benjamin, "every second of time was the strait gate through which the Messiah might enter" (Benjamin 1968, p. 264). However, Agamben should heed the words of Benjamin that the "Messiah comes not only as the Redeemer, he comes as the subduer of the Antichrist" (Benjamin 1968, p. 255). Thus if the figure of the Messiah remains somewhat ambiguous in Benjamin, for Agamben, it is clear that the post-Christian self is an immanentized parousic and messianic figuration whose own *conatus essendi* is the operator of "anthropogenesis" after the profanation of Christian glory and its economy of salvation (Agamben 2011, p. 251).

In seeking to deactivate Christian glory, Christian history and the Christian self, Agamben has effectively removed metaphysical heteronomy, salvation as God's free initiative and hence a view of the Christian self as inherently responsive and doxological. Agamben's man, then, like Heidegger's *Dasein* whispers to itself, it its sabbatical 'live-ability' and possibility, 'I am who I am' thus denying the heart of the Christian doxological self, namely the loving recognition of *being-a-creature*.

Desmond's Reactivation of Christian Glory

The work of William Desmond, like Agamben's, is one of the most significant intellectual events of our time. This is seen especially, but by no means exclusively, in the great trilogy of the *Between: Being and the Between* (1995), *Ethics and the Between* (2001) and *God and the Between* (2008). Yet how to get to the heart of the significance and fecundity of Desmond's work? I have already suggested that his work must be seen as a creative reactivation of Christian metaphysical glory. Indeed, that his style of thought is an instantiation of the kind of Christian metaphysics needed today in light of the eclipse of Christian glory. Desmond's style of thought, then, must be characterized as a metaphysical doxology in so far as his thinking is itself a performance, a song of praise and glorification to the Giver of all being and the good of the 'to be.' In order to show this, I reflect on the themes of the Sabbath and glory, suggesting that they flow from the very springs of Desmond's thought and the springs from which his thought continually draw are, I claim, metaphysical astonishment and metaphysical peace. However, to think these springs means to trace the Source of these springs and thus what *draws* Desmond's thought. For the Source must be ever-active and flowing forth in the very movement of the springs. Thus, to think the Source of this drawing, as traced in the springs, in relation to the Sabbath and glory, is to think performatively—along with Desmond—ways of reactivating Christian metaphysical glory. Metaphysical thinking must turn again to the wealth of the metaphysical poverty of creaturely existence. Which is another way of saying that existence must again become song.

The voice and thought of Desmond could not be more different than Agamben's. Desmond's work is certainly post-Heideggerian and post-Hegelian, but the nature of the 'post' is of a rare sort. Desmond's thinking is anything but historicist, insofar as his thinking is in no way beholden to a thinking of being historically predetermined by Hegel or Heidegger.[11] In this, Desmond has bucked the trend of the majority of Continental thinkers, insofar as he has shifted his vision away from a seemingly all-encompassing nihilistic atheism in an attempt to resurrect two archaic words: metaphysics and God. To many, this might seem a naïve enterprise of an idiotic voice crying in the desert; a voice that fails to see adequately the autistic darkness for what it is: nothing. Yet Desmond sees the darkness for what it is, because he knows that despite its power, the darkness has not extinguished the light. Desmond's thinking is a thinking after 'postulatory finitism' enacted by a 'posthumous' mind that has awakened after long sleep of finitude and the forgetting of being and God (GB, for references to 'Posthumous mind' see: 32, 33, 98, 184, 186, 201, 220, 223, 249, 304, for references to 'Postulatory finitism' see: xi, 2, 8, 11, 129, 312, 313). Desmond's posthumous thinking does not refuse to look into darkness, but it does, like the apocalyptic martyrs of the prophetic Erik Peterson, refuse to utter a word against God's creation (Peterson 2011, p. 171).

In other words, the heart of Desmond's thought is a metaphysics of creation. I further suggest that Desmond's metaphysics of creation is best characterized as a postmodern form of Augustinianism. Yet to be a non-identical repetition of Augustine is to also be a non-identical repetition of Plato. This is to say that Desmond's thinking exhibits a hermeneutic tactic, in the spirit of Clement of Alexandria, which sees that the old is disclosed in the new and the new lies hidden in the old: *vetus in novo patet, novum in vetere latet*. Plato: a pagan philosopher of astonishment and peace fulfilled in *the* Christian philosopher of astonishment and peace: Augustine. Desmond's indebtedness to Plato and Augustine is nowhere more evident than in his unending reminder that metaphysics will always be a loving activity of astonishment. Desmond thus deploys this Platonic-Augustinian spirit contra the *conatus* of self-foundation of philosophical modernity to show, in the words of Przywara, that philosophy is *reductio in mysterium* (Przywara 2014, pp. 181–188). That is, philosophy cannot be understood unless being is that mystery of otherness which cannot be mastered.

However, Desmond could not truly partake in the Platonic-Augustinian spirit, if he himself was not astonished at the 'thing itself,' that is, being in its abiding mystery. This is why, for Desmond, metaphysical mindfulness is a *"being beholden"* and a being true to being's hyperbolic over-determination

---

[11] For more on Desmond's opposition to the Heideggerian trend of current Continental thought, in relation to Badiou, see Gonzales (2019).

(BB 10). To be mindful, metaphysically, is to be taken up into, and by, the otherness of being's abiding mystery. Thinking, in the between, is the very space of the communication of otherness and transcendence within man's ineluctable in-between condition. Thus, thought's dwelling space is the very indwelling of a mystery which, in keeping with Augustine, is both interior and exterior to thought's in-between condition. Desmond's mindfulness thus springs from metaphysical astonishment before being's abiding otherness. Being's mystery thus surmounts the violence of the voyeuristic eye of consciousness' self-identical *clarté* and the *polemos* of dialectical identity. And it surmounts because being is itself convertible with peace, the other spring of Desmond's thought.

Desmond claims that there is a Sabbath for thought and that peace should exist between philosophy and religion. Yet he claims that to obtain this peace thinking must learn to pray, that is to sing the glory of God and his creation. This singing glorification was rendered obsolete by Agamben's circular and dialectical interpretation of glory which denied the analogical interval. This denial effectively cut off metaphysical heteronomy and God's salvific event, in the name of a parousic self, which parodies Christian glory in the glorification of man's inoperativity. Yet Desmond is a metaxological thinker, and thus he is able to secure the difference between God and creation. That is, Desmond secures that God is not his kingdom, thereby rending glory possible again. Desmond's thinking, as a metaxological metaphysics of creation, is not bound to what Agamben sees to be the legacy of Christianity in the West, namely the thinking of an infinite being's finite history and the figure which survives this history. No, Desmond's metaphysical mindfulness is rooted in the analogical interval and thus he thinks a story of being which is rooted in creation *ex nihilo* and the whyless love which this event expresses and continues to express. For Desmond, there is always a coming to be prior to becoming. A being given to be which is the genuine coming to be of otherness in the metaphysical gift of difference which creation itself is (GB 241–258). Creation and the self is an event of gifting which expresses the *commercium* of love and metaphysical peace between the Agapeic Origin and his creation.

Yet how to understand this peace? This peace is granted, in the Genesis account, on the Seventh day, the last day, the day of rest from the work of creation, the day set apart, made holy. However, this peaceful rest could not have been given if what was first made was itself not good: very good (Genesis 1:31). God's restful beholding of the goodness of creation is the absolving consecration of creation's otherness: an absolution which

Agamben's profaning mind refused to receive. God's metaphysical creative beholding of creation is God's own Amen to the created otherness of being. To think the peace of God's Sabbath is thus to metaphysically reiterate, to repeat non-identically and perform this great creative Amen to being. Our creaturely beholding vision is thus a response to the call of communication given by God's unspeakably generous love which, to the attentive questioner (Augustine 1991, Book X, 9), is everywhere present in the peaceful glory of the between of creation.

To think the Sabbath is not to immanentize it in the void of inoperativity, understood as the self's contemplation of its power-as-possibility. Rather it is to think the creative gift of God's peace which is the "perpetual re-creation of the world" (IST 356). It is to think the self as given to be: a *passio essendi* prior to the *conatus essendi* of power-as-possibility. To respond to this gift is to perform the poverty of creatureliness, where we become—a resounding—existing in pouring forth seraphic canticles (think of Desmond's ten metaphysical cantos) (GB 281–327). In our poverty lies our wealth. To think the glory of the God of the Sabbath is to think the Source of our creatureliness, and this is what *draws* Desmond's thought. To do this is to dwell within the peace of metaphysical astonishment of the good of the 'to be' of the between where the immemorial moment of the giving emergence of created being, out of the depths of God's creative love, is communicated. To fully think this one's entire existence must become song, thereby performatively and dramatically reactivating the pleromatic tradition of Christian metaphysical glory on the other side of its eclipse, in an age of ever-intensifying profanity and counterfeiting.

Bibliography

Agamben, Giorgio. 1998. *Homo Sacer: Sovereign Power and Bare Life*. Trans. Daniel Heller-Roazen. Stanford: Stanford University Press.

———. 2011. *The Kingdom and the Glory: For a Theological Genealogy of Economy and Government (Homo Sacer II, 2)*. Trans. Lorenzo Chiesa. Stanford, CA: Stanford University Press.

———. 2012. *The Church and the Kingdom*. Trans. Leland De La Durantaye. London/New York/Calcutta: Seagull Books.

———. 2017. *The Mystery of Evil: Benedict XVI and the End of Days*. Trans. Adam Kotsko. Stanford, CA: Stanford University Press.

Augustine. 1991. *The Confession*. Trans. Henry Chadwick. Oxford: Oxford University Press.

———. 2000. *The City of God*. Trans. Marcus Dod, D.D. New York: The Modern Library.
Balthasar, Hans Urs von. 1988. *Theo-Drama: Theological Dramatic Theory: Volume I: Prolegomena*. Trans. Graham Harrison. San Francisco: Ignatius Press.
———. 1989. *The Glory of the Lord: A Theological Aesthetics: Volume IV: The Realm of Metaphysics in Antiquity*. Trans. Brian Mc Neil, C.R.V. et al. San Francisco: Ignatius Press.
———. 1994. *Theo-Drama: Theological Dramatic Theory: Volume IV: The Action*. Trans. Graham Harrison. San Francisco: Ignatius Press.
———. 1998. *Theo-Drama: Theological Dramatic Theory: Volume V: The Last Act*. Trans. Graham Harrison. San Francisco: Ignatius Press.
Benjamin, Walter. 1968. Theses on the Philosophy of History. In *Illuminations: Essays and Reflections*. Trans. Harry Zohn. New York: Schocken Books.
Buber, Martin. 1957. Prophecy, Apocalyptic, and the Historical Hour. In *Pointing the Way: Collected Essays*. Trans. Maurice Friedman. New York: Harper & Brothers.
Derrida, Jacques. 1993. On the Newly Arisen Apocalyptic Tone in Philosophy. In *Raising the Tone of Philosophy: Late Essays by Emmanuel Kant, Transformative Critique by Jacques Derrida*, ed. Peter Fenves. Trans. John Leavey. Baltimore: The John Hopkins University Press.
Girard, Rene, and Benoît Chantre. 2009. *Battling to the End: Conversations with Benoît Chantre*. Trans. Mary Backer. East Lansing, MI: Michigan State University Press.
Gonzales, Philip John Paul. 2019. *Reimagining the Analogia Entis: The Future of Erich Przywara's Christian Vision*. Grand Rapids, MI: William B. Eerdmans Publishing Company.
———. forthcoming. Between Philosophy and Theology: The Theological Implications of William Desmond's Thought: An Interview with John Milbank. *Radical Orthodoxy: Theology, Philosophy, Politics*.
O'Regan, Cyril. 2012. Girard and the Spaces of Apocalyptic. *Modern Theology* 28: 123–124.
Peterson, Erik. 2011. *Theological Tractates*. Ed. Michael J. Hollerich and Trans. Michael J. Hollerich. Stanford, CA: Stanford University Press.
Przywara, Erich. 2014. *Analogia Entis: Metaphysics: Original Structure and Universal Rhythm*. Trans. John R. Betz and David Bentley Hart. Grand Rapids, MI: William B. Eerdmans Publishing Company.
Schmidt, Christoph. 2014. The Return of the Katechon: Giorgio Agamben contra Erik Peterson. *The Journal of Religion* 94 (2): 182–203.
Taubes, Jacob. 2013. *To Carl Schmitt: Letters and Reflections*. Trans. Keith Tribe. New York: Columbia University Press.

PART IV

On Wholeness, Hegel and Pan(en)theism

CHAPTER 13

The Real and the Glitter: Apropos William Desmond's *Hegel's God*

Sander Griffioen

Ten years ago, on the occasion of my valedictory address at the Vrije Universiteit Amsterdam, William Desmond presented me with a small-sized replica of a boat which is thought to show St Brendan, the Navigator, on his voyage across the ocean. Although the original carving points upwards, the replica can be hung both horizontally and vertically, with both dimensions giving expression to the same meaning: the church ferrying the people of God to heaven through a world of difficulties. Interestingly enough, the backside of the replica adds a possible reading that will prove to be pertinent to this chapter. The text says that it may also be viewed as "in Jungian psychology, the psyche constellating the four functions in unison to voyage to wholeness".[1]

---

[1] Replica from the Kilnaruane carved pillar stone, made at the Wild Goose Studio, Kinsale, Ireland.

Krina Huisman edited this article. She suggested improvements and helped repair a few unclear passages.

S. Griffioen (✉)
VU Amsterdam, Amsterdam, Netherlands

The longing for a 'voyage to wholeness' is, I think, precisely what Desmond's category of the 'counterfeit double' is all about. His concern is that such striving for innerworldly wholeness, of which Jung's psychology is just one expression, threatens to destroy what makes human life *human*: an essential openness, or 'porosity', as he prefers, to the whole of creation. The critique of holism is central in the first part of this study, both in the sections on *Hegel's God* and in the section dedicated to the notion of 'counterfeit'. The issue remains present in the second and third part, albeit less prominently, where the emphasis will shift to the anonymity of the good. Our main sources in the first part will be *Hegel's God* (HG) and *Is there a Sabbath for Thought?* (IST), while in the second part we will discuss IST once more as well as *The Intimate Universal* (IU). A few words of caution to conclude this introduction. I do not want anyone to think that the notion of 'counterfeit doubles' provides a universal key for Desmond's work as a whole. One salient feature of Desmond's work is its multilayered and multifaceted composition. This rich texture makes it hard to draw straightforward conclusions in a relatively short chapter.

Hegel's God

William Desmond confided to me in an email that the publisher preferred not to have 'counterfeit double' in the title (June 2, 2002). This was probably since it would not recommend the book to a contemporary public that, just as in the days of the apostle Paul, comes to philosophy "to hear some new thing" (Acts 17: 21) and prefers not to be reminded of thorny issues of falsehood and idolatry. It would recommend itself even less to Hegel scholars who immerse themselves so fully in Hegel's system that any reference to a meta-standard of falsehood or truth becomes impossible.

In his contribution to my *Festschrift*, Desmond related one reaction of bewilderment we encountered in the summer of 1993 on travelling together in Japan and Korea. It was a response to his address to the Korean Hegel society, "a reply in German by a Korean professor who had studied in Germany, and who had assumed the ways of Hegel scholars who do not quite get the point of my apostasy from the church of Hegelian true believers" (Desmond 2006, p. 126). In academic philosophy, the appeal to meta-standards is immediately branded as external criticism, with all the attendant connotations of 'biased', 'dogmatic', and so on. Whereas Hegel himself, in fact, appealed to meta-standards again and again—most clearly when proclaiming in his later years to have paved the way for a reconciliation, or even a unison, of philosophy and Christian religion. One wonders how Hegel scholars can deal with this claim without asking themselves whether their patron's understanding of Christian religion measured up to what Christian churches had confessed for centuries.

In assessing the reception it received in the Korean Hegel society (and possibly elsewhere), we have to take into account that Desmond's work differs strongly from regular Hegel studies since its focus is not on much discussed controversies, and also because references to secondary literature are relatively scarce. *Hegel's God* is least of all a work in which an author positions him- or herself by criticizing others. As we will see, rather than just criticizing, Desmond engages in a lively interchange with Hegel, granting strong points, showing fascination with the development of certain themes, expressing agreements with others, and so on, while consistently questioning the overall direction. *Hegel's God*, I suggest, is best seen as a study in which the interpreter openly departs from his "own presuppositions and possibilities", as Gadamer put it in his preface to a collection of essays on Heidegger.[2] Part of his 'presuppositions and possibilities' is the grid of categorical distinctions. For this chapter, the categories of the 'erotic' and the 'agapeic' will prove vital.[3] He does not smuggle these into his discourse (as often happens) but is open about weaving his own discourse into that of Hegel's. Also in this regard, he could have appealed to Hegel, who was frank about the need to take one's reason along in order to be able to discern reason in the world.[4]

It is no surprise then that this book does not follow the downtrodden path of the sharp divisions between expository and evaluating sections. From the start, it engages in a lively dialogue in which exposition and critique go hand in hand. Let me add that its critique is never without appreciation. Some examples: on the theme of love in the early writings:

---

[2] "Es ging mir auch in allen meinen späteren Heidegger-Aufsätzen darum, von meinen Voraussetzungen und Möglichkeiten aus die Denkaufgabe sichtbar zu machen, der sich Heidegger gestellt hat..." (1983, Vorwort). The analogy is not strict: whereas Gadamer's affinity with Heidegger is palpable on every page, Desmond's relation to Hegel is one of proximity and distance.

[3] In an earlier study, I listed two groups of basic categories: the first one comprising the univocal, the equivocal, the dialectical, and the metaxological; the second consisting of the idiotic, the aesthetic, the erotic, and the agapeic (Griffioen 2010, p. 121).

[4] "Wer die Welt vernünftig ansieht, den sieht sie auch vernünftig an. Beides ist in Wechselbestimmung" (*Vorlesungen über die Philosophie der Geschichte*, Einleitung, Hegel 1955, p. 31).

"Hegel is close to the heart of the matter, and also very distant" (HG 41); On the theme of worship in the early writings: "Clearly Hegel understands the conjunction of difference and relation in worship" (HG 59); On the *Phenomenology of Spirit*: "The details of that work are fascinating in their own right" (HG 82); On the relativity of boundaries: the argument that "every limit is in principle surpassable by its being stated as a limit" is called 'powerful' and 'persuasive': "Hegel undoubtedly has much persuasive power on his side" (HG 84); On the progress of subjectivity from naïve self-affirmation via loss of self to mature reaffirmation: "Hegel is right to draw attention to these things"; adding: "I dwell on this because there is clearly a lot to what Hegel says. The powers of subjectivity are mindful and they are dynamic and they are forming's of selving and also of self-transcendence, hence also relations to other-being" (HG 91).[5] However, here we arrive at a juncture where their respective roads diverge: in Hegel, the further development of subjectivity shows a subject endlessly circling within itself in a process of self-mediation,[6] whereas Desmond rejects this "model of inclusive self-knowledge" (HG 92) and insists instead on the finiteness and porosity of the self. Here, finiteness does not indicate a deficiency, but rather an openness to the 'between'. As he explained elsewhere: "There are forms of selving and othering that do not yield to Hegel's scheme to render the way in speculative dialectic. The between, like the way, is an open passage. In finitude, it remains porous to what exceeds determination in terms of what can be immanently given" (Desmond 2006, p. 125). For Desmond, the essential porosity can only be safeguarded if and as long as the temptation to immanentize the 'beyond' is resisted. Here lies the reason for "his apostasy from the church of the Hegelians" of which he spoke apropos his address to the Korean Hegel society.

If we would sum up *Hegel's God*, it would be 'God within the whole'. Holism is the pivot on which Desmond's critique turns. He draws a dividing line between visions of an inclusive whole that leave no room for 'God

---

[5] More recently in a similar vein: "there is an important point for human existence here, and it is Hegel's point too, namely, that we must adventure in otherness to come to ourselves" (IU 324).

[6] As he put it concisely in an earlier publication, when dealing with Hegel's category of the *Entäusserung* (self-externalization/alienation): instead of a real reaching out towards the other as other, "there is erotic transcendence for, to put it briefly, the one itself in the one as othering itself" (BB 220). Compare Franz Rosenzweig on idealism as a "dreamland of self-seeking" ("Idealismus: traumland der eigensucht", Rosenzweig 1988, p. 394).

beyond the whole' and of an open whole that remains porous. Whenever he arrives at this point, his tone tends to become passionate—for instance apropos the axiom 'the truth is the whole': "But if there is a truth here, *is it the whole truth? Is it the truth of the whole?* Hegel will say 'yes'. But are there crucial omissions needed to make this claim? If so, the Hegelian whole will not be the 'whole'. Why?" (HG 91). It is this holism that Desmond's critique targets relentlessly. He points at asymmetries being absolved in an "inclusive process of holistic self-mediation" (HG 60); despite a "flicker here and there" of unmediated otherness, he signals a triumph of "holistic immanence" (HG 115). The dialectical method results in a "speculative self-mediating whole" (HG 183), hereby turning Hegel's philosophy into a "speculative holism" (HG 196). There is no denying that this holism permeates Hegel's work as a whole, from the early manuscripts to the great lecture series which he held in the last phase of his life. So in principle Desmond is right to apply his critique to the whole corpus.

Yet, Desmond fails to register the role of Protestantism in Hegel's later political philosophy. Hegel's early works do indeed express hostility to the Christian church, while, as Desmond puts it, "a Te Deum is sung to autonomous reason" (HG 33). In his later work, however, the Protestant church becomes the guardian of the public order (the realm of *Sittlichkeit*). The former subordination of religion to philosophy makes place for a mix of subordination and partition. What determines the composition of the mixture is that religion is subordinated in one respect, while being allotted freedom in another: *subordination* because Hegel posits that religion can only survive under the tutelage of philosophy and *freedom* because he concedes that this refuge stands apart from the world, and therefore cannot guide the development of the state and (more broadly) the public realm. These realms then remain dependent on a free, non-transformed religion (*in casu* protestant Christianity).[7] The dual approach to the relation of philosophy and religion, of course, was bound to give rise to divergent interpretations. Once the emphasis falls on subordination, Desmond's

---

[7] Nowhere this Janus-faced solution is drawn more sharply than in the closing paragraphs of his lectures on philosophy of religion. I quote from his notes (dated August 25, 1821): "Religion in die Philosophie sich flüchten—.... Welt ihnen ein Vergehen in ihr.... Aber Philosophie partiell – Priesterstand isolirt—Heiligthum—Unbekümmert wie es der Welt gehen mag ... Wie sich gestalte ist nicht unsere Sache" (Hegel 1987, p. 300). Only by finding refuge in philosophy, religion will escape the onslaught of historical critique; yet this refuge is isolated from the world.

holism-critique is hard to refute. However, once it shifts to the juxtaposition, a more benign interpretation becomes possible, such as the one set forth by Merold Westphal, who argues that the subordination of religious representation (*Vorstellung*) to speculative concepts (*Begriff*) should not be taken as the key to Hegel's philosophy: "I have little doubt that placing the question of the relation of religion to philosophy in the context of the relation of religion to the state will significantly change the discussion of the former issue" (Westphal 1992, p. 181). I do not think, however, that both interpretations are on a par. Note that *partition* is secondary to and dependent on *subordination*: the freedom of the Protestant church is a 'let be' granted from some *superordinate* position (as such it is the counterfeit double of the divine *let be*). Therefore, I side with Desmond's diagnosis, while granting that it would have gained by considering the other position as well.

Counterfeits

The term 'counterfeit' seems to have emerged in Desmond's work only around the turn of the century. As a technical term, it is absent in *Perplexity and Ultimacy* (1995), while five years later it is prominently present in an essay on Soloviev and Shestov (2000), republished five years later in *Is There a Sabbath for Thought?* From there on it was to retain a strong presence: a word count shows that in *The Intimate Universal* (2016) it occurs more than 150 times, against only 6 hits for 'holism'.

The inspiration for the introduction of this category must have been Soloviev's *A Story of Anti-Christ* (1900). In this story 'counterfeit' not only plays a strategic role, but is the defining element of the anti-Christ's power. The concluding pages of *Hegel's God* strongly echo this story, especially the passage about "the problem of the anti-Christ" being that he "appears the same as Christ and so can successfully pose as the true Christ" (HG 205).[8] When used emphatically,[9] 'counterfeit' is synonymous with 'idol', a relation made explicit in *The Intimate Universal*: "Idols, or what I call the counterfeit doubles of God" (IU 345). The assumption is that

---

[8] A footnote refers to the essay on Soloviev and Sjestov mentioned above. We'll return to this statement on introducing the second type of counterfeits.

[9] Which is not always the case—so for instance on the development of the French Revolution: "The brothers have become the hindering others, the counterfeiting comrades..." (IU 145).

an idol deceitfully duplicates something that is good, deriving its power from this deceit.[10]

A further assumption is that evil is to be understood primarily from this vantage point. It does not mean that there would be no evil outside of this connection, but without exception, texts relevant to the subject matter of my contribution do link evil and counterfeits. The road to evil is paved with glittering falsehoods, for instance the promise of homecoming for mankind and a final liberation of creativity: In truth, this 'saving' of immanence is a return to evil, though it announces itself as humanity finally at home with itself (Hegel's *zuhause sein*), or the final liberation of creativity (Nietzsche).[11] More specifically, regarding counterfeits: could one say that an idol is nothing more than a glitter losing its power once the fraud is discovered? That the spell is broken once the glitter is washed off? This conclusion is stated in so many words in Soloviev's *Story*. At the end of the story, the narrator—introduced as 'Mr. Z'—answers questions from bystanders to whom he had just related the story of an apocalyptic battle between the Pope and the Last Emperor (representing the anti-Christ). When asked whether the Emperor is essentially evil, he answers with a proverb: "All that glitters is not gold", adding: "You know too well this glitter of counterfeit gold. Take it away and no real force remains—none" (Soloviev 2012, p. 36).

The same question is more difficult to answer in Desmond's case. Some of the pertinent texts suggest indeed a situation in which no force remains once the glitter is removed, while others suggest that the hold of idols is more tenacious than Soloviev's Mr. Z assumes.[12] By distinguishing two different types of counterfeits I will try to obtain a clearer understanding

---

[10] In Timothy Keller's *Counterfeit Gods* (2010), 'counterfeit' and 'idol' are also synonymous. However, the theme of 'perplexity' is without parallel in Keller.

[11] The 'saving of immanence' refers to Hegel's claim, reiterated by Nietzsche, that a 'holistic immanence' would rehabilitate the phenomenal world (allegedly reduced to a mere chimera by transcendent religion) (HG 204).

[12] I doubt though whether Mr. Z. fully represents Soloviev's 'message'. If I had been among the bystanders, I would have asked the narrator to explain the obvious discrepancy between his solution ("Take it away and no real force remains") and what he related earlier about the struggle between Emperor and Pope, a story climaxing with Pope Peter's anathema: "By the authority of Christ, I, the servant of the servants of God, cast you out forever, foul dog, from the city of God, and deliver you up to your father Satan!" (Soloviev 2012, p. 28). Mr. Z.'s opinion comes closer to Thomas More's Utopians, who "wonder how any Man should be so much taken with the glaring doubtful Lustre of a Jewel or Stone, that can look up to a Star or to the Sun himself..." (Moore 1743, p. 73).

of Desmond's ideas. My demarcation runs between two forms of doubling: a one-to-one correspondence of original and counterfeit and a doubling of *functions* rather than of *things*, not implying by necessity a likeness all across the board. The distinction is my explication of what remains implicit in the text.

A prime example of a counterfeit of the first kind is the illustration Desmond himself offers on occasion: the false money dropped in England by German warplanes in order to upset the money circulation. The resemblance the false money bore to the real was so perfect that it evoked suspicion. It was the true money that showed wear and tear because of use, whereas the false money glittered from being unused.[13] Desmond's comments on Hegel's changed attitude towards Protestant religion provide us with another instance of the first type of counterfeit. Remember, I suggested that this change presented a turn to the good compared to his earlier hostility. Desmond, however, views the same development as a token that "the mature Hegel" became a more "mature counterfeiter of God":

> The mature Hegel became a more mature counterfeiter of God; became so, because he rightly sees more in the original than he is trying to match and double with concepts. His maturity as counterfeiter, in that regard, is *more open and true* to the original—and this is the source of the persuasion he exerts on many. (HG 205)

Note the assumption of a strong resemblance, nothing short of a one-to-one correspondence of all salient features. Of course, once the falsehood is discovered, the spell is broken.[14]

An example of the second type of counterfeit is to be found in the immediate context of the previous quote. The resemblance now appears

---

[13] "During World War II German counterfeits of British currency were very successful in sowing confusion, until it was noticed that the notes of the counterfeits were 'perfect', while the notes of true currency always had a small flaw. The true with flaws were backed by creditworthiness, the perfect and false by nothing trustworthy" (IU 447n; in similar wordings in IST 148–149).

[14] I do not imply that 'counterfeit' in *Hegel's God* is only used in this sense. I cannot imagine that Desmond would hold that the 'absolute idea' (or 'absolute spirit') is a spitting image of the biblical God. Hegel's contemporaries certainly did not think so. When Hegel (as mentioned earlier) proclaimed the reconciliation of speculative philosophy and Christian religion, the public's reaction was sceptical and unbelieving: some took it as a proof of dishonesty, others as an early symptom of dementia (Rosenkranz 1844, pp. 400–401).

to be a (deceiving) similarity between *ways of functioning*: a matter of substitution in which something arrogates a position while seemingly carrying on with the functions pertaining to that position:

> But—once again—what if the dynamic of spiritual energy is not the same as the original, perhaps even runs counter to it? Do we not then have exactly the problem of the anti-Christ who appears the same as Christ and so can successfully pose as the true Christ? How then do we distinguish the true original and the counterfeit? (HG 205)

As indicated before, the passage has a distinctly Solovievian touch—consider for instance that 'counterfeit' is taken as the defining element of the anti-Christ's power. By looking closely at the text, however, we can discern relevant differences. It turns out to be not simply a matter of something real being replaced by a glittering but inherently fake surrogate. The text speaks of a dynamic of spiritual energy that differs not just from the original, but possibly runs counter to it. Apparently, it is a basically wholesome development that is deflected to serve another goal, yet in such a way that an appearance of similarity is kept up. In Desmondian terms: an erotic curving of a basically agapeic dynamic. The substitution then is not a substitution of one thing for something real (false money etc.), but involves a change of direction effected by a dissimulated change of function. Think of Augustine's (as well as Luther's) definition of sin as a *curvatus in se*, that is, a process in which a reaching out for something good is curved backwards towards some self-serving purpose.

The dissimulation may be the work of specific individuals (philosophers, for instance) but may also be the effect of group dynamics or cultural shifts, possibly even of epochal dimensions. In fact, it is possible to adduce illustrations of both possibilities. *The Intimate Universal*, for instance, offers this instance of a 'curving backwards' at an individual level: "This is where affirming the good of the 'to be' as my self-affirming begins a turn into evil. The selving is seduced, seduces itself to absolutize its own self-affirming" (IU 220).[15] On the other hand, the passage on the 'problem of the anti-Christ' quoted before points to changes on an epochal scale. Apparently, Desmond's position is that individual idolatry always affects the larger community, while epochal changes on the other hand do not absolve individuals from their personal responsibility.

---

[15] Compare: "A closure of the *conatus essendi* on itself" (IST 295).

Perplexity

It may suffice to show that the second type of counterfeits belie Mr. Z's claim that once their glitter is taken away, no real force would remain. A directional change is likely to create its own historical continuity; it may take generations to undo the consequences (if at all). Hence the almost audible bewilderment in the very last sentence of *Hegel's God*: "I often wonder if we have not woken yet, though we have denied Hegel, or rebelled, times out of number" (HG 207).

This bewilderment, or *perplexity*, is the theme to which we turn now. The Augustinian idea of evil as a *privatio boni* will provide us with a key to decode a number of statements on good and evil that seem contradictory at first glance. Comparing the texts that speak about perplexity, bewilderment and so on, one finds many references to a confusing symbiosis of good and evil. So, for instance, in these passages from *Perplexity and Ultimacy*: "All being is good, even the evil" (PU 241); "We fail to understand an unconstrained gift" (PU 221); "This means that God's generosity is horrifying, since it seems to suggest: All is permitted. Freedom means all is permitted" (ibid.). Jumping to *The Intimate Universal*, written two decades later, we find similar expressions of bewilderment, for instance concerning the soothing effect of beauty. Apropos Keats's adage 'a thing of beauty is a joy forever', Desmond relates a story about a tyrant with blood on his hands being entertained by lovely music: "This is the perplexity the story poses for us: Is this what beauty is—music wrung from hell, concealing hell as it is, and making it look like a heaven?" (IU 312)[16]; "Backstage of beauty we see the mechanisms of hell. Recall Nietzsche: we need the 'lies' of art to save us from the 'truth'" (IU 312–313). It seems we are left in a permanent state of confusion, with little light to guide us. Light is good—yes!—but the false glitter of counterfeits also participate in the light: "The daimon and the angel are intermediaries, but the daimonic can become diabolical, and the first angels fell. (…) By what light tell this counterfeit light, since it too is in the light? How could light counterfeit light?" (IST 147). No use seeking one's inner light through a voyage inward:

---

[16] Compare the almost identical wordings in ISB 51, the only difference being that here the contrast is more explicitly put as one between *surface* (the musical beauty) and the *deeper* reality of violence: "The surface of the beautiful hides the working of hell" (ibid.). I will return to this quote below, when dealing with the 'incognito'.

It is just in the desert that the torment of the counterfeits of God makes itself most felt; for it is in our deepest emptiness that idols seem to appear as from nothing, and tempt us with their different salvations. Who will show us the difference between salvation and salvation, salvation and perdition? This is another side of the radical perplexity the issue of the anti-Christ raises. (IST 191)

The key to rightly understanding the "all is permitted" is the assumption of a fundamental goodness, the "goodness of creation" (Desmond 1995, p. 221), coupled to a peculiar application of the Augustinian *privatio boni*. 'Goodness of creation' only rarely occurs in so many words in the texts I consulted. We encounter 'being given to be' or simply 'given to be', always with the connotation of a *good* gift, far more frequently. Over against current postulates of self-creation, Desmond posits "a 'being given to be' that is prior to striving" (IST 330). But note that this 'striving' potentially goes awry from the start. The idea that freedom implies that all is permitted must be taken in this light, as meaning that 'given to be' as such does not pose a restriction on what is permitted. As quoted above: the 'given to be' is an 'unrestrained gift' that does not dictate or prescribe any proper use. Although Desmond subscribes to the Augustinian definition of evil as a *privatio boni*, meaning literally that evil has 'to take away' from the good to do its corrupting work, hardly any limits are set to the 'taking away'.[17] This is why statements such as those quoted above leave the impression (wrong as it may be) that good and evil are equiprimordial. Nothing characterizes Desmond's philosophy more, I believe, than the combination of a basic trust in the goodness of creation and the affirmation of a perplexing potency of human freedom, with no restricting power to prevent it from running the whole gamut of possibilities, even to the point where, as *Hegel's God* puts it: "There will be no other god but ourselves to remind us of our hubris, now dancing around itself and flattering itself with intoxicating and holy names like 'creativity'" (HG 204).

---

[17] In this respect Desmond's philosophy differs strongly from the tradition from which I stem, neo-Calvinism with its stress on structures and norms holding for and protecting the good creation. As I said elsewhere of Herman Dooyeweerd, the foremost philosopher in this milieu: he "had an unyielding trust that the creation order can be bent but never broken or by-passed. He held that hypostatizing one aspect of the normative order at the expense of other norms cannot but lead to the normative order bouncing back in the course of history—a reaction interpreted as immanent justice" (Griffioen 2015, pp. 196-198). Understandably, 'perplexity' in his thought lacks the intensity it has in Desmond.

Thus far only two types of counterfeits were distinguished. In fact, we encountered already instances of idols that cannot be subsumed under either one. Take for instance our last quote: "There will be no other god but ourselves to remind us of our hubris" (HG 204). Can this 'god' still be called a 'counterfeit double'? If this god can at all be called a counterfeit, it is not in the sense of a copy bearing a close resemblance to an original, be it in appearance or in its functioning. The hubris mentioned in the text does not pose as a force to good, dissimulating its will to power. There is no keeping up of appearances while hell is causing havoc behind the façade.[18] Instead, the pose is one of a brutal "I am, and there is none beside me",[19] without even attempting to make itself acceptable by mimicking something else.

When we compare *The Intimate Universal* to *Hegel's God* and other texts from that time, we perceive a shift towards the 'third type'. One indication is the increased frequency of terms like 'secret', 'hidden', and especially 'incognito' (occurring almost 60 times), all of which signal a retreat of the good, be it as real presence or as counterfeit (first and second type). Concomitantly, perplexity displays a paralleled differentiation. In texts we considered before, it refers to similitudes that were so close as to be utterly confusing. In contrast, the perplexity linked to the incognito appears to be caused by a blatant disconnection. What Desmond has registered is an increased indifference in our culture to any pre-given standards. The prevailing attitude in much of modern life is one of *ni dieu ni maître*. The flipside to this is that there is little need to counterfeit those standards.[20] However, the 'given to be' remains constitutive, also once the relation to present-day culture has become tenuous. This is borne out by the following passages: "There is relation even in what is separate. It is impossible to confine agapeic service to any one space or sphere—even though it is more than happy to abide as incognito" (IU 55); "Still Caesar

---

[18] Remember the earlier example of music "wrung from hell": "The surface of the beautiful hides the working of hell" (Section 4.1).

[19] "This is the rejoicing city that dwelt carelessly, that said in her heart, I am, and there is none beside me...": Zephaniah 2: 15, KJV, compare Isaiah 47: 8: "Therefore hear now this, thou that art given to pleasures, that dwellest carelessly, that sayest in thine heart, I am, and none else beside me..." (KJV).

[20] For simplicity's sake, I express myself in terms of 'standards'. I trust it has become clear already that these standards should not be conceived as transcendent and invariable. Instead, for Desmond, the source of normativity is the Logos, the 'intimate universal', expressing itself as the 'agapeic dynamics' mentioned above.

and his empire come second, are derivative from the incognito of the agapeics" (IU 363).

Sure enough, the agapeic is "more than happy to abide as incognito", but what about the *ordo cognoscendi*? How do we, who "do not see our signs" (Psalm 74:9), know that the good is present, albeit incognito, and will prevail in the end?

From this, one can gather that the tone of *The Intimate Universal* must seem rather sombre, if not pessimistic. This is not the case, however, as the book ends on a positive note. It speaks of "the heart purged of its idols", and of "the porosity of the soul unclogged" (IU 418). The final part deals as a whole with the *praxis pietatis* within the bounds of the family. It is here that "the incognito divine is mixed in with the family" (IU 417). So, what is due to remain incognito in the public realm may yet become tangible in other forms of communal life! The message is definitely not that hope will survive in private niches only. It is not a home sweet home. Rather, the family is viewed as a bridgehead for redirecting other domains of communal life—provided its piety stays intact:

> The incognito divine is mixed in with the family. We have seen here an intimate piety and in this elemental form of sociality, if this piety is not guarded, it is made all the more difficult that proper reverence for divine measure will flourish outside the family in other public commons. The intimate is not only in the familial commons, but if its piety is not there, there are repercussions in other forms of community, social, political, and religious. (IU 416–417)

To be redirected in this sense would mean for public life to become porous both in its horizontal and vertical relations—recall the double use of the replica of St Brendan's boat. It means living under an open heaven, yet remaining finite. This is, of course, what Desmond captures as *the between*. The distinctions between three types of counterfeits are mine, not Desmond's. I trust they will help to appreciate the depth and richness of his texts.

Bibliography

Desmond, William. 1995. *Perplexity and Ultimacy*. Albany: SUNY.
———. 2006. On the Way: Travelling with Sander Griffioen. In *Sander Griffioen, Een weg gaan*. Budel: Damon.

———. 2016. *The Intimate Universal: The Hidden Porosity Among Religion, Art, Philosophy, and Politics*. New York: Cambridge University Press.
Gadamer, H.G. 1983. *Heideggers Wege. Studien zum Spätwerk*. Tübingen: Mohr.
Griffioen, Sander. 2010. Towards a Philosophy of God: A Study in William Desmond's Thought. *Philosophia Reformata* 75: 117–140.
———. 2015. Action & Reflection, II. *Philosophia Reformata* 80: 178–203.
Hegel, G.W.F. 1955. *Vorlesungen über die Philosophie der Geschichte*. Ed. J. Hoffmeister, Band I. Hamburg: Meiner.
———. 1987. *Vorlesungsmanuskripte I (1816–1831)*. In *Georg Wilhelm Friedrich Hegel. Gesammelte Werke*, ed. Walter Jaeschke. Band 17. Hamburg: Meiner.
Keller, Timothy. 2010. *Counterfeit Gods: When the Empty Promises of Love, Money and Power Let You Down*. London: Hodder & Stoughton.
Moore, Thomas. 1743. *Utopia or the Happy Republic [1516]*. Trans. Robert Foulis. Glasgow: Gilbert Burnet.
Rosenkranz, Karl. 1844. *G.W.F. Hegels Leben*. Berlin: Dunker & Humblot.
Rosenzweig, Fr. 1988. *Der Stern der Erlösung*. Frankfurt: Bibliothek Suhrkamp.
Soloviev, Vladimir Sergaevitch. 2012. *A Story of Anti-Christ [1900]*. Trans. Unnamed. Lexington: Kassock Bros.
Westphal, Merold. 1992. *Hegel, Freedom and Modernity*. Albany: State University of New York Press.

CHAPTER 14

Transcendence in Metaxology and Sophiology

Josephien van Kessel

The first time I came across *metaxu* as a philosophical notion was in the social philosophy, or better Sophiology, of Sergei Bulgakov (1871–1944). Bulgakov points to the origin of the term from Plato's *Symposium*, meaning the 'in-between' or 'middle ground:' "In creating the world, God put a *gran'* (border) between himself and the world, which unites and separates the one from the other (a kind of *metaxu* in the sense of Plato)" (Bulgakov 1999, p. 193). Bulgakov names this *metaxu* Sophia, God's Wisdom, Love and *Providenie* (Providence).[1] In my search for this term on the Internet, it was not for long that I discovered William Desmond's metaxology. It struck me as more than a coincidence that both Bulgakov and Desmond call their philosophical projects, Sophiology and metaxology, after this 'between' of God and world, that is, of transcendence and immanence.

[1] The Russian and English words have the same Latin stem. Sophia is a common female name and often endowed with a feminine nature in Russian Sophiology. I write Sophia and Sophiology with a capital letter, but 'it' when referring to Sophia in order to stress its nature as a principle. I write a lower-case initial letter when it is used as an adjective, for example, sophiological or sophic.

J. van Kessel (✉)
Radboud University Nijmegen, Nijmegen, Netherlands

© The Author(s) 2018
D. Vanden Auweele (ed.), *William Desmond's Philosophy between Metaphysics, Religion, Ethics, and Aesthetics*,
https://doi.org/10.1007/978-3-319-98992-1_14

A short but intensive perusal of Desmond's works only confirmed my intuition that metaxology and Sophiology are similar projects. In the first place, in the broadness of their fields of application: sociology, philosophy (i.e. metaphysics, ethics, aesthetics etc.) and religion or theology. In the second place, because their explicit task is to understand Sophia/*metaxu* in all these realms. I found further confirmation in Desmond's article 'God Beyond the Whole: Between Solov'ëv and Shestov' in which he compared his thought with that of two important Russian religious philosophers, Vladimir Solov'ëv (1853–1900) and Lev Shestov (1866–1938).

Solov'ëv is considered to be the father of Russian Sophiology, although he never called his own philosophy Sophiology (Bulgakov would be the first to call it as such), but 'theosophy,' nor did he write openly on Sophia in his philosophical works, only in his poetry. Lev Shestov is a contemporary of Bulgakov and belonged to the same class[2] of Russian religious intelligentsia in the Silver Age (1890–1920) that was occupied with the interpretation of Solov'ëv's legacy. Some were, like Shestov, critical of this legacy, others, like Bulgakov, felt themselves the spiritual heirs of Solov'ëv, and tried to develop his philosophical thought further. In his article, Desmond positions himself and metaxology "[B]between Solov'ëv and Shestov" regarding the subject of "God Beyond the Whole" (IST 167–199).

In this chapter, I will initially try to answer the following questions: whether Desmond's interpretation of Solov'ëv's philosophy is correct and whether he is right in positioning himself between Solov'ëv and Shestov. My further question concerns the implications of Desmond's interpretation of Bulgakov's Sophiology, when I speak of Sophiology and metaxology as analogous developments or similar projects. To answer these questions, in the first section, I will give a short overview of Bulgakov's Sophiology in the context of Russian religious philosophical thought, with specific attention to his characterization of Sophia as *metaxu* of God and world. In the second section, I will turn to Desmond's criticism of Solov'ëv's presumed holism, idealism and rationalism, which will highlight the position of both metaxology and Sophiology with regard to these -isms. In the third section, I will try to answer Desmond's six questions at the end of his article, regarding "the limitations of the holistic God," from Bulgakov's sophiological perspective. This will make clear whether

---

[2] The Russian intelligentsia is often called a 'classless class' consisting of people with similar education. The religious intelligentsia is a relatively small subgroup.

Desmond's criticism of Solov'ëv holds in case of Bulgakov's Sophiology. In the fourth section, I present metaxology and Sophiology as similar philosophical projects, not only in content, subject matter, formal aspects, presuppositions and so on, but also in legitimation and objectives.

Sophia as *Metaxu*

For Bulgakov, Sophia is the hidden order of creation that reveals itself in this world, for example, as beauty in art and in nature, as truth in science and philosophy and as good in society. As Bulgakov writes in his posthumously published autobiographical notes: "Yes, here[3] I took into my heart the revelation of Sophia (*otkrovenie Sofii*),[4] here into my soul was put the jewel that I looked for in the course of my whole blind and troubled life" (Bulgakov 1946, p. 13). He would be occupied with the study of Sophia, that is, Sophiology, throughout his professional career: from its start in the late 1880s as young Marxist political economist, who denied all religious experiences, during his reorientation into an Idealist social philosopher in the early 1900s, and into a Christian religious philosopher and Christian socialist 'publicist' (*publitsist*[5]) in the late 1900s and early 1910s, as an ordained priest from 1918 on, and as a theologian during his subsequent career in exile in Paris from 1924 until his death in 1944.

Sophiology is, furthermore, an attempt to acquire *positive* knowledge of Sophia, which is not in line with the Orthodox tradition of *apophasis*, and which is also the reason that both Bulgakov and Solov'ëv were often accused of gnosticism (Vaganova 2011, p. 64ff).[6] The same reproach can be made at the address of Desmond's metaxology, since this also tries to find a logos of *metaxu*. In the course of his work, Bulgakov gave many characterizations (or identifications) of Sophia. Sophia is *Slava* (Glory), *Krasota* (Beauty), *Mudrost'* (Wisdom), *Tserkov'* (Church), to name only a

---

[3] He was baptized in the parish church of Livny.
[4] Bulgakov writes 'otkrovenie Sofii' and 'Sofiia otkryvaetsia': Sophia is an agent that can reveal itself. On the other hand, Russian grammar allows an interpretation of a God who reveals his Sophia.
[5] *Publitsist* and *publitsistika* are untranslatable like many Russian terms. It is a kind of political journalism. See also Schrooyen (2006, p. 7).
[6] Sophiology is therefore *cataphatic*, and not *apophatic* as traditional Orthodox philosophy and theology that deny the possibility of positive knowledge of God, who is absolutely transcendent to human thought. On *apophasis* as a characteristic of Orthodox spirituality, see van den Bercken (2011, p. 125).

few of its identifications. One of Sophia's central qualifications, however, is *gran'* (border) and *sviaz'* (connection) between transcendence and immanence, between Divine and human worlds: Sophia is the ultimate *metaxu* (between/*mezhdu*) (Bulgakov 1999, p. 193), both absolutely transcendent to created order as its source and fully immanent in created order as its ontological root and principle.

For Bulgakov, the between of God and world has the important connotation of *and*, which is an antinomic[7] reality: Sophia is both God *and* not God, earthly *and* Divine, created *and* uncreated. According to Bulgakov, an antinomy is a "contradiction for rational thought," and the main antinomy of religious consciousness is the simultaneous absolute transcendence *and* immanence of God (Bulgakov 1999-I, p. 100). Desmond likewise signals a metaxological 'not' that "separates and allows communication" (p. 172) and is part of "hyperbolic thought." Desmond's theory of creation is also consonant with Bulgakov's theory of creation from 'nothing' (*mè-on*, not *ouk-on*). Sophia is exactly the between (*metaxu*) of transcendence *and* immanence, and is both the relation *and* the distinction. This *metaxic* quality of Sophia is also the ultimate precondition of the ideal form of human sociality/community, that is, Orthodox *sobornost'* (Bulgakov 2003, p. 119).[8] This sense of community is crucial for Desmond's metaxology as well.

Desmond's Criticism of Solov'ëv's Holism and Rationalism: What About His 'Sophia-Doctrine'?

In his article, Desmond criticizes Solov'ëv's philosophy via Shestov.[9] At first, he seems to agree with Shestov's criticism of Solov'ëv's holism and abstract rationalism.[10] Further on, however, Desmond repeatedly defends Solov'ëv against Shestov's attacks, and does this in a 'negative' way, that is, by attacking Shestov's position as having no sense of "God beyond the

---

[7] Bulgakov derives his use of antinomy from his friend and Orthodox priest Pavel Florenskii (2004 [1914]).

[8] See also Van Kessel (2010) on Bulgakov's interpretation of *sobornost'*.

[9] Desmond uses Shestov's article on Solov'ëv: "Speculation and Apocalypse The Religious Philosophy of Vladimir Solovyov," first published in *Sovremeniye zapiski*, nrs. 33–34 (1927–1928).

[10] This was a frequent criticism of Solov'ëv's philosophy by Russian religious philosophers of the Silver Age, amongst others by Bulgakov, who confesses he is more inspired by Solov'ëv's poetry than by his philosophy (Bulgakov 2008, p. 70).

Whole" (IST 181) and being unable to "distinguish between Christ and anti-Christ" (IST 192). He, furthermore, asks, whether Solov'ëv in this respect can do more and, more specifically, his "doctrine of Sophia." (IST 181).

Desmond's main aim in the text is to explore some of the philosophical and religious ambiguities that are attached to "the idea of the whole" especially in relation to God (IST 167). He uses Solov'ëv and Shestov with this aim in mind and more, in particular, the "nonnegotiable differences between the two" (ibid.). The first difference is that Solov'ëv wants philosophically to affirm an 'All-unity' (*vseedinstvo*), while Shestov protests against All-unity in calling it 'omnitude' (*vsemstvo*), "on behalf of the free singularity of the human, and the personalism of the creator God" (IST 168). Another difference is Solov'ëv's presumed rationalism versus Shestov's irrationalism.

Referring to an early work of Solov'ëv, *Lectures on Divine Humanity* (1995), Desmond concludes that there are indeed "idealist currents in Solov'ëv's thought" (IST 177) and "resonances of this holistic God in Solov'ëv" (IST 169) because in idealism God is the ultimate whole of wholes. According to Desmond, this is also the reason for idealism to favor emanation to creation. Emanation suggests the continuity of the world and God, and the immanence in the world of the divine and of the world in the divine, whereas creation suggests the transcendence of the divine, hence the non-divinity of the world: "The holistic God stresses the sameness of world and God, the God of creation the difference" (IST 170). The holistic God assimilates, whereas the God of creation "keeps open an essential difference" (IST 172): "As with idealism, opposition and fragmentation are not denied, but they are situated within the compass of a more inclusive unity" (IST 178). This unity ultimately is the telos of differences and many-ness. Desmond allows that Solov'ëv's All-unity is "not the block unity or absorbing God," for he tries to "grant some qualified independence to the members of the 'All-unity'" (ibid.). He, however, also stresses Solov'ëv's negative attitude to the self-assertion of difference and singularity over against the whole, that is, to egoism.

The deeper kernel of Shestov's criticism of Solov'ëv (and of Desmond's criticism of Sophiology) is the connection of rationalism and necessity, and thus the un-freedom of the singular (IST 172–173). Shestov pleads for the freedom of creation and of revelation. Every revelation comes from beyond the whole, from transcendence, but every rationalization tries to include this beyond into the whole, to make it immanent (IST 175).

Furthermore, Desmond follows Shestov's criticism of the rationalism contained in Solov'ëv's idealism, and calls for a meta-logical logic, that is, a logic that is not univocal. The problem is more specifically rationalistic universalism, which ends up hostile to the intimate singularities of life. However, already in his master dissertation *Crisis of Western Philosophy Against the Positivists* (1874) and continuing in his doctoral dissertation *Criticism of Abstract Principles* (1877–1880), Solov'ëv criticizes the abstract principles of rationality and strives for integral knowledge (*tsel'noe znanie*), a notion he took from the Slavophiles (Zenkovskii 2011, p. 461).

Furthermore, according to Desmond, Solov'ëv continues the more progressive historical *teleologies* such as we find in idealist thought (i.e. in Plato, Plotinus, Kant, Hegel and Schelling) and identifies Compte's *Grand-Être* (p. 179) with his own divine-human 'All-unity,' that is, with *Bogochelovechestvo*. This 'absolutization of humanity' is compared by Shestov with idolatry, that is, with being the counterfeit double of God. Bulgakov would defend Solov'ëv's *Bogochelovechestvo* against this accusation of being an idol, but he attacks Marxism and populism in exactly this vein because it puts mere humanity—and even the individual human being—in this position of idol. Desmond, in this respect, likewise does not agree with Shestov: not Solov'ëv's Divine humanity is the idol, but Comte's *Grand-Être*.

As Desmond, furthermore, confirms, Solov'ëv's thought about 'community' is essentially different from thoughts of Hegel, Spinoza and Schelling, despite "idealistic resonances" (IST 179). He starts to suspect that "participation in the intimate universal of a worshipping community puts brakes on the temptation to render the 'All-unity' in terms closer to a homogeneous, neutral, impersonal universal," and "it is closer to this that his [Solov'ëv's] heart lies rather than to the idol of rational necessity or indeed the holistic God of idealistic philosophy" (IST 179).

Sophia and Anti-Christ

According to Desmond, Solov'ëv started to suspect these problems of a counterfeit double of the absolute whole/God and related these to the problem of the anti-Christ: "The holistic god usurping the God beyond the whole" (IST 180). Desmond points to "the doctrine of Sophia which gives some sense of the God beyond the whole" of idealist holism, and which "might be seen as intending to *keep open the ontological difference* of Creator and creation" (IST 181): "Is not the doctrine of Sophia a pointer to a *middle between* utter transcendence and an otherwise godless immanence?" (IST 181). Even if Shestov would call this Sophia an idol, why not consider it as "a name for a community of wisdom and love between the God beyond the whole and the divine-human community coming to be within the finite whole" (IST 181).

Furthermore, according to Desmond, the maternal and feminine metaphorics of Solov'ëv's Sophia are as *intimately personal* as the dominant "paternal metaphorics of the Old Testament transcendence" that Shestov prefers, and love of the mother is "more a fleshed bond, hence has an incarnational dimension," than love via the father (IST 182, italics Desmond). In his spirituality, Solov'ëv "had an intensely aesthetic, embodied sense of the feminine Sophia." (IST 182), and his Sophia-doctrine, according to Desmond, seems more the result of *theia mania*, than of idolatry of the rational concept of which Shestov accused him. Desmond's last 'reproach' to Solov'ëv regards trying to make sense of this fire and madness in the idealistic language of the 'All-unity'. The reproach regards not 'trying to make sense' as such, which is the task of philosophy, but of Solov'ëv doing this in the wrong language: "The language of the whole is not adequate to this beyond" (IST 182). In my view, this is exactly the reason that Bulgakov developed his 'sophiological language,' which follows Desmond's recommendation "to find a better language may be as much a task for philosophy as it is a matter of willingness to listen to the sacred languages of holy scripture" (IST 182).

The deeper problem of idealism is, according to Desmond, the problem of the anti-Christ and the dualism of worldly and spiritual power. Power as *superbia* is the usurpation of spiritual power (IST 183).[11] The God beyond is a god beyond this power "claiming 'nothing beyond'" (ibid.). Those, who do not bow for the anti-Christ, do this in name of the one that is beyond. Here, Desmond refers to the three temptations of Christ. The temptation of the anti-Christ is the third temptation of spiritual pride. The first of bread is the temptation of economics and of worldly comfort. The second is that of autocracy and worldly power. The third is of spiritual power, which is also Nietzsche's great temptation, according to Desmond (IST 184), the same Nietzsche, who was so admired by Shestov.

Solov'ëv's anti-Christ is saved by the counterfeit double from this last temptation of *superbia*, and not by a power of God. As Desmond acknowledges, "there is a *difference* between the City of God and the City of Man

[11] This connects to the political philosophical meaning of Sophiology, see van Kessel (2012).

(Augustine)" (IST 185, italics by Desmond). Time, according to Desmond, is the mixture (or the medium/between of that mixture) of the two cities. A counterfeit double of God is an idol "made by man for man." Idols are social ideals that are "inwardly corrupted by the will-to-power of *superbia*" (IST 186). From the outside, the anti-Christ looks like the God-man, but, inwardly, he is corrupted. As Desmond admits, Solov'ëv's superman (*sverkhchelovek*) and Nietzsche's *Übermensch* "seem to be very like doubles of each other. Yet, while seeming very close, they are entirely opposed: in the refusal of God in the second, and in the impossibility of the first without God" (IST 187). Although Nietzsche "is said to have brought us to the twilight of the idols, but did he? Or did he manufacture a new idol?" (ibid.). Desmond answers these rhetorical questions in the affirmative.

Furthermore, even Nietzsche "seems (in *Will to Power*) very sympathetic to a new pantheism" (ibid.). This is, however, not "the rational whole of idealism, but the rhapsodic Dionysian whole of will-to-power and Amor fati" (IST 189). Both are counterfeit doubles of God: it is a "*war among pretenders to prophecy*" (IST 191), in which Solov'ëv and his short story of anti-Christ are of more help than Shestov, who "seems unable to distinguish between Christ and anti-Christ" (IST 192). Shestov is right in demanding 'singular finesse', but Solov'ëv is also right in demanding systematic understanding, that is, philosophy (IST 190).

Six Questions to Sophiology and Holism

Desmond's six questions to holism concern what he calls the limitations of the holistic God, which address: the origin of difference, the fall in time, the necessity of the arising of the many, the space for freedom, the status of the singular individual and the character of the community of God and creation (IST 193–199). To exactly these questions, Bulgakov gave an ideal-realist answer by means of Sophiology.

Regarding the first point, Bulgakov agrees with Desmond that to see difference only as the result of the fall is to see it too negatively: both want to affirm plurality as positive. Furthermore, according to Desmond, the fall degrades the temporal, instead of elevating it: speaking in these terms of the good of the plural and the temporal "is not adequate to the good" (IST 193). Being in the between "does not fall; it arises into being" (ibid.). In Desmond's metaxology, the origin of difference is not the fall in time, but an arising in time: time is supported on the love of eternity, which cannot be an erotic love, but only an agapeic love. He suspects in Solov'ëv's interpretation of love in *Smysl liubvi* (*The Meaning of Love*, 1991) more eroticism than agapeism, as important emphases are lacking in Solov'ëv's conception of love: the agapeic release of finite creation as other, the 'nothing' between god and world, the community within creation and between creation and God (IST 194). In his theological Sophiology, Bulgakov would develop exactly this criticism of Solov'ëv's overly erotic love for Divine Sophia, as well as these emphases: the empirical world is created by God from 'nothing,' which is not the absolute *ouk-on*, but the relative *mè-on*,[12] and it is not the result of emanation; the act of creation was a voluntary act, not a necessary act; the central importance and abundance of God's love as love for Its other, that is, Sophia and so on.

Desmond's third question on the necessity of the arising of the many is a basic question for Bulgakov as well, as it undermines both the freedom of God as creator and of human freedom as created, that is, the possibility of "the contingency of finite beings in the between" (IST 195). If necessity rules creation, mankind does not have to do anything, and, concerning Desmond's fourth question, there is no "space for freedom," that is, for the unfinished and the open, in view of the holistic God (ibid.). According to Bulgakov, the question of creaturely freedom can only be answered in a *Philosophy of Economy*,[13] because economy is this fight, and synthesis between freedom and necessity (Bulgakov 2000, p. 196ff).

Desmond's agapeic God, furthermore, "loves the idiotic, and delights in the sweet singularity that dances or dares before it" (IST 195). This formulation strongly reminds of both Solov'ëv's and Bulgakov's Sophia, who is the "love of Love, i.e. the eternal object of Divine Love," "enjoyment, joyous feeling and play" (Bulgakov 1999-I, pp. 193–194) and who, according to Proverbs 8: 30–32, "was His delight day by day, Frolicking before Him at all times."[14] This characterization strongly connects Sophia with singularity, and with Desmond's fifth question on the status of the singular individual, that is, the 'person' in Russian religious philosophy. In holism, this idiotic singularity should vanish into the more encompassing whole, or is estranged from the whole, and in some cases is seen as the

---

[12] See Bulgakov (2000, p. 328), Glossary of Greek Terms; Bulgakov (1999-I, pp. 170–171).

[13] *Philosophy of Economy*, in which Bulgakov introduced Sophia as a social principle, is both his doctor's dissertation in and goodbye to political economy as a science.

[14] Bulgakov (2000, pp. 57, 69, 99). See also Kornblatt (2009, p. 36), who stresses the connection of Sophia with laughter in Solov'ëv's Sophia-poems (p. 91).

center of evil. Desmond connects this point of the singular individual as the source of evil also with Solov'ëv's philosophy. Although it is true that Solov'ëv is very negative about egoism of the individual in *Smysl liubvi* (1991, p. 170), he is also very negative of any egoism *à deux* (and more). Furthermore, Solov'ëv would never consent to make idiotic singularity disappear into a more encompassing whole, nor is this his definition of a successful love relation between two or more persons, or in a successful love relation between man and God. According to Solov'ëv (1991, p. 179), in their ideal form, all relations are characterized by *syzygia* (conjunction).

Love allows the difference of self and other, and even demands it. Desmond sees the singular as a particular whole in itself but also tries to articulate a "community of open wholes" in the between, beyond the dialectical language of parts and wholes (IST 197). This resembles what Desmond calls Solov'ëv's "ecumenical community," and what Bulgakov calls *sobornost* (catholicity), which is the ideal form of Orthodox (ecclesiastical) society (ibid.). Furthermore, Bulgakov sees willful self-assertiveness, what he names 'heroism,' as the wrong attitude of the individual.[15] He would agree fully with Desmond's assertion: "Such willful self-assertive humanity is not the truth of singularity. To come anew to the porosity of being it must pass through a penitential un-selving" (ibid.). This "penitential un-selving," Bulgakov (1997, p. 114) called *poslushanie* (obedience) and identified with Weber's inner-worldly asceticism.

According to Bulgakov, as well as Augustine, evil is not a quality of the world itself, nor is the plurality or contingency of being after the fall in history. Evil is only in the choice of the individual against God or its refusal of community with God. Regarding Desmond's sixth question on the character of community of god and creation, Bulgakov would agree with his disapproval of the holistic model of community as self-communication. A holistic community seeks to reconcile oppositions, "But all otherness is not opposition," as Desmond affirms, and some othernesses "are not merely provisional," but essential (IST 198). Bulgakov tried to understand this difference in an antinomical, and not in a dialectical, way.

---

[15] In his famous Vekhi-article "Heroism and Asceticism," published in 1909.

Metaxology and Sophiology

On the one hand, both Desmond's metaxology and Bulgakov's Sophiology attack 'pure idealism' for its abstract holism, which Bulgakov called 'monism,' and its abstract rationalism. On the other hand, both try to save from idealism what is valuable. Sergei Khoruzhii (in Florenskii 2004, p. 215) not without reason calls Florenskii, Solov'ëv and Bulgakov 'religious materialists.' Likewise, Bulgakov in his doctoral speech on September 21, 1912, called his own approach "mystical or religious materialism" (Bulgakov 2009, p. 373). Both Desmond and Bulgakov engage in dialogue with Hegelian dialectics. Bulgakov would find an alternative in 'anti-nomism,' while Desmond tries to replace univocal logic, that is, dialectics, with a meta-logical, that is, a metaxological approach. Both in a similar sense try to keep us open or make us open up to the "porosity of being" in the between.

In my opinion, Desmond accuses Solov'ëv too lightly of a tendency to holism, and too lightly identifies the ancient *Hen kai pan* (One the All, IST 169) with Solov'ëv's and Bulgakov's *vseedinstvo* (All-unity). Bulgakov speaks of his own 'holism' as pan-en-theism in opposition to pan-theism (Zenkovskii 2011, p. 821), while Desmond identifies the two from the start (IST 168). According to me, in this way, Desmond allows for less difference in the whole, that is, only addresses the reductive whole of idealistic holism. Desmond's response to Solov'ëv resembles a rhetorical device, that is, the straw man argument. Through Shestov's criticism of Solov'ëv, Desmond criticizes something or someone else, and this something has to do with 'contemporary panentheism' (IST 170), and "a particular formation of the *dialectical way* of thinking" (i.e. Hegelian 'univocal logic'), all forms of "modern Eleaticism, followed in the essentials by all the major thinkers" (IST 174), referring to Spinoza, Solov'ëv, Schleiermacher, Kant, Hegel and Schelling, and forms of postmodern thought, that is, Nietzsche and his followers (IST 187).

Clearly, Desmond singles out the doctrine of Sophia as pointing to the possibility of a language that is adequate to this beyond. It is perhaps significant that Solov'ëv did not openly speak about Sophia in his published philosophical works,[16] but he did evoke her and was in communication with her in his poetry. Interestingly, Bulgakov valued Solov'ëv's poetry

---

[16] He did so only in his unpublished work *La Sophia*, which he wrote before his published philosophical dissertations, and in his published poetry.

more than his philosophical works, where Solov'ëv used Hegelian dialectics in a rather strict way. Bulgakov developed instead an antinomical way of thinking and speaking about Sophia. For Bulgakov, Sophia is not God, even though God at times may identify with his Sophia, nor is Sophia a hypostasis or 'person,' which she clearly is for Solov'ëv, and which is highly valued by Desmond. In my opinion, Bulgakov is the least personalistic of 'Sophiologues,' as his Sophia is not a hypostasis or person, although sometimes coming close to this qualification, for example, in *Svet nevechernii* (1917), but the principle of 'hypostas-ity,' Sophia is not a woman, but the principle of femininity, is not Jesus-Logos, but his bride, that is, the Church. For Bulgakov, clearly, Solov'ëv's too personal interpretation of Divine Wisdom is a problem: if Solov'ëv is serious about his personal 'love-affair' with Sophia, what does this reveal about his self-evaluation? Did he see himself as a prophet? As Christ? Did Solov'ëv himself discern between Christ and anti-Christ? These are important questions, which Bulgakov wanted to answer in his Sophiology, in which Sophia is not an individual person, but Church, and the community of *sobornost'*, a metaphysical Divine-human relationship, to be realized in this world, and as such very similar to Desmond's description of *metaxu* and 'ecumical community.'

Conclusion

Both Desmond and Bulgakov try to think the *metaxu*, and their philosophical projects are very similar, although their historical positions are a century apart. Whereas in Bulgakov's lifetime, Christianity still seemed an eligible alternative, in our lifetime this choice seems archaic, and needs more defense. This, in my view, accounts for Desmond's criticism of Solov'ëv by way of a straw man, but maybe also for his impersonal description of *metaxu*. In his criticism of Solov'ëv, Desmond clearly fights his own demons, that is, Hegel's rationalism and idealism but more, in particular, the modern 'equivocal' ethos.

Bulgakov, however, would have agreed for the greater part with Desmond's criticism of this 'equivocal' ethos of the philosophy of modernity. In his own Sophiology, although a further development of Solov'ëv's 'Sopia-thought,' Bulgakov criticized Solov'ëv's too intimate relation with Divine Sophia, and what this implied for Solov'ëv's self-evaluation. Bulgakov would agree, however, with Desmond's admiration *and* criticism of Hegel's absolute idealism. Bulgakov is closer to developing his own sophiological language in sociology, philosophy and theology than Solov'ëv was, who was only able to express his "Sophia-doctrine" in his poetry. Bulgakov proposes the language of antinomy, which enabled him to transcend the univocal logic of dialectics, which is also Desmond's greatest enemy.

As I argued above, Desmond incorrectly positions himself between Solov'ëv and Shestov. In fact, he is much closer to Solov'ëv, and clearly expects more from him, than from Shestov, more in particular from his 'Sophia-thought'. I demonstrated as well that Desmond's metaxology and Bulgakov's Sophiology share important characteristics, goals and even enemies, that is, abstract rationalism, holism and idealism, in name of 'God beyond the whole.' Both try to develop another philosophical language which is not univocal nor dialectical, but antinomical or hyperbolic. In short, despite a difference of almost 100 years, metaxology and Sophiology are indeed analogous developments in philosophy, pointing to the importance of a possible 'beyond,' including a beyond of dualistic 'either/or' thinking, by way of concentrating on the between/Sophia.

Bibliography

Bulgakov, Sergei. 1946. *Avtobiograficheskie zametki (Autobiographical Notes)*. Ed. L.A. Zander. Paris: IMKA.

———. 1997. *Dva grada. Issledovanie o prirode obshchestvennykh idealov (Two Cities. A Research into the Nature of Social Ideals)*. Ed. V.V. Sapov. Sankt Peterburg: RKhGI (Originally Published Moskva: Put' 1911).

———. 1999. *Pervoobraz i obraz (Proto-image and image). Tom 1. Svet nevechernij. Sozertsaniia i umozreniia (Vol. I: The Unfading Light Observations and Reflections)*. Moskva: Iskusstvo/Sankt-Peterburg: Inapress (Originally published in 1917 as *Svet nevechernii. Sozertsaniia i umozreniia.* Moskva: Put'). *Tom 2. Filosofiia imeni. Ikona i ikonopochitanie (Vol. II: Philosophy of the Name. The Icon and the Veneration of Icons)*.

———. 2000. *Philosophy of Economy: The World as Household*. Trans. Catherine Evtuhov. New Haven: Yale University Press. (Originally Published in 1912 as *Filosofiia khoziaistva.* Chast' pervaia Mir kak khoziaistvo. Moskva: Put').

Bulgakov, Sergii (Prot.). 2003. Muzhkoe i zhenskoe v bozhestve (The Male and the Female in the Deity), 343–364; Muzhskoe i zhenskoe (Male and Female), 365–388. S.N. Bulgakov: Religiozno-filosofskii put'. Mezhdunarodnaia nauchnaia konferentsiia, posviashchennaia 130-letiiu so dnia rozhdeniia 5–7 marta 2001 (S.N. Bulgakov: Religious Philosophical Way. International Scientific Conference in Memory of the 130th Anniversary of His Birthday). Ed. A.P. Kozyrev. Moskva: Russkii Put'.

———. 2008. *Tikhie dumy: ètika, kul'tura, sofiologiia (Quiet Thoughts: Ethics, Culture, Sophiology)*. Izdatel'stvo Olega Abyshko. First Published as *Tikhie dumy: iz statiei* 1911–1915-gg. (Quiet Thoughts. Essays 1911–1915). 1918. Moskva: Leman i Sakharov.

Bulgakov, Sergei. 2009. *Filosofiia khoziaistva*. Moskva: Institut russkoi tsivilizatsii. [First Published in 1912. English Translation by Catherine Evtuhov, see Bulgakov, 2000a].

van den Bercken, Wil. 2011. *Christian Fiction and Religious Realism in the Novels of Dostoevsky*. London-New York-Delhi: Anthem Press.

Florenskii, Pavel. 2004. *The Pillar and Ground of the Truth: An Essay in Orthodox Theodicy in Twelve Letters*. Trans. Boris Jakim. Princeton University Press. Paperback Edition. Originally Published in Russian in 1914 as *Stolp i utverzhdenie Istiny: Opyt pravoslavnoi feoditsei v dvenadtsati pis'makh*.

van Kessel, Josephien H.J. 2010. Sophia and Sobornost': Cement and Organizing Principle of Orthodox Society. In *Sofiologiia, seriia 'Bogoslovie i nauka'*, ed. Vladimir Porus, 208–220. Moskva: BBI.

———. 2012. Bulgakov's Sophiology: Towards an Orthodox Economic-Theological Engagement with the Modern World. *Studies in East European Thought* 64: 251–267.

Kornblatt, Judith Deutsch. 2009. *Divine Sophia. The Wisdom Writings of Vladimir Solovyov*. Including Annotated Trans. Boris Jakim, Judith Kornblatt, and Laury Magnus. Ithaca and London: Cornell University Press.

Schrooyen, Pauline. 2006. *Vladimir Solov'ëv in the Rising Public Sphere. A Reconstruction and Analysis of the Concept of Christian Politics in the publitsistika of Vladimir Solov'ëv*. PhD thesis at Radboud University Nijmegen, Nijmegen, PrintPartners Ipskamp.

Solov'ëv, Vladimir. 1991. *Smysl liubvi: Izbrannye proizvedeniia*. Editor N.I. Tsimbaeva, Moskva: Sovremennik. Smysl liubvi (1892–1894), pp. 125–182; Trans. Jane Marshall as Solov'ëv, V. 1985. *The Meaning of Love*. Trans. Jane Marshall. 1945. Revised by Thomas R. Beyer, Jr., 1985.

———. 1995. *Lectures on Divine Humanity*. Trans. and Ed. Jakim, Boris. Lindisfarne Press. (Translation of Chteniia o Bogochelovechestve (1877–1891). Also Translated as Lectures on Godmanhood by Peter Zouboff. 1948.

Vaganova, N.A. 2011. *Sofiologiia protoiereia Sergiia Bulgakova (The Sophiology of Archpriest Sergii Bulgakov)*. Moskva: Izd-vo PSTGU.

Zenkovskii, Vasilii. 2011 [1950]. Istoriia russkoi filosofii. Moskva: Akademicheskii Proekt.

CHAPTER 15

Panentheism and Hegelian Controversies

Philip A. Gottschalk

William Desmond is a well-known Hegel scholar. As such, he has engaged other Hegel scholars who are panentheistic in their interpretation of Hegel. We will focus our discussion on the theme of pan(en)theism and examine Desmond's engagement and interaction with two who advocate this view, specifically Peter C. Hodgson and Sergei Bulgakov, an inheritor of Vladimir Solov'ëv. The first section will focus on Desmond's treatment of Hegel and Hodgson on the issue of pan(en)theism. In the second section we will consider Desmond's interaction with Solov'ëv and introduce the panentheism of Sergei Bulgakov, who is an inheritor of Solov'ëv. In conclusion we will entertain differences between Desmond's 'Between' and the dipolar god of panentheism (GB 225–240).

Hodgson Versus Desmond: The Clash of the Hegelians

The debate between Peter C. Hodgson and Desmond about Hegel's view of religious community can be seen as an illustrative encounter between Desmond and his others. Hodgson has translated Hegel's *Lectures on*

P. A. Gottschalk (✉)
Tyndale Theological Seminary, Badhoevedorp, Netherlands
e-mail: pgottschalk@tyndale-europe.eu

© The Author(s) 2018
D. Vanden Auweele (ed.), *William Desmond's Philosophy between Metaphysics, Religion, Ethics, and Aesthetics*,
https://doi.org/10.1007/978-3-319-98992-1_15

Philosophy of Religion into English. In a commentary volume to his translation of Hegel's work, Hodgson has taken issue with Desmond's interpretation of Hegel.

Hodgson's main claim is that Desmond's understanding of Hegel in terms of pantheism (or panentheism) is not subtle enough. According to him, Hegel is not, as Desmond suggests, a 'totalizer' who "cannot count to two" (Hodgson 2005, p. 157). Hodgson maintains that Hegel's 'holism' does, in fact, include a robust sense of otherness and difference. Secondly, Hodgson claims that Desmond is a follower of Kierkegaard in that he cannot abide or understand dialectical thinking. Hodgson does not believe that Desmond does justice to Hegel's subtle dialectic, but rather flattens it into a merely totalizing force. Hodgson supposes that Hegel's view of kenosis, the descent of God into humanity, can be read differently and more generously towards Hegel's view than Desmond's reading allows. Thirdly, Hodgson repeatedly ripostes Desmond as simply a Christian thinker, that is, that Desmond is merely a theist and is limited in his ability to appreciate differences within the Christian theological community.

Hodgson maintains that Hegel's God is not monistic or pantheistic, but holistic. For Hodgson, holistic means that God encompasses the whole, but is not the whole. In Hodgson's view the sublation of humanity into Godhood is not a totalizing of the One reducing the other into itself, but rather means that God gives himself to community. God comes into community and is realized through community. Without both God and the other, there is no community. Hodgson sees no problem with God and community being one without God subsuming or sublating community into himself. Desmond, on the other hand, believes Hodgson's concept of religious community to be Hodgson's own interpretation of Hegel. Desmond believes that Hegel's dialectic is much more erotic (to use Desmond's term) than agapeic. Hegel's God, on Desmond's reading, is realizing himself, creating himself, by sublating community. Desmond is not sanguine about Hegel's God desiring to be a part of community. Desmond drives this wedge further by showing how left-wing Hegelians were perhaps more honest than Hodgson in seeing religious community as giving way to a kingdom, in their view a social democracy (HG 179; BHD 170–172). Right-wing Hegelians, on the other hand, saw this final community as the Kingdom of Prussia. Desmond's point is that Hodgson's generous reading of Hegel owes more to Hodgson himself than to Hegel.

Desmond is at pains to maintain that God must be an overdetermined other (someone who exceeds our concepts and can inform us). God must also be agapeic. God must be free to create others for themselves and not for his own self-aggrandizement or self-development. It is true that Desmond mentions Aquinas in regard to God, but this does not mean that Aquinas informed Desmond's critique of Hegel, but rather that Desmond is aware that Aquinas has a similar view: "A god that creates itself would have to be itself to create itself" (2005, p. 197). Desmond believes God must be 'beyond' the whole. Desmond's desire is to protect both the independence (transcendence) of God and the independence (freedom) of the individual. God must be free to create, and the individual must be free to renege or make good on his or her promise; the individual, in Desmond's system, is "freely given to be with a promise". Desmond also desires free individuals who can choose to do good or evil as they will without coercion. Hodgson somehow supposes that there is freedom from coercion in Hegelian dialectic (Hodgson 2005, p. 159). However, Desmond does not read Hegel so. Desmond does not believe that Hegel's sublation is as generous as Hodgson does. Desmond sees the final sublation as reducing the Same and Other to the Same. Desmond's critique of Hegel is not merely a Christian or theistic one; rather, he has developed a subtle system of metaxology, which includes a *finesse*, which surpasses Hegel and Hodgson.

Hodgson accuses Desmond of being a follower of Kierkegaard and similar in his view of Hegel to Feuerbach. Kierkegaard and Feuerbach cannot accept dialectic. Kierkegaard ends with a Christian personalist view that rejects dialectic and mediation. Feuerbach rejects Hegel's intermediated whole with its Spirit and settles for a materialism which is this worldly. Hodgson accuses Desmond of projecting his own (theistic) view onto God, while refusing Hegel's more subtle approach.

Desmond repudiates this simplistic identification with Kierkegaard. Desmond is sympathetic to Kierkegaard's personalism and his defense of the freedom of the individual, but Desmond's metaxological approach is more than a return to mere univocity and binary oppositions (equivocity). The issue with regard to Hegel is whether Desmond has understood Hegel correctly and surpassed him or whether Hodgson's interpretation of Hegel is the correct one. Hodgson argues that Desmond does not do justice to Hegel's views of intermediation or sublation/dialectic. Desmond, on the other hand, argues that Hodgson is guilty of 'hermeneutical naïveté' with regard to Hegel's language (Desmond 2005, p. 190).

Hodgson is far too generous to Hegel. Hodgson is entirely convinced by Hegel's arguments, while Desmond remains dubious. According to Desmond, despite Hegel's language of intermediation, dialectic leads finally to the sublation of the other into the One. Desmond's metaxological system is intended to incorporate the best of dialectic, while admitting dialectic's failure with regard to Sameness and Otherness. Hegel's thought is unable or unwilling to accept that which it cannot absorb or comprehend. Metaxological thought admits that thought is not able to comprehend the other. Metaxology does not need to absorb or comprehend or incorporate the other to know the other. The other, whether another or God, gives itself to be known. Others are overdetermined. In other words, in Desmond's system, individuals always exceed what is known of them. Hegel's system seeks to incorporate all into a whole. According to Desmond, Hodgson's whole, which includes God and parts, is Hodgson's own panentheistic reading of Hegel. The logic of Hegel's system, according to Desmond, is not so 'open'. If one accepts Hegel's own logic, finally, art and religion are sublated into philosophy (thought thinking itself). Hodgson does have some worries on this score. Desmond agrees that there is something to be worried about and that Hodgson's emendations of Hegel show that there is more of Hodgson in them than Hegel. Desmond also argues that if Hodgson may emend Hegel, then so may Desmond. Desmond, though, would argue that Hegel cannot be so emended, but that we must go beyond Hegel and dialectic to metaxology.

Hodgson accuses Desmond of promoting a "dualism of classic theology" (2005, p. 153). Hodgson says that Desmond "brings the criteria of Christian doctrine" to bear when critiquing Hegel (2005, p. 155). Apparently, Hodgson believes that this is sufficient to rule Desmond's view out of court. The question remains: Has Desmond developed a philosophical system which accounts for Hegel and goes beyond him? Either Desmond's metaxological approach accounts for community and intermediation, and origins and creation, or it does not.

Two further issues can be considered: creation and evil. In either reading of Hegel, God others himself in creation to come to himself. Whether God finally sublates or encompasses the others in or into himself is a point of difference. Hodgson does not wish to see a final sublation of religious community into political community or indeed of religion into philosophy. Desmond agrees with Hodgson that this is a bad sort of sublation. Hodgson, though, believes one can read Hegel more generously and allow for a religious community, which is not sublated by either the body politic or philosophy. Desmond disagrees. Dialectic leads to sublation; the true is the whole. Desmond, then, offers with his metaxological view the creation of others by God who are genuinely free from God. They are not created to help God realize himself. They are 'for itself', not modes of another being coming to itself through these modes. Hegel's world is one of teleology. All things move inexorably toward their goal, their telos. Desmond dislikes such teleology. God is agapeic in Desmond's view. He creates others for their own good. He gives them being (existence) and possibility. God is the "possibilizing possibility" (BB 335–339). He not only gives being but also gives a 'promise', not a teleology, but a germ, a possibility, which they may freely realize or renege on. Hodgson argues that God creates *ex Deo* rather than ex nihilo. Desmond, on the other hand, argues that God must remain other, though he can relate to his creation. Creation must be ex nihilo, insofar as it is not from God's essence, and it does not lead back to fulfilling itself by becoming one with God or becoming enmeshed and included in a greater whole, in which God and the world are now one. Desmond's concern is to maintain a Christian personalism, but if he is to be believed, his commitment to personalism comes as a result of his overall system.

The question of evil is a central point in the Hodgson-Desmond debate. If God is realizing himself in the world, then evil must be a part of God. This would seem to be an honest interpretation of Hegel. Other panentheists have embraced this idea wholeheartedly. One must hold an aesthetic theodicy and make evil only apparent. If only we had the right perspective, God's perspective, we would see that our suffering is inconsequential and is a part of the overall "plan of God". Desmond keeps evil outside of God (2005, p. 197). Hodgson believes that God takes evil into himself and redeems it kenotically. Desmond disagrees. A god who cannot overcome evil but becomes one with the community and can only work within it without guarantee of success is no God. For Hegel, evil can be sublated and made sense of. Desmond, following Kierkegaard and Lev Shestov, sees some evil as radical and impossible of being sublated into community, much less into God (EB 114ff). In Desmond's view, God as an agapeic origin can also come independently from outside the between to offer redemption and reconciliation.

Desmond has developed a system, his metaxological system, by which he has advanced a view that God is beyond the whole. He has given a philosophical exposition of Hegel and responded from a philosophical position (his metaxological approach) to Hodgson. Desmond argues against Hodgson disputing Hodgson's panentheistic emendation of Hegel. Desmond maintains the independence of God and creation. He rejects Hegelian dialectic. He is unsatisfied with an aesthetic theodicy.

Panentheism in a Russian Key: Solov'ëv and His Inheritors

In 'God beyond the whole: Between Solov'ëv and Shestov', Desmond treats several issues with regard to Vladimir S. Solov'ëv, which are reminiscent of Desmond's treatment of Hegel. (IST 167–199). Desmond uses Lev Shestov, the Russian fideist and anti-systematician, as foil to Solov'ëv, who is, in a Russian way, a systematician (1998, pp. 45–80). Desmond is correct to criticize Solov'ëv for his panentheism. Solov'ëv's panentheism, though, is tied to his Sophiology, that is, his belief that in effect Sophia, the eternal feminine, is the world soul. Though Solov'ëv's panentheism can be seen as an outgrowth of his reading of Hegel, it is also a result of Solov'ëv's own experience, his 'vision' of the 'eternal feminine', the divine Sophia. Desmond is right to focus on Solov'ëv's attempt to reconcile humanity and Godhead. Solov'ëv is seeking a bridge, it seems a metaphysical bridge, between creation and the Creator. Desmond notes also that Solov'ëv's concept of All-unity or Total-unity (всеедиство *vseedinstvo*) has difficulties (Valliere 2000, pp. 333–336). When attempting to think everything together, there is a tendency to diminish the individuals in favor of the one or the whole. As Desmond points out, there is a loss of 'open wholes' and even with the idea of Godmanhood (Богочеловечество *Bogochelovechestvo*), which supposedly allows humanity to grow into the likeness of God. One senses a reabsorption of the individual into the deity. The concept of deification (обожение *obozheniie* in Russian and θεωσις *theosis* in Greek), which is supposed to exalt humanity, raising it from fallenness to a semi-divine state, seems questionable, since it depends on the neo-Platonic idea of participation.

One of Solov'ëv's heirs was Pavel Florensky. Florensky was a Russian Orthodox priest known for his large work *The Pillar and Foundation of Truth*. Florensky was the teacher of another Russian Orthodox thinker, Sergei Bulgakov (Lossky 1951, p. 192). Florensky, in his attempt to systematize Solov'ëv's ideas, advanced the idea that Sophia was a 'fourth' hypostasis (person) of the Godhead (Zenkovsky 1953, p. 888). The motivation to deify Sophia is for Sophia to become a metaphysical bridge between the creation and the Godhead (Lossky 1951, p. 215). This argument was not accepted by the Russian church at that time (Gottschalk 2004, p. 175).

Bulgakov sought to develop Solov'ëv's and Florensky's Sophiology. Bulgakov saw that a simple pantheism would not be acceptable (Valliere 2000, p. 335). He sought to emphasize Sophia and her role, and yet to maintain a distinction between God and the world. He accepted the term panentheism for his view (Lossky 1951, p. 229; Zenkovsky 1953, p. 905). Andrew Louth in *Modern Orthodox Thinkers* notes that panentheism is being considered again, even by Bishop Kallistos Ware (Louth 2015, p. 347). Bulgakov's Sophiology was condemned by the Russian Metropolitan in exile, Sergius. This condemnation was the result of an examination of Bulgakov's views by Vladimir N. Lossky, who had produced a booklet called *The Argument about Sophia* in 1936 (Lossky 1936). Aside from the claim about Sophia being the 'fourth' hypostasis, which Bulgakov denied, the issue of Bulgakov's panentheism was a key problem (Valliere 2000, pp. 333–336). V.N. and N.O. Lossky held to the Patristic (Athanasian) concept of deification ("God became man, that man might become god".). Still they saw Bulgakov's panentheism as compromising both the nature and the individuality of created beings, and individuality of God. In the view of N.O. Lossky, a critic of Bulgakov, the entire world must be such a concretely real being or concrete consubstantiality for it to exist at all (Gottschalk 2004, p. 266, 267). Still N.O. Lossky himself also subscribed to a revised form of Sophiology. That is, he believed that the world is a consubstantial being governed by a head substantival agent or soul (similar to Plato's world soul), whom some of the Russian thinkers identify with Lady Wisdom or Sophia (or the Virgin Mary) (Lossky 1951, p. 266).

Though N.O. Lossky maintained that the entire world is an 'organic whole' due to this consubstantiality, he did not subscribe to the panentheism of these other Russian thinkers, for example, Solov'ëv, Florensky or Bulgakov. Rather N.O. Lossky maintained that panentheism cannot answer three important questions, which a theistic view can answer. That is, panentheism cannot explain the freedom of individual agents, it cannot explain the existence of evil and it is logically unfounded.

With regard to the first point, N.O. Lossky attempted to maintain a strong personalism. Despite Bulgakov's panentheism, Bulgakov himself also wished to maintain a strong sense of the individual. Bulgakov believed in deification or обожение *obozheniie* in Russian or θεωσις *theosis* in Greek, as noted above. Both Bulgakov and N.O. Lossky believed in deification as the final goal of all individuals. Though both also believed in apocatastasis or universal salvation, N.O. Lossky felt that Bulgakov's approximation of the entire creation to the Godhead through the Divine Sophia allowed no real personalism. In his *History of Russian Philosophy*, N.O. Lossky refers to this as Bulgakov's "Sophian determinism" (Lossky 1951, p. 222). Bulgakov's panentheism, entailing as it does a telelogy of the whole or the All-unity, does not really allow individuals freedom. In Desmond's terms each individual is given to be in the Between as a "for itself", which is "given to be with a promise" (BB 377ff.). The Creator does not foreordain the choices of each individual. He gives a potential, a 'promise', which the individual is free to own and strive to attain this promise. The individual can also renege on it and fail to achieve all that he or she could. Perhaps in Bulgakov's panentheism, similar to Hegel's, there is no individual in the end. Still to be fair to Bulgakov, he wishes there to be both a community (соборность *sobornost'* in Russian) of free worshippers and an organic world whole. Desmond's criticism of Solov'ëv's All-unity seems to haunt all of Solov'ëv's heirs. Though they wish to have free and robust individuals in the whole, the whole seems to become a closed whole, rather than a whole of 'open wholes', which Desmond advocates. Bulgakov saw God as the possibilizing possibility, as Desmond does. Despite his desire to have a metaphysical bridge, Sophia, between humanity and the Godhead, Bulgakov could not help but see individuals as given for themselves with a promise. However, Bulgakov and N.O. Lossky were unwilling that any should be lost. Apocatastasis or universal salvation, it seems, must in the end remain an insult to the individual. Due to the neo-Platonic idealism under which both labor: 'to be is to be good', no individual can exist who does not have some good within (even Satan). Since there is good within, all must eventually return to oneness with God. However kind or expansive this goal of recovering all individuals might seem, it does not allow ultimate freedom to the individual. Desmond, on the other hand, points out there is radical evil in the world, evil which is not redeemable, evil which is irrational. Solov'ëv, Bulgakov, N.O. Lossky and other heirs of Solov'ëv are unwilling to endorse such awful freedom (Lossky 1951, p. 225; Lossky 1949, p. 81).

The Question of Evil

As concerns the question of evil, Solov'ëv's and Bulgakov's panentheism cannot explain either the origin of evil or the existence of radical evil. Panentheism does not allow real freedom to the individual. It is also impossible to explain how evil arose in a panentheistic world. However, the larger issue, as far as evil is concerned, is that there is no reason for evil to arise at all. Why would God give a fallen Sophia to be the organic whole of the earth? Why does creation occur at all? Individuals may have more robust individuality in Bulgakov than in Hegel, but it seems in the end to be only an apparent individuality. Perhaps the Sophiologists could not escape the Hegelian origins or other German idealist origins of their metaphysical system. The Russian Orthodox tradition is quick to assert that the deification of humankind does not mean that humans become God, that is, part of the Godhead. Yet, it is hard to understand how deification does not in some sense lead to oneness or even Oneness. Relying on the metaphysics of (Pseudo-)Dionysius, the Eastern Church tends to fall into a "return to the One". As Desmond has pointed out with regard to Hegel, if one assumes a panentheism, there seems to be a necessity to maintain an aesthetic theodicy. In other words, evil is only apparent. There is no real evil, but that it will be redeemed and brought back into the Whole. It is difficult to imagine how the crimes of genocide through the twentieth century could be included in an aesthetic theodicy (EB 378 n10). Humans are demiurges and can do real, irredeemable evil. Unfortunately, this is a part of what being a free being means.

Desmond's engagement with Solov'ëv and Shestov show his interest in these two particular Russian thinkers and their form of philosophical engagement: Solov'ëv's more metaphysical approach and Shestov's more "Lutheran fideistic" or "Kierkegaardian", irrationalist approach (Maia Neto 1995). While Desmond's engagement with Solov'ëv in the aforementioned article is quite interesting and engaging, it would be interesting to see Desmond engage some of Solov'ëv's heirs like Pavel Florensky, Semyon Frank and, particularly, Sergei Bulgakov. Since there is currently a renewal of interest in Bulgakov's thought, it would be very interesting to see how Desmond would understand Bulgakov's creation à la Sophia and his All-unity. Bulgakov spends a lot of time defending and expounding his version of personalism. Desmond also believes in a strong personalism. If Desmond would show just how or where Bulgakov goes wrong, it would be instructive. Bulgakov, like Solov'ëv, seeks a robust form of ecumenism.

Bulgakov seeks to explain real connections between worldly wholes, which Desmond explains through his 'Between', a space for worldly wholes of 'open wholes' to be fostered. Tracing a line from Solov'ëv to Florensky to Bulgakov in terms of metaphysics would be a worthwhile task.

Conclusion

At the outset of this chapter, our goal was to analyze Desmond's engagement with panentheism by focusing on his replies to Peter C. Hodgson and Vladimir Solov'ëv. We expanded our purview to include Sergei Bulgakov, an inheritor of Solov'ëv, to show how Russian thinkers have developed Solov'ëv's thought and to show how Desmond could further entertain their thought.

With regard to Solov'ëv and his inheritors, there would seem to be a wide space for Desmond's further exploration of Russian heirs of Hegel or German Idealism. Desmond's interest in the idea of community would be a good comparison to Bulgakov's ideas of *sobornost'* (community) and his view of the world as an organic whole. Desmond's concern for a whole of 'open wholes' could find good counterexamples or helpful foils. Desmond's own understanding of the interplay of religion, philosophy and literature would be further sharpened by a few more Russian encounters. Bulgakov's attempts to explain and foster a generous ecumenism would be fruitful ground for Desmond's explorations. One could ask: How far off is Bulgakov's personalism from Desmond's, which would allow for open wholes? What might Desmond gain by this interaction? Desmond has shown his willingness to engage with other Hegel scholars. He has also been open to cross-pollination from other fields, for example, art, literature and religion. He has also been a persistent critic of panentheism, questioning its overly imminent god and panentheism's ability to deal with the problem of evil.

Bibliography

Desmond, William. 1998. Philosophical Audacity – Shestov's Piety. *Lev Shestov Journal* 2: 45–80.
———. 2005. Response to Hodgson. *Owl of Minerva* 36 (2): 198–200.
Gottschalk, Philip A. 2004. *Between Fideism and Dogmatic Rationalism*. PhD thesis, Katholieke Universiteit Leuven, Belgium.

Hodgson, Peter C. 2005. Hegel's God: Counterfeit or Real? *Owl of Minerva* 36 (2): 153–163.
Lossky, Vladimir N. 1936. *Spor o Sofii (Argument About Sophiia.)*. Paris: YMCA Press.
Lossky, Nicholas O. 1949. Resurrection of the Body. *Anglican Theological Review* XXXI (2): 71–82.
———. 1951. *The History of Russian Philosophy*. New York: International Universities Press.
Louth, Andrew. 2015. *Modern Orthodox Thinkers: From the Philokalia to the Present*. London: SPCK.
Maia Neto, Jose. 1995. *The Christianization of Pyrrhonism: Scepticism and Faith in Pascal, Kierkegaard, and Shestov*. New York: Springer.
Valliere, Paul. 2000. *Modern Russian Theology: Bukharev, Soloviev and Bulgakov: Orthodox Theology in a New Key*. Grand Rapids: Eerdmans.
Zenkovsky, Vasilii V. 1953. *The History of Russian Philosophy*. Vol. II. London: Routledge & Kegan Paul.

PART V

Creation, Embodied Being and Beauty

CHAPTER 16

The Gift of Creation

Richard Kearney

It is an honor to pay homage to the work of William Desmond in this volume. I have known William for almost 40 years as both friend, colleague and fellow Irish philosopher. We have had many exchanges over four decades of intellectual conversation including pieces in the *William Desmond Reader* and *After God*, not to mention numerous reviews and critical papers in learned journals and conferences on both sides of the Atlantic. In what follows I will revisit some of these past conversations as they pertain to Desmond's philosophy of religion as well as addressing some of William's most recent thinking on the subject. In doing so I will be paying particular attention to what I see as a series of critical productive paradoxes 'between' apparent opposites—divine creation and human creativity, gift and imagination, theology and philosophy, ethics and poetics, othering and selving. I offer these few reflections as a set of appreciative meditative commentaries on Desmond's poetic-metaphysical pondering of the sacred.

Let me begin with some introductory remarks on Desmond's approach to the question of God. Desmond speaks of a 'companionship of religion and metaphysics' which resists the secularist framework of much contem-

R. Kearney (✉)
Philosophy Department, Boston College, Chestnut Hill, MA, USA
e-mail: kearneyr@bc.edu

© The Author(s) 2018
D. Vanden Auweele (ed.), *William Desmond's Philosophy between Metaphysics, Religion, Ethics, and Aesthetics*,
https://doi.org/10.1007/978-3-319-98992-1_16

porary philosophy. He challenges the sway of what Charles Taylor calls 'exclusivist secularism' which dismisses religion as an eligible subject for serious philosophical consideration or, at best, consigns it to the realm of private conviction (Taylor 2014). Desmond equally obviates the 'phenomenological reduction' of religion, carried out by Husserl, Heidegger and most of the French existential phenomenologists, which 'suspended' or 'bracketed' the question of faith as an interference with the pure questioning of Being. (Heidegger goes so far in the *Introduction to Metaphysics*, as to declare that 'a Christian Philosophy is a round square and a misunderstanding'.) And Desmond also chaffs at the methodological neutralism of certain current trends in Biblical studies which reduce sacred scriptures to philological tracts or historical-sociological data with little appreciation of their spiritual, theological or metaphysical truth claims. Against such pervasive ostracizing of religious faith from philosophical discussion, Desmond offers a deep metaphysical engagement with religion as an experience of 'passion and compassion' (a *passio essendi* and a *compassio essendi*).

But if Desmond circumvents the modern embargos on philosophizing about God, what does he actually say about reason and faith? In what follows, I propose to look at five specific texts where I believe Desmond positively addresses the liaison between philosophy and religion. I want to suggest that this affirmative kinship 'between' (metaxu) the questions of Being and God is a central leitmotif of Desmond's metaxology, albeit often discreet and poetic in its articulation.

I

In chapter eight of *The Intimate Strangeness of Being* (2012), entitled "The Confidence of Thought: Between Belief and Metaphysics", Desmond calls for a new form of thinking about the sacred. He writes: "The confidence of thought asks a willingness to hearken to what is worthy in the beliefs of religion. Once again an old companionship calls for renewal, after the great divorce of modernity" (ISB 204–205). He goes on to state the need for "a new postmodern porosity between the religious and the metaphysical. Of old in modernity we knew the self-understanding of the philosopher as a scientist or technician or revolutionary and latterly as perhaps even a poet after his or her own fashion. But the more archaic companionship of the philosopher with the religious and its vocation is worth new thinking and renewal" (ibid.). Later in the same chapter, Desmond links this new thinking to a special kind of 'affirmation' or 'confidence' in the metaphysical nature of Being itself—a certain "ontological love that is present in being truthful" (ISB 225).

Such a rethinking of the kinship between faith and metaphysics entails a series of important affirmations across a broad existential spectrum. It involves a fundamental ontological confidence expressed as much

> in religious faith as in the trust in reason itself, as much admonitory of the overreaching ambitions of human power as in solidarity with human poverty, as much rejoicing in the excellence of human nobility as compassionate in sight of the tragedies of failure, as much tender to human limitations as laughing with its folly. (ISB 225)

Desmond even goes so far as to name this consoling affirmation of the spirit a "mysticism of deeper communication ... in love with the good of mortal things because secretly the divine love of mortal things has been confided to them" (ISB 226). Striking this mystical note, Desmond dares realign the perennial questions of Being and of God under the guidance of the unmentionable word 'love'. Confidence in Being, he implies, is ultimately expressed as caritas. And the consequences of this primacy of love are real and multiple for our lived existence. They express the great mystery of what Desmond calls the intimate universal:

> We would be infinitely loved. In our most idiotic intimacy, we live ourselves never as a neutral replaceable something but as intimately singular. God is the endowing source of the intimate universal. Only the personal, transpersonal God could endow the trusted singular with the universal as the intimate universal. Bist du bei mir: the air quickens our confidence, heartens it, but it is love that the air consecrates. (ISB 230)

In this same text Desmond makes what I take to be a powerful distinction between divine 'investiture' and human 'investment' (ISB 207). The first, he explains, operates according to a sacred economy where a reserve of enabling power is passed over from a source to a recipient. Thus, we find ourselves invested with certain powers as gifts, as grateful recipients of prior ontological investitures, before we ever invest our own powers in the world of give-and-take, before we subscribe to a finite material economy of credit and debit. Our very being, as Desmond puts it, our very esse or 'to be' may be seen as an endowment. "There are enabling powers, resources, first given before they can be invested in something further" (ibid.). Desmond is at his theopoetic best, I find, when writing about the gift of investiture as a form of divine agape, an enabling power or resource which is invested in us before we reinvest it in anything else:

> It is the generosity of the endowing God who calls to agapeic return. This is not a surplus in the sense of adding this or that to a determinate store. It is simply generosity and thankfulness lived as both self-enabling and more than self-enabling. It is participation in the overdeterminacy of a surplus good which in being given away is not depleted but augmented. (Ibid.)

And is there a return on such divine investiture? Yes. The return is

> to give away the gift, in the sense of passing on the endowment with the generosity fitting to the gift. We own nothing and we are most profitable when we make no profit for ourselves, but pass on the increase in generosity that cannot be increased, and that is itself nothing but increase of participation in the good of the 'to be'. (ISB 207)

This divine circle of endless kenotic giving is an excellent answer to the anthropology of the gift explored by Marcel Mauss and Maurice Godelier. And one might add to the neutral impersonality of Heidegger's *es gibt*. By contrast, it serves as a fitting gloss on the Pauline notion of kenosis as an act of endless self-giving, an act powerfully captured in Andrei Rublev's famous icon of the three persons of the Trinity, called the 'The Hospitality of Abraham'. The image of divine *perichoresis* par excellence. Father giving to Son giving to Spirit in an open circle of inexhaustible generosity and gratuity.[1]

II

The second text I wish to look at deals with the notion of divine creation as 'possibility' or *posse*. This particular discussion is part of an ongoing critical conversation with Desmond, begun in a number of journal reviews and culminating in his piece, "Maybe Maybe Not: Richard Kearney and God" published in *After God: Richard Kearney and the Religious Turn in Continental Philosophy* (2006). Here, Desmond offers a constructive critique of my philosophical exploration of God in *The God Who May Be* (Kearney 2001), most specifically as it pertains to the idea of creation as

---

[1] See my essay 'Making God: An essay in Theopoetic Imagination' (Kearney 2017).

posse or 'possibilization'. Questioning my eschatological take on *posse* as being too future oriented, Desmond offers a more archeological interpretation of the act of creation:

> This is the giving to be of finite being by the origin (arche). Creation can refer to an activity or an outcome of activity, and I refer here primarily to the 'act' of creating rather than the 'product' created. This is a possibilizing, but it is more than that, since it is not just the reduction of possibility to actuality, but the bringing to be of actuality and possibility. (Desmond 2006, p. 68)

And there is something 'hyperbolic' here about creative possibilizing, "since without this nothing finite would be or become" (ibid.).

Invoking the traditional doctrine of *creatio ex nihilo*, Desmond reads creative possibilizing as a response to a prior and primordial giving of an originating gift. A giving which, he insists, is closer to archeological *agape* than eschatological *eros*. The origin is not creating itself in creating finite being: it is bringing to be the finite other as genuinely Other, endowed with promise, ontological, aesthetic, ethical and religious. He suggests that

> creation is best thought in terms of the hyperbole of agapaeic bringing to be. We might respond to this suggestion by saying 'may be, may be not'. Very fair, since we glean something of this agapeic bringing to be from the finite creation as already given. In that given creation, we are always tested between a maybe and a may be not. (Desmond 2006, pp. 68–69)

Desmond appears to suspect the eschatology of Maybe of a latent activism or voluntarism which underestimates the anterior givenness of the gift. But I do not think this is the case. My notion of divine creation speaks of a possibilizing from the future understood as the loving act of a *deus adventurus*, a perpetually coming and becoming God, a theopoetic calling of and by *posse* toward *esse*, the eventual task being the co-creation of the Kingdom of *Possest*, as Nicholas of Cusa put it. Such a divine May Be (or *Peut-Etre*) deconstructs the old scholastic concept of God as First Cause or Pure Act (*actus purus non habens aliquid de potentialitate*, as Aquinas put it)—a concept which become known in continental philosophy as the Omni-God of ontotheology (Heidegger, Vattimo), the logocentric metaphysics of Presence (Derrida, Caputo) and the totalizing ontology of the

Same (Levinas, Irigaray). Desmond boldly defends metaphysics against these descriptions, which he sees as caricatures, and against what he sees as the lure of an overly dynamic God of becoming (the divine *posse* having its roots in the Greek term *dunamis*)—where God possibilizes and humanity actualizes. I think he would say: too much *conatus* and not enough *passio*. Or as he himself puts it, we need to construe creation with reference to a "primal givenness of being ... a *passio essendi*, prior to the becoming of any and all *conatus essendi*" (Desmond 2006, p. 69).

While I would defend the eschatology of *posse* as a mediation between *conatus* and *passio*, I do agree with Desmond's resistance to the idealist trends of much modern philosophy where an 'anthropological reduction' (to use Martin Buber's phrase) seeks to confine creation to a purely human/humanist activity. In such an exclusively 'immanent frame', as Charles Taylor notes, the sacred transcendence of the Other is overshadowed, if not ostracized. Here Desmond and I find ourselves on common ground, both acknowledging the creative life of *Posse* in terms of Gift and surprise, a divine creation calling out for human re-creation in its turn. In this respect, both Desmond's metaphysical God of *agape* and my eschatological God of *eros*—working from the past and future, respectively—reject the modern Cult of Constructivism, where the other (human or divine) becomes little more than a projection of our finite consciousness, an idea that we produce out of our own autonomous projections. (Think here, e.g., of the influential constructivist lineage running from Hegel, Marx and Feuerbach down to Freud, Sartre and Ernst Bloch).

Desmond proposes the idea of God as creative Gift as a bridge between our respective positions, and I think he is right. He writes accordingly of a

> sense of the possible emergent beyond the self-becoming in which the other possibilizes a freedom released beyond our own powers of self-determination. This enabling of release makes possible a transfiguration of our own efforts and claims to be self-determining. Since the openness to the other comes to form for us here in this release, there emerges a more radical possibilizing of self-becoming that is creatively there for the other in an ethical and religious mode. (Desmond 2006, p. 71)

But Desmond rightly insists, this possibilizing is not first what we do—rather

> it is received by us as a gift from the other'. He elaborates on this point thus: 'The surprise of the generous other is in this gift—itself calling forth our 'being generous'. It is here, more than anywhere else, that I think Kearney's notion of the eschatological 'may be' finds its opportunity of greatest moment. (Ibid.)

And he asks: "What here emerges as possible and possibilizing?" (ibid.) To which he responds: "The most intimate and often incognito creativity which does not insist on itself, in that it is in the image of the origin and the first creation. This is the communicative creativity whose generosity of being is agapeically released beyond itself, making way for the other" (ibid.). Here is no closed circle, but rather a dialectical between of re-creation defined as a 'space of porosity'. A metaxological openness where "communication is enabled, possibilised, sparked between humans, and between humans and God" (ibid.). And he concludes, tellingly, with a discreet nod to confessional practice: "Prayer happens in the intimacy of this porosity" (ibid.).

III

The third text I wish to address is Desmond's first chapter of *The Intimate Universal: The hidden porosity among Religion, Art, Philosophy and Politics* (2016), entitled "Religion and the Intimate Universal". Here, Desmond works from the inside out, locating the openness to the sacred in the gap or cleft of 'nothing' at the very heart of the human self. He returns to his central notion of the gap between self and other as a porous between-space where the finite and infinite can cross and commune (while never collapsing into each other). He sees this experience of the nothing-gap as a call beyond the reign of "erotic sovereignty" which dominates in our modern age, to a loving experience of "agapaeic service" (IU 52). Reflecting also on the internal 'nothing' between oneself and oneself, Desmond makes the intriguing claim that in the solitude of such intimacy there is, in fact, no solitude. Raising the question "what is the nothing here?", he affirms that it the between-space where the "enabling communication of the power of being gives us to be what we are and are to be" (IU 49). There is, he insists, an 'inward otherness' marking one's deepest intimacy to oneself. And this is where we may find the communication of the incognito God in the deepest ontological porosity of one's soul, so deep that it seems like nothing, since the porosity is itself nothing—the open between space in which communication of the power to be is given and different selvings take determinate form. One is never alone even when one is alone. (Ibid.)

Developing this quasi-mystical theme of the 'luminous dark night'—reminiscent of both John of the Cross and Augustine's discovery of the divine in the interior *intimo meo* (Confessions)—Desmond contrasts the prevalent modern turn from the other toward the self (think of the modern idealist movement running from Descartes, Kant and Hegel to Husserl and Sartre) with the "religious turn toward porosity to the divine in the intimate universal" (IU 50). But Desmond vigorously resists the tendency to separate the individual experience of intimacy from the public community at large, especially insofar it concerns our social and ethical responsibility to others. On the contrary, he boldly suggests that "religious community alone is able truly to reconcile the singular and the universal" (IU 51). The Beatitudes whisper while never being directly invoked. (This is philosophy after all.) And he goes further still to claim that religion, like love, is the most intimate thing for the human being—more intimate to me than I am to myself but with an intimacy that is not narcissistic or autistic but serves, paradoxically, as a rich resource for "communication and communicability" (IU 51). In this sense, pace Kierkegaard in *Fear and Trembling*, the intimacy of the Single One is deeply compatible with the universal in its deepest sense. In Desmond's philosophy the mystical, the ethical and the religious are not competing either/or stages on life's way, but mutually interanimating spheres of dwelling between the singular and the absolute. In authentic religion the most intimate interiority reconnects with the most far-reaching exteriority of the 'whole'; not to exert some kind of totalitarian hegemony over our lives, but to foster a disposition of openness to the all, in a spirit of 'agapeic service' to the community (IU 52). This exchange between the singular and the absolute occurs at the level of our most "primal porosity" and requires an active-passive response to the sacred—both a commitment to service for others and a fundamental "patience of being" (IU 57).

This double fidelity is not always easy to sustain and may earn the name of 'sacred idiocy'; it is a primordial ontological metaxu between apparent opposites (the most interior immanence and the most ulterior transcendence) which exemplifies Cusanus' mystical notion of the *coincidentia oppositorum*, though Desmond rarely cites Cusa or indeed any of the great mystics by name. But if the mystics go largely incognito in Desmond's work, they continue, I suspect, to ghost his pages and guide his steps. He always observes a certain discretion of naming in his meditation of the mystical—the unnamability of the sacred serving its multinamability. And he is also aware of potential misreadings and misdemeanors. Experiencing the mystical 'nothing' at the heart of Being can lead to a liberating interpretation of the teaching—"Blessed are the poor in spirit"—in terms of an "essential poverty of the human spirit"—but the same nothing, if we are not careful, can be a gateway to the demonic. To nothingness as an absence of the good (*privatio boni*). Or to put it in another way: the gap in Being may express itself either (1) as a 'fertile void' of sacred idiotic intimacy, where the self experiences an 'ecstasis' of kenosis and self-emptying moving beyond itself toward the other or (2) as a plunge inward to a darkness that curls up in itself (similar to Luther's notion of 'self-incurvature'). The best can also be the worst, and vice versa. There is a drama of choice and freedom here. Desmond's metaphysics of the void is never sanguine or rosy-eyed. It never forgets the medieval adage '*corruptio optimi pessima*'.

IV

The fourth passage I wish to comment on is in chapter seven of *The Intimate Strangeness of Being* (2012), which bears the title "Pluralism, Truthfulness and the Patience of Being". Here, we find one of Desmond's most sustained and dramatic treatments to the sacred as it pertains to the distinction between creation and construction. Human creativity is at its best, he argues, when it construes itself not as a willful act of *homo faber* but as a re-creation of a prior creation, a creative mimesis expressing a second yes in response to the primary yes of divine genesis—an act we experience existentially as call and gift. It is interesting to note that here, as elsewhere, when engaging with the sacred, Desmond rarely, if ever, cites the authority of sacred scripture—any more than the great spiritual masters or church fathers. He seems resolved to remain within a philosophical idiom of discourse. Or to be more exact, he writes as a philosopher of religion rather than a theologian or biblical scholar. (This is an important distinction which I have sought to articulate in my own writing and thinking, especially in recent works like *Anatheism* (Kearney 2010) and *Reimagining the Sacred* (Kearney 2016).)

Addressing the phenomenon of artistic creation, he describes art as the receipt of a gift before it becomes a construction of human will. "Gift is prior to construction", he insists, as "[t]here is a call of truth on us that is coeval with our being ... It releases us into a certain freedom of seeking, but this freedom and release are not themselves self-produced" (ISB 189). Let's be clear: Desmond is not denying the importance of human invention and imagination; he is simply resisting the relativization of efforts to absolutize the claims of human productivity in conformity with the dominant cult of *homo faber*. He is not against human action per se, only a self-inflated activism which denies that our *conatus essendi* is always preceded ontologically by a *passio essendi*. And, here, Desmond returns to the idea of 'gifted' humans as "creatures of an absolute source that gives us to be and give us to be as good". This is the good of the 'to be' (esse) in which we participate and which empowers us to create and re-create in turn. A view which depends on our recognizing an "otherness more original than our own self-definition". We are only self-defining, Desmond argues, because we are originally given to be as selves. Our selving is preceded by our othering, so to speak, giving a new connotation to Rimbaud's maxim, "Je est un autre". As Desmond pithily sums up: we are "only creative because created; only courageous because encouraged; only loving because already loved and shown to be worthy of love" (ISB 196). In this sense one might say that being patient is not an ordeal but an invitation to participate in the patience of being itself, understood as the intimate giving and givenness of creation. The highest action of philosophy is thus revealed to be isomorphic with the greatest passion of religion in the common experience of 'wonder'. Ontology becomes donatology: being as gift.

> In an ontological patience before the surplus happening there is for us the offer of an agapeic astonishment.... Wonder, marvel, reverence all reveal something of what is good and worthy of affirmation in the patience of being, even apart from any construction or further mediations by our own endeavor to be. (ISB 197)

Desmond can thus conclude that the best kind of metaphysics is a "mindful love of being" which expresses itself as movement beyond the *passio essendi* to a fuller form of *compassio essendi*: a compassion of existence which "communicates a sign of what a more divine love might be for mortals" (ISB 201). Again, one senses a proximity here to the great Abrahamic mystics and Buddhist Bodhisattva, without any ever being cited by name.

But what does become explicitly evident, at this juncture of ontological compassion, is that Desmond's poetics of creation embraces an ethics of care. "We become witnesses to the *compassio essendi*", he writes, "in the care we take of the other for the sake of the other. In this care, we may be released beyond ourselves in a minding of the other potentially agapeic" (ISB 201). Desmond intimates that such ontological empathy with finite others is traversed by the infinite Other. The passion of patience yields to the action of compassion in laying us "open to secret sources of strengthening that make us porous to the religious intermediation with the divine" (ISB 201). Abraham, Jesus, Hafiz and the Buddha would concur.

V

The fifth and final text I wish to address is a recent essay named, felicitously, 'Godsends' (Desmond 2016). Perhaps more than any other text, we find here Desmond, the poet of the everyday, taking his rightful place beside Desmond, the philosopher of religion. The very title itself suggests a compelling, engaged reflection on the connotations of 'ordinary language' for the relationship with the divine—the colloquial term 'godsend' being a typical example.

Godsend conjures up multiple everyday epiphanies of gifting and gracing expressing the mystical truth that the world is a theophany. This is something, as Desmond notes in a rare invocation of names, that his compatriots, John Scotus Eriugena and George Berkeley, have both attested—Eriugena with his notion of the divine as a *deus currens*, running like a tide of genesis through the flesh and blood of the natural universe and Berkeley with his theory of perception—*esse est percipere aut percipi*—as an empirical sign language of God (Desmond 2016, p. 12). Here 'revelation' ceases to be a proposition, thesis or syllogism, but expresses itself in quotidian acts of creation. These godsends can run from the most simple epiphanies of the everyday—as attested in the poems of Gerard Manly Hopkins celebrating the 'pied beauty' of the sacramental universe (viz 'Glory be to God for dappled things')—to the great Revelations of Abraham, Jesus and the prophets (to mention just the Judeo-Christian tradition). Citing the latter in an unusual moment, Desmond muses whether Christ might be an "absolute godsend—the single absolute, absolutely intimate with the absolute sender, and yet absolute as sent … through a kenotic intermediary absolutely porous to the sending source" (Desmond 2006, p. 13). A musing which he translates into a claim for an "absolute community" of

God and Godsend (Father and Son) which in no way signals a diminishing of the "transcendent mystery of the source, even while revealed in absolute immanence" (ibid.). Desmond concludes his meditation with this double hypothesis: "The prophets: singular godsends of the absolute? Christ: the absolved and absolving godsend?" (ibid.). While hinting here at his own personal Christian commitment, Desmond retains his position as a philosopher of religion rather than a proponent of dogmatic theology in leaving us with Christ as a question.

It is telling, I think, that in this most recent sortie into the God question—as a godsend combining the work of philosophical reasoning and spiritual revelation—Desmond returns to a key insight about the metaphysics of the gap. Expressing the opinion that the word 'gap' need not be treated as a bad word, he retrieves the idea of a cleft or fracture in being as a potential breaching of the 'immanent frame'. He speaks of "chinks in the closure of immanence on itself" (Desmond 2016, p. 21), echoing Leonard Cohen's famous lyric—"there is a crack in everything that's how the light gets in". Harking back implicitly to the nihil at the heart of the Judeo-Christian *creatio ex nihilo*, and explicitly to the ancient Greek word 'chaos', Desmond speaks of how the "giving creativity of the origin can often be most striking in this between space—in this gap" (Desmond 2016, p. 21). And he pursues this central metaxological intuition as follows:

> A gap is a medium of openness, a middle of communication. In and across such gaps, godsends may be sent. There need be nothing otiose about such a 'gap' at all. And especially so if our too solid world is actually subtended by the more original porosity of being. Godsends happen in the medium of this porosity. (Desmond 2016, p. 21)

If space permitted, it would be interesting to engage here in a deeper critical reflection of how one might relate this porosity of the godsend to the four 'hyperboles of being' outlined by Desmond in *God and the Between*, namely, the idiocy of being, the aesthetics of happening, the erotics of serving and the agapeics of communication (GB 22). But that is work for another day. Suffice it to end this meditation on 'godsends' with a nod to Desmond's compelling final suggestion that the giving of the intimate universal in the godsend is basically a 'birthing with'—a co-natus. This particular notion reminds me of Eckhart's beautiful notion of the divine birthing itself in and through each human being, as well as Maurice Claudel's idea of poetics as a perpetual *co-naissance* between the human and the divine—an idea taken up by Merleau-Ponty in his later writings. But, as I have already remarked, Desmond is not prone to the hermeneutic penchant for philosophizing with proper names and prefers to speak boldly in his own words with his own voice. He thinks in personal insights not quotes. And for this originality of thinking, as for much else, we can be grateful.

Conclusion

I would like to conclude my modest commentary on Desmond's philosophy of religion, with a final word on his metaxology understood as a "mindful love of being" (ISB 226). I believe that while Desmond is essentially discreet in his mentions of the divine—one often has to weasel them out of his ingeniously intricate metaphysical speculations—the ultimate task of metaphysics remains for him a 'patient mindfulness' of the *metaxu* as openness to the absolute. But I repeat: patient here has nothing to do with supine passivity or subordination to some Supreme Omni-God or Sovereign Cause. It has to do with a passion of being-between which acknowledges that all our most creative acts are themselves responses to a prior and original gift of creation. Creation is this two-way com-passion which runs from sacred genesis down to our ordinary acts of making and praying, doing and thinking. This is finally where philosophy can reenter a dialogue with faith, reason with revelation—a robust and productive dialogue for so long censored in the modern prejudice of what Taylor calls 'exclusivist secularist humanism'. Addressing the vocation of the metaphysical thinker of being between light and darkness, Desmond pens this quintessentially metaxological credo:

> Patient mindfulness must open itself again to this passion of thinking—passion as an undergoing and a receiving—passion, one might also say, as an inspiration that already carries us in an arc of transcending, unchosen at first by us and rather choosing us before we, always late(r) choose for it. This confidence is ecstasis into a darkness that is not grim but listening'. (Ibid.)

It is precisely here that we see the 'family resemblance to religious faith'. Desmond clarifies this paradox thus: "This is no univocal light but a trust that comes to hold steady, to be held steady in the light and darkness, in the equivocal twilight, or dawn, that marks our metaxological condition" (ibid.). In the final analysis, Desmond gives the last word to 'love' as a primordial confiding in being. Love is faith because *fides* is, at bottom, con-fidens. The truth of love is troth—trust:

> When all things are considered, this mystery is what, in our heart of hearts, we love as ultimate. Love is in confiding. We are loved when another takes us into his or her confidence. We love another when we are taken into confidence. We are by our very being taken into confidence. The call on our being is to take what is given into our own confidence. (ISB 226)

It would be hard to find a more fitting philosophical hymn to the caritas of creation.

Bibliography

Desmond, William. 2006. Maybe, Maybe Not: Richard Kearney and God. In *After God: Richard Kearney and the Religious Turn in Continental Philosophy*, ed. John Manoussakis. New York: Fordham University Press.

———. 2016. Godsends: On the Surprise of Revelation. *Ephemerides Theologicae Lovanienses* 92: 7–28.

Kearney, Richard. 2001. *The God Who May Be: A Hermeneutics of Religion*. Evanston: Indiana University Press.

———. 2010. *Anatheism: Returning to God After God*. New York: Columbia University Press.

———. 2016. In *Reimagining the Sacred: Richard Kearney Debates God*, ed. Jens Zimmerman and Richard Kearney. New York: Columbia University Press.

———. 2017. God Making: An Essay in Theopoetic Imagination. *Journal of Aesthetics and Phenomenology* 4: 31–44.

Taylor, Charles. 2014. *A Secular Age*. Cambridge, MA: Harvard University Press.

CHAPTER 17

On Speaking the Amen: Augustinian Soliloquy in Shakespeare's *Metaxu*

Renée Köhler-Ryan

In Shakespeare's Scottish play, mired as it is in evil that refuses to abate, there is a moment, after the Macbeths have murdered the king, when the main protagonist is on the stage alone. His act of soliloquy not only meets the standard of theatrical convention.[1] At the same time, he carries out the philosophical act of Augustinian soliloquy in reverse. Macbeth questions himself, and reveals how closed off he is to his moral community, how impermeable to divine communication. He cannot even pray, having found that when he tried, 'Amen' stuck in his throat. This is but one of the forms of what Desmond calls 'sticky evil' in the play. Desmond's analysis of equivocity in that work draws from his development of a philosophy of the *metaxu*. When that concept of equivocity is seen for its indebtedness to Augustine's insistence on self-reflection, it brings to light

[1] For more on the definition of soliloquy, see Stock (2010, 2011, 2017), Fox (2003), Arnold (1911), Hirsch (1997), and Skiffington (1985).

R. Köhler-Ryan (✉)
The University of Notre Dame Australia, Sydney, NSW, Australia
e-mail: Renee.Kohler-Ryan@nd.edu.au

© The Author(s) 2018
D. Vanden Auweele (ed.), *William Desmond's Philosophy between Metaphysics, Religion, Ethics, and Aesthetics,*
https://doi.org/10.1007/978-3-319-98992-1_17

that the true tragedy of Macbeth is that because Macbeth has harmed his kin, he can know neither himself nor God.

Read in light of Desmond's statement that *Macbeth* is a play "saturated with equivocity" (BB 112), the murderer's few lines of thwarted soliloquy illuminate the pathway of Augustinian journey both forwards and backwards. At the same time, such analysis accentuates the importance of self-reflection as an antidote to tragedy. Macbeth's downward spiral into further, stickier, evil (he is "in blood stepped in so far" that he cannot stop (3.4.142)), inverts the Augustinian order of knowledge of God and soul. Desmond's articulation of this shows how mired humans can be in evil when they refuse, in word and deed, divine communication. According to Augustine, when one journeys from the exterior to the interior, the self expands so as to move further, from the inferior to the superior. For Augustine and Desmond, both moments of movement are needed: progressing from exterior to interior requires a sound and humble relationship to the world; extending toward God intensifies self-knowledge. At that point, possibilities for communication of transcendence, in a community with God and others, become possible. Macbeth forfeits all this with a murder; his refusal to stop there and to repent, retracing fully a journey toward his maker, is the source of tragedy in the play. Macbeth knows what he is at this moment, but he refuses to change. All this and more is better known when Macbeth is considered in light of the features of Augustinian soliloquy and of Desmond's articulation of equivocity.

Augustine's *Soliloquies*

While the term 'soliloquy' is associated with some of the most profound and self-reflective words spoken by Shakespeare's characters on stage, it has specifically philosophical, Augustinian roots. Augustine coins the word because he needs something to describe a very particular way of speaking to oneself while in the presence of God. The freshness of this approach is highlighted by Augustine's astonishing moment of self-discovery at the beginning of the text of the *Soliloquies*. Laboring to find the answers for many philosophical questions directly related to Augustine's understanding of himself, he hears a voice. Where it comes from, he does not really know. Is it inside him or outside? Is it him or "someone else"? (2000, I.1,1) That voice reveals itself as Reason, which then makes certain demands on Augustine: he must write down his discoveries so that an audience of a few can later read them. There can, however, be no such intrusion now. There must be no one to whom Augustine will dictate his thoughts; he alone must be the scribe. For the moment, there should be only one other listener. At this point, three are involved in the dialogue—all listening, porous to each other; but the audience only hears the words of two— Augustine and Reason. God's presence is constantly inferred, known by a degree removed, through the words of those speaking. Nonetheless, that divine proximity makes all the difference. Augustine truly knows himself only when he first opens himself up in prayer; philosophical investigation depends upon openness to God. As the text proceeds, Reason lays out the demands that are at the same time the agenda for the remaining work: first will come prayer that Augustine will have the stamina to find what he is looking for; then he must write down what he finds, "that [his] confidence may be increased by what [he has] done" (2000, I.1,1). Finally, he will need to record conclusions. Augustine's answers will not only be for him; they will also speak to "a few ... fellow citizens" (2000, I.1,1) who, like him, are porous to divinely inspired reason.

These 'fellow citizens', as we know from his later work, *City of God*, will be defined by their inner life of *caritas*, which is characterized by properly ordered desire.[2] Community thrives only when its members are able to love well. Augustine makes clear that a soliloquy can only achieve its integrative aims if it begins with prayer that orientates one's desires. Otherwise, the soliloquist goes mad, being out of synch with reality. This raises a major theme in the *Soliloquies*, which is that God heals the soliloquist's disordered appreciation of reality. The one who lacks such knowledge is unhealthy or, in Latin, 'insane', where insanity refers to sickness of physical, psychological, and spiritual dimensions. Reason's role in the work of becoming healthy is to reveal, rather than conceal, any improper loves or desires. Disordered love thereby equates with incapacity to explore and know the self with the powers of reason, which means that when Reason falters, or turns itself to the work of deception rather than illumination, it is an accomplice in foul play. It becomes destructive double-speak, turning to the darker side of equivocity, which obfuscates, instead of finding and considering the potencies of selfhood.[3] Equivocity at its best discovers mystery, rather than skips over what one must honestly consider.

In other words, avoiding the pitfalls of equivocity means seeing things as they really are in their ineffability. To achieve this is the work of a lifetime, undertaken first with faith and then hope and love (Augustine 2000,

---

[2] See, for instance, Augustine, *City of God*, XIV, 28.
[3] See ISB 51–56, where Desmond speaks of the possibility of double-speak to be both revelatory and duplicitous.

I.5 and I.6,12–I.7,14). Such vision entails true health of the whole person, directed by that person's mind (Augustine 2000, I.13). As alluded to, Augustine's use of terms for 'health' slips into equivocity within the Latin text so that health, while referring to physical well-being, more often emphasizes what happens when health of the mind is no longer present. In Book I in particular, such health (sane) is a central theme. For instance, within his first longer prayer, Augustine invokes God as the one who neither drives his people mad, nor allows anyone else to do so (Augustine 2000, I.3). Then, Augustine asks that God purge him of any madness (*insaniam*)[4] and instead make him healthy (*sanis*). In order to become 'sane', Reason reminds Augustine that his focus must be on heavenly, more than earthly, delights. In other words, love can no longer be *cupiditas* (Augustine 2000, I.19) driven by a soulless desire for that which will one day cease to be, shrouding the deceived lover in darkness, and leading to spiritual sickness. By contrast, the one with *caritas* is illuminated from within, by Reason that is virtuous—that is, well directed—toward its proper purpose. We see things as they are when we view their inner wisdom, which is their participation in God's love (Augustine 2000, I.13,22–23). This heals us from an illness that Augustine thinks of as a kind of madness whereby reason cannot see what it must. Thus, the journey toward such sight begins with faith; one may not yet be able to fully see but must believe that there is something there to see—a Beauty beyond all, which, when discerned, heals completely (Augustine 2000, I.7,14). Hope is also essential so that one does not despair at ever achieving such a state. Finally, and most importantly, *caritas* infuses the entire person, turning him away from darkness and leading him toward an eternal cure; only this love never leaves, even when faith and hope are no longer necessary.

This is the quest for comprehensive understanding, where the eyes of the body are but a beginning point. Only with eyes that work, or are healthy, can we look—but Augustine emphasizes that looking is different from seeing (Augustine 2000, I.6,12). To see God is to understand him. This, finally, brings true health. Thus, the eyes look to the exterior so as to inform the inner man, who then sees what is above: God. This means that knowing and loving are the work of constant integration; health cannot be

---

[4] The Latin terms can be found in the original text published by James J. O'Donnell at: http://faculty.georgetown.edu/jod/latinconf/latinconf.html. I am referring to these throughout, to emphasize the way in which Augustine is playing on the double of mental and physical health.

gained in what is excessively abstract. In particular, there can be no sanity when self-deception is at play. Augustine finds quite quickly how mistaken and hubristic it is to think that the mind alone can save. Under interrogation by Reason, Augustine proclaims that in particular the pleasures of sexual intercourse mean nothing to him: he is so much enraptured with the pursuit of wisdom that he has transcended these trappings of concupiscence. The next day, however, he is forced to admit otherwise, acknowledging what Reason is right to point out: that while he now experiences differently the imagined pleasurable activities of the flesh, they are not completely removed from his horizon of desires. This realization through experience, says Reason (Augustine 2000, I.6,12), is God's way of treating his patient—by showing Augustine that there are still significant vestiges of what he needs to abandon in order to be truly virtuous, motivated by more holy love.

Augustine is devastated by what has been brought to light. In the darkness, he found something in himself that he would want purged. In the light, he can acknowledge this, but it is painful. He begs: "Why do you probe and pierce so deeply?" (Augustine 2000, I.14,26) This moment of porosity enables greater closeness to God. Brought to nothing,[5] he proclaims himself no longer capable of either taking for granted or making promises. He thought he knew himself, but now he knows otherwise: that he utterly relies upon God to show him what he is. Until he truly sees the Beauty that is God, he cannot pretend to know himself. This is at the same time perhaps the most personal moment of the text: Augustine realizes that in this vision of himself, he is the one at stake; he will be lost if he refuses to acknowledge what he would rather ignore, before Reason and in the presence of God.[6] This is a moment very much like that in the *Confessions*, where he sees himself for what he is (1997, VIII.7,16). As such, it reminds that the work of self-reflection is at the heart of much-needed continual conversion. This, then, is a moment of self-reflection and orientation. He had been so certain the day before that he had achieved a purity of spirit that enabled him to rise up completely above physical pleasure. Realizing otherwise, he is thrown back upon God, reminded of his need for the restoration of health. God's healing will make

---

[5] For the implications of being brought to nothing, or zero, see in particular: GB 28–30 and 33–35; Köhler-Ryan (2017).

[6] For a similar moment, see Augustine (1997, VIII.12,28).

him sound in mind and body; it will make him sane but only if he has the humility to work with God to achieve that healing.

Such sanity is brought about by divine illumination. Acknowledging his creaturely dependence on God, Augustine can know himself; he can emerge into the light. Thus Reason admonishes him to turn away from shadows and toward his true self—which is imperishable, unlike his body (Augustine 2000, II.19,33). Furthermore, to find the self is at the same time to find God; true self-knowledge only occurs in knowing at least something. In turn, seeing the self depends upon humility. Healing relies on us first acknowledging our darkness, our nothingness in the face of God. Again one finds the Augustinian order of movement: from the exterior to the interior; the inferior to the superior. As Augustine soliloquizes, he *looks* with his physical eyes, before *seeing*, realizing that he needs to focus on what is within. Such introspection helps him to realize what he is, in face of the infinite light and love of God. The more Augustine can honestly reflect, the more he knows himself as creature, as well as the debt of love that he has to God and to the world in which he lives.

Crucial to all this is Augustine's view that forgiveness and healing are only possible when one is honest with oneself. As is even more evident in *Macbeth*, without the healing balm of divine forgiveness, some morally significant, evil actions have the power to destroy every imaginable aspect of selfhood, including self-knowledge. This insight deepens awareness of the need at every point of movement, from exterior to interior, and inferior to superior, to be porous to the divine. As a general principle, this entails having the humility to place God first in the order of love. Practically speaking, it necessitates honest and rigorous self-reflection, and knowing when one has breached a moral law and stands in need of forgiveness. One needs to think prayerfully and pray thoughtfully, as prayer and thought mutually disclose. At the same time, such prayer and thought are affected by the exterior. A rich matrix of interrelationships is at play, such that a rupture at any one point affects the whole person in relationship to God, self, and world. Ignoring this risks one's overall well-being—or one's sanity, taken in Augustine's broad scope of meaning. At the same time, it jeopardizes the health of the society in which one lives. For, as Shakespeare's *Macbeth* illustrates, an evil deed pollutes when it goes unacknowledged and unrepentant. Macbeth realizes this sooner than his wife, when he is unable to pray—to speak 'Amen'. At this moment, Macbeth seems to glimpse himself as he must look in the sight of God. He has the opportunity to undo what he has done, but instead chooses for an equivocity that closes off possibilities of communication. He is lost.

Equivocity and Being at a Loss

Macbeth's being at a loss can be explained in philosophical terms developed by William Desmond, who emphasizes that equivocity refers to the manyness and the flux of reality, which derives from the overdeterminacy of being.[7] That is, being always exceeds what we can find, or determine, about it. We can therefore experience excess that occludes our ability to express and communicate. Positively understood, equivocity reminds that the world is so rich in meaning that no matter how much we discover, there will still be more to appreciate. Our use of language reminds us of this. "Words", Desmond points out, are "overdetermined; they mean more than they say explicitly, and carry around within themselves unacknowledged origins. Words are excess: they express reserves of meaning but also reserve recesses" (ISB 181). Put otherwise: precisely the strength of equivocity—the richness of its overdeterminacy—can be exploited, so that words can only seem to mean what they say, and the listener is left to guess the intention behind an act of speech. More troubling is that the speaker might hide from himself through equivocation; further still, that a political climate can be so oppressive that the self is lost along with inability to speak freely. Here, equivocity can be as harmful, as tyrannical, as univocity, as the self becomes infected; words and reality cannot harmonize. Equivocity descends into oppressive double-speak. This is decidedly the world of *Macbeth*.

Again, such despotic equivocity has its counterpart in tyrannical univocity. It should be remembered that doubleness in speech is not, *per se*, harmful. Dialogue explicitly relies on such doubleness, whereby two speakers each present their perspectives. As is being argued, a prior doubleness is necessary to such healthy dialogue, in soliloquy, where the self questions and reflects upon the self. Thus the difficulty of recognizing oneself is emphasized precisely by indicating doubleness. In contrast, a dictatorial thinker can willfully overlook ambiguity and decide on one meaning alone where more than one is actually at play. This is where tyran-

---

[7] For the significance of overdeterminacy, see in particular: EB 163–177; GB 35–40 and 128–134; BB 63–75; ISB 38–43; IU 400–404.

nical univocity becomes realized. Desmond considers how dialectic can become dominated and consumed by a modern rational (Hegelian) univocal voice: the "dia" becomes univocalized to the point that the voice of doubleness is ruled out (ISB 46). The difference inherent in doubling plays into an overarching synthesis that is then absorbed into oneness.

Dangerous in a different way is the refusal to acknowledge the doubles upon which the ethical dialectic rests. That is, Macbeth finds himself not *beyond* but instead *between* good and evil (Desmond 2002, p. 146). Shakespeare's presentation of Macbeth's world, Desmond argues, could actually form a response to Nietzsche's refusal of this ethical dialectic. Rejecting all systems, Nietzsche settles on the necessity of flux. In such a vision, all is equivocal—nothing is settled except what the striving will ordains. The relativism of the will to power refuses to find good and evil at play in the overdetermined *metaxu*. Nothing is determined already, and no action is determinable as either good or evil. Nietzsche offers us the unstable footing of Macbeth, who *wants* to be right that being sovereign in subjective power is all. Standing there with the murderer though, something else is apparent. Nietzsche detests the notion that the sovereign master should sometimes seek forgiveness and repent. Macbeth voices the despair of someone who *knows*, deep down, that he has "most need of blessing" (2.2.32). Listening to Lady Macbeth as well as to his fear at having breached the boundaries of ethical community, he dare not look on what he has done. The contrast with Augustine at his lowest point in the *Soliloquies* is stark (Augustine 2000, I.14.26). A Nietzschean might interpret this as the cowardice of someone unable to look into the abyss.[8] Is it not instead the case that Macbeth knows all too well that reality is not a state of flux overcome by acts of an amoral sovereign? This moment of ethical awareness is possibly the most honest in the whole play. Macbeth will not listen, and without the help of an ethically aware companion—let alone of God—he is too afraid to look. He cannot see nor can he repent. And yet, he knows himself bereft.

This brings to bear that dialogue, which relies on openness to the other and commitment to state as clearly as possible what one means, implodes when conversants withhold the real import of the words being used or

---

[8] As Desmond points out, Nietzsche has "contempt for the criminal who cannot live up to his deed" (2002, p. 146). The unrelenting Nietzsche demands self-knowledge that is at the same time knowledge of the deed. Simultaneously, he leaves no possibility for repentance. This is another way of thinking about a closure to transcendence, and at the same time to Augustinian movement.

when they misunderstand or misinterpret what is being said. A two-sided conversation in quest for what is true becomes a disunity parading as robust discourse. Dialogue can in this way become monologue without the porous characteristics of soliloquy. The disjointed exchanges between Macbeth and his wife, in Act II, Scene ii, sound out what happens when dialogue is not porous to the self-reflective work operative in soliloquy. Out of tune with the ethical dialectic between good and evil, all forms of intercommunication break down. Destructive equivocity usurps meaningful dialogue. Augustine, Shakespeare, and Desmond all emerge here as thinkers porous to the ways good and evil announce themselves in the *metaxu*. Human action and reflection strive to respond to such communications.

Macbeth, Equivocity, and Soliloquy

Essentially, these three thinkers emphasize the power of language and the significance of words. In the overdetermined matrix of the *metaxu*, there is a real difficulty to strike a balance between univocity and equivocity. Overdetermination does not constitute disharmony and meaninglessness, but mystery and plenitude. Augustine theorizes about the importance of words and communication, and shows what happens when words open to all forms of transcendence work well. Shakespeare's Scottish play gives existential depth to the perils of miscommunication, of univocalized equivocity.[9] The playwright is acutely aware that when words lose their facility to resonate, all we are left with is an empty echo that defies meaningful interpretation. Macbeth is a fragmented self. Unable to discern meaning, he cannot become integrated. This, the result of the Augustinian journey in reverse, affects not only Macbeth and those who immediately surround him. His actions influence the kingdom and, he acknowledges, the whole created order, reminding that what we say and do always affects more than the self alone; such is the interconnected nature of reality. Reading *Macbeth* with an Augustinian framework in the background, and with the possibilities and potential perils of an equivocal milieu in view, throws into relief the implications of Macbeth's introspection. A close reading of this now illustrates the implications of refusing to move from world to inner self, from lesser self to God.

[9] See also Garber (2004, pp. 700–771), on details of equivocation in *Macbeth*, and in particular on the use of 'double' in the play.

It is illuminating to consider that equivocity in its more destructive form is at work throughout the various social dimensions of *Macbeth*, blocking possibilities for self-understanding. James Shapiro's analysis of the year in which the play was written underscores Shakespeare's personal awareness of how communities fracture when communication is impossible. The year 1606 in Jacobean London was a climate of fear; it was also the year during which a shift occurred in the meaning of the term 'equivocation'. From meaning simply 'ambiguous', equivocation moved to signify "concealing the truth by saying one thing while deceptively thinking another" (Shapiro 2015, pp. 178–179). Constantly in fear of capture, torture, and death, Jesuits attending to the spiritual needs of Roman Catholics still living in England argued that one could use words with the intention that they be understood one way by the human listener and another by God. A secret treatise at the time listed four kinds of deception, the last of which argued that a lie was not essentially a lie "if you believed that God knew your thoughts, even if the person questioning you could not" (Shapiro 2015, p. 182). The very notion of lying is here contested, forcing a gap between what is (intention of the speaker, known only to him and God) and what is presented to others (what the hearer understands, based on the words used). This concerns far more than ambiguity and creates fissures where there should be continuities—between intention and deed (here, the words spoken), and more fundamentally, between self, others, and God.[10]

The milieu of *Macbeth*, like that in London of 1606, could not be in greater contrast to that of *Soliloquies*. In the latter, Augustine deliberately opens up a space in which one can freely and openly articulate one's thoughts, beliefs, and even fears. There, in the presence of God, he strives for increased aptitude to say what he truly means. As a case in point, this is where Lady Macbeth systematically refuses to go. She chides her husband, telling him not to think beyond a calculus of who to kill, when, and how, in order to gain power. She severs her imagination, refusing to see blood for what it is. She declines to recognize the true nature of her acts, as homicide and regicide. These are the ruptures in the potencies of hospitality and community, into whose gaping wound she descends. All this is done in the name of reason and power—and of a love of her husband so disordered that it cannot be love at all. The lady speaks in tones of spousal

---

[10] For some of the political implications of saying 'Amen' in a religious context in the time that Shakespeare was writing, and with particular discussions of *Richard III*, see Targoff (2002).

affection but raves with a lust for power, whose consequences she cannot grieve in the open. Her guilt, nonetheless, is revealed to others when she does not know it—in her manic, restless sleep.

As she pines and wails, the truth of what she has done emerges and engulfs. The Macbeths are both bogged in what Desmond calls 'sticky evil': the crime may have seemed simple in thought—something that once done could be forgotten and referred to as a 'deed' or 'business' or 'enterprise' but not as murder. The reality is otherwise: the murder is primal and messy, and it leads to more and more letting of blood. Right after the deed, Macbeth is the one who realizes this, knowing that his hands will never be clean again (2.2.61–62). Lady Macbeth sees this only later. At the time of the murder she nonchalantly chides her husband, "A little water clears us of this deed. / How easy it is then" (2.2.68–69). Later, in the night, when conscience pricks, her underlying alarm can speak: "Who would have thought the old man to have had so much blood in him?" (5.1.39–40) We cannot see the blood on Lady Macbeth's hands, but it stays. Such stickiness, in sleep, brings with it nightmares of hell (5.1.36)—a form of non-sleeping—for Macbeth, the clinginess of evil is obvious far sooner—but then even more systematically ignored. His is the stickiness of an 'Amen', lodged in his throat and now unspeakable (Desmond 2002, p. 153).[11] In both cases, a deed has closed off all passage of communication, but the porous passages of disclosure had already become partially clogged. In the face of equivocity, where fair and foul are indistinguishable, Macbeth has opted for what he wants, rather than what is. Sharp indeed is the difference between Macbeth's inability to speak 'Amen' and Augustine's outbursts of prayer and praise. Macbeth cannot pray because he has refused to let the exterior speak in unison with interior—by violating the moral order, murdering his king and guest, but above all, another human person—and because he cannot acknowledge his own inferiority before the divine gifts of life, freedom, and goodness. In other words, now lacking his bearings, he can only be confused by what is otherwise the gift of equivocity.

The play thus demonstrates the problems of univocity when it is taken too far, thereby illuminating the balance that it is necessary to maintain between univocity and equivocity. Univocity is true to being when it reminds of the importance of forms of certainty, which can be spoken and lived. However, it is potentially dangerous, when it leads to one voice

---

[11] Also see BB 254n.

speaking, drowning out all others, demanding to be taken as the only determination possible on a given matter. This, one might say, is monologue without the characteristics of soliloquy. The Macbeths are in this way univocal tyrants—unwilling to listen to innocent, truthful, and warning voices, they silence through violence. The root of their univocity is in the reversed Augustinian trajectory already indicated. Macbeth's univocity is most evident in that he thinks himself superior; inattentive to the nuanced expressions of others and in particular of the witches, he reads signs in the way that he wants to: his intention overrides any other possible motivations behind the words of others. Macbeth thinks he is able to outrun the supernatural; he prioritizes what seems over what is, to such an extent that no human life is anything more than "a tale / Told by an idiot, full of sound and fury / Signifying nothing" (5.5.25–27). The emptiness results from Macbeth's loss of self, which is first indicated very early in the play, after the moment of the murder. It is in these lines, when Macbeth, alone for just a moment, speaks, that he is most aware of what he has done, and of how he is now separated from God and the whole of creation. He describes after the killing that he had overheard a servant laugh in his sleep, whereupon another called out 'murder'. Thus awake, the young men prayed together—one saying "God bless us" and the other "Amen" (2.2.27). It is as if, Macbeth says, they had seen his bloody hands and called for supernatural aid. Macbeth is terrified by this incident because he found himself, in the moment, unable to pray. He asks his wife: "But wherefore could I not pronounce 'Amen'? / I had most need of blessing, and 'Amen' / Stuck in my throat" (2.2.32–34). Lady Macbeth demands that such stickiness, the result and counterpart of his earlier "screwing his courage to the sticking place" (1.7.61) and murdering Duncan, must not be thought about. If they dwell too deeply on such thoughts, they will go mad. Tragically of course, Lady Macbeth does lose her sanity. Here, an unwillingness to recognize the full import of their deeds leads to madness. A healing double-speak is missing. She succumbs to the insanity that Augustine explicitly seeks to avoid. Where Augustine is willing to find and imbibe a bitter medicine, Lady Macbeth refuses to acknowledge her illness.

Also in contrast to Lady Macbeth, Macbeth can acknowledge immediately what he has done, and he realizes the effects of murder. The implications of his deed can be readily analyzed by examining his few moments of theatrical soliloquy in Act II. For just a few lines, Macbeth is alone on stage, and what he says can be analyzed in light of Augustine's main points in the *Soliloquies* and Desmond's metaxological philosophy. Thereby, Macbeth comes into focus as having reversed the Augustinian movement of self-knowledge. At the moment in the play in question, Lady Macbeth has just left the stage to smear the sleeping grooms (possibly those who had prayed earlier[12]) with blood. Macbeth speaks as follows:

> Whence is that knocking?
> How is't with me, when every noise appals me?
> What hands are here? Ha: they pluck out mine eyes.
> Will all great Neptune's ocean wash this blood
> Clean from my hand? No, this my hand will rather
> The multitudinous seas incarnadine,
> Making the green, one red. (2.2.58–64)

In these brief lines, several considered themes are evident. First, while Macbeth's soliloquy meets some of the formal criteria of that form of speech on stage, it neglects the Augustinian dimension, whereby one questions oneself in the presence of God. Macbeth cannot pray. God is missing, and so Macbeth cannot find himself. Second, Macbeth is afraid that he will go mad. Finally and decidedly, interior and exterior, inferior and superior, are all decoupled, because equivocity in its more sinister form has taken hold.

These few lines articulate that when members of a political community cannot pray and really be heard when they speak the truth, stabilizing self-knowledge is impossible. Macbeth interrogates both interior and exterior worlds, trying to find and make links where he experiences only disconnections. The knocking at the door, the blood on his hands, the sight of the hands he wants to be clean, the image of a green sea turning red if he were to wash his hands there: all bombard his senses. What he wants to be the case simply is not. The contrast between how he feels—pale, literally 'appalled' by every sound—and the red blood on his hands is striking,

---

[12] Editors of the *Arden Shakespeare* edition of Macbeth note that while some assume those who cried out to be Malcolm and Donalbain, "it is more likely that they are the sleepy grooms referred to later [at 2.2.51], and subsequently made Macbeth's scapegoats" (Shakespeare 2015, p. 180). If this is the case, and these are the sleepy grooms, then a breakdown of community is even more evident here. While they can pray, the inability of another to echo their prayer, or pray with them, is a foreshadowing of the violence that will be done to them by that same outsider.

indicating disjunctions between what he wants (to be cleansed of sin) and what appears (evidence of his evil actions).[13]

Then comes Macbeth's moment of true self-realization. In a gradual process of self-analysis, he knows that he is severed from God, and from creation. The greenness of the sea would not take away the taint of the murder. Putting his hands in "all great Neptune's ocean", no washing would occur. Instead, the blood on his hands would discolor every ocean. A few lines later, Lady Macbeth glibly declares "a little water clears us of this deed" (2.2.68). She demands her husband not be lost in thought. Right now, Macbeth can still think the deed for what it is. The moment passes and becomes a rejection of guilty self-knowledge. This is the decisive moment when he closes off porosity between introspection and transcendence: "To know my deed, 'twere best not know myself" (2.2.74). To think about what he has done, in the exterior world, is to acknowledge what he is. He would rather not know himself now. Fully aware of the intrinsic connection between what he has done and what he is, Macbeth at this point decides not to be aware. He will do everything that he can to distance himself from the deed, and thereby from himself. The violence with which this invention occurs will, of course, only bring him further toward its inner source: his severance from God and Reason.

Conclusion

This moment of Shakespeare's soliloquy, read via Desmond's analysis of equivocity in relation to sticky evil, grants depth to the age-old philosophical maxim: know thyself. Such knowledge involves not only the self, but creation, and depends upon a relationship with God that witnesses to the fecundity of equivocity. It is the foundation of a metaxologically grounded community, and the source for all moral action. Again, Macbeth's inability to say 'Amen' is crucial when considered from Augustine's main points in the *Soliloquies* and Desmond's metaxological philosophy, in turn influenced by Augustine's anthropology. For Augustine, the root of spiritual illness is the inability to acknowledge the order of being. Derived from this is the incapacity to pray and to listen to Reason. Further, the unhealthy one cannot define or communicate what is

---

[13] Macbeth's dramatic situation could be compared with Augustine's use of the structures of theater in the *Soliloquies*. For a discussion of the latter, see Foley 2014.

real and true. This inability to speak bleeds too upon those surrounding the unhealthy. One thinks of Lady Macbeth's doctor, who "thinks" but "dare[s] not speak" (5.2.5) about the evidence he has seen of sticky evil. Unequivocal honesty with the self, before God, is necessary for 'sanity' and the health of an entire community at the same time. It is, then, crucial to this analysis to recognize that having reversed the Augustinian journey, Macbeth can neither pray nor listen to reason in its fullest, most porous, sense. This enables a fuller understanding of reason's role in self-knowledge, and thereby facilitates a deeper appreciation of what reason, in its more ancient, metaxological roots, entails.

Namely, Reason in Augustine's *Soliloquies* is both univocal and equivocal—a richly metaxological interlocutor. Augustine does not know whether to think of Reason as himself or someone else, as interior or exterior. As a *dramatis persona*, Reason uncompromisingly drives Augustine to state as clearly as possible what he means and what he wants; at the same time, Reason is compassionate and patient. Reason is porous to otherness, and particularly attentive to the desires of the whole person, as well as the communications of the divine. Reason helps Augustine to think clearly about who he is and what he wants. With Reason, his speech has focus and is directed toward God, whose presence illuminates what he most desires to know. He is porous to what he knows; it affects him as he receives it, and it changes him within. This is best articulated in his prayers—at the beginning his prayer is long-winded, looking for the point. Later, he can speak succinctly to God what he wants to know: only two things, God and the soul, 'nothing more'. Following Reason's direction, he prays: "God, who is always the same, may I know myself, may I know you. This is my prayer" (Augustine 2000, II.1,1). Thus, knowledge of God coincides with self-realization. This short prayer, the result of much labor, states clearly what Augustine intends. His speeches in the *Soliloquies* run in the opposite direction to Macbeth's language in Shakespeare's play, which becomes increasingly difficult to decipher.

Tragedy has thus developed out of a failure of self-knowledge that recognizes the ethical space *between* good and evil. This is a domain where transcendence constantly announces itself. Augustine's trajectory, taken in reverse, is applicable to dramatic tragedy only in a secondary sense. When Augustine, Shakespeare, and Desmond indicate the interdependencies and communications between self, world, others, and God, they emphasize a deep mystery within the primal Judeo-Christian story of the lure of evil and the destructive nature of sin. Macbeth and Lady Macbeth are like another Adam and Eve.[14] As such, they remind that self-reflection porous to transcendence and ethical knowledge is important for each and every human person. Only in learning from what I have been given, as it communicates to me, can I know myself, and only then can I see myself as I am—quintessentially desiring God. Two things only are necessary to know the potencies of being human: God and the soul. Such knowledge, though, is forged using the fire of an ethical life that depends upon open communication. Tragedy occurs when saying what one means, in the presence of God, cannot happen in either exterior or interior dimensions.

Bibliography

Arnold, Morris LeRoy. 1911. *The Soliloquies of Shakespeare: A Study in Technic.* New York: Columbia University Press.
Augustine. 1997. *The Confessions.* Trans. Maria Boulding, OSB. Hyde Park, NY: New City Press.
———. 2000. *Soliloquies: Augustine's Inner Dialogue.* Trans. Kim Paffenroth. Hyde Park, NY: New City Press.
Colston, Ken. 2010. *Macbeth* and the Tragedy of Sin. *Logos: A Journal of Catholic Thought and Culture* 13 (4): 60–95.
Desmond, William. 2002. Sticky Evil. In *God, Literature and Process Thought*, ed. D. Middleton, 133–155. Aldershot: Ashgate.
Foley, Michael P. 2014. A Spectacle to the World: The Theatrical Meaning of St. Augustine's Soliloquies. *Journal of Early Christian Studies* 22 (2): 243–260.
Fox, Robin Lane. 2003. Augustine's *Soliloquies* and the Historian. In *Studia Patristica XLIII: Augustine and Other Latin Writers*, ed. F. Young et al., 173–189. Leuven: Peeters.
Garber, Marjorie. 2004. *Shakespeare After All.* New York: Anchor.
Hirsch, James. 1997. Shakespeare and the History of Soliloquies. *Modern Language Quarterly* 58 (1): 1–26.
Köhler-Ryan, Renée. 2017. Thinking Transcendence, Transcending the Mask: Desmond Pondering Augustine and Thomas Aquinas. In *William Desmond and Contemporary Theology*, ed. Christopher Ben Simpson and Brendan Thomas Sammon, 191–216. Notre Dame: University of Notre Dame Press.
Shakespeare, William. 2015. *Macbeth*, Bloomsbury: *The Arden Shakespeare*, ed. Sandra Clark and Pamela Mason. London: Bloomsbury.

---

[14] This is evident in several ways. There is a parallel between Lady Macbeth and Eve as temptress; the way that sin infects the whole world, about which Macbeth is very aware, as discussed, is another parallel idea. For more on this, see Colston (2010).

Shapiro, James. 2015. *1606: William Shakespeare and the Year of Lear*. London: Faber & Faber.
Skiffington, Lloyd A. 1985. *The History of English Soliloquy: Aeschylus to Shakespeare*. Lanham, MD: University Press of America.
Stock, Brian. 2010. *Augustine's Inner Dialogue: The Philosophical Soliloquy in Late Antiquity*. Cambridge: Cambridge University Press.
———. 2011. Self, Soliloquy, and Spiritual Exercises in Augustine and Some Later Authors. *The Journal of Religion* 91 (1): 5–23.
———. 2017. The Philosophical Soliloquy. In *The Integrated Self: Augustine, the Bible, and Ancient Thought*, 98–126. Philadelphia: University of Pennsylvania.
Targoff, Ramie. 2002. 'Dirty' Amens: Devotion, Applause and Consent in Richard III. *Renaissance Drama* 31: 61–84.

CHAPTER 18

Metaxology and Environmental Ethics: On the Ethical Response to the Aesthetics of Nature as Other in the Between

Alexandra Romanyshyn

William Desmond's diagnosis of ethical problems that arise in modernity is applicable to some of the current issues in environmental ethics. In this chapter, I will concentrate primarily on Desmond's account of the devaluation of being, which leads to instrumentalization. I will apply the loss of perceived value of the 'other' to environmental ethics, with nature being the 'other'. I will also explain modernity's misuse of nature in light of Desmond's views of the devaluation and instrumentalization of nature. Finally, I will argue that Desmond's metaxological metaphysics provides the basis for a more appropriate view of nature, which will promote a more ethical treatment of the environment.

Environmental philosophy has a number of challenges, some of which Desmond's metaxological metaphysics can assist in answering. One such problem is that of anthropocentrism—namely, a tendency within Western thought to view human beings as the only possessors of intrinsic value, while all else has merely instrumental value (Brennan and Lo 2016).

A. Romanyshyn (✉)
Saint Louis University, St. Louis, MO, USA
e-mail: alexandra.romanyshyn@slu.edu

© The Author(s) 2018
D. Vanden Auweele (ed.), *William Desmond's Philosophy between Metaphysics, Religion, Ethics, and Aesthetics*,
https://doi.org/10.1007/978-3-319-98992-1_18

Desmond's metaxological worldview combats such anthropocentrism, first, because it counteracts the belief that we possess absolute power over nature, and second, because it defends the transcendence and intrinsic value of nature. In this chapter, then, I will elucidate the portions of Desmond's philosophy that will explain the rising mistreatment of nature and that will help us motivate a better attitude towards nature.

Agapeic Origin and *Ways of Wondering*

Mankind begins in a state of astonishment at the goodness of being. Imagine the wonder of a baby, discovering for the first time commonplace items that adults take for granted: a door swinging on its hinge, the sound of a rattle, a splash of water. Yet with age and experience, the innocence of the wonder becomes tainted: hinges can pinch, rattles can herald a threat, and water can burn the lungs. Through a process of disillusionment, humans come to realize the danger of the 'other'—a being outside of themselves, or specifically another human outside of oneself. The original, innocent wonder is tarnished by the perception of threat. One may merely weather the threat of the other, or one may cope with the threat by moving towards a devaluation of the other. Once that which posed a threat is devalued, one can dominate it more easily. Consider, for instance, the reaction of one who is insulted by a close friend; while continuing to value the friend's opinion, one will feel deeply hurt by the insult. One may weather the hurt, but there is a more palatable option: to eradicate it. How often, then, will one react by disavowing the friendship, or by claiming that the friend's opinion is meaningless, groundless, false, and not worth consideration. Such a reaction is one of *devaluing* what is hurtful—ignoring or eliminating its value—and thus depriving it of the power to hurt. Note, such devaluation may spare one pain in the here and now, but perhaps at the cost of greater goods.

Now I should observe that while Desmond criticizes the above loss of wonder at otherness, he is not necessarily calling us to return to an immature, childish wonder. There are in fact three ways of wondering, as Desmond outlines in "Ways of Wondering" (ISB 260–300). First, the original astonishment: pre-reflective and pre-intentional. Desmond writes,

> [T]his idiocy of astonishment sounds negative, not our negation but our being negated. And yet it is more the affirmative 'too-muchness' of the happening that is outlined in the event of astonishment. There is an intrusion of ontological frailty in the unpremeditated event of coming to be: it might not have come to be, it might not have been at all. (ISB 264)

We wonder at creation around us, not because we are weak or lesser, but because of the abundant goodness of the being of the other. This astonishment is not a failing or weakness on our part, but rather a recognition of the magnificence of the other.

The initial, pre-reflective astonishment must give way to a more considered view of the world. While it can go wrong and lead to a more determinate, even positivist, perspective, it can also give way to perplexity. Perplexity is a more mature way of wondering; it is

> a modality of wondering that brings us more into the *equivocity of being:* the play of light and darkness, the chiaroscuro of things and ourselves; the dark light of unformed things and things forming; of ourselves formless and seeking form and being returned to formlessness; of all things enigmatic and intimating; of ourselves the most baffling of beings, at once shouting absurdly and absurdly singing. (ISB 275)

This way of wondering is more reflective as it reacts to the equivocity of being, that is, a bewilderment that the previously perceived good is equivocally good—that it is in some sense threatening. Perplexity provokes us towards a more complex awareness of the other, perceiving it as not just idiotically good, as we once thought.

Finally, perplexity can give way to curiosity, which Desmond describes as follows: "Finally, positive science for the maturity of the human race: now disciplined, regulated curiosity knows positively of reality in all its detail. The teleology of knowing is mapped onto an inexorable move from the indeterminate to the determinative" (ISB 299). This is a more intellectual way of wondering, a way that promises an understanding of the other, without limiting the other or viewing it as wholly graspable within the confines of our intellect. It is the most matured and intellectual way of wondering, which allows us to both know and marvel at the other.

Loss of Astonishment: The Move to Devaluation, Subjectification, and Instrumentalization

Astonishment can go awry when we become aware of the equivocity of being. Instead of yielding to a more sophisticated sort of wonder, we can lose astonishment and begin to devalue the other. The devaluation of nature as 'other' comes in response to the threat of nature which issues as desire for a more comprehensive sense of autonomy (EB 25–30). We can understand this more clearly when we consider that devaluation, in some ways, seems to create both ethical and logical space for control and domination of the other. The devaluation of which Desmond speaks is a rejection of intrinsic value in the other, leaving merely instrumental value. If something has no value besides instrumental value, then it is permissible for us to use this thing in ways most profitable to us. We no longer see any good in the thing itself. For example, if it is more profitable for us to destroy a tool, such as a hammer, rather than to hammer nails with it, then it is morally permissible to destroy the hammer, since the hammer has no intrinsic value. The very existence of the hammer is not good; the hammer is only good insofar as it is a useful tool for humans. It may then be used or destroyed in whatever way provides the greatest utility. When one rejects the intrinsic value of nature, or of things within nature, then one likewise instrumentalizes nature; we thus subjectivize value, valuing things only relative to ourselves (EB 39). If nature has no intrinsic value, then it can be used like a hammer: a tool, only valuable insofar as it can profit us.

A desire for autonomy, as well as recognition of the equivocity of the other, motivates subjectification of the other. As Desmond writes, "it is the self who is the power so to place the other, and to do so, not for the other as other, but for its own self, and indeed for the securing of its own self-determining power, or its own power as self-determining" (EB 35). The desire for pure autonomy leads us to treat the other as having no autonomy of its own—for if it did, we would have to acknowledge our own heteronomy, our own dependence upon the being of things around us. We desire perfect control over the other because only then can we be truly autonomous. Thus, failure to recognize our own limitations and heteronomy, that is, a desire for complete autonomy, leads to a subjectification of the value of the other.

Even a cursory perusal of philosophy of nature during the nineteenth century reveals a predominant conception of nature as being merely mechanistic. With the rise of science and the positivist worldview, nature began to seem less a mystery and more purely determined or determinate:

> Teleological explanations generally were rejected, and, at a time when Darwin's doctrine had not yet been received, in its place the materialists set the claim that what looked like purposive behavior or development was nothing but the result of increasingly complex physical and chemical processes. (Rueger 2012, n.p.)

With increasingly scientific explanation of natural phenomena, there was less of an inclination to recognize purpose within or beyond nature, leaving room for us to impose our own purposes upon it. The "apparently mechanistic world of nineteenth-century science" thus facilitated the subjectification of value within nature (ibid., n.p.). The prevailing view of nature as lacking intrinsic purpose or value primed people to view nature as something to be bent to their own purposes, and to only be of value insofar as it was valuable to them.

We thus have multiple concomitant reasons for the devaluation of nature and the subjectification of value. Nature was seen as a threat, brimming with powerful forces that can potentially destroy. A palatable response is to neutralize the source of the threat, a perceptible theme in modern philosophy. Or, a more Nietzschean response, one of positing man as the source of all value in a valueless world, places man in the position of power.[1] We become that which determines value. Our rejection of the other, the result of perceiving it as a threat, is trifold: a rejection of its autonomy, helping us view nature as something within our control; a rejection of its intrinsic value, leaving it only instrumental value; and a rejection of its 'overdeterminacy', a term by which Desmond expresses that something is not indeterminate, but also not purely determinable by man.[2] This trifold rejection of nature, prompted by the perception of nature as a threat, can explain the use and misuse of nature in modernity: all over the world, natural resources are being depleted. The philosophy behind this is clear: if nature is not with us but against us, we must control it to make it work *for* us; if nature has no intrinsic value, we have the right to alter it for any of our purposes; if it has no overdeterminacy or intrinsic good, then we should determine and modify it to make it good for us.

One may object that not all ill-treatment of nature is the result of perceiving it as a threat; for example, we pillage many resources that would not have been threats if left to their own devices, such as forests or other natural habitats. However, we need not posit that every act of control is the direct result of perceiving a threat; even if we do not view nature as a threat, yet we still question its inherent goodness, there is logical space for

---

[1] See: "So we can restate the point concerning the grounding milieu of value: modernity's shaping of the ethos grows out of distrust of equivocity, expressed in the univocalizing mentality of dualistic opposition that produces a devaluing objectification of being on one side and a subjectification of value on the other side" (EB 41).

[2] For a helpful example of 'overdeterminacy', see EB 163.

us to control and determine nature. As Francis Van den Noortgaete notes, "in modernity—especially so in its current late form—the given goodness of being has been progressively called into doubt, resulting in a decoupling of being and the good, as notions of inherent value were increasingly replaced by humanly attributed potential use value" (2016, pp. 122–123). So, merely believing that being and good do not necessarily correspond to one another creates space for us to deny the intrinsic good of nature and determine it at our own scrutiny. Once mankind views nature as something we should control or determine, then it is easier for us to rationalize using it, or even abusing it, for our own purposes, exactly as we would do with a tool or anything else upon which we impose value.

Loss of Perplexity and Implications on Nature

Desmond diagnoses modernity as also lacking 'erotic perplexity'; such a lack is the inability to recognize that some aesthetic value cannot be perfectly grasped by human intellection. As Desmond describes in *Perplexity and Ultimacy*, perplexity arises in response to the mysteriousness of the Good, for "the Good suggests an enigma which will not let us excuse ourselves from thinking. Quite to the contrary, this enigma renews perplexity and makes the mind sleepless. Beyond every determinate problem and every univocal answer, there is another, second perplexity, beyond all determinacy" (PU 173). Erotic perplexity is the natural response to recognizing that the other is known, only in part; there is a part of it that transcends the limitations of our intellects. Such recognition implies a sort of scepticism, which is not necessarily bad: "Whether it crushes or releases, skepticism can be an expression of philosophical truthfulness" (PU 184). Such scepticism, however, can prompt a form of self-transcendence, for "there is an implicit orientation of honest self-transcendence towards the absolute truth as other to our own self-transcendence" (PU 175). Realizing that the other is transcendent, and consequently, transcending our powers of comprehension, directs us towards what is higher, rather than reducing all to the finite, or the determinate. Erotic perplexity turns us beyond ourselves.

Enlightenment philosophy lost such erotic perplexity and tends towards reductionism. As Holmes Rolston III describes modernity's worldview, "Animals were mindless, living matter; biology was mechanistic" (1989, p. 126). Reducing everything to mechanism both deprives it of value and deprives us of wonder. The loss of wonder parallels a quest for control and complete understanding, at the expense of the failure to recognize those things which might transcend our understanding. For example, we might try to understand something exhaustively, using science, but there are some aspects of a thing's being that science cannot capture, and so our methodology will be limited. Consider, for instance, a scientific analysis of a painting: it would yield a comprehensive account of the chemical composition of the paint, the dimensions of the painting, and the proportions of its figures; however, it would not be able to tell you, quite importantly, whether the painting counted as good *art*; science would not have the correct methodology to measure something's aesthetic value.[3]

On Desmond's account, something like nature exceeds the capacities of not only particular disciplines, but also of our finite intellectual powers. Thus, our observation of nature is characterized not only by the limitations of our methodologies, but also of our understanding. Something unquantifiable, immeasurable, and undeterminable, such as the beauty of a sunset or the sublimity of a thunderstorm, is not valuable to one who seeks thorough comprehension of nature, because such values cannot be measured and determined by human powers. The scientific explanations of sunsets and thunderstorms do not capture their aesthetic goodness. Consequently, the desire to eliminate perplexity causes a desire both to make nature purely determinate and to ignore its aesthetic qualities.

Meanwhile, modern philosophy is the perfect companion for industrialization: the devaluation of nature means we can exhaust natural resources for our own gain, since there is no value except in relation to us. Desmond refers to such a phenomenon as the "subjectification of value", that is, value becoming relative only to oneself, the subject. The subjectification of value, concurrent with instrumentalization, easily complements Nietzschean will to power. Nietzsche, questing for higher autonomy and self-transcendence, rejects the possibility of a power or determiner higher than man: without a higher power beyond man, there is no source of value external to man, enabling man to determine the value of all things (see EB 153). While Nietzsche wishes to maintain transcendence within man, at least within the human will, his desire to escape inherent value leaves him trapped in nihilism, "despite his excess of rhetoric about overcoming nihilism" (EB 154). Nietzsche quests for value and transcendence, but ultimately devalues being, for "Nietzsche knew the devaluation of being in modernity, though

---

[3] For more of Desmond's thoughts on a scientific worldview, see EB 213, 238 and 379–380.

he took this valuelessness for the *truth of being*: no inherent value—value is what we stamp on the flux. Nietzsche recommends a more radical process of creative self-becoming" (EB 153). However, "his aestheticization of the good and the world is such that there can be no good, no rank, will it otherwise though he may" (EB 156). There is a desire for value in Nietzsche, without a metaphysical basis for such value. How can we give value to a valueless world, when we are indeed part of that valueless world?

As Desmond explains then, Nietzsche becomes the equivocal doppelganger of Kant. In Nietzsche, Kant's self-legislation becomes autonomy that is not under moral law, since it is the source of the law. Thus, "postulating God becomes postulating self, and self becomes the *summum bonum*" (EB 153). Because Kant's argument for the existence of God is roughly a postulation of a higher power, Nietzsche can go a step further to postulate *man* as that higher power. Such will to power then contributes to the subjectification of value, and thus, of the value of nature.

Aesthetics and Environmental Ethics

Desmond recounts various approaches to 'aesthetics', which I understand to be the desirable aspect of the good, and I will apply these senses of aesthetics to environmental issues. The ways of considering aesthetics are the univocal, equivocal, dialectical, and finally metaxological. First, the univocal: this way considers one objective good. To be, is to be good, and this good is completely determined. Such univocity relates to aesthetics insofar as aesthetics refers to what we find desirable; what we desire is simply the good.[4] Univocity, thus, roughly parallels the original astonishment into which we are born; there is no doubt that the baby wants the puppy, or that the puppy is good. That moment when the puppy bites, disillusioning one to its purely determined goodness, reveals the equivocity of being, as well as the equivocity of the good, leading to the second sense of the aesthetic. Being can be good in one sense, bad in another, and our desires will shift accordingly. Furthermore, some goods will fuel, not satisfy, our appetites, and so we find that the more we acquire, the more we desire. Equivocity lies both in our shifting perception of the good and in

---

[4] Desmond writes, "This aesthetic univocity of value is a pre-reflective univocity: lived in very definite ways, especially as defined by the common sense of communities; not made an object of determinate thinking unless there is a breakdown, an unforeseen change, or a deprivation" (EB 57).

the tendency of one good to propagate further desires for that good, or for other desires (see EB 87). Thus, the good becomes indeterminate, or indeterminable, and our desires are indeterminate in the sense that they know neither constancy nor bounds.

The interplay between determinacy and indeterminacy, univocity and equivocity, leads to dialectical self-determinacy. Desmond writes, "passing into the determinate, and thence into significant indefiniteness, the dialectical way approaches the overdetermined ethos in terms of *self-determination*. If to be is to be good, here to be good is to be self-determining" (EB 117). The indeterminate is intolerable, and so one seeks to determine things oneself, to control things. Consider the Kierkegaardian aesthete, a character consumed by sensual pleasures and immediate gratification; the infinity of sensual desires is intolerable, and quite often such characters will mellow to the life of asceticism, a form of ultimate control over desires. To determine things so completely, however, one must be the source of determination, but we are ultimately not the source of determination (see EB 231). Being is 'overdetermined'; it points to something beyond itself (perhaps God), which has determined it, although this determination exceeds the capacity of human understanding. To make oneself the determiner of what is overdetermined, then, necessitates a self-transcendence, making oneself a higher power than one already is, as a Nietzschean account would have. But this is also intolerable, to Desmond, for it seems we cannot be the source of determination, and thus the source of value, goodness, and power, when we are a part of the very creation that we have stripped of these things (see EB 19 and 35–37). Recall that the ability to determine another's value flows from the devaluation of that other. How can we give value to a valueless world, when we are ourselves part of that valueless world? Only when we recognize our heteronomy—that is, acknowledging that we are not purely autonomous, that there are other partially determined, partially autonomous powers, and hence other sources of value and other holders of value—only then do we see reality as it actually is, which brings us to metaxology.

Since we cannot be the source of everything—value, goodness, power, even being itself—we must recognize the transcendence of the other and the givenness of being. That is, there is a way in which nature transcends us, and its very existence is a gift from a more transcendent origin. As Desmond writes, "The relation to the good as other is more complex than dialectic comprehends; the mystery is more affirmative than equivocity knows; determination is more open than univocity allows" (EB 219).

Recognizing the overdeterminacy, the complexity, the 'givenness' of nature helps us appreciate nature *as* other, in its own right, not merely in relation to ourselves; recognizing its origin as something beyond us helps us appreciate its intrinsic value. Thus, we return to original astonishment at nature, and by extension, the environment. Interacting with nature becomes an aesthetic experience: we return to appreciating the goodness of the other, and even its terrible moments are transfigured into an aesthetic experience of the sublime. A lightning storm is no longer perceived as a threat, but as something to behold with awe, as well as with awareness that it has the power to obliterate us. Lightning is beautiful, but it can kill you; it is striking in two senses of the word! The aesthetic experience of the Sublime—"a finite manifestation of the infinite"—reminds us of the overdeterminacy of nature: that is, it is neither purely determined nor undetermined; it both transcends us, and comes from something more transcendent than itself (EB 183). The sublimity within nature is "beyond the measure of our moral evaluations of good and evil" (ibid.). It has a source greater than us, and a purpose greater than ours.

Metaxology, then, by pointing to the origin of being as something beyond us, re-elevates the very nature, the very environment that modernity has devalued. By helping us experience, aesthetically, the overdeterminacy and the intrinsic good of the other, a metaxological worldview shows us that nature has value beyond our instrumental uses for it. It is not something we can determine; our will to power is futile. But more importantly, nature is *good*. There is no need to determine it, dominate it, control it; nature is not a threat to us, but a gift, rife with awe-filling, perplexing beauty.

Metaxology, as a metaphysical system that points to the origin or *metaxu* of a being, restores the original astonishment that was tarnished at the discovery of being's equivocity. Van den Noortgaete says, "to Desmond, precisely this renewed astonishment about the plenitude of being forms the basis of ontological gratitude" (2016, p. 123). Furthermore, gratitude "due to its acknowledgement of a goodness that is not self-authored" helps us not only recognize a source of value beyond ourselves, but also it makes us *want* to uphold the bearer of that value, because we appreciate it (ibid.). As we will see, such an attitude helps immensely in environmental ethics.

Regarding nature and the environment, metaxology tells us to look beyond our own transcendence, for though there is a transcendence of man, there is the transcendence of the other, in this case nature, as well.

Another key point of metaxology is being "in the between", neither wholly separate from the other nor wholly one with the other. We humans are in nature, but not of nature; although we do transcend it in a sense, our existence is interwoven with nature. We are neither purely autonomous nor purely heteronomous; we can act in ways not determined by nature, but there are other senses in which we are still determined by nature: one cannot, for example, plant a garden without earth, water, seeds, and so on. Our most basic sustenance is dependent upon nature. This betweenness, then, helps us value the other insofar as we are interrelated with it; betweenness humbles us through the acknowledgement of our own heteronomy (see EB 200). Meanwhile, by revealing the transcendence of nature as something that points towards an origin higher than both itself and us, metaxology prevents us from viewing our dependence upon nature as the only source of its value. Thus, metaxology makes a twofold contribution to environmental ethics; by asserting our heteronomy, a metaxological worldview prevents us from believing that we can have absolute power over nature, and by defending the transcendence of nature as other, metaxology preserves the intrinsic value of all beings in nature. Metaxological metaphysics, by pointing to the agapeic origin of being, shows us that we are not self-created, self-determined, or self-made, and neither is nature determined by us.

Applied specifically to aesthetics, metaxology shows us that to be is to be good. Thus, the existence of nature and its constituents is good. Furthermore, metaxological aesthetics reveals *incarnate* goodness; existence as *physical, fleshed* being is good. Nature, in all its sensuality, and our corporality that makes us dependent upon nature, are good in virtue of being physical things. The aesthetic value of flesh is given, as well as a task, for it refers us to the other; through the aesthetics of embodiment, we sense others and are sensed. Aesthetics thus relates us even more to the other.

In nature, aesthetic qualities, including sublimity, point to the otherness and transcendence of nature's origin, and consequently to the otherness and transcendence of nature. Because aesthetics involves our desires as well, such recognition of aesthetic good in nature is not merely an epistemological recognition, but a recognition of desire; one sees the good of nature and *wants* it. This connects to gratitude, gratitude for the good of the other, without which "environmental ethics risks being reduced to a duty, and hence limited in its impact" (Van den Noortgaete 2016, p. 125). Desmond's metaxological account of aesthetics, as well as of ethics and metaphysics, yields an approach to environmental ethics by which the ethical behaviour is desirable, not onerous, for "gratitude apparently fosters a tendency for cooperative behavior exceeding what is required by, or esteemed as appropriate in view of, social norms. It increases the inclination to help, even when this is effortful or costly, and thereby extends to include strangers" (ibid., p. 126). Thus, a metaxological perspective on aesthetics, as well as on metaphysics, can induce us towards a more ethical treatment of the environment.

Conclusion

A metaxological worldview can vastly promote respect and consideration for nature. Desmond uncovers the shortcomings of the very aspects of modern philosophy that make the misuse of environmental resources appear permissible. He replaces such metaphysics with metaxology, which preserves the dignity of nature as other, consequently, as something partially independent from us, with value and transcendence of its own. The implications of Desmond's view are that nature has intrinsic value, as well as a purpose other than our instrumental purposes for it. Therefore we ought to respect nature as other. Furthermore, ethical treatment of nature is not onerous, but something delightful, if we return to our original astonishment at nature as good, along with erotic perplexity at beholding its aesthetic qualities. Thus, by not only preserving the value of the other, but also calling us to enjoyment, appreciation, and awe at the good and beauty of the other, Desmond's view would make respectful treatment of nature and the environment not only obligatory, but also pleasurable, as one delights in all aesthetic goods.

Bibliography

Brennan, Andrew, and Yeuk-Sze Lo. 2016. Environmental Ethics. *The Stanford Encyclopedia of Philosophy*. Winter Ed.

Desmond, William. 1995. *Perplexity and Ultimacy: Metaphyscal Thoughts from the Middle*. Albany: State University of New York Press.

———. 2001. *Ethics and the Between*. New York: SUNY Press.

———. 2012. *The Intimate Strangeness of Being: Metaphysics After Dialectic*. Washington, DC: Catholic University of America Press.

Rolston, Holmes, III. 1989. Environmental Ethics: Values in and Duties to the Natural World. *Ethics and the Environment* 11: 363–368.

Rueger, Alexander. 2012. Conceptions of the Natural World, 1790–1870. In *The Cambridge History of Philosophy in the Nineteenth Century (1790–1870)*, ed. Allen Wood and Songsuk Susan Hahn. Cambridge: Cambridge University Press.

Van Den Noortgaete, Francis. 2016. Generous Being: The Environmental-Ethical Relevance of Ontological Gratitude. *Ethics and the Environment* 21 (2): 119–142.

CHAPTER 19

Responding Metaxologically

William Desmond

The themes of this book are very fitting for the preoccupations that have perplexed me. There is hardly a book I have written, from *Art and the Absolute* to *The Intimate Universal*, in which the interplay between art, religion and philosophy (in a metaphysical register) has not been at issue.[1] These three, in addition to our being ethical, are of significance for themselves and for philosophical reflection. All honor to Hegel for placing art, religion and philosophy at the highest level of absolute spirit. I am at one with the imputation of ultimate importance, though I am not fully at one with the way Hegel relates them. I hold that there is a metaxological intermediation among art, religion and philosophy rather than a dialectical sublation, as Hegel held. The metaxological intermediations of the spaces between art, religion and philosophy are plurivocal rather than univocal, or even dialectical. There can be intermediations between philosophy and

[1] See especially AA and IU.

W. Desmond (✉)
Villanova University, Villanova, PA, USA

Maynooth University, Maynooth, Ireland

KU Leuven, Leuven, Belgium
e-mail: William.Desmond@kuleuven.be

the aesthetic, as there can be between philosophy and our being religious, as well as between the aesthetic and the religious.[2] Being ethical is not to be neglected, and I have also written extensively on this.[3] Kierkegaard is not wrong in speaking of the aesthetic, ethical and religious spheres of life. The question for me is, as with Hegel, how he understands them. How they overlap or pass into each other demands thought more subtle than laying them contiguously side by side in an existential self-becoming. Kierkegaard does not do this, of course, though I would say that the aesthetic and art, as much as our being religious and ethical, participate in a saturated equivocity in which significant ambiguity comes from the porosity of our being rather than from an endeavor to move from the aesthetic, to the ethical, to the religious, otherwise contiguously placed side by side. There is something about the permeability of these that continually resists their each being placed in their autonomous spheres.

About all three, in themselves and in relation, as well as in connection with our being ethical, there are saturated equivocities that resist the univocal literalness of prosaic thought. These equivocities find a place in thought somewhere between system and poetics. At the same time these equivocities are not to be dialectically superseded by the higher univocity of a speculative system. Hegel's philosophy of absolute spirit has been recurrently a source of fascination and resistance in my own thought which differently treats this saturated equivocity. The equivocity is to be dwelt in metaxologically: as a sign of the surplus signifying of the overdeterminate ethos of the between, not as a medium allowing passage to conceptual thought, simply thinking itself at the end of all self-becoming. There is an aesthetic/artistic wording of the between, just as there is a religious and a philosophical wording. Being ethical is the incarnation of that wording in a form of human life in fidelity to the call of being good.[4] Instead of the triadic sublation of art, religion and philosophy in the unity of the concept at home with itself, there are metaxological intermediations which have a more fourfold character. The wording of the between is a crossing of the between. We can cross from in to out, from out to in, from below to

---

[2] If AOO answers the intermediations of art and philosophy, and IST responds to the intermediations of religion and philosophy, *The Gift of Beauty and the Passion of Being: On the Threshold between the Aesthetic and the Religious* (Eugene, OR: Wipf and Stock, 2018) addresses intermediations between the aesthetic and the religious.

[3] Most fully in EB but also in PO.

[4] See 'Wording the Between', in *The William Desmond Reader*. Ed. Christopher Simpson (Albany: SUNY Press, 2012), 195–227.

above, from above to below. This seems simple enough at first glance, but there is nothing univocal about it. There is something about it hard to determine, something exceeding our self-determination, something not merely indeterminate but in excess as overdeterminate. In what sometimes seems almost nothing there is a too-muchness that shows finite being on a threshold, in a communicative, even revelatory sense. A metaxological dwelling with the saturated equivocity tries to think these crossings, tries to word plurivocal passages in the wording of the between.

This book presents to me a rich collection of impressive discussions ranging over an equally impressive range of themes and figures. On each of them I could have, and would have liked to have, said something fuller in response, but space forbids this. I have tried to make an important point or two as I respond to each of them. I am grateful for the care with which my work has been read and honored. I am full of appreciation for the acumen in commenting on my work, and the charity in correcting it. I take each of the contributors as companioning my own thoughts. I hope that my remarks are not too impressionistic but I have listened to my companions, and if I raise issues I see related to the exchange, I often want to amplify or supplement the given contribution. Of course, as happens in the conversation of companions, explicit responses do not preclude silent accords and unspoken communities of shared understanding. There is always more to say.

1

As one would expect from John Milbank, he offers a bold and very interesting reflection, with imaginative and surprising turns of thought and connections that highlight hitherto unnoticed possibilities. I appreciate the connections he draws of my own work with a longer historical unfolding. I would remark on my own long meditations on the relations between the *esprit de finesse* and the *esprit de géométrie*. Perhaps the rigors of mathematics have not enough engaged me in thinking through the equivocities of the *metaxu*. I once was a dab hand at mathematics when I was young, but it is a language I have left unused later. That said, the tense combination of the ordered thinking of mathematics and the wayward intuitions of the poetic was important in the formation of my mind. I suppose the *esprit de finesse* has assumed a kind of priority in my thoughts over the *esprit de géométrie*. This is not because I am lacking in respect for the latter. Quite the contrary, the extraordinary univocities of the mathematical quest are perplexingly interesting insofar as they lead to certain equivocities and paradoxes at certain extreme thresholds. I take this territory of paradox to be home ground for John Milbank's penetrating reflections. I do touch on some of these matters briefly in articulating the transition from being as univocal to being as equivocal in BB (see the end of Chap. 2 and the beginning of Chap. 3). I have put stress on diverse conceptions of infinity in my work, right from the beginning with DDO: the infinite of succession, intentional infinitude and the actual infinitude—these are at the core of this first effort to stage the metaxological philosophy. I speak of different conceptions of infinity also in connection, for instance, with the understanding of the world we find in Pascal and Hegel. I remain a companion of Plato in thinking that there is a noetic and ontological level beyond the mathematical level of thinking of *dianoia*. (I am not sure Badiou gets this.) Reflecting the long tradition stretching back to the Pythagoreans, Leibniz has an interesting remark about arithmetic and music: 'Music is a hidden arithmetic exercise of the soul, which does not know that it is counting' (*Musica est exercitium arithmeticae occultum nescientis se numerare animi*. Letter to Christian Goldbach, April 17, 1712). It is cleverly altered by Schopenhauer: 'Music is a hidden metaphysical exercise of the soul, which does not know that it is philosophizing' (*Musica est exercitium metaphysicis occultum nescientis se philosophari animi*). I would alter it again in wondering if music is 'before' calculating. The word sings the world into being; the word sings mathematical intelligibility into being. It is not just that music is secretly mathematics, but that mathematics is a music the intellect does not always know it is singing. Leibniz's God sometimes comes across more as a God of geometry than a God of finesse.[5] In reading John Milbank I am reminded how George Cantor believed he was hearing the voice of God in connection with transfinites. Alas, *theia mania* also may be shadowed with the risk of real madness. I can identify with the Pythagorean-Platonic strain whose music is still to be heard in Kepler but which has gone silent in Galileo. Among the many important things John Milbank points to in this splendid exploration is the admission of 'logical mystery beyond logic alone' which allows us to think the thought of God anew, and this without exiling, with Wittgenstein, ethical and religious matters to the 'sublime margins'. And this in the worthy company of thinkers like Nicolas of Cusa and Erich Przywara.

The reflection of David Schindler is a very searching and sensitive exploration on the importance of truth and being truthful. There are

---

[5] See GB Chap. 3 on the Gods of geometry.

many things I like about it, but I will just mention his delving into the relevance of some of the thoughts I elaborate in ISB. He offers a probing discussion of Vattimo full of insight, and while I will not comment on Vattimo, I will offer a supplementary remark, in the spirit of this contribution, on a certain overlap in concerns between myself and Heidegger. I agree that it is an important point to move to a level of considerations that are not confined to the terms of propositional truth(s) alone. Heidegger tries to name this order of being in the truth with his notion of *alētheia*. I would rather speak about the more original porosity of being, in and through which truth as other to us comes to communicate itself in and to our own immanent being truthful. In BB, there is an important chapter entitled 'Being True' in which I try to articulate the connection between different senses of being and different modalities of being true, culminating with the metaxological sense. I talk about being true as the agapeic service of transcendence. In relation to this, I would say that Heidegger's concern with *alētheia* is only half-true, and seems to me to be untrue to our more primordial participation in being true in our own being truthful. What I mean is betrayed in the way that in *Being and Time* (§29) he uses the language of robbery (*ein Raub*) to describe *alētheia*: we wrest truth from its hiddenness, we steal it from its being withheld in itself. I think of Prometheus stealing fire from the gods. In Heidegger's robbery I do not find the agapeic manifestation of the true which offers itself to us in generous communication. We do not steal the true from its hiddenness. If we were to play with perhaps related metaphors, the agapeic communication of the true is more like Pascal's fire (*feu*): it comes to us, comes over us. The true words itself in tongues of fire. How Heidegger gets from his robbery (or from *Polemos*) to *Gelassenheit* is never made clear. He is moving in the right direction but I have always wondered if the terms of his earlier commitments hinder his truer release into the clear, the truer release in the porosity of being and being true. Among David's work is the first-rate *Plato's Critique of Impure Reason* (2008): it shows an admirably finessed sense of the plurivocal Plato, between system and poetics. Christ's remark comes to mind about those who become scribes for the kingdom: they are like householders who bring out from the storeroom things both old and new. I sense an agapeic mindfulness, stretched between what was, what is and what is to be, at work in his writings.

Daniel Minch addresses the issue of the relative silence about God in recent philosophy, especially since Kant, but reminds us very helpfully that the issue is one for theology also. Theology also has had to come to terms with its own ongoing 'crisis of metaphysics', partly sourced in a problematic understanding of finitude that has come down from Neo-Scholasticism. He offers us an eminently lucid account that takes in a longer historical view that shows the prefigurement of current crises in earlier understandings. I am illuminated by his way of situating the 'crisis of metaphysics' in theology, and he makes impressive sense in applying the scheme of the fourfold sense of being to the hermeneutics of experience, as Schillebeeckx understands this. I confess to not being as knowledgeable about Schillebeeckx as Daniel Minch's illuminating chapter persuaded me that I should be. I learned much from it about his thought, and I am struck by the intelligent and engaging way Daniel puts my own thought into a mutually illuminating contrast with Schillebeeckx's work. I do have some hesitations about the transcendental approach in philosophy, and am too much of a Platonist (perhaps in a heterodox or reformed sense) to make me hesitant about the aporias generated by a too unsuspecting historicist or hermeneutical approach to things. The relation of time and eternity has been a too-much-neglected issue in historicist thought since Hegel. It is hard to drive out of mind what Dostoevsky calls 'those cursed, eternal questions'. I wonder also if one were to stress more the porosity of being and the *passio essendi*, whether one might modify the tendency to privilege some kind of *futurity* we find in much modern thought. It is a serious question for me how teleology and eschatology need to be rethought in light of an ontological/metaphysical and theological archeology of the absolute origin which bring us closer to the truth of the porosity of being and the *passio essendi*. This is not absent here, but Daniel's worthy reflection makes me wonder about the future tilt of Schillebeeckx.

The hesitation about Kantian 'correlationism', and hence the legacy of transcendental thought, is at stake in Sandra Lehman's very interesting and well-thought-out study of how the realist impulse is present in the new realist thinking and my own work. She is quite right to note a fundamental difference in the overall design of the two approaches. Whereas a metaxological philosophy opens to a form of metaphysical theism, the new realism seems predicated on the groundless character of the absolute, if indeed there can be an absolute at all on its terms. That said, she helpfully offers a lucid and well-structured account of a kinship between metaxology and the new realisms, the result of shared ontological concerns. In agreement, I must celebrate the liberation of ontology/metaphysics from the dogmatic dead-end produced by the orthodoxies of post-metaphysical thinking. In tune with the spirit of her thoughts, I have worried whether this new realism is too much in agon with forms of philosophizing dominating the French landscape in the twentieth century, without enough hermeneutical self-consciousness that the realistic impulse is both as old as the philosophical tradition and as ontologically rooted in the deep constitution of the human being as the porosity to being, expressed diversely in different formations of the desire to know. Vis-à-vis correlationism, I have wrestled with what I take to be the one-sidedness of the transcendental approach when it comes to the knowing of the other qua other (in DDO, for instance), but that granted, I think we cannot think ourselves out of the picture in a full accounting of the ontological field. To think ourselves out of the picture (apart from the incoherence) would be a philosophically reactive reply to the one-sidedness of correlationism. The deeper truth of selving and othering is in this porosity of being and indeed various reformed shapes of correlationism that articulate the being of the between. I find that Sandra says very apposite things on these scores, as well as welcome things about Heidegger, which I also endorse.

2

I am very grateful to Brendan Sammon for bringing his impressive knowledge of the work of Dionysus the Areopagite to bear on the possible metaxology of the divine names. While some recent philosophical thinkers, such as Jean-Luc Marion and John Manoussakis, have shown sympathies for this tradition, contemporary philosophy generally finds itself out of sorts in dealing with these themes. There are analytical discussions of the divine attributes, but I think it safe to say that the mode of treatment lacks the feeling of appreciative, reverent participation we find in earlier forms. I am illuminated by the work of Sammon, and I note his concern elsewhere with beauty in his excellent *The God who is Beauty*, a concern I share. What I call the hyperboles of being, and the finding of indirect direction to God through these hyperboles, can be seen to belong to this Dionysian tradition. I will only add that Part 4 of GB, entitled 'God' (following godlessness, ways to God, Gods), can well be seen in that tradition and in a genuinely participatory way. The names of God, the so-called attributes, are thought through by means of what I call 'metaphysical cantos', of which I sing ten. A metaphysical canto is a sung riposte to those post-metaphysicians who purse their lips when pronouncing the word metaphysics and indeed God. Brendan Sammon is also a singer in his attunement to the beauty of the divine. The metaphysical cantos, surface appearances notwithstanding, are full-throated efforts at being mindful of God: they give voice to thought singing its other (as I put it in PO). I am at home in singing with Dionysus and with Brendan. Singing and metaphysics can make divine love to each other.

Mark Novak rightly sees a continuing friendly dialogue with Richard Kearney with whose work I have kept in touch over many years. He outlines helpfully some of the salient features of both of our approaches. His voice enters mindfully into that continuing conversation. Richard Kearney himself contributes to this volume, and I will say a further word or two in due course. That said, Mark Novak's exploration is helpfully relevant to the theme of aesthetics, religion and metaphysics. I wonder if there are slightly different slants to these in my own and Richard's works. My relation to the metaphysical tradition is more sympathetic than his, who has been more accepting of something closer to the Heideggerian characterization of the tradition. This has consequences for the God of metaphysics, so-called, consequences I do not find myself at home with. That said, the convergences that Mark foregrounds are well worth stressing. Theopoetics: this is mirrored in my own concern with the poetics of the religious, though the terms 'between system and poetics' tell something of the different sense of conversation between metaphysics and the aesthetic I would have. Mark Novak picks up on this very well in the later parts of his chapter. In one light my engagement with art, religion and philosophy is a kind of metaxological redoing of Hegel's absolute spirit, and perhaps overall more of a (re-)sacralization of the aesthetic rather than an aestheticization of the sacred. A forthcoming book, *The Gift of Beauty and the Passion of Being*, brings this out. Do I have a slightly different take on the creative power of the imagination which, I think, more truly finds itself endowed by the *passio essendi*, and nurtured to figural wording out of the more primal porosity of being? If it is true I am trying to recall the agapeics of the divine (something philosophers have not done, or even attempted), Richard Kearney and I are at one in thinking that eros and agape do not have to be set over against each. The hyperboles of being are figures that word metaxological thresholds, thresholds where we can begin to hear again the divine wording of being as a given between. I have significant things to say about metaphor, analogy, symbol and hyperbole that give metaxological precision and nuance to our wording(s) of the divine *metaxu*.

I am heartened by Patrick Cooper's welcome attention to the idiotics of the divine woo. I take us to be at one in the face of the amazing forgetfulness of the mystical in the moralization of the religious in our time. Moralization can become a project of our autonomy, but mysticism lies in the agonizing delight and delicacy of the divine woo. Mysticism comes in many forms, but recurrent is the ecstasy and torment of being called to love, of being in love where idiotics, aesthetics, erotics and agapeics promiscuously mingle. Patrick perceptively picks up on central Augustinian registers from early in my work and to which I return again and again. I found illuminating the contrast with Blondel that he offers us on that score. Also very illuminating was the community of echo and reecho with the work of Russbroec. I am grateful to Patrick for helping me better see my own work in this echoing and reechoing. One is struck by the significance of Russbroec as an important interlocutor. He is not as attractive to the fashionable postmodern admirers of Eckhart, and it would be an interesting question to ask why. Yet he is a worthy interlocutor, the quiet richness of whose work deserves honoring, and which Patrick honors nobly. I found very engaging Patrick Cooper's deployment of *The Intimate Universal,* coupled with a precise reminder of how Augustine or Augustinian themes are companions to my thinking over the long haul. Part of the brilliance of Augustine lies in his capturing in a concise formulation an entire sense of the world, of self and of God, and yet what is captured is not captive but rather releases in us an awakening to divine mystery. It is captivating to us but we cannot make it captive and so is not unlike the mystical woo of the divine idiotics.

3

Cyril O'Regan offers a very fine exploration of evil in my work and in that of others. Cyril is perhaps the person who has most engaged my work, and I am grateful for the finesse and friendship of his companioning presence over a long time. Evil is a recurrent perplexity in all my work in some form or other, and I have written a significant number of articles on different dimensions of the mystery of evil. I have hopes to write a trilogy in which the first volume will be called *Desecrations,* to be followed by *Purgations* and *Consecrations.* I hubristically model this trilogy on *La Divina Commedia.* I did start on *Desecrations* but put it aside for the moment, and the difficulty of the matter (or anti-matter) is brought home to me by Cyril's exploration. Instead I turned to *The Gift of Beauty and the Passion of Being.* In that book, the opening reflection on the gift of beauty ended with an encounter with the mockery of evil in relation to the beautiful: a séance with hell. Even with beauty I could not escape encountering hell. It is very difficult to enter intimately into the mystery of evil, and one risks being perplexed to the utmost, indeed being tormented and shattered by the mystery. While I hesitate about theodicy as practiced by rationalistic philosophers, I do find that the contemporary rejection of theodicy makes it a bit too easy to side-step the perplexity that generates the torment of soul about the justice (*dike*) of the divine (*theos*). Gnosticism I share an interest in, but defer to Cyril O'Regan's superior knowledge. I have learned more than I can say from his exceptional work on Gnosticism. His approach to Gnosticism is more oriented to narrative hermeneutics, while mine has perhaps more of an ontological-existential pathos. His very helpful contribution here helps me gather some of my thoughts to date, and also points in very helpful directions with regard to other resources and thinkers. I have high respect for Paul Ricoeur, perhaps to a degree more for the earlier Ricoeur of *Fallible Man*, and also his exceptional *Symbolism of Evil*. I do find a version of Kant haunting the later Ricoeur, to which I cannot subscribe unreservedly; admittedly Ricoeur is equivocal. George Bataille, Cormac McCarthy and Jerzy Kosinski are illuminatingly cited. The excremental mysticism of the first I found both fascinating and repulsive. Concerning the second I did have an earlier interest but let it lapse through a mixture of laziness and lack of time. The third precipitated me into unresolved rumination, occasioned by his suicide. In my own engagement with evil, I would mention Shakespeare, John Milton, Flannery O'Connor, William Golding, Gerard Manley Hopkins (the dark sonnets) and Dante. Cyril is spot on to focus on the Medusa theme, which has engaged me probably most in connection with Schopenhauer and Nietzsche. I recall an early study of Hegel's dialectical account of evil, how to interpret it and how it is limited. In tune with Cyril's suggestion, I argue for the indispensable need of the image to deal with what I call the idiocy of the monstrous: indispensable not to know the evil in the sense of providing a determinate rational explanation, but in the sense of helping us acknowledge and remember what lies on the threshold of determinate conceptualization and pointing beyond such determination to our intimacy with the *mysterium iniquitatis*.

Roberto Del'Oro provides us with a very nuanced discussion of some central ethical issues connected with the thresholds of life and death: coming to be and passing away. It provides a first-rate mingling of philosophical and anthropological dimensions to address ultimate issues that have been recessed in many discussions of medical ethics or bioethics. Roberto is a theologian with serious philosophical credentials, willing to enter into dialogue with currents of thought, some of which are not either hospitable or even antagonistic to the theological dimension of bio-ethical issues. It is often forgotten how in this matter ethical concerns were first raised by those with religious or theological concerns. Medical ethics or bioethics risks being overtaken as a professional area of concern by thinkers not at all sensitive to the issues of philosophical and theological anthropology. The results are a kind of wasteland of medical ethics, so well described here, and against which Roberto struggles honorably. One wonders if the second ethos we have reconfigured in the light of our uses of science and technology, in the dominion of serviceable disposability, makes us lose intimacy with the deeper sources, not only of our humanity but of being at all. This chapter is a recall and wake-up call to what is elementally constitutive of our condition of being. It makes first-class use of my own notions of the *passio essendi*, the *conatus essendi* and so on. It is admirable in the way it brings these thoughts to issues in bioethics which reveal the recessed ontological and theological issues in patterns of thinking which are overtly in flight from metaphysics and theology. He is very sensitive to how, though rooted in nature, we risk denaturing ourselves in remaking ourselves according to a second nature. This remaking runs roughshod over the *passio essendi* and lacks reverence for subtleties of the endowed powers that constitute our incarnate being. In echoing my own thoughts, he reveals them to me in new lights, not so evident to me before. I find it heartening that the ideas have lives beyond the ones they have lived or are living in my own work. For myself I grow more somber and fearful of the wasteland, not as the desert before the rejuvenating rains, but as the degraded soil that follows misuse of the earth, misuse too of our own bodies as the earth of our singular and communal selves that endow us as extraordinary beings in creation.

Dennis Vanden Auweele's chapter is a very interesting and insightful study of the plurivocal nature of silence. However, I cannot be silent in regard to my gratitude for Dennis's indispensable support and tireless work in organizing the gathering out of which the current book emerged. He was a kind of *primum mobile*, for nothing would have happened without him, nor would this collection of chapters have come to be. He has more than generously offered my work the gifts of his own engagements. I endorse his appreciation of the playfulness of Socrates-Plato (in the dialogue *Euthydemus*) in comparing us as philosophers to children chasing after larks. I like the twinning of seriousness and playfulness: seriousness, since if one has watched the way a child might try to catch a lark, the child can be absolutely absorbed in the chase; and yet when the lark escapes, what we sometimes witness is a squeal of delight! There is something tender rather than disparaging about this image: children, closest to immediate wonder, and tireless in seeking and yet not paralyzed by the discouragements of the already defeated. Look at a child chasing a bird on a beach: it is not the will to capture but the delight of surprise that captivates us, the joy in seeking to touch the mysterious creature of flight that alights, tantalizes us and flies off, if we do not woo it to stay a while. A number of significant discussions of silences are gathered and remarked upon, and I very much endorse the indispensable need of silence. I once wrote a piece entitled 'The Solitudes of Philosophy', in which what was at stake was the corrective and convalescent power of silence, about which Dennis's reflection writes in salutary reminder. *Beata solitudo, sola beatitudo*. This is a wise saying, much forgotten in the professionalization of philosophy as an academic specialty for which we are not promoted for our silences. It would be interesting to connect what Dennis says on silence with the soliloquy about which Renée Kohler-Ryan speaks: a soliloquy, spoken by one alone, is meant to be heard, or overheard—either by fellow humans or by the divine; it is not absolutely alone. There are many silences, of course, and not all of them benign. I am interested in mystical silence; the silences of nature; the silences of lovers; the autistic silence into which religion is driven in an age idolizing secular autonomy. Dennis properly notes the apophatic dimension of silence and suggestively says much about silence in Dostoyevsky and Nietzsche. I am struck here how the Grand Inquisitor does all the talking while Christ says nothing. The Grand Inquisitor talks himself out of his intention to execute Christ again. His talk provides the rope by which he hangs himself. Christ says nothing in response to being told to depart and never return. He silently kisses the Grand Inquisitor. Christ is neither a judge nor executioner; he is who he is, and in his company, our truth is reflected back to ourselves, and sometimes we become our own judges and executioners. Until we are kissed. Silently. One thinks too of the silences of Christ in the company of Pontius Pilate. Sometime a silent kiss is the true answer. It meets the kiss of Judas in a doing of the good, an act of love, not a theory. There is much more I would like to say, but alas on this occasion, I must now be silent.

 I am intrigued to be coupled with Giorgo Agamben, but my intrigue is answered very well by this exploration of Philip Gonzales. Part of this intrigue concerns a movement in thought which exhibits a kind of post-Christian colonization of Christian symbols. This is cause of joy to some theologians, but I find myself hesitant. I worry that it answers to what I called (in connection with Hegel's God) the production of counterfeit doubles. (This is central to the contribution of Sander Griffioen and I will say a word or two about it next.) Agamben is undoubtedly intriguing, and not least in connection with displays of what looks like an extraordinary mastery of arcane erudition. We are lured and allured by this teasing erudition but wonder to what pass the entire performance brings us. Philip's excellent reflection put me in mind of the question of eschatology about which I have been asked more than once. I explain my diffidence in terms of the idolization of any (to me) questionable teleology of immanent history. Such a teleology risks being false if deprived of a proper archeology of the good of the 'to be'. Without what in more theological terms is called 'creation', we find it hard to articulate an ontology of the 'to be' and its good, and what follows is not recreation but our reconstruction of the future as a this-worldly redeeming beyond. This may not be Agamben, though if memory serves me correctly, in *The Coming Community*, he speaks of *limbo* in terms with an echo of Aquinas, though not with the significance of Aquinas: limbo as the state of natural happiness one might enjoy without the beatific vision. That happiness might be deemed happiness enough. Limbo is thus, perhaps, a certain take on what Charles Taylor calls the 'immanent frame'. I am struck by how 'eschaton' has the meaning of 'edge' (as well as 'end'). 'Edge' is a threshold and a cutting. I would speak of the need to be at the edge of things in which the clogged porosity is cut open again, pierced by a beyond that cannot be contained by any immanent historicist teleology—communicating immanently the infinite qualitative difference of divine transcendence as other. Such would refer to an *archē* or origin 'before' creation or coming to be and to an overdeterminate fullness beyond every determinate and self-determining completion. This is divine grace not human work, and it qualifies the meaning of glory differently with regard to erotic sovereignty and agapeic service. It is not a matter of either servility or sovereignty. Beyond this contrast what is at stake for us is the right alignment of self-affirming love, eros, philia and agape. The point is not a strike against erotic sovereignty. There is glory there too. But the fuller glory is the coursing of the companioning power through all the loves. This means that, beyond any 'immanent frame', we must do what we can to keep the porosity to the divine open.

4

I very much appreciate the discerning attention that Sander Griffioen devotes to my engagement with Hegel. I am glad he sees that my relation to Hegel is not any dualistic opposition which simply rejects him but a metaxological intermediation which opens to him as the other as well as receiving from him, though there may be tensions and sometimes even hostility, hopefully righteous, between interlocutors. Sometimes I wonder if I have more philosophical appreciation for Hegel in my dissent than some of his devoted acolytes who repeat verbatim the words but sometimes miss the spirit of the *Sache selbst*. I am gladdened by Sander's memories of some of our own exchanges—always invigorating—on our peregrinations in the Far East. Indeed these memories bring back to me the pleasures of finding philosophy and friendship alive together. I am intrigued by his reference to the role of Hegel's Protestantism in the more mature writings. I have been asked by pious Hegelians, even atheistically pious Hegelians, if my arguments with Hegel have to do with my being Catholic. I am suspected of being happy with the unhappy consciousness and the mortal sin for any modern, namely, being in love with the 'beyond'. I do find myself perplexed about the exact place of religion in Hegel's thought. There is something paradoxical in placing religion at the level of absolute spirit and affirming Christianity as the consummate religion, and yet from the standpoint of the immanent historical realization of freedom, claiming that the religious community, while needful as providing some foundation to the modern state, is too 'spiritual', while the modern state is the more complete worldly realization of freedom. I find myself resonating with Kierkegaard's warnings about the idolization of the modern state. A secular community can be an idol if it counterfeits the religious community. I have wondered if this is closer to the question of nihilism: not that the highest values devalue themselves, but that counterfeits of the highest values masquerade as higher than the highest values. I am made to think again by this chapter about the counterfeit double as a *parodia sacra*. Extraordinary mimicries of the highest are hard to distinguish from the highest, since they mimic them so faithfully—a paradox since the faithful mimicry is unfaithful. Nihilism is not how the highest values devalue themselves but how an economy of counterfeit doubles of such values becomes indistinguishable from these values themselves—the faithful mimicry is without faith. I think of the secular moralization of the religious mystery that preaches to the religious that is it not moral enough and hence to be superseded. The new configuration seems very like the original but something is missing, something has been hollowed out, or subject to a mutation, and the new doubling or redoubling has the character of a counterfeit. It claims to have the currency, claims perhaps to have more currency than the original, but it is evacuated of what made possible our confidence in the original. We can invest confidence in what we call a 'con job', but it is backed up by nothing in which we can place our confidence, our true trust.

I am glad to be better instructed about Sergei Bulgakov by Josephien van Kessel, and I defer to her knowledge of Vladimir Solov'ëv. I am happy also to confess that given the way I try to orchestrate the interchange of considerations between Lev Shestov and Solov'ëv, while also trying to communicate something of the metaxological approach, all the nuances of Solov'ëv might have well merited further consideration. I am also glad that there are convergences between Bulgakov and my own work, and need my attention. I would still say in my own work that something like a reformed Shestovian impulse is at work, against the abstract universal. The notion of all-unity has for me too many associations of an enclosing totality, though I sense that this is not Solov'ëv's intention. As best as I can in GB, I try to distinguish between the God of the whole, whether of pantheism or panentheism, and the God beyond the whole, the God of creation. I still think panentheism has questions to answer and that the God of creation offers subtler possibilities than its critics always allow. My own explorations of the intimate universal might be seen as partaking of a Shestovian as well as a Solov'ëvien impulse. The thought of the anti-Christ cannot be fitted into the logic of any immanent holism. Likewise, there is a refusal of the whole at work in evil which cannot be rendered in holistic terms. The singular mutation of the intimate is at the source of the idiocy of the monstrous. Christ and anti-Christ look like twins but they are not, and no logic of the universal alone, or the whole, will do justice to what is at stake. What Sander Griffioen says regarding the nature of the counterfeit double is insightful on the issue. Perhaps the point is too crude, but in suitably qualified ways, I see that Solov'ëv is to Shestov as Hegel is to Kierkegaard. Paul Weiss once remarked about BB that it was a rewriting of Hegel from a Kierkegaardian interior, something he had previously thought was impossible. He compared BB to the *Phenomenology of Spirit* and advised me now to write my *Science of Logic*. I did not think this was possible, given that the apotheosis of metaxological mindfulness is not thought thinking itself. Though not a science of logic in Hegel's sense, perhaps IU is a kind of attempt to meet Weiss's request. Now being better instructed about Bulgakov and Solov'ëv, I take Josephien's appreciated thoughts as an opportune invitation to turn to them again.

The chapter of Philip Gottschalk presents a contrast with Josephien van Kessel. He is a serious student of Shestov and Nicholas O. Lossky, and he perhaps puts more emphasis on what motivates my hesitations about pantheism and panentheism and rightly so. He carefully outlines what Peter Hodgson says in critique of my interpretation of Hegel and I will say something below on this. My distance from panentheism is not sourced in any dualistic opposition of immanence and transcendence but more positively comes from a space beyond dualism and immanent dialectic of the Hegelian form. There is a strong sense of affirming the divine transcendence as other to the immanent transcendence of nature as a whole, or the self-transcending of the human being as willing to complete its own immanent and autonomous self-determination. Philip offers a thoughtful and lucid exploration of why I am not a panentheist. He is right that 'strong' transcendence is not fashionable today, partly because it is misinterpreted in terms of a dualistic opposition of finite and infinite, partly because of the antinomy of autonomy and transcendence relative to which we choose the ultimacy of immanent self-transcending. Philip rightly mentions that I stand back from teleology of the Hegelian sort, and I would refer to remarks above in reference to eschatology as beyond this form of immanent teleology. Hegel has had many offspring on this score in relation to immanent history, even among those whose philosophical idiom is markedly anti-Hegelian. The philosophical and theological option for some form of immanent holism, at best with a weak sense of something 'more', is chosen over the transcendence that follows from the absolute singularity of the divine. An agapeic sense of that singularity is entirely compatible with an affirmation of divine community, such as we find in a Trinitarian theology, and the thought of the absolute intimacy of the divine with finite creation. Absolute transcendence and absolute intimacy are not opposites in the metaxological orientation. I am happy Philip brought Hodgson into the discussion. Hodgson favors something closer to panentheism, but I note a last long footnote which indeed are the last words of his book. They recount remarks by a reader for Oxford University Press. They raise questions about his interpretation, questions Hodgson grants as needing to be addressed and allowing another interpretation of Hegel. These words are mine. I was the reader. I have said this in printed exchange with Hodgson, though the words might have been taken ironically.

Ironically, perhaps in a deeper sense, Hodgson was not entirely without agreement with me, though he did not know it, in confessing agreement with the 'reader'.

5

I am warmly grateful to Richard Kearney for these searching reflections on chosen passages and aspects of my work, grateful for their mindful attention, itself attendant with the friendly spirit of companioning thought. I have said one or two things already in response to Mark Novak's study. There are companioning convergences in both of our works, even if some of our intellectual places of departure are not exactly the same. Our shared concerns with the aesthetic, the ethical and the religious are marked in Richard's case by efforts to formulate a theopoetics, while mine, perhaps more metaphysically inflected, take place between system and poetics. He asks about being and God, and I would not univocally identify the two. I recall visiting Paul Weiss as an old man, and on entering his apartment, he would immediately almost shout (he was a bit deaf): "How do you get from being to God?" I sensed he wanted a direct answer, whereas my suggestion was to find direction by indirection. My sense is that this answer would be approved by Richard, even if his indirections are more mediated by hermeneutical narrative (understood in a broad sense). The figurative dimension of the exploration, even in metaphysics, is not to be slighted. I do think that a metaxological metaphysician has to be a 'lover' as well as a 'theorist', as I put it in IST. He is right to say that I have often tended to stress the *archē* by contrast with his tendency to tilt toward the 'end'. I do think his sense of eschatology in small things; his 'micro-eschatology' is very consonant with the spirit informing the notion of the *intimate* universal. I said above how 'eschaton' has also the sense of 'edge', even down to the cutting edge that opens up the closure upon themselves of immanent historicist teleologies. The eschaton in the micro cuts into time, all the time. If I am not mistaken, this is at work in his more recent departures in anatheism. It is not accidental that I am also interested in consecrations. Richard intriguingly talks about a 'whisper' of the beatitudes in my work. I note that I have written on Aquinas and the beatitudes, and am concerned, among other things, with how the beatitudes as 'exceeding virtue' break out of the terms of reference of Aristotelian ethics, and not without what I detect is a hint of discomfort here and there on Aquinas's part. I like the suggestion that the mystics 'ghost my pages', especially if we invest 'ghost' with its secret, saturated meanings. I am not so sure I am as reticent about God as I take him to suggest. I am more reticent in some books, true. But I have the sense that some in the confraternity of Continental philosophers cross to the other side of the street when they see me coming: I smell too much of God! In fairness to myself, nobody talks about God today in quite the way I do in GB (granting the book is understood). I think that the penultimate chapter on the mystic God, in light of the idiotics of the divine and the mystic woo, is worthy of mention (as Patrick Cooper does). If I am not mistaken about myself, the final Part, simply entitled God, with its ten 'metaphysical cantos' (and there is a tale in these terms), is all but shamelessly religious for a contemporary philosopher.

Renée Kohler-Ryan makes a profound connection between Shakespeare's dramatic deployment of the soliloquy and the specifically philosophical roots that it has in Augustine. As she rightly underscores, Augustine coins the word in calling attention to the particular way one speaks to oneself while in the presence of God. I mentioned in response to Dennis Vanden Auweele how soliloquy paradoxically is meant to be heard or overheard. Who 'over'-hears when a humanistically oriented sense of things takes over? Not least, something of the startling freshness of Augustine's astonishing process of (over-heard) self-discovery is weakened or lost. I do not hide my admiration for Augustine, and how I am taken by the way he describes his own itinerary of thought: from the exterior to the interior, from the inferior to the superior. The superior agapeically over-hears the inferior in the reserved depths of its most intimate quest(ion). Renée gives a lovely meditation on speaking the amen with reference to *Macbeth* and the Augustinian soliloquy. She knows how much I love and honor this play as perhaps the supreme dramatic exploration of the equivocity of being, under the doom of sacrilegious evil, and how it blocks the porous flow of true communication. Renée offers some fascinating discussion of the ethos of equivocity prevalent in Shakespeare's London around the time of the writing of the play. Killing the anointed king is an attempted deicide of God in one's own soul, and eventually, in the tyrannical mutation of erotic sovereignty, it is also the self-murder of one's own soul. The theme is handled with aplomb, rightly bringing in Nietzsche and the potentially infernal equivocity of seeking to be beyond (moral) good and evil. The step beyond is not into the innocence of becoming but potentially into the infernal de-creation of the integrity of the soul, the ethical community and the political order. The Augustinian soliloquy is always porous, beyond selving, to the superior good of the divine companioning power. Porous to this companioning in its being, selving becomes clogged on itself when it insists on itself alone, sometimes to the extreme of closing the giving source of the porosity, closing into itself in being *incurvatus in se*. Absolute selving is the death of self, if being absolute is only being for itself. There is equivocal mimicry: absolute selving counterfeits the absolute—without the porosity. There is no absolution, if the absolute self claims to confer it on itself. Renée's reflections put me in the mind of how Shakespeare, in the words of Macbeth himself before the crime is committed, offers us a different take to Nietzsche on pity and the tyrannical will to power: 'And pity, like a naked newborn babe,/Striding the blast, or heaven's cherubim, horsed/Upon the sightless couriers of the of the air,/Shall blow the horrid deed in every eye,/That tears shall drown the wind'. I believe that in Shakespeare's time a pictorial representation of the crucified Christ was called a 'Pity'. Macbeth too knows that beyond the equivocation of evil there is judgment. He knew the 'Doom' would come. (At that time the representation of the Last Judgement was called the 'Doom'.) The Doom and the Pity: both the working out of the divine amen and our responsive amen to it that affirms it again, or not.

I am pleased to see Alexandra Romanyshyn lucidly and intelligently taking up the ecological implications of my thought. She recounts finely how the claims stemming from the modern anthropocentric standpoint risk landing us in a wasteland where nature's being and worth for itself come under threat. Her reflection is a very good complement to the work of Francis Van Den Noortgaete who recently completed a fine doctoral dissertation, 'Being Beholden: An Iconic-Liturgical Perspective on Nature and the Role of Ontological Gratitude in Environmental Ethics'. The ongoing work of Peter Scheers also merits mention. Her concern has been an important theme from early on in my thought, and she represents it well. I am thinking, for instance, of some reflections in the final chapter of PO, 'Thought Singing its Other'. There in 'Songs of the Elemental' the changed orientation to the land in Ireland struck me as full with ominous possibilities, even while the official views sang a *te deum* to the land as an exploitable resource in the dominion of serviceable disposability. Something stirred that was profoundly at odds with the older Irish attitude to the land, and I do not single out Ireland for reasons of ethnic piety, but because of something elemental being at stake. There was something ominous about the situation whose dangers have only increased with the intervening years. Has mindfulness of the elemental become more widespread? Yes, and no. Yes, in that we face more publicly the loss; no, in that often the response is taken primarily to be more efficient technologies in the running of the dominion of serviceable disposability. Alexandra sees that this will not be enough. One might say that what we need rather is an *ontological metanoia* in relation to the givenness of creation. *Metanoia* is often translated as a repentance, and surely we need that, but it is also a matter of a new noetics of being, a noetics that is *meta* in the double sense of the Greek: in the midst and also beyond. Metaxology is a form of metanoetics in this regard. (The work of Takeshi Morisato is very helpful in pursuing this point in dialogue with Hajime Tanabe.) Alexandra's reflection contributes to the communication of this mindfulness and this *metanoia*. It is very perceptive in seeing the need for permeability between aesthetic, ethical, religious and metaphysical considerations. Often treatments of ecological issues make one unsure about whether the fullness of these considerations enters the picture. Ecological thought asks a metaxological metanoetics. I see Alexandra's welcome reflections as pointing in this direction.

Bibliography

Desmond, William. 2012. Wording the Between. In *The William Desmond Reader*, ed. Christopher Simpson, 195–227. Albany: SUNY Press.
———. 2018. *The Gift of Beauty and the Passion of Being: On the Threshold Between the Aesthetic and the Religious*. Eugene, OR: Wipf and Stock.
Schindler, David. 2008. *Plato's Critique of Impure Reason: On Goodness and Truth in the Republic*. Washington: CUA Press.

Index[1]

A

Agamben, Giorgio, 10, 155, 155n6, 209–224, 328, 329
Agape, 8, 10, 49n2, 52, 114, 120–123, 274–276, 324
Agapeic love, 16, 116, 121, 133, 251
Amen, 174, 224, 285–300, 334, 335
Anti-Christ, 234, 235, 237, 239, 247–250, 254, 331
Aquinas, Thomas, 16, 19, 49, 49n3, 81, 136, 259, 275, 329, 333
Arche, 114, 120, 123, 206, 275, 329, 333
Augustine, 11, 45, 57, 129, 132, 133, 136, 137, 141, 144, 152, 153, 158, 161, 163–166, 163n19, 163n20, 165n23, 165n24, 168, 212, 216, 222–224, 237, 250, 252, 278, 285–296, 298, 299, 325, 334
Autonomy, 5, 8, 10, 54, 73, 142, 182, 186, 187, 190, 191, 195–207, 305–307, 309, 310, 325, 328, 332

B

Badiou, Alain, 18, 35n15, 40, 41, 210, 213, 222n11, 320
Bataille, Georges, 155, 155n5, 160, 160n13, 169, 170, 172, 326
Bioethics, 10, 177, 181, 188, 189, 326, 327
Blondel, Maurice, 136, 137, 325
Boole, George, 19, 38
Bruno, Giordano, 17, 27, 27n6, 28
Bulgakov, Sergei, 11, 243–246, 245n4, 246n7, 246n10, 248–255, 251n13, 251n14, 257, 262–266, 331, 332

---

[1] Note: Page numbers followed by 'n' refer to notes.

C

Cantor, George, 22, 29–41, 32n12, 320
Caputo, John D., 113, 124, 210, 213, 275
Caritas, 8, 45–47, 57, 273, 284, 287, 288
Catholic, 9, 30, 33, 61–63, 156n8, 204, 218–220, 294, 330
Community, 5, 7, 8, 10, 46, 52, 53, 56, 97, 100, 105–110, 116, 131, 134, 146, 147, 151, 160, 168, 207, 237, 241, 246, 248–252, 254, 257, 258, 260, 261, 264, 266, 278, 281, 285–287, 292, 294, 297–299, 297n12, 310n4, 319, 325, 330, 332, 334
Conatus essendi, 55, 56, 107, 156, 156n9, 157, 167, 184, 186, 187, 206, 220, 224, 276, 280, 327
Concrete ideal-realism
   real beings; concrete consubstantiality, 263
Confidence, x, 53, 77, 272, 273, 283, 284, 287, 331
Copernican turn, 17
Correlationism, 79–87, 322, 323
Counterfeit double, 51, 60, 197, 211, 230, 234, 240, 248–250, 329–331
Creation, 9–11, 27, 62, 64, 65, 70, 71, 73, 88, 102, 103, 120, 162n17, 164, 188, 189, 219, 222–224, 230, 239, 239n17, 245–248, 250–252, 260–265, 271–284, 296, 298, 305, 311, 327, 329, 331, 332, 336
Cusa, Nicholas, 17, 19, 20, 27, 27n6, 28, 31, 35n14, 119, 173, 275, 279, 320

D

Dante, 3, 167, 326
Dasein, 80, 85, 153n2, 221
de Lubac, Henri, 61, 63, 140, 187
Death of God, 47n1, 118, 209, 212
Deconstruction, 1, 9, 23, 115, 140, 180, 275
Deleuze, Gilles, 18
Descartes, René, 18, 19, 24, 26, 28, 29, 35, 278
Dialectics, 4, 7, 16, 18, 19, 69, 89, 118, 120, 122, 134, 139, 158, 160n13, 160n14, 232, 253, 255, 258–262, 292, 293, 311, 332
Dionysius the Areopagite, 9, 97–99, 101–108
Divine names, 9, 323
Dostoyevsky, Fyodor, 1, 2, 154, 166–168, 195, 212, 328

E

Eckhart, Meister, 144, 282, 325
Equivocal, 16, 17, 67–69, 72, 90, 90n4, 115, 118, 136, 138, 140, 141, 144, 195, 201, 231n3, 254, 283, 292, 293, 299, 310, 320, 326, 335
Eros, 121, 122, 132, 138, 139, 141, 174
Erotic, 16, 49, 51, 71n8, 85, 117–119, 121, 122, 131, 133, 134, 138–140, 142–147, 154–156, 159, 190, 191, 205, 231, 231n3, 232n6, 237, 251, 258, 277, 282, 308, 314, 325, 329, 334
Ethos, 5, 6, 104, 108, 109, 131, 141, 147, 167, 177–191, 254, 307n1, 311, 318, 327, 334

Event, 7, 48, 85, 98, 99, 109, 113, 115, 159, 187, 188, 199, 209–214, 216, 218, 221, 223, 304
Evil, 3, 10, 26n4, 124, 124n3, 151–174, 215, 235, 237–239, 252, 259–261, 263–266, 285, 286, 290, 292, 293, 295, 298, 299, 312, 325, 326, 331, 334, 335

F

Factiality, 79, 81, 82, 82n2, 88, 89
Fate, 153, 162, 172, 204
Fichte, J.G., 18, 18n1
Fidelity, 53, 55, 169, 278, 318
Finesse, x, 5, 7, 50, 131, 133, 147, 196, 197, 203, 250, 320, 321, 325
Florensky, Pavel, 262–263, 265, 266
Fragility, 101, 131, 145, 153
Freedom, 46, 52–55, 64, 66, 73, 155, 165n23, 187, 190, 191, 196, 233, 234, 238, 239, 247, 250, 251, 259, 263–265, 276, 279, 280, 295, 330

G

Gabriel, Markus, 77
Gadamer, H.G., 65–67, 178, 179, 231, 231n2
Gelassenheit, 124, 321
Givenness, 10, 55, 79, 80, 89, 105, 125, 131–133, 145, 146, 155, 157, 189, 196, 200, 212, 275, 276, 280, 311, 312, 336
Glory, 168, 196, 209–224, 245, 281, 329
Gnosticism, 134, 161, 161n16, 164, 245, 326
God, 2, 4, 6, 9–11, 21, 27, 27n6, 28n8, 31, 33, 41, 48, 55, 60–65, 70, 72, 73, 81, 98–109, 129, 131–135, 138, 139, 141, 143–147, 159, 162n17, 168, 188, 191, 196–199, 197n1, 201–203, 207, 210, 211, 217n8, 218–224, 229–241, 243, 244, 245n6, 246–252, 254, 255, 257–266, 271–278, 281, 282, 286–290, 292–294, 296–300, 310, 311, 320, 321, 323–325, 329, 331, 333, 334

H

Health, 159, 186, 288–290, 288n4, 299
Hegel, G.W.F., ix, 3–5, 7, 8, 10, 11, 15, 18, 18n1, 49, 89, 135, 151, 158–161, 163, 163n18, 212, 217, 222, 230–236, 238, 248, 253, 254, 257–262, 264–266, 276, 278, 317, 318, 320, 322, 324, 326, 329–332
Heidegger, Martin, 3, 6, 9, 53, 55, 65, 77, 79, 80, 83–88, 90, 114, 115, 118, 126, 127, 127n4, 153, 153n2, 162, 163, 174, 197, 212, 215, 216, 216n7, 221, 222, 231, 231n2, 272, 274, 275, 321, 323
Hermeneutics, 9, 21, 54n11, 59–74, 118, 119, 183, 213, 222, 283, 322, 326
Heterodox, 145, 322
Holism, 230, 232–234, 244, 246–248, 250–253, 255, 258, 331, 332
Humanism, 18, 283
Husserl, Edmund, 38, 39, 179, 272, 278
Hyperbole, 6, 104, 116, 132, 140, 144, 275, 282, 323, 324

I

Immanence, 59–62, 101, 105, 115, 116, 122, 136, 137, 139–142, 144, 235, 243, 246–249, 278, 282, 332
Instrumentalization, 11, 70, 303, 305–309
Intimate universal, 7, 48, 49, 53, 56, 57, 122, 130, 131, 141, 143, 177–180, 190, 240n20, 248, 273, 277, 278, 282, 331

J

Jacobi, F.H., 17, 40
Justice, 48–50, 56, 78, 85, 100, 101, 105, 113, 125, 199, 239n17, 258, 259, 326, 331

K

Kant, Immanuel, ix, 4, 8, 17, 18, 29, 40, 77–80, 136, 152, 153, 156, 158n12, 167, 167n27, 185, 196, 199, 201–203, 248, 253, 278, 310, 321, 326
Kearney, Richard, 9–11, 210, 213, 277, 324, 333
Kierkegaard, Sören, 153, 258, 259, 261, 278, 318, 330, 331
Kristeva, Julia, 113

L

Levinas, Emmanuel, 113, 156, 209, 210n1, 276
Logic, 8, 19–21, 23, 30, 32, 35, 38–41, 50n4, 54, 118, 136, 160, 180, 186, 187, 201, 248, 253, 255, 260, 320, 331
Love, x, 16, 30, 46–50, 49n2, 50n7, 52, 56, 98, 99, 116, 121, 122, 133, 143, 145, 172, 172n32, 177–191, 204, 205, 215, 219, 223, 224, 231, 243, 249–252, 273, 278, 280, 283, 284, 287–290, 294, 324, 325, 328–330, 334

M

Macbeth, 11, 154, 166, 285, 286, 290–300, 334, 335
Maréchal, Joseph, 10, 129, 135–142, 144
Marion, Jean-Luc, 34, 34n13, 35n14, 36, 84, 113, 173, 173n34, 197, 211, 323
Materialism, 77, 79–83, 87, 89, 253, 259
Mathematics, 8, 17, 19, 20, 22–28, 30, 34, 35n14, 38–41, 319, 320
May-be, 82, 119
McCarthy, Cormac, 170–172, 170n30, 326
Mediation, 5, 16, 28n8, 69, 72, 90, 100, 129, 130, 132, 138, 141, 142, 144–147, 259, 276, 280
Medicine, 177–180, 182, 185
Medusa, 152, 169–174, 326
Meillassouc, Quentin, 9, 78–83, 82n2, 87–90
Merleau-Ponty, Maurice, 80, 80n1, 283
Messianism, 209–211, 214, 216–218, 220
Metaphysics, 2, 5, 6, 8–10, 15, 19, 21, 40, 41, 45–57, 59–74, 77, 78, 88, 95, 98, 106, 115, 117–119, 129, 130, 132, 133, 137, 139–141, 147, 151, 152, 156n8, 156n9, 159, 182, 189, 191, 197–200, 202, 211, 213, 215, 216, 221–223, 265, 266, 271, 273, 275, 276, 279, 282, 283, 303, 313, 314, 322–324, 327, 333

INDEX   341

Metaxology, x, xi, 2–4, 7–11, 45–57, 77–90, 156n8, 205, 219, 243–255, 259, 260, 272, 283, 303–314, 317–336
Metaxu, 3, 5, 15, 97, 104, 107, 114–117, 126, 243–246, 254, 272, 278, 283, 285–300, 312, 319, 324
Middle, 1, 9, 31, 97, 102, 104, 105, 113, 115–127, 131–133, 141, 142, 166, 167, 243, 282
Mindfulness, 51, 52, 78, 83, 85, 86, 89, 104, 117, 125, 130, 131, 137, 142, 145, 147, 188, 212, 222, 223, 283, 321, 331, 336
Moral law, 199, 202–204, 290, 310
Murdoch, Iris, 154, 154n3, 168

N
Nancy, Jean-Luc, 158n12
Naturalism, 17
Neoplatonism, 26, 28, 97, 98, 164, 165, 173
Neoscholasticism, 39, 60, 62, 63, 67, 322
Neo-Thomism, 1, 2
Newman, John, 62
New realism, 9, 78, 90, 322, 323
Nietzsche, Friedrich, ix, x, 2, 4, 5, 45, 47, 52, 60n2, 155, 157, 160–163, 202, 203, 205–207, 212, 235, 235n11, 238, 249, 250, 253, 292, 292n8, 309, 310, 326, 328, 334, 335
Novalis, 18n1

O
Ontology, 18, 27, 35, 36, 67, 77, 78, 85, 117, 118, 120, 159, 212, 275, 280, 322, 329
Orthodox, 41, 245, 245n6, 246, 246n7, 252, 262, 265, 322

Otherness, 3, 4, 54, 66, 68, 70–72, 85, 89, 101, 103, 104, 116, 118, 120, 123, 130–133, 135, 137, 138, 141–143, 145, 147, 184, 185, 188, 190, 199, 205, 206, 219, 222, 223, 232n5, 233, 252, 258, 260, 277, 280, 299, 304, 313
Overdeterminacy, 115–117, 133, 136, 142, 196, 274, 291, 307, 312
Overdeterminate, 3, 101, 103, 104, 131, 134, 135, 197, 293, 318, 319, 329

P
Panentheism, 253, 257–266, 332
Pantheism, 8, 10, 159, 250, 258, 263, 331, 332
Pascal, Blaise, 3, 27, 163, 163n20, 166, 204, 212, 320
Passio essendi, 55, 56, 107, 131, 156, 156n9, 157, 167, 184, 187, 189, 206, 224, 272, 276, 280, 322, 324, 327
Patience, 55, 107, 206, 278, 280, 281
Paul, St., 46, 56, 163, 163n19, 174, 230
Perplexity, 2, 5, 6, 11, 31, 182, 235n10, 238–241, 305, 308–310, 314, 325, 326
Plato, 2, 6, 19–23, 25n3, 26, 28, 40, 97, 154, 158, 161, 163, 163n20, 200, 212, 222, 243, 248, 263, 320, 321
Plurivocal, 3, 104, 105, 109, 125, 133, 134, 317, 319, 321, 327
Poetry, 6, 124, 125, 197, 198, 204, 244, 253, 253n16, 255
Porosity, 3, 6–9, 105, 108, 129–134, 138, 143, 145, 157, 167, 177, 186, 189–191, 196, 197n1, 230, 232, 241, 252, 253, 272, 277, 278, 282, 289, 298, 318, 321–324, 329, 335

342 INDEX

Postmodern, 7, 8, 15, 46, 49, 50n4, 51, 53, 151, 155, 158n12, 197–199, 222, 253, 272, 325
Postulatory finitism, 9, 59–61, 73, 222
Prayer, 117, 188, 277, 287, 288, 290, 295, 297n12, 299
Privatio boni, 156n8, 238, 239, 279
Providence, 161, 243
Przywara, Erich, 8, 41, 213, 213n4, 219, 222, 320

R

Religion, 5, 7, 8, 10, 40, 55, 113, 118, 119, 130, 151, 152, 157, 158, 164–166, 190, 196, 197n1, 198, 223, 231, 233, 233n7, 234, 235n11, 236, 236n14, 244, 260, 266, 271, 272, 278–283, 317, 318, 318n2, 324, 328, 330
Ricoeur, Paul, 10, 152, 162–168, 174, 326
Rublev, Andrei, 274
Ruusbroec, Jan van, 10, 130, 132, 142–147

S

Sabbath, 10, 197, 213, 216, 220, 221, 223, 224
Schelling, F.W.J., 4, 5, 15, 17, 18, 18n1, 157, 157n10, 217, 248, 253
Scheuer, Pierre, 10, 129, 135–142, 144
Schillebeeckx, Edward, 9, 61–70, 72, 73, 322
Schlegel, K.W.F., 18n1
Scholasticism, 96, 101
Schopenhauer, Arthur, 2, 153, 320, 326
Second Vatican Council, 61, 63

Selving, 59–74, 104, 122, 142, 144, 155, 189, 212, 232, 271, 278, 280, 323, 335
Shestov, Lev, 11, 212, 234, 244, 246–250, 253, 255, 261, 262, 265, 331, 332
Silence, 10, 60, 133–135, 137, 139–141, 174, 181, 188, 195–207, 296, 321, 327, 328
Skepticism, 60, 308
Socrates, 200
Soliloquy, 11, 285–300, 328, 334, 335
Solovyov, Vladimir Sergeievich, 11, 244–255, 257, 262–266, 331, 332
Sophia, 127, 243–251, 251n13, 251n14, 253–255, 262–265
Sophiology, 11, 243–255, 262, 263
Soul, 263
Sovereignty, 51, 122, 154–156, 160, 169, 215n5, 216, 277, 329, 334
Spinoza, 17, 28, 40, 55, 56, 56n13, 159, 161, 185, 212, 220, 248, 253
Subjectification, 185, 305–310
Sublation, 118, 122, 258–261, 317, 318
Substantival agent, 263

T

Taylor, Charles, 100, 101, 181, 183, 190, 210, 213, 272, 276, 283, 329
Teleology, 73, 248, 261, 305, 322, 329, 332, 333
Telos, 134, 206, 247, 261
Theism
  theistic, 263

Theodicy, 4, 152, 156n9, 157–160, 162, 165, 167n27, 168, 261, 262, 265, 326
Theopoetics, 10, 114, 114n1, 117, 123–128, 274, 275, 324, 333
Transcendence, 5, 9, 49, 51, 59–61, 85–87, 89, 90, 90n4, 97, 100–106, 108–110, 115, 116, 123, 131, 132, 136, 144, 147, 154, 173, 174, 191, 197, 223, 232n6, 243–255, 286, 292n8, 293, 298–300, 304, 309, 311–314, 321, 329, 332

U
Univocal, 4, 6, 15, 17, 18, 24, 67, 69, 70, 84n3, 90n4, 104, 105, 109, 115, 118, 138, 144, 161, 162, 185, 231n3, 248, 253, 255, 283, 292, 296, 299, 308, 310, 317–320

V
Vattimo, Gianni, 9, 46–48, 51–55, 51n8, 210, 213, 275, 321
Vector, 85, 86, 90n4, 96, 102, 103, 131
Veritas, 8, 9, 45–47, 57
Vico, Giambattista, 20, 28, 35n14, 38

W
Weak thought, 51
Weil, Simone, 154, 154n3, 168, 171
Wittgenstein, Ludwig, 22, 25, 30, 33–40, 79, 320
World Organic Whole
  organic whole, 263
World soul, 263

Z
Zero, 18, 22–24, 25n3, 29, 34, 41, 289n5
Žižek, Slavoj, 113, 210, 213